Memory Consolidation
Psychobiology of Cognition

Memory Consolidation
Psychobiology of Cognition

Edited by
Herbert Weingartner
National Institute of Mental Health

Elizabeth S. Parker
National Institute on Alcohol Abuse and Alcoholism

LEA

LAWRENCE ERLBAUM ASSOCIATES, PUBLISHERS

1984   Hillsdale, New Jersey   London

Lawrence Erlbaum Associates, Inc., Publishers
365 Broadway
Hillsdale, New Jersey 07642

Library of Congress Cataloging in Publication Data
Main entry under title:
Memory consolidation.

  Bibliography: p.
  Includes index.
  1. Memory   2. Memory—Physiological aspects.
I. Weingartner, Herbert.   II. Parker, Elizabeth S.
BF371.M453   1984   612'.82   84-1508
ISBN 0-89859-323-9

Printed in the United States of America
10 9 8 7 6 5 4 3 2 1

Contents

Preface

The first book devoted to memory consolidation was prepared by James McGaugh and Michael Herz. In the preface to that volume, which appeared in 1972, McGaugh and Herz were explicit about the fact that the book dealt with animal research. At that time, major advances in understanding consolidation processes were based on the study of psychobiological processes of learning and memory in lower animals. It was our belief that this concept is valuable in considering memory phenomena in humans, the area from which the concept originated around the turn of the century.

This volume was organized for students of human memory and related cognitive processes. The issues deal not only with memory in unimpaired individuals, but also with impaired patients and with consolidation in lower animals. The chapters in this volume demonstrate that consolidation is a flourishing and controversial concept in memory research today. More than ten years after the seminal book of McGaugh and Herz, questions about consolidation are re-examined in light of current models of human memory, its pathology, and its modulation by drugs.

The editing of this book has gone through several stages. We thought it might be useful to share some of that history. Five years ago, the editors (Weingartner and Parker) began to work together at the NIMH. As two psychologists with strong interests in the altered states of human memory, we found ourselves working in a neurobiological research milieu. Our conversations with one another covered a broad range of topics, but none so persistently recurred as memory consolidation, and questions about the notable absence of this concept from contemporary systems of information processing, memory and learning.

HW found the concept useful in trying to define the memory-learning changes evident in disorders of mood, in relation to the effects of cholinergic drug treatments in humans, in characterizing the neuropeptide cognitive response, and in trying to find a role for activation processes in cognition. EP was perplexed by the facilitating effect of alcohol on consolidation, a research topic that owes its start to work she did with Ronald Alkana. As graduate students at the University of California–Irvine, Alkana and Parker conducted a series of animal studies to test the hypothesis that alcohol impairs memory by disrupting consolidation. This research began in 1973 in Jim McGaugh's laboratory. Because of the unexpected facilitating effect of alcohol, the research still continues. Perhaps it will be relevant only to understanding the memory change produced by alcohol. Perhaps it will allow us to examine how stimulation of reward systems affects memory storage.

Thus in 1978, when we began to work together, HW expressed interest in memory and the cholinergic system, memory consolidation in pathological states—particularly depression—and the role of arousal in cognition; and EP was interested in consolidation and alcohol's stimulating and rewarding effects. This started us thinking not only about these specific topics, but about more general questions as well. Why is the consolidation hypothesis necessary? Why has it been so ignored by investigators of normal human memory? What types of phenomena are amenable to understanding through a consolidation perspective? Is memory consolidation best viewed as an instrumental concept to enable a bridging of the gap between psychobiological and experimental studies of memory? Do researchers avoid consolidation explanations because these imply some type of unconscious, or automatic process? Have investigators of altered storage processes in animal memory begun to use consolidation without thinking about its relation to other aspects of memory?

These questions led us to turn to our colleagues. Our first step was to organize a symposium to formalize data, concerns, thoughts and questions dealing with memory consolidation. The issues raised at that APA symposium in 1979 clarified certain key questions and debates. We felt that others would want to think about these issues as well. The book represents our attempt to embellish the perspectives presented at that original symposium.

We are deeply grateful to the authors of the chapters in this volume who shared concern for clarifying and developing questions about memory consolidation. They have been dedicated, creative and responsive throughout the preparation of the volume. They were eager to state their views clearly, knowing that the volume would present opposing perspectives. The volume reflects significant contributions from all participants.

We are indebted to a number of colleagues who have helped us along the paths of our research. We thank and acknowledge the efforts of our many research colleagues who have helped us in thinking about memory consolidation, and in struggling with us to translate our thoughts into researchable hypotheses. We particularly want to thank some of our students who brought to us a freshness and an open curiosity about how we might consider memory from different vantage points, and who weren't already sure what was and was not worth studying about memory. We especially want to thank Rita Diebel, Erika Fergeson, Sheila Smallberg and Barbara Schwartz for being just the students for whom the volume was intended, and for their enthusiastic help in critiquing our ideas. A few of the many investigators whose critical input has been invaluable to HW in examining a psychobiology of memory consolidation are Robert Cohen, Dennis Murphy, Edward Silberman, and Barbara Strupp. Ralph Esposito has been enormously helpful to us both, with his invaluable knowledge about the reward system of the brain and behavior. We thank Richard Wyatt for his encouragement in pursuing research that does not fit neatly into disciplinary niches and for thinking about neurobiological models of the facilitation effect. To Richard Stillman, we owe thanks for his constant support of cognitive research in his laboratory.

1 Memory Consolidation: A Cognitive Perspective

Herbert Weingartner
Laboratory of Psychology and Psychopathology
National Institute of Mental Health

Elizabeth S. Parker
Laboratory of Clinical Studies
National Institute on Alcohol Abuse and Alcoholism

AIMS

This volume is concerned with characteristics of memory consolidation. It addresses a historically classic concept that has been used to define aspects of learning, retention, memory, and related cognitive operations. The contributors to this volume explore a variety of issues that describe facets of memory consolidation. These include the biology, pathology, neuropsychology, neuropharmacology, and the behavioral events that are elements of the structure of such a construct. Questions are raised and discussed, such as: Is memory consolidation a useful metaphor? Under what circumstances? What types of biological and behavioral events are relevant in considering such a construct? What aspects of memory and memory phenomena require a memory consolidation explanation?

The volume has a second related agenda, namely to bring together historically disparate approaches to the study of learning and memory. Considerations of the biology, psychology, and pathology of human and lower animal learning and memory have progressed separately. This has seriously compromised what we might learn about complex memory-learning-cognitive phenomena. We believe that if we are to make substantial progress in understanding the *psychobiological* determinants of cognitive processes, then we must be prepared to integrate theory and data from these different areas of investigation. Without such a

1

synthesis we will continue to ask weak questions and generate incomplete data. On the other hand, with an appropriate merging of those approaches, it should be possible to learn a great deal about the structure of cognitive processes.

We would hope that this volume will challenge current metaphors and concepts now used in memory research. The cognitive psychologist should obtain a picture of biological and clinical phenomena that are ordinarily outside his or her area of study but may in fact be relevant and important in defining aspects of memory and learning. Likewise, those interested in learning and memory in lower animals will find a discussion of memory consolidation based on the study of information processing in man equally worthwhile. Such a view of human memory may provide new insights about memory processes in lower animals. The volume may also be important for the neuroscientists who remain frustrated in relating brain events to behavior. If neuroscientists are going to help define the biological bases of higher mental processes, they must be as appreciative of the complexities and structure of cognitive behaviors as they are of biological tools and theories about the brain. Ultimately, it is of little value to map vague behaviors onto precise biological events.

POINT OF VIEW

Understanding the structure and determinants of how living systems adaptively respond to their environment, learn, and remember has persisted as a most important issue in psychology. Survival depends on effective appreciation and integration of information from the internal and external environment. To associate and respond to an event requires access to information about relevant prior experience, and the integration of the consequences of responses to ongoing stimulus events (information). Many psychologists have emphasized the importance of acquisition processes and, to a lesser extent, retrieval processes, in defining learning and memory; others have demonstrated the importance of postprocessing events in the establishment and maintenance of memory traces. In general, cognitive psychologists have shown relatively little interest in defining mediational-rehearsal processes that succeed initial acquisition of information. Other experimentalists have sustained their interest in the nature of postprocessing biological and behavioral events that may modify some central nervous system representation of previously processed experience. Scientists concerned with the biology of animal learning and memory have been most persistent in their interest in these postprocessing events. They, rather than investigators of human learning and memory, have found memory consolidation a useful working concept for considering how brain events might mediate memory processes. They have demonstrated that many types of treatments introduced after acquisition modulate and alter memory. The very fact that postprocessing events can affect what is ''remembered'' in lower animals is considered a reflection of the

consolidation process at work. The period of time in which memory is susceptible to change may vary from milliseconds to hours, days, even years after
training or learning. It would also appear that a number of different types of
biological (and behavioral) systems may be involved in memory consolidation.
Some of these systems are described by contributors to this book.

For those interested in human learning and memory, a memory consolidation
construct has not been considered useful. Cognitivists have found other types of
explanations and metaphors much more helpful in describing memory phenomena. These involve descriptors that can be more easily tied to observable
behavioral events. Consolidation processes, as perhaps passive "unconscious"
operations, are inconsistent with the behavioral operationalism of contemporary
information-processing research. Nevertheless, the notion of memory consolidation merits reconsideration in light of recent advances in other areas of memory
research. The contributors of the chapters that follow consider the value and
structure of memory consolidation in a critical, evaluative, and integrative
fashion.

BASES FOR CONSIDERING MEMORY
CONSOLIDATION

Despite the fact that memory consolidation refers to a subset of postprocessing
events, it can mean a variety of things and imply varying processes to different
investigators. It is not likely to be a single process or event.

Most of the data base for considering memory consolidation comes from
psychobiological studies of lower animals with an emphasis on biological rather
than behavioral events. Notions and theories about memory consolidation have
also relied upon findings of the effects of various neuropharmacological agents
introduced either before or after the acquisition of information in animals and more
recently in humans. Other concepts of memory consolidation have also been based
upon studies of impairments in memory and learning as seen in a variety of clinical
syndromes. In contrast, cognitive psychologists have developed models and
theories that have not included memory consolidation. For human memory researchers, postprocessing events have been considered in terms of cognitive
operations and processes that would be expected to alter acquisition through
changes in encoding. Furthermore, a consideration of postprocessing events, from
a cognitive perspective, has not been logically or psychologically linked to
consolidation processes in lower animals. Together, all of these research efforts
have suggested a role for memory consolidation processes in particular and
postprocessing events in general, in the development, maintenance, and retrieval
of memories. A consideration of how memory consolidation might be useful in
understanding cognitive phenomena may also provide a framework for bringing
together the divergent approaches that have persisted in the study of memory and

learning. As such, it may invite us to reformulate how we think about memory phenomena. These areas of study are reviewed by the contributors to this volume. We begin with a brief historical overview of learning and memory research because that may be helpful for understanding current differences in theory and approach to cognitive phenomena.

A HISTORICAL CONTEXT FOR CONSIDERING MEMORY CONSOLIDATION

Any area of science can be seen as an evolution or unfolding of theory, metaphor, and models leading to experimental tests and new findings, which can then be used to support, modify, and sometimes refute our theoretical notions about a set of phenomena. This leads to new theories and descriptors for better defining our observations about a set of events. The metaphors, models, and theories we use determines the types of questions we ask, and what we consider important and worth explaining. This process by which our view of an area is altered is most frequently smooth, orderly, and continuous, with few dramatic shifts in theory and approach to problems. Part of the orderliness is artificially created by a consensually arrived at set of assumptions and accepted domain of theory that guides the behavior of a scientific community and determines how we ask questions, which questions are important, and which methods of research we employ. Theory also guides how we interpret findings. Occasionally there are dramatic changes in thinking about phenomena and the paradigms used to investigate them. Such upheaval is built upon new dramatic types of findings, rediscovery of important old findings, or fresh formulations of old theories and findings. Such paradigm shifts often produce changes in our thinking that go well beyond the areas of study that triggered these changes in viewpoint, method, and theory. There have been relatively few such sharp breaks in thinking about cognition, at least within experimental psychology. This is so despite the fact that we know little more about bases of learning and memory than we did 50 years ago. Perhaps this is because experimental psychologists, more so than physical scientists, focus more on how they do science than how they can solve the problems addressed. They are particularly vocal and explicit about what they consider psychologically and scientifically defensible approaches and what types of metaphors they find acceptable for describing and defining aspects of behavior. Perhaps we have been trapped in a historical rut and tradition which will be ineffective in solving how learning and memory work.

What is our historical heritage that determines how we examine learning and memory? All memory researchers have agreed on what questions need to be explored: What determines the acquisition (learning), retention, elaboration, and persistence of memory, and what influences the retrieval or performance of what has been learned? Many approaches to the study of these phenomena have evolved, and these have been pursued separately in human and animal learning.

At one time it was hoped that "laws" of learning and memory that were derived from the study of lower animals would be equally useful in accounting for human learning and memory. Lawful stimulus-response relationships were described in the form of mathematical statements based on notions of drive, motivation, the probabilities and strength of some response in a hierarchy of responses, or the relationship between stimuli. With behaviorism, general laws of learning and memory were stripped of concepts without clear behavioral referents such as many poorly understood intervening biological events (see Boring [1950] for an excellent treatment of this history).

For the past 30 years human learning and memory research has proceeded separately from the earlier tradition of a generalized approach to learning and memory. It has involved the study of acquisition and retreival processes but not of retention processes. That is, studies performed in the human learning laboratory have focused on the events that occur just before or at the time of information processing or at the time of the retrieval or performance of some learned behavior. The events that succeed information storage have been largely ignored, except by students of interference theories of memory. Within this research context cognitive psychologists have determined a great deal about the processes that mark the establishment of memory traces. Research has successfully defined some of the characteristics of stimuli that make them more or less noticeable, differentially encodable, easily learned, or learned with greater difficulty. Other research has characterized the capacity of our attentional memory system: still other studies have dealt with the ways in which organizational properties of stimuli can alter what is learned and what is remembered. We have learned something about how retrieval context in relation to encoding conditions determine whether a subject can successfully remember some information. These findings and related theory are discussed in all volumes on memory, learning, or information processing. Basic questions about what maintains information in memory are not asked by cognitive psychologists. A research void remains. Similarly, little is known, and there is little inquiry about, the plasticity of memory traces. Unlike animal learning and memory research, little work has been done relating postprocessing events that may take place immediately after learning with the ways these events alter what might be remembered at a later point in time. These postprocessing events would include biological as well as behavioral processes that occur during retention periods of various lengths.

When human learning and memory researchers shifted their efforts away from attempts to account for cognitive processes on the basis of theories of learning and memory in lower animals, they attempted to develop models of information processing that would isolate and define different components of acquisition. It was assumed that this could be done by studying unimpaired subjects in the human laboratory. They would provide the data base necessary to specify distinct stages of information processing that are part of the establishment of memories. Computer models and metaphors were first used to define how events are stored in memory. There was relatively little interest in what maintains memory traces. Little research was accomplished concerning the retrieval of information from memory. No effort was made to understand underlying biological processes. The research emphasis on acquisition processes for defining learning and memory continued with the recent development of single process theories of learning and memory. Although these levels of processing, or elaboration-encoding theories, were thought to provide a contrasting and perhaps competing framework for the analysis of memory, few new methods (or problems) were introduced to study memory phenomena.

All of the cognitive information-processing models that have been developed in the past three decades were designed to link the complex set of events that begin with receptor stimulation and end with some performance measure that would indicate memory or learning had taken place. A heritage of logical positivism and operationalism assured that the concepts, metaphors, and descriptors used to define aspects of information-processing models were limited to observable, verifiable behaviors that could be measured. One could manipulate the nature of stimuli and response conditions but not events inside a subject's head. Unconscious, passive, subjective, mediational processes were therefore appropriately excluded as data and with it a concept such as memory consolidation was also omitted. Memory consolidation was difficult to operationalize, within the context of contemporary human memory research, and therefore could not be adequately studied in the human learning laboratory. In addition, most cognitive researchers were convinced that biological processes need not be a part of information-processing research—that memory and learning could be adequately studied in terms of behavioral events in the unimpaired subject. In fact, some contemporary cognitive psychologists such as Wickelgren, Landauer, and Bjork have used memory consolidation explanations (see Wickelgren, 1977, for a review). They are the exceptions, and this aspect of their research has had relatively little influence on other cognitive psychologists. Finally, the concept of memory consolidation was outside the domain of contemporary information-processing research, which was primarily concerned with how memories get formed or established during the brief period after stimulus exposure, at acquisition. Processes that extend well into the time in which subjects are attending to other stimuli were not of interest.

The study of impaired learning and memory has been of interest to yet another group of psychologists. Their training was often clinically focused and therefore different from those interested in the study of cognitive processes within the tradition of experimental psychology. The general focus of this clinical research was the cognitive dysfunction associated with some syndrome rather than laws that might govern memory processes. Nevertheless, these clinical research efforts, particularly those directed at describing memory pathology in neuro-psychiatric populations, also resulted in the development of models, paradigms, and frameworks for defining aspects of memory. These models of disturbed memory relied more heavily on neurological metaphors and concepts and less on models of information processing based on the study of unimpaired subjects. Failures in recent memory, disruptions in accessing knowledge structures in semantic memory, and time-dependent retrograde amnesias were some of the phenomena of particular interest to these neuropsychologists. To the clinical neuropsychologist the notion of memory consolidation was considered particularly useful in accounting for retrograde amnestic effects. Descriptions of cognitive dysfunctions were detailed in patients with various kinds of relatively specifiable brain lesions that included structures such as unilateral or bilateral lesions of the temporal lobe, frontal lesions, limbic structures, etc., as well as studies of patients with reversible brain insults such as head trauma or those receiving electroconvulsive therapy. Single case studies of patients with rare and difficult to define lesions, the study of patients with temporal lobe dysfunctions, Korsakoff syndrome, progressive dementias, and localized head injury patients all served to provide an important clinical base for studying the pathologies of memory. There was relatively little integration of data or theory that emerged from the study of unimpaired individuals and the views of disordered human memory that grew from neuropsychological research. In general, the study of impairments in memory were either ignored by model builders investigating memory and learning in unimpaired subjects, or viewed with curiosity, sometimes interest, but no more so than other unusual or rare accidents of nature.

A behavioral tradition for the study of animal learning is well established. There is a well-established consensus about the key problems, questions, and concepts that remain unresolved in accounting for learning and performance in lower animals. What are the elements, conditions, structure, topography of learning a set of stimulus-response relationships? Observable behavior is the basis of such theorizing; hypothetical constructs are unacceptable. In addition, it is internally consistent to argue that the same lawful relationships that define animal learning should serve to account for how man learns and remembers. Findings from the study of human information processing, learning, and memory, and its pathology have not been considered particularly useful for those interested in how animals learn and remember (perform some behavior). The study of the biology of animal learning and memory has also been largely ignored by most behaviorists interested in laws of learning and memory.

The study of the biology of learning and memory has also developed separately from the study of the psychology of learning and memory. Although research efforts have provided an increasingly detailed picture of brain events that may be relevant for learning and memory, they have been mapped onto vague and poorly defined behavioral measures. This has been the case precisely because studies of biological determinants of memory have been pursued in relative isolation from the study of human learning, behavioral studies of animal learning, and cognitive pathologies. The neuroscientist has considered "going it alone" as his tools have become increasingly sophisticated. In general, the developments in the neurosciences have been well outside the domain of psychology and have produced a wealth of theory and tools that can be used to define brain events. For example, it is with rapidly increasing precision that one can examine the neuroanatomical sites that may play a role in memory. Similarly, neurochemical events can be characterized in great detail. Many brain events can be measured in man through noninvasive techniques. It is now possible to begin to characterize regional brain activities that may be involved in thinking, learning, and memory. Techniques include both traditional and new forms of psychophysiology such as event-related evoked responses, cerebral blood flow, and biochemical assays that measure, albeit indirectly, neurochemical central nervous system changes. Recent methods for studying regional brain metabolism have further expanded our capabilities to define some of the biological events that may be important in cognition. In addition, increasingly specific pharmacological tools have allowed us to temporarily alter the activity of relatively specific aggregates of neurons and relate such changes to cognitive events. Similarly, it is possible to measure in detail specific characteristics of the neurochemical response of the brain to many drug stimuli.

The combination of neurophysiological, neurochemical, and neuroanatomical measure of brain activity can be used to provide us with a picture of the biology of cognitive processing in man. However, to be of more value to both cognitivist and neuroscientist, the effects of such biological probes should be mapped onto detailed descriptions of cognitive events. Many neuroscientists have become interested in relating brain events to behavior, but most are content to relate brain events to each other. In either case the cognitive psychologist should seize the opportunity to exploit some obviously powerful tools to begin to define a biology of cognitive processes. For these tools and concepts to be effective requires that we ask not only intelligent cognitive questions but project and map them onto appropriate biological systems. Many brain systems may have some role in the formation, maintenance, and retrieval of memories. Little research has been accomplished that would define the role of these different systems for different types of cognitive activities. What has been lacking is the development of a biological taxonomy of memory that includes the detail of biological and component cognitive relationships.

The concept of memory consolidation has been used most frequently in research directed at discovering the biological determinants of memory. Consolidation models have offered a seductively useful construct to account for disruptions or enhancements in memory performance of some previously learned behavior. Here, the concept of memory consolidation has not only been used as a theoretical construct but has also determined the types of experiments and designs for studying learning and memory phenomena. Typically, treatments are introduced after learning. These treatments might then alter the characteristics and integrity of memory traces that have already been established or laid down in some temporary or plastic form. These, biological processes, that follow acquisition and precede performance (retrieval), have been the concern of those interested in animal memory consolidation. What is implied and explained by memory consolidation in lower animals remains open to much debate.

ISSUES TO BE CONSIDERED IN DEFINING A PSYCHOBIOLOGY OF MEMORY CONSOLIDATION

What can one make of the concept of memory consolidation in the historical contexts described above? Is the concept of memory consolidation a useful one in defining aspects of information processing? Does memory consolidation suggest new methods of approach or new formulations of current findings that, when applied to human learning and memory research, tell us something new about memory phenomena? Are there phenomena that are not readily explicable on the basis of contemporary models of memory and learning that can be better understood using a concept like memory consolidation? Might such a notion be of value in describing the establishment, maintenance, and retrieval of memories? Memory consolidation, when considered by human learning and memory researchers, is quite different from how the concept is used in the study of disorders of learning and memory or by those scientists interested in drug-altered cognition in humans; or in the study of the biology or psychology of learning and memory in lower animals. If the construct is of value, then what might it explain or describe about memory? Does the concept, memory consolidation, account for some phenomena we associate with memory processes that cannot be readily explained on the basis of other existing notions? Does it add to our descriptive and predictive capabilities in defining the circumstances under which learning or memory are likely to be more or less complete? Does it suggest new approaches to the study of memory phenomena? The fact that psychologists often ask different questions about memory makes it inherently difficult to answer such questions in a general way.

There have been three broad types of issues and concerns that have persisted as research themes in memory consolidation: 1) What is the nature of the biological factors that mediate such processes? 2) What are, if any, the cognitive behaviors that are part of the processing operations that follow acquisition and of memory consolidation, in particular? 3) What is the joint role of biological and psychological determinants or psychobiological determinants that defines memory consolidation processes? The classic biological issues that have been of major concern include the following: What are the biological bases of memory consolidation processes? What is the time frame during which information in memory store continues to be vulnerable to change? Do consolidation processes occur over a period of seconds, hours, days or even years after information has been acquired and is represented in memory? Is the time frame of such consolidation processes different for different types or components of postprocessing events? Do the time-dependent retrograde amnestic phenomena in lower animals, as well as in man, represent one kind of empirical basis for examining the issue of time-dependent memory consolidation processes? Linked to the issue of the timing of memory consolidation processes are questions about the nature of the perhaps differentiated biological processes that may take place after acquisition. What brain systems are involved? For example, to what extent do memory consolidation processes depend upon the integrity of limbic and diencephalic structures? To what extent do consolidation processes act through changes in dendritic branching, alterations in neuronal competition, changes in synaptic plasticity? What are the chemical changes that may be important in determining how memories become fixed or changed in their form? These would include regional changes in neurotransmitter activity, or altered neuroendocrine function, both in the central as well as the peripheral nervous system. These physiological determinants may or may not also be reflected in the kinds of encoding processes that are used to reformat information, making it less vulnerable to disruption or decay.

As we pointed out earlier, cognitive psychologists have generally avoided the use of memory consolidation as an explanatory metaphor in accounting for memory phenomena. Nevertheless, it is clear that recently acquired information appears to change over time, and this is not easily explained on the basis of retrieval factors. It is also difficult to account for the maintenance of information in memory on the basis of current cognitive theory and data. Regardless of whether one uses any facet of a memory consolidation concept, it is clear that memory traces are subject to change, through active as well as passive (perhaps ''unconscious'') processes. It would also appear that some reworking and re-structuring of what is in memory occurs long after acquisition. Postprocessing, rehearsal, mediation, and related types of cognitive operations may account for some of these changes in recently acquired information. The role of schemata, introduced a half century ago as a way of describing alterations in the structure of what is in memory, can be seen as one kind of postprocessing memory consolidation explanation (Bartlett, 1932). Freud's notion of consolidation as a kind of forgetting that can make way for the development of new concepts may also fit a schematic interpretation of how memories change after acquisition. The broad question of how information in episodic memory may gradually be recoded so that it becomes part of knowledge memory (a memory system that is highly structured but dissociated from the context in which that information was acquired) may also be an example of memory consolidation (Tulving & Donaldson, 1972).

The role of retrieval processes in defining what is in memory continues to be an important issue in the psychology of information processing. In relation to consolidation processes, retrieval processes may include periodic reactivation of information that is in episodic memory and concurrent restructuring of knowledge memory (e.g., a kind of updating of information in memory. See the Miller and Marlin chapter in this volume.) Perhaps such persistent and periodic retrieval and restructuring of what is in memory may serve to stabilize and maintain memory traces. This may be yet another cognitive reflection of a type of memory consolidation process.

In organizing this volume we had to consider several issues. First, would it be possible to bring together the diversity of problems, metaphors, questions, and types of explanations that have been considered part of the domain of memory consolidation? What kind of picture of memory processes would emerge from such a synthesis? Who would find such a synthesis of views of interest and value? Would such a presentation of viewpoints about memory consolidation provide an opportunity to consider some phenomena ordinarily ignored? Certainly the contributors to this volume have found our exchange of views extremely valuable. It has altered how we think about memory phenomena. Whether this interchange can be of value to others remains to be seen.

In developing an overview and synthesis of the psychobiology of memory consolidation as well as providing a generalized framework for considering cognitive issues we move from a biological view of memory consolidation to a psychobiological picture of memory processes in lower animals. We then consider the psychology and biology of memory consolidation in cognitively impaired patients. The first chapter provides an overview of the relationship between brain systems that are involved in reinforcement, reward, and self-stimulation and those areas of the brain that play some role in memory and learning. In this chapter Ralph Esposito develops both a neuroanatomical and neurochemical basis for linking brain-reward systems and memory. The next three chapters are concerned with memory consolidation from the vantage point of animal memory research. Gold and McGaugh consider the time-dependent processes that define memory consolidation. They emphasize the role of the peripheral as well as central nervous system, neuroendocrine factors, and particularly the catecholamine system. Miller and Marlin, as well as Spear and Mueller, consider, in detail, the role of retrieval processes in memory consolidation. Miller and Marlin consider how reactivation of previously stored information, as part of a process of updating catalogues of knowledge in memory, may be at the heart of consolidation processes. Spear and Mueller highlight the importance of retrieval context conditions in determining access to memory traces and link these events to memory consolidation. Keppel, in considering what is known about human memory and learning, provides a critical review of the value of notions of memory consolidation for our understanding of human memory. He points out that in the past such a concept has not served to teach cognitive psychologists much about learning and memory phenomena and argues that existing cognitive models and methods are not strengthened or enhanced by memory consolidation metaphors. Other concepts serve well enough to account for how we learn, remember, or forget information. In contrast, Loftus and Paivio consider some of the dynamic changes that occur in the form and structure of memories in terms of postprocessing events ordinarily not considered in detail in current human learning and memory research. They rely heavily on memory phenomena that occur outside the traditional laboratory setting. In considering clinical and pharmacological studies of memory consolidation processes in man, Squire, Cohen, and Nadel, then Albert, and finally Parker and Weingartner, describe a rather diverse set of observations about memory phenomena that would appear to require some type of memory consolidation explanation. These include different types of time-dependent retrograde amnesias that share similarities to those seen in studies of lower animal learning. In addition, findings based on drug manipulations, following an acquisition phase of learning, can, in some instances, disrupt or enhance the probability of recalling a set of events at a much later point in time. These kinds of findings suggest that memory traces remain plastic long after acquisition.

In summary, the volume provides a picture of memory consolidation from many different points of view. It should also serve as a synthesis that can be used to develop a psychobiology of cognition. We feel that animal learning and memory research can teach us much about the psychobiology of memory formation in humans. A detailed analysis of brain events associated with human and lower animal learning and memory should be relevant to contemporary cognitive research. Findings based on studies of unimpaired subjects, patients with reversible or irreversible disruption of various brain regions, and neuropharmacological studies of both unimpaired subjects and cognitively impaired patients are also relevant for the development of theories that describe memory mechanisms. It is the convergence of information about the nature of memory processes in general and memory consolidation in particular that is viewed as the appropriate framework for the analysis of memory.

A CONSIDERATION OF POSTPROCESSING EVENTS: A FRAMEWORK FOR THE ANALYSIS OF HUMAN MEMORY CONSOLIDATION

We consider three different types of processes part of memory consolidation. All succeed the aquisition of information and play different roles in determining the integrity of memory traces.

The best described of these processes are the sustained, passive, automatic, biological operations that occur over a period of time and in stages after learning. These processes may persist long after an event has been stored in memory and can take place in parallel with other behavioral and biological events. These multiphasic biological events occur in a fixed sequence, each mediated by different but overlapping neuroanatomical and neurochemical systems. We would view these biological processes as involved in "stabilizing" memory traces; they need not be reflected in conscious active cognitive operations. Furthermore, this type of memory consolidation process is one that is relatively ubiquitous and nonspecific, affecting all kinds of stored information.

We postulate that a second set of consolidation processes are involved in selectively altering the strength and form of only some highly discriminable, recently formed trace events in memory. This learning may be particularly important for effective adaptation to the environment and is associated and tied to definable consequences. Brain systems involved in mediating affect, motivation and reward would be particularly involved in this type of memory consolidation process. One manifestation of such a memory consolidation process would be changes in arousal or activation (Weingartner, Hall, Murphy, & Weinstein, 1976) as well as selective reinforcement or reward that related to some learned information (Esposito, this volume). This type of memory consolidation process would also be reflected in cognitive operations used to encode experiences. Unlike the slower passive consolidation processes, this postprocessing biological process would be initiated rapidly and decay in a short period of time and would serve to selectively mark and highlight some information in working memory. This type of process may represent the biological basis of the now classic Thorndike law of effect.

A third type of postprocessing event that may be important in defining the persistence and changes in memory traces is essentially cognitive in nature and therefore may not fit traditional or classic concepts of memory consolidation.

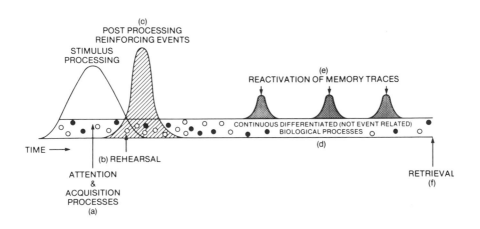

FIG. 1.1.   Some component memory consolidation processes.

These cognitive processes are involved in relating recently processed events to previously established structures in memory that represent the organism's previously acquired knowledge base (e.g., semantic memory). These structures can be seen as providing a context for the rehearsal of information in working memory. These same structures may be continually reactivated long after an event has been processed and encoded (even weeks later) and may be involved in recoding information in episodic memory so that it is integrated with information in knowledge memory. This process would include the reorganization of information in episodic memory, and this cognitive operation may occur in stages and over an extended period of time.

These three processes that are viewed as different types of memory consolidation are portrayed in Fig. 1.1. It explicitly tries to link cognitive and biological processes in a manner that can be applied to the analysis of memory phenomena. As such it has provided us with a useful heuristic and framework for thinking about memory consolidation.

REFERENCES

Bartlett, F. C. *Remembering: A study in experimental and social psychology.* Cambridge: Cambridge University Press, 1932.

Boring, E. G. *A history of experimental psychology.* New York: Appleton-Century-Crofts, 1950.

Tulving, E. & Donaldson, W., Eds. *Organization of memory.* New York: Academic Press, 1972.

Weingartner, H., Hall, B., Murphy, D. C., & Weinstein, S. *Nature,* 1976, *263*, 311.

Wickelgren, W. A. *Learning and memory.* Englewood Cliffs, N.J.: Prentice Hall, 1977.

2 Cognitive-Affective Integration: Some Recent Trends From a Neurobiological Perspective

Ralph U. Esposito
National Institute of Mental Health

Recent advances in neuroanatomy, electrophysiology, and neuropharmacology have contributed enormously to our understanding of the neural structures that support rewarding brain stimulation in animals and of their functions during more naturalistic behaviors. It has been proposed that these so-called "reward pathways" constitute a brain "system" that appears to have evolved to amplify the effects of biologically significant stimuli and related responses in order to modify the organism's adaptive repertoire. This biological function would of necessity be related to the psychological constructs of attention, reward, and memory.

Various biochemical, anatomical, and pharmacological studies have indicated a critical role for the central catecholamines, particularly dopamine, in the mediation of brain stimulation reward. The evidence for dopamine involvement in the mediation of mesotelencephalic self-stimulation is particularly cogent. It is hypothesized herein that these *ventral midbrain dopaminergic neurons*, in conjunction with *opiate-mu* receptors, function to bias the sensitivity of certain forebrain structures (i.e. *frontal cortex, cingulate cortex, amygdala*) involved in the integration of higher order perceptual input with information concerning stimulus significance. This "reward-selective" attentional process serves to activate the organism to orient and respond to motivationally significant stimuli. Sustained activity in dopaminergic pathways, in conjunction with *opiate-delta* neurons, provides immediate feedback for continuation of behavioral sequences that result in positive hedonic consequences. Thus, *opiate-mu* receptors may function as filters in "reward-selective" attention for external stimuli whereas *opiate-delta* receptors may be involved in the concurrent filtering for internal stimuli of significance based on past associations and internal drive states. This latter

15

internal hedonic feedback serves the dual purpose of maintaining adaptive behavioral sequences while also initiating mechanisms involved with the consolidation of the memory process for the experience. *This hypothesis essentially conceives of the dopaminergic-enkephalinergic "reward" pathways as an integral part of a complex neuronal network involved with the sensitization and desensitization of organisms to exogenous, and particularly endogenous, stimuli of significance.* The degree of functional activity encountered in this neural system has relevance both for normal cognition and disturbances in thought, affect, and attention encountered in certain psychiatric disease states.

INTRODUCTION

Numerous attempts have been made to relate specific fiber systems, which support rewarding brain stimulation in animals, to specific drive-oriented behaviors such as sexual activity, feeding, etc. In retrospect, it is clear that these attempts to localize classes of behavior to circumscribed "reward" pathways have generally been unsuccessful (for a review, see Morgane, 1979). Essentially, these endeavors have yielded to more general considerations that have attempted to account for the marked plasticity and situational dependency of behaviors elicited by electrical (or chemical) stimulation to any particular brain site (e.g., Valenstein, Cox, & Kakolewski, 1968). The fact that rewarding brain stimulation can be reliably demonstrated in diverse species, extending from fish to man (German & Bowden, 1974), suggests a very basic neurophysiological mechanism of some widespread and fundamental evolutionary significance. Thus, in lower animals such as the rat, it has been suggested that the neural pathways that both support self-stimulation behavior and yield various stimulation-induced behaviors (such as feeding, drinking, sexual activity, etc.) may be conceptualized as a "command motor system" for exploratory-investigatory, goal-seeking, or simple appetitive behavior in general (Panksepp, 1981). In logical extension, it has been proposed that in higher animals and man these so-called "reward pathways" constitute a brain system that has evolved to amplify the effects of significant stimuli and related responses in order to increase their likelihood of retention (Valenstein, 1977). Thus, neural "reward systems" may be conceived of as facilitators of goal-directed or purposeful behavior. When considering human purposeful behavior in particular, the concepts of direction and purpose should not be limited to analysis of overt behaviors, for cognition must have logical, sequential, goal-directed cohesion if it is to be appropriately manifest at the behavioral level. At the level of neuronal behavior, recent advances in neuroanatomy, electrophysiology, and particularly neuropharmacology have contributed enormously to our basic understanding of the neural structures that support rewarding brain stimulation and the functions of these structures during more naturalistic behaviors.

Various converging lines of evidence have indicated a critical role for the central catecholamines (Crow, 1976; Fibiger, 1978, German & Bowden, 1974), particularly dopamine (DA) (Fibiger, 1978; Phillips & Fibiger, 1978; Wise, 1978), in the mediation of this behavior. The evidence implicating dopamine in the mediation of mesotelencephalic rewarding brain stimulation is particularly cogent (Clavier & Routtenberg, 1980; Phillips & Fibiger, 1978).[1] Perhaps the most exciting discovery of the neuroanatomical "renaissance," sparked by the initial application of the Falck and Hillarp histochemical fluorescence technique (Falck, Hillarp, Thieme, & Torp, 1962), and its subsequent refinements, was the description of this extensive DA projection system, ascending in close association with the medial forebrain bundle to innervate several telencephalic areas. In the rat, the cell bodies of origin of this system arise from the ventral mesencephalon, comprising areas A_8, A_9, and A_{10} according to the nomenclature of Dahlström and Fuxe (1964), and ascend within the projection pathways roughly congruent with the nigrostriatal and mesolimbic pathways as described by Ungerstedt (1971). From a general morphological viewpoint (and, to some extent, a functional view), the ascending fibers of the mesotelencephalic DA system should be considered a unitary system with a lateral to medial, though partially overlapping, topographic arrangement of projections to the striatal and limbic cortices (Björklund & Lindvall, 1978). Thus, in a certain sense, the limbic forebrain may be said to have a crude topographic DA representation in the ventral mesencephalon. Björklund and Lindvall (1978) contend that the mesotelencephalic DA system, from a phylogenetic perspective, should be regarded as an old component of the reticular formation, and as such may represent a reification of Nauta's (1963) conceptualization of a limbic-midbrain connection. The major terminal structures include the caudate and putamen of the basal ganglia, nucleus accumbens, olfactory turbercle, septum, bed nucleus of the stria terminalis, amygdala, anterior-medial cortex, and the suprarhinal (sulcar) frontal cortex (for detail, see Björklund & Lindvall, 1978). The cortical projections to the anterior-medial frontal and anterior cingulate areas have been the most intensively studied terminal areas. Their pattern of innervation from the mesencephalon has been detailed in a number of studies (Hökfelt, Fuxe, Johansson, & Ljungdahl, 1974; Lindvall, Björklund, Moore, & Stenevi, 1974; Lindvall, Björklund, & Divac, 1979; Thierry, Blanc, Sobel, Stinus, & Glowinski, 1973). Also, in these areas DA sensitive adenylate cyclase has been characterized (Tas-

---

[1]Although evidence indicating *critical* involvement of DA neurons in mesotelencephalic self-stimulation is virtually incontrovertible, recent electrophysiological studies concerned with conduction velocity and refractory periods of self-stimulation neurons (Shizgal, Bielajew, & Yeomans, 1979; Shizgal, Bielajew, Corbett, Skelton, & Yeomans, 1980; Yeomans, 1979) also indicate the necessary involvement of neurochemically unidentified, descending, myelinated, rapid-firing neurons, that probably project back to the DA cells in the ventral tegmental area, and other more caudal brainstem sites. Some prominent fiber systems likely to fulfill such a role in reward circuitry will be discussed in the section titled "The Maintenance of Behavior".

sin, Thierry, Blanc, & Glowinski, 1974), specific uptake mechanisms for DA have been identified (Trabucchi, Spano, Tonson, & Eratola, 1976), cellular responses to DA have been localized and identified electrophysiologically (Bunney & Aghajanian, 1978), and marked apomorphine-induced metabolic activation, as assessed by regional glucose utilization, has been noted (McCulloch, Saviki, McCulloch, & Sokoloff, 1979). In the primate brain, DA concentration is highest in the frontal cortex and decreases precipitously along the fronto-occipital axis (Brown, Crane, & Goldman, 1979). Extensive reciprocal interconnections between target areas of these DA projections, particularly the ventromedial frontal area, anterior cingulate area, and the amygdala in the primate, have been documented by anterograde and retrograde tracing methods (Porrino, Crane, & Goldman-Rakic, 1981). The ventromedial frontal region, including the anterior cingulate gyrus, receives both direct and indirect (amygdalo-thalamo-cortical) input from the amygdala, in contrast to the dorsolateral frontal region, which is essentially devoid of direct or indirect amygdalofugal input. On the basis of its selective relationship with the amygdala, this ventromedial region may be considered the "limbic" portion of the frontal association cortex (Porrino et al., 1981). The past decade has witnessed a great deal of speculation implicating this DA system and its forebrain target structures (with particular emphasis on the limbic-frontal sites) in numerous cognitive and affective processes and various psychiatric disease states, despite the fact that very little is known concerning the basic neuropsychological significance of this system. It has been suggested that these pathways function to affect the intensity by which an organism may perceive and respond to affectively significant stimuli (Ungerstedt & Ljungberg, 1974). In this chapter, experimental evidence will be reviewed, indicating that components of this ventral midbrain DA system, which support rewarding brain stimulation in animals, function to bias the sensitivity of forebrain structures (i.e., frontal, cingulate cortices, and amygdala) concerned with the integration of higher order perceptual input with information concerning affective state.

Highly relevant to the present discussion is the striking congruence of opioid peptides near the dopaminergic cell bodies, in the ventral mesencephalon, and the terminal projection sites, both in the striatal and limbic areas (Elde, Hökfelt, Johansson, & Terenius, 1976: Pollard, Llorens, Bonnet, Costentin, & Schwartz, 1977a; Pollard, Llorens-Cortes, & Schwartz, 1977b: Uhl, Kuhar, Goodman, & Snyder, 1979). This anatomical and biochemical interface has received considerable experimental attention and has recently been extended to the behavioral realm where it has been proposed that the enkephalins exert a modulatory control over the rewarding brain stimulation (Esposito, Perry, & Kornetsky, 1980, 1981) and other, more naturalistic, behaviors mediated by the mesotelencephalic dopaminergic system. Of particular relevance to the issue of opioid modulation of monoaminergic activity is the recent pharmacological evidence suggestive of a multiplicity (Lord, Waterfield, Hughes, & Kosterlitz,

1977; Martin, Eades, Thompson, Huppler, & Gilbert, 1976) and regional heterogeneity of opiate receptors in rat (Chang, Cooper, Hazum, & Cuatrecasas, 1979; Goodman, Snyder, Kuhar, & Young, 1980; Pert, Taylor, Pert, Herkenham, & Kent, 1980; Simon, Bonnet, Crain, Groth, Hiller, & Smith, 1980), monkey (Lewis, Mishkin, Bragin, Brown, Pert, & Pert, 1981), and human (Bonnet, Groth, Gigannini, Cortes, & Simon, 1981) brain. A thorough discussion of the data bearing on this burgeoning and controversial topic of putative multiple opiate receptors (i.e., their exact numbers, specific biosynthetic processes, putative endogenous ligands, and regional distribution) is beyond the scope of the present discussion. However, it will be imperative for the reader to be cognizant of the important distinction between the classic opiate-μ (morphine-preferring highly naloxone sensitive), and the opiate-δ (enkephalin-preferring relatively naloxone insensitive) receptors (Lord et al., 1977).[2] With respect to neuroanatomical distribution of the relative amounts of morphine (μ) versus enkephalin (δ) receptors, some preliminary data have been reported. High density opiate-μ binding has been reported in brainstem areas which have been implicated in the mediation of the analgesic effects of opiates (Chang et al., 1979; Goodman et al., 1980). In contrast, high opiate-δ binding sites, relative to opiate-μ binding, has been reported in the midbrain and frontal cortex (Chang et al., 1979; Goodman et al., 1980; Zhang & Pasternack, 1980).

Another approach to receptor classification has distinguished between Type I and Type II opiate receptors, which seem to be closely related to μ and δ receptors, respectively (Pert, 1981; Pert et al., 1980). Utilizing autoradiographic techniques, this research group has found Type I receptors to be high in areas related to pain transmission and opioid mediation of analgesia (e.g., spinal cord, nucleus gigantocellularis). In contrast, Type II receptors are located predominantly within the limbic forebrain structures, such as the nucleus accumbens, amygdala, and hypothalamus, as well as the frontal cortex (Pert, 1981; Pert et al., 1980). It may be suggested that Type I opiate receptors are involved in the mediation of the sedative and analgesic actions of the opiates, whereas Type II receptors may mediate the excitatory and euphorigenic properties of these compounds. More recently, this same laboratory has also presented some rather provocative data concerning the relative distribution of opiate-μ and -δ receptors in the primate cerebral cortex. They reported that in contrast to -δ receptors, which have been found to be evenly distributed throughout the rhesus cortex,

---

[2]Despite the fact that several distinct opiate receptors have been proposed on pharmacological grounds (Lord et al., 1977; Martin et al., 1976), present biochemical data support only a dichotomy of opiate receptors with differential distribution patterns as revealed by in vitro autoradiography (Pert, 1981, Pert et al., 1980). Recently, this latter research group has presented evidence to suggest that opiate-μ and δ receptors may in fact represent different configurations of a single allosteric receptor complex (Bowen, Gentleman, Herkenham, & Pert, 1981; Quirion, Bowen, & Pert, 1981a). The functional implications of this intriguing "dynamic receptor" hypothesis must await future research.

opiate-μ receptors increased in a gradient along hierarchically related organized systems that sequentially process modality-specific sensory information (visual, auditory, and somatosensory) of an increasingly complex nature. This gradient culminated in the amygdala with the highest opiate-μ receptor density (Lewis et al., 1981). Thus, although the functional significance of these two opiate receptor systems remains uncertain, some general directions may be gleaned from current data. There is general agreement that the *opiate-μ* (or Type I) receptors are likely to be involved with the sedative and analgesic effects of the opiates. Recent data (reviewed by Lewis et al., 1981) also indicate a potentially significant role for these receptors in the affective filtering of external sensory input. On the other hand, it seems plausible that opiate-δ (or Type II) receptors mediate the excitatory and possibly euphorigenic effects of the opiates. In this chapter, evidence relating different aspects of opioid functioning to DA functions, with particular focus on attention-reward mechanisms, will be covered. Although a complete analysis of mesotelencephalic DA functioning should take into account the actions of other closely related putative neurotransmitter systems (e.g., acetylcholine, gamma-aminobutyric acid, thyrotrophin-releasing hormone, substance P, cholecystokinin, neurotensin, etc.), I believe that this selective focus on enkephalinergic-dopaminergic interactions will yield valuable information concerning the significance and general functional interrelationships between peptidergic and aminergic systems throughout the brain. Such interrelationships (peptidergic-aminergic) will undoubtedly play an increasingly critical role in our understanding of brain behavior relationships.

REWARD-SELECTIVE ATTENTION

Attention encompasses a wide spectrum of psychological processes ranging from simple orientation and habituation responses to sustained vigilance in a complex and varying environment. Within this general domain, it is legitimate to consider and discuss level of consciousness, variation in terms of the sleep-wakefulness continuum, focal attention, attentional shifts (otherwise known as the ability to change set), etc. A somewhat neglected area of attention (particularly from the neuropsychological perspective) constitutes what I will call perceptual-motivational integration. Although this process may involve only a dimension of attentional processes in general, it is critical. Behavioral adaption requires attention to motivationally significant stimuli. The biological utility of ''arousal'' or ''selective filter'' mechanisms, which alert organisms to stimuli without regard to their positive or negative consequences for survival, is rather dubious. In complex and varied environments, survival dictates that animals have considerable behavioral flexibility. It should not be unexpected, therefore, that neural mechanisms would evolve for the amplification of stimuli and related responses that have adaptive significance.

Orientation to Significant Stimuli

Olds (1962) noted that in lower organisms the phenomenon of rewarding brain stimulation is almost entirely related directly or phylogenetically to olfactory functions. Thus, in lower organisms it appears that "reward" mechanisms may have evolved from a primitive, rostral, chemoreceptive mechanism, thus enabling simple appetitive behaviors, such as the pursuit of food or potential mates. In higher organisms, the anatomy of rewarding brain stimulation is still related (in a phylogenetic sense) to "olfactory" structures, but insofar as the predominance of olfactory control of behavior diminishes, there seems to have been a corresponding gradual change in "reward" functions. Other sensory modalities gain "input" and consequently polysensory input can now activate "reward" mechanisms. Crow (1973) described rewarding brain stimulation in rats derived from a system of DA neurons arising from the ventral mesencephalic area around the interpeduncular nucleus with terminals in the corpus striatum, nucleus accumbens, olfactory tuberculum, and the interstitial nucleus of the stria terminalis. Crow noted that this mesencephalic DA system received afferent input from the habenular nuclei (indirect evidence for reciprocal connections have recently been demonstrated: Nauta & Domesick, 1978), which is supplied directly with olfactory fibers (Herrick, 1908, 1948). The tratus olfactopeduncularis also terminates in the region of the interpeduncular nucleus, suggesting an important role for olfactory input in determining the function of this DA system. Olfaction is directed toward objects in the environment, and the activation of movements towards these stimuli. Crow speculated that if there exists an association between the mesencephalic DA neurons and the central olfactory structures, then the DA neurons constitute a final motor pathway for the mediation of the general effects on motor behavior of positively rewarding olfactory stimuli. Further, in the course of evolution, this DA system came to be activated by stimuli (in modalities other than olfaction), which, by past experience, have acquired significance for the organism. These mechanisms, according to Crow, could be the physiological basis for the development of what learning theorists generally term incentive motivation, or incentive induction effects. This proposition is consonant with Old's conception of a primitive forebrain olfactory appendage, which, in the course of evolution, came under increasing complex polysensory control, finally existing as the fundamental substrate for learning in higher animals.

In rats, electrical stimulation delivered to the cell bodies of the mesencephalic DA (areas A_9, A_{10} of Dahlström & Fuxe, 1964) results in increased forward locomotor-exploratory activity accompanied by sniffing. This is similar to the range of behaviors induced by low doses of amphetamine (Moore, 1977). The increased DA-mediated behavior, induced either electrically or by low doses of amphetamine, results in behaviors that can be described as "appetitive" in the sense that they involve active exploratory-investigatory behavior. After destruction of the mesolimbic and mesocortical DA terminals by 6-hydroxydopamine injections, rats manifest a greatly diminished capacity to investigate novel environmental objects (Fink & Smith, 1980). Systemic administration of the dopamine agonist apomorphine to these DA denervated animals increases investigatory responses to novel, but not familiar, environmental objects. (Fink & Smith, 1980). Similar exploratory and oral stereotyped behaviors can be observed in the rat after stimulation of the pyriform cortex, olfactory tubercle, amygdala, and the insulo-orbital cortex (Ellinwood, Sudilovsky, & Nelson, 1973). In a similar vein, Iversen (1977) has recently summarized evidence implicating the so-called mesolimbic components of the mesotelencephalic dopaminergic system in the selection or orientation toward meaningful stimuli, while nigrostriatal fibers initiate appropriate responses. Further, single-unit electrophysiological studies have demonstrated the responsiveness of dopaminergic neurons to external sensory stimuli, which serve as conditioned cues for reinforced responding (Rolls, Thorpe, Perret, Boytim, Wilson, & Szaba, 1981). Thus, dopamine fibers seem to play a significant role at the interface between motivation and movement. The functional significance of the ventral mesencephalic DA ''reward'' neurons may be that of a general system concerned with the facilitation of appetitive behaviors by mediating the effects of rewarding stimulation on performance (Crow & Gilbe, 1974). Students of learning theory should recognize the close similarity of this to Miller's ''go'' or ''activating'' mechanism, which acts to intensify ongoing responsiveness to relevant cues (Miller, 1963), or Sheffield's postulated ''drive induction system,'' whereby the motivating effects of reward feed back into instrumental acts (Sheffield, 1966), or Hull's generalized drive, D (Hull, 1943). Thus, in sum, the DA ''reward'' neurons of the ventral mesencephalon, which are phylogenetically related to olfactory pathways, have developed into a neural mechanism whereby diverse sensory stimuli exert activating or ''drive-inducing'' effects on behavior. Finally, Crow predicted that pathophysiology of the ''incentive-motivational'' system would be expected to seriously impair responsiveness to affectively significant stimuli, thus implying a rather subtle but pervasive role for DA in behavioral regulation (Crow & Arbuthnott, 1972; Crow & Gilbe, 1974). As noted, similar activation of postural and motor mechanisms, generally associated with exploration and attention in the rat, can be elicited by the acute administration of psychostimulants, such as amphetamine. These effects are mediated by the ''so-called'' mesolimbic-mesocortical components of the mesotelencephalic dopamine system (Moore, 1977). Amphetamine-induced behaviors include locomotor stimulation, gnawing, sniffing, licking, grooming, and/or other oral stereotypies. In infrahuman primates, amphetamine will elicit related behavioral patterns with the addition of more head movements, eye-hand coordinated movements, and search-examining activities. In man, curious preparative searching and sorting patterns may emerge (Ellinwood, 1969). These behaviors may be accompanied by feelings of marked perceptual enhancement and sense of satisfaction associated with these repetitive, compulsive behaviors (Ellinwood, 1969; Ellinwood et al., 1973).

Several studies suggest that DA-mediated exploratory investigatory activity may be subject to modulation by enkephalin neurons. The recent finding of enkephalinergic neurons on dopaminergic axon terminals (Pollard et al., 1977a, 1977b) has provided one anatomical basis for interaction between the endogenous opioids and DA. Katz, Carroll, and Baldrighi (1978) reported that synthetic analogues of both leucine and methionine (leu-, met-) enkephalin produced naloxone reversible, dose-related increases in locomotor activity in mice. Naloxone administered to a separate group of mice reduced the initial activation usually seen after exposure to a novel environment. Naloxone has also been found to depress hole-board exploratory activity, entries into a novel environment, and responding for sensory stimulation in mice (Katz & Gelbart, 1978). The latter study also demonstrated a direct correlation between enkephalin-induced behavioral activation and exploratory behavior. Katz (1979) and Rodgers and Deacon (1979) have reported quite similar findings in the rat. Similar findings by Arnsten and Segal (1979) demonstrated that naloxone produced dose-related reductions in frequency of contact with environmental stimuli. Because exploratory behavior is clearly motivated behavior and novel stimuli have been demonstrated to have rewarding value (Berlyne, 1960; Christopher & Butter, 1968), Katz has suggested that naloxone may interfere with the rewarding potential of novel stimuli. In this view, stimuli would lose activating and reinforcing properties and, therefore, cease to reinforce exploratory behavior. Thus, feedback from enkephalin neurons may be necessary in order to sustain DA-mediated orientation and exploration. Microinjections of the long-lasting analog of met-enkephalin, D-Ala^2-met^5-enkephalinamide (DALA-MET), into both area A_{10} (Broekkamp, Phillips, & Cools, 1979b) and the nucleus accumbens (Pert & Sivet, 1977) produced a short latency behavioral stimulation effect. This effect was quite similar to effects produced by electrical stimulation of the A_{10} area (as described by Crow & Gilbe, 1974, see above) or microinjections of DA into the nucleus accumbens (Pijenberg & Van Rossum, 1973). Further unilateral intranigral injections of DALA-MET have been shown to produce contraversive turning behavior in rats (Welzl, Flack, & Huston, 1982), a behavior indicative of DA agonist activity (Ungerstedt, 1971). Similar contraversive turning is also induced by unilateral nigral injections of morphine and more potently by the opiate-δ agonist D-Ala^2-D-Leu^5-enkephalinamide (DALA-LEU) (Pert, 1983). Kelly, Stinus, and Iverson (1980) recently reported that infusion of DALA-MET into the ventral tegmental area of rats induced behavioral activation, which was characterized by increased locomotion, rearing, and number of hole-box investigations. These effects were reversed by nalaxone and blocked entirely by the 6-hydroxydopamine neurotoxic destruction of catecholaminergic cells within the nucleus accumbens. Amphetamine-induced behavioral activation was potentiated by the concurrent infusion of DALA-MET into the ventral tegmental area. These findings, as those above, strongly suggest that the enkephalins may exert a modulatory influence over the mesencephalic DA functioning. Kelly et al. (1980), as did Katz and Gelbart (1978), suggest that this modulation may involve a reward-related function of the enkephalins. Recently, Chesselet, Cheramy, Reisine, and Glowinski (1981) reported data concerning the in vivo local effects of opiates on DA release in the cat caudate nucleus. Both morphine, and more markedly, DALA-MET, stimulated DA release. Morphine's effect was antagonized by nalaxone, but that of the synthetic enkephalin was not. These observations, taken together with the similarity in effects between DALA-MET and peripheral opiate-δ agonists, indicated that enkephalin may increase DA release via an action at presynaptic opiate-δ receptors. Alternatively, recent single unit recording and turning behavior studies suggest an indirect DA agonistic action of enkephalin within the substantia nigra mediated via a disinhibition of inhibitory (possibly gabaergic) interneurons (Pert, 1983). Thus, the exploratory-investigatory behavior related to mesotelencephalic DA may be subject to modulation by opiate-δ neurons. Specifically, feedback from presynaptic (and possibly transynaptic) opiate-δ neurons may be required for sustained DA-mediated exploratory-investigatory behaviors in rodents and more complex DA-mediated attentional behaviors in infrahuman primates and man. As noted in monkeys, the exploratory-investigatory responses include more tactile and visual activities, whereas in humans the range of behaviors is quite variable and can include writing or other cognitive activities.

Complex Perceptual Analysis

If dopaminergic neurons are involved in orientation to meaningful environmental stimuli, then damage to these fibers should result in sensory impairment. Accordingly, Ungerstedt (1974) has described a sensory neglect syndrome produced by unilateral 6-hydroxydopamine-induced striatal lesions in rats. These animals fail to orient toward tactile, auditory, and olfactory stimuli presented to the side contralateral to the lesion; conversely, they respond normally to ipsilaterally presented stimuli. Loss of self-stimulation behavior is also noted and shows a high correlation with total DA loss. There is gradual recovery of some sensory abilities (e.g., after one week the rats will begin to react to smell and after seven weeks, most will respond to visual stimuli), but appropriate reaction to tactile stimulation may not return even after months. This differential rate of recovery argues against a strict motor deficiency and suggests a more subtle inability to integrate sensory and motor functions to perform an appropriate response. The sensory disturbances are believed to be related to more rostral brain sites innervated by the ascending DA fibers (i.e., striatal and limbic forebrain areas), DA terminal degeneration will undoubtedly affect the activity of postsynaptic neurons in the terminal forebrain areas. As noted, the specific function of these ascending DA neurons may be to affect the intensity with which an organism perceives and/or responds to sensory imput (Ungerstedt & Ljungberg, 1974). Thus, as stated, the general functional significance of the ascending DA fibers, which support rewarding brain stimulation in animals, may be to affect the sensitivity of specific forebrain structures (i.e., frontal cortex, cingulate, amygdala) that are concerned with the integration of higher order perceptual information, with information concerning affective state.

Unilateral neglect or inattention to stimuli has been observed clinically in humans with fairly well-circumscribed lesions. Lesions in three particular cortical areas have frequently been associated with neglect syndromes: the inferior parietal lobule, the dorsolateral frontal cortex, and the cingulate gyrus (Heilman, 1979). The inferior parietal area receives input from somatosensory, auditory, and visual association cortex (Pandya & Kuypers, 1969), plus limbic and reticular input (Mesulam & Van Hoesen, 1977). In the monkey, multimodal neglect has been produced by lesions confined to this area (Heilman, Pandya, & Geschwind, 1970). The dorsolateral frontal cortex also receives input from visual, somesthetic, and auditory modalities as well as direct input from the inferior parietal lobule (Pandya & Kuypers, 1969). In addition, biochemical evidence has indicated the presence of DA in this area (Brown et al., 1979), and tracing studies tend to implicate the midbrain as the source of the DA projections to the frontal cortex (Porrino & Goldman-Rakic, 1982). Lesions of the dorsolateral frontal lobe produce a polysensory neglect in the monkey (Kennard & Ectors, 1938; Welch & Stuteville, 1958) and in man (Heilman & Valenstein, 1972). Heilman and Watson (1979) also described unilateral neglect in patients with discrete lesions of the cingulate. Accordingly, Watson, Heilman, Cauthen, and King (1973) experimentally demonstrated that discrete unilateral lesions of the anterior cingulate gyrus produced neglect in monkeys. Pandya and Kuypers (1969) demonstrated projections from the dorsolateral frontal area to the anterior cingulate in the monkey. In the rat, mesencephalic DA projections to the anterior cingulate (Björklund & Lindvall, 1978) have been demonstrated. Studies in the monkey suggest a similar pattern of innervation (Porrino & Goldman-Rakic, 1982). Thus, all cortical areas associated with "sensory" neglect have extensive reciprocal interconnections; in addition, the frontal cortex and anterior cingulate cortex receive DA projections from the midbrain (Björklund & Lindvall, 1978). These two areas also have been functionally linked by extensive electrophysiological and behavioral investigations (Damasio, 1979; Desiraju, 1979).

Heilman and Watson (1979) have postulated an attention-arousal hypothesis of sensory neglect. They have argued that simple sensory or perceptual hypotheses are inadequate to explain neglect because the syndrome is usually multimodal and can be produced by lesions outside of traditional sensory pathways. They note that all three cortical areas have prominent direct and indirect connections with the brainstem reticular formation. The specific importance of the mesencephalic reticular formation has been underscored by the demonstration that discrete lesions to this area will produce neglect in cats (Reeves & Hagamen, 1971) and in monkeys (Watson, Heilman, Miller, & King, 1974). Heilman and Watson (1979) have hypothesized that unilateral neglect is, in actuality, a unilateral attention or alerting defect in a cortico-limbic-reticular circuit. They speculated that the cortex is involved in basic stimulus analysis as it distinguishes novel from non-novel and biologically significant from nonsignificant stimuli. In this scheme, biologically significant stimuli activate corticofugal impulses, which direct the reticular formation to activate the cortex.

The speculation that cortical structures implicated in neglect syndromes are responsive to novel and biologically significant stimuli has received firm support from single unit electrophysiological studies in monkeys. Yin & Mountcastle (1978) have reported neurons in the posterior parietal area, which fire selectively when monkeys visually fixate motivationally significant stimuli. Mirsky and colleagues have reported attention related cells in the reticular formation and prefrontal cortex of monkeys working on a go, no-go visual discrimination task (Pragay, Mirsky, Ray, Turner, & Mirsky, 1978; Pragay, Mirsky, Mirsky, & Scales, 1980; Ray, Mirsky, & Pragay, 1982). These units manifested significant changes either following or anticipating conditioned stimuli that signaled the availability of response-independent reward. Thus, the cells were not related to the response, nor were they responsive to the physical parameters of the task stimuli in the absence of reinforcement conditions. In addition, these cells were responsive to changes in reinforcement conditions, such as variations in the interstimulus interval. They have characterized their cells as attention-reward units. Suzuki and Azuma (1977) reported on cells around the sulcas principalis of the frontal cortex that fired during fixation of a lightspot that controlled behavior by subtle changes in brightness. Kojima (1980) reported on prefrontal units in the monkey that differentiated between behaviorally significant and nonsignificant visual stimuli. Like the units reported by Pragay et al., (1980), these cells were insensitive to physical changes in the stimuli and were also response-independent. More recently, Watanabe (1981) reported prefrontal units in the monkey that also respond to the meaning of a stimulus in a delayed conditional discrimination task, independent of its physical properties. In an interesting study, Rosenkilde, Bauer, & Fuster (1981) reported two types of reward-related cellular activity in the monkey ventral prefrontal cortex. "Type I" cells fired following choice reinforcement or gratuitous reward, apparently indicating reward availability. "Type II" cells fired following changes in reward contingencies. The former were located in the lateral aspect of the ventral prefrontal cortex, while the latter were located more medially. Rolls, Caan, Griffiths, Murzi, Perret, Thorpe, and Wilson (1982) reported on orbitofrontal cells in monkeys that were responsive to changes in reward expectancies (i.e., extinction) or alterations in reward contingencies (i.e., reversal trials in a discrimination paradigm). Niki and Watanabe (1979) reported single units in the cingulate and prefrontal areas of the monkey brain that responded to changes in the reinforcement contingencies, whereas other units fired in an anticipatory manner to reinforcement-related responses. The former may be related to the genesis of the P300 component of the cortical evoked potential, which seems to correlate with this type of information (Sutton, Braren, & Zubin, 1965), whereas the latter may be related to the cortical CNV, which is elicited by anticipation of reinforcement-related responses (Walter, Cooper, Aldridge, McCallum, & Winter, 1964). Finally, in an elegant series of related experiments (with rabbits), Orona, Foster, Lambert, and Gabriel (1972) have shown that units in the deep laminae (V and VI) of the cingulate cortex develop differential responsiveness to the positive and negative conditioned stimuli shortly after the onset of avoidance conditioning (predictive of overt conditioned behavior); during reversal training the units in this area undergo a transition in parallel with appropriate behavioral reversal. In sum, these data strongly suggest the involvement of these cells in the earliest aspects of associative learning.

The attention-arousal hypothesis of neglect (Heilman & Watson, 1979) also postulates the existence of corticofugal projections to the reticular formation and reticular projections to the cortex. Cortico-limbic-reticular projections have been amply demonstrated (Astruc, 1971; French, Hernandez-Peon, & Livingston, 1955; Nauta, 1964). In terms of reticulocortical activity, two ascending routes have been proposed: (1) a ventral basal forebrain pathway, including the lateral hypothalamus, and substantia innominata, believed to mediate EEG desynchronization; and (2) a dorsal route via the thalamus, believed to be important for recruitment phenomenon (Brodal, 1969). The lateral hypothalamus and the substantia innominata both receive fibers from the reticular formation, leading to the suggestion that they may be part of the critical reciprocal reticular-cortico-loop proposed by Heilman and Watson (1979). Marshall, Turner, and Teitelbaum (1971) and Marshall and Teitelbaum (1974) provided some empirical support for this notion by producing neglect in rats with lateral hypothalamic lesions. Unilateral lesions of lateral hypothalamic "reward" sites (i.e., capable of supporting self-stimulation behavior) in split-brain cats (Wright & Craggs, 1979) also result in contralateral neglect and ipsilateral EEG synchrony over a wide frequency range. Thus, it may be inferred that neurons at the level of the lateral hypothalamus, which support rewarding brain stimulation, have pervasive effects on information processing in the cortex. It has been noted by many investigators that these pathways are comparable in many respects to the ascending monoaminergic pathways (Ungerstedt, 1971), and it is remarkable that Ungerstedt (1974) has produced the neglect and related behaviors (aphasia, adipsia, etc.) with specific neurochemical lesions of the ascending DA fibers. Further, unilateral 6-hydroxydopamine lesions in the substantia nigra of rats leads to assymmetrical electroencephalograms, suggestive of lowered arousal, and associated with ipsilateral neglect (Siegfried & Bures, 1978). Finally, Mintz, Tomer, Radwan, and Myslobodsky (1982) reported that in patients with hemi-Parkinsonism (i.e., unilateral), the amplitude of the contralateral visual-evoked potential is significantly reduced. Chronic 1-dopa therapy or simple attentional-task demands can reverse this asymmetry. Interestingly, Parkinson patients also manifest specific increased latencies to the P300 component of the event-related evoked potential, which has been strongly implicated in psychological processes related to selective attention and stimulus evaluation (Hansch, Syndulko, Cohen, Goldberg, Potrin, & Tourtellotte, 1982).

Thus, in sum, substantial evidence exists relating DA fibers and their target forebrain structures in complex sensory analysis (i.e., "attentiveness"). This is consistent with Heilman and Watson's (1979) "attentional" theory of neglect, which postulates a critical cortico-limbic-reticular circuit necessary for attention to biologically significant stimuli. The mesotelencephalic DA system (a phylogenetically old component of the reticular formation) may represent a critical component of the hypothesized cortico-limbic-reticular loop. Accordingly, current evidence suggests that this DA "reward" system, subject to modulation by opioid peptides, biases the sensitivity of certain forebrain targets, thereby affecting the intensity by which an organism perceives and responds to affectively significant stimuli.

External-Internal Integration

Once motivationally significant stimuli have alerted an organism, goal-oriented, purposeful behavior ensues. The maintenance of appropriate behavior sequences (or cognitive events) requires the integration of incoming sensory input with information concerning relevant past associations, present needs, and drive states. This integration will maintain adaptive behavior, and secondarily, initiate memory mechanisms responsible for encoding the experience. The amygdala and closely related limbic-forebrain structures, play a central role in these integrative processes. The dopaminergic input to these areas seems to serve as a critical mechanism for biasing or modulating important input to these forebrain structures and their efferent outputs to striatal pathways, thereby influencing cognitive "acts." This is analogous to the manner by which DA neurons modulate striatal outflow to influence motor behavior. The particular role of the amygdala is perhaps unique, due to its extensive interconnections with neocortical, striatal, and limbic structures (Gloor, 1978).

Major afferent imput to the amygdala derives from orbitofrontal cortex, hypothalamus, pyriform cortex, and the thalamus. In addition, virtually all other limbic structures and every sensory modality projects directly or indirectly to the amygdala (Richardson, 1973), Although early theories of amygdaloid functioning primarily encompassed visceral and olfactory functions, more recent theories, based on lesion and electrophysiological studies, have implied a role for this structure in the ability to incorporate changes in reinforcement contingencies into new adaptive behavioral patterns (Jones & Mishkin, 1972) and in the acquisition of stimulus-reward associations (Mishkin & Aggleton, 1981; Spiegler & Mishkin, 1981). Studies involving radiotelemetered activity from the amygdala in freely moving monkeys engaged in naturalistic interaction have found the highest electrical activity related to social encounters associated with a high degree of ambiguity and emotional significance, i.e., sexual and aggressive encounters (Kling, Steklis, & Deutsch, 1979). In man, depth recordings from epileptic patients have revealed stimulus-elicited electrical activity in the amygdala during tasks that normally generate scalp potentials related to aspects of attention (Halgren, 1980). These findings are in accordance with Gloor's (1978) general psychobiological hypothesis, which conceives of the amygdala as a link between neocortical information for higher order perceptual-mnemonic material and the basic drive mechanisms of the hypothalamus. Recent research has continued to amplify the extensive interrelationships between sensory neocortical areas, the amygdala, and related limbic structures.

Single unit electrophysiological experiments (Prelevíc, Burnham, & Gloor, 1976) in cats have demonstrated an extensive, diffuse, nontopographic excitatory influence exerted upon the lateral, basal, and central nucleus of the amygdala by the lateral temporal neocortex, an area presumed to be involved with complex sensory processing. Research on the neocortical afferent connections to the amygdala in the monkey (Herzog & Van Hoesen, 1976) has revealed an even greater proportion of the temporal neocortex projecting to the amygdala, rendering further support to the view that the amygdala occupies a critical anatomical junction between the diencephalon and the neocortex. Utilizing the horseradish peroxidase retrograde transport technique, Llamas, Avendano, and Reinoso-Suárez (1977) demonstrated ipsilateral amygdaloid projections to virtually the entire prefrontal cortex in the cat. On the basis of these findings the authors note that, in addition to its role in the evaluation of stimulus significance and internal state, the amygdala should exert an important influence on frontal lobe function. In a phylogenetic sense, they have suggested that higher development may, in general, be correlated with increasingly intricate limbic-neocortical connections, thereby permitting increasing complex behavioral patterns. In this vein, the aforementioned results of Porrino et al. (1981) are of interest. Utilizing anterograde and retrograde tracing methods, these investigators demonstrated direct amygdaloid projections to the orbitofrontal cortex and the anterior cingulate gyrus in the rhesus monkey. Interestingly, the dorsolateral frontal region was found to be without direct or indirect amygdalofugal projections. On the basis of the ventromedial frontal region's "select" relationship with the amygdala, they suggest that it be considered a "limbic" portion of the frontal association cortex. It is noteworthy that this particular area of the primate cortex has been implicated on the basis of single cell analysis (see above), in the evaluation of reward and reward-related stimuli (Orona et al., 1982; Rolls, et al., 1982; Rosenkilde et al., 1981; Watanabe, 1981). Amygdaloid unit activity has also been associated with reward-related integrative functions. Thus, in cats, single units in the amygdala, which had habituated to an auditory stimulus, began to fire again when the stimulus was paired with paw shocks (Ben Ari & le Gal la Salle, 1972). Fuster and Uyeda (1971) reported amygdaloid units in the monkey that responded differentially to conditioned signals preceding reward (food) or punishment (shock). Interestingly, under extinction conditions the absolute number of units in the amygdala that responded to the conditioned stimuli decreased. Rolls et al. (1982) also found certain amygdaloid units that fired in response to conditioned stimuli associated with food reward. Thus, the close anatomical and functional interrelationship between the frontal-cingulate cortex and the amygdala is critical for the mediation of stimulus-reward associations. It is also important to note that amygdala lesions disrupt tasks that are dependent on internally generated signals or cues, such as discrimination reversals (Schwartzbaum & Poulous, 1965), timing behavior (Pelligrino, 1968; Pubols, 1966), and learning set problems (Barrett, 1969). Thus, the amygdala may be involved in the integration of both external and internal stimuli with changes in reinforcement contingencies in order to adaptively modify behavior.

As previously mentioned (see introduction), Lewis et al. (1981) reported data concerning the cortical distribution of opiate-μ receptors as assessed by selective binding of [³H] naloxone in the monkey cerebral cortex. They noted that opiate-μ receptors increased in a graded manner along hierarchically organized cortical visual systems that sequentially process sensory input of a progressively more complex nature. Similar gradients were noted for both auditory and somato-sensory systems. For example, in the primate visual system, sensory input is processed along a series of specific, cytoarchitecturally defined cortical areas that correspond to an increasing perceptual complexity (Turner, Mishkin, & Knapp, 1980). In a general manner, once visual information has reached the striate cortex, it is projected anteriorly to prestriate cortex, continues on to inferotemporal cortex, thence to the ventral temporal pole, and from there to the amygdala. Progressively increasing and more widespread cortico-amygdaloid projections arise along the same gradient, suggesting an increasing cortical influence on amygdala activity, coinciding with increasing complexity of the visual input. Lewis and colleagues reported a gradient of increasing receptor density strikingly congruent with the anatomical-functional gradients, culminating with the highest opiate-μ receptor concentration in the amygdala. A similar opiate-μ receptor gradient was reported for both the auditory and somatosensory systems, as they projected from the primary sensory areas along various stages to termina-tions in the amygdala. These authors suggest that, as in the anatomical-functional gradients, opiate-μ receptors may exert a progressively greater influence on increasingly complex perceptual input. Thus, opiate-μ neurons may play a role in the filtering of sensory input at the cortical level. Together, given the amyg-dala's emotional-motivational involvement, they specifically suggest that the opiate receptors may be involved in "emotion-induced selective attention." Conversely, they also hypothesize that amygdaloid afferents back to the cortical sensory areas may constitute a "reverse" gradient of opiate neurons, whereby limbic information relevant to affective state may influence sensory attention. This latter proposition asserts a type of "motivational" corollary discharge, as proposed in motor systems (Teuber, 1964, 1966), which provides affective feedback and influence on sensory input via opiate-μ receptors, thus proposing a possible mechanism by which limbic states could influence sensory mechanisms of selective attention. Outside the posterior sensory processing areas, the highest concentration of opiate receptors was found in the ventromedial frontal cortex. This is of interest because as mentioned previously, this frontal area has extensive interconnections with the amygdala (Porrino & Goldman-Rakic, 1982) and has been strongly implicated in attention and reward-related behaviors on the basis of lesion (Butter, Mishkin, & Mirsky, 1968; Butter, Mishkin, & Rosvold, 1963) and single-unit studies in animals (Rolls et al., 1982; Rosenkilde, 1981; Watanabe, 1981), and clinical observations in man (Damasio, 1979; Jouandet & Gazzaniga, 1979). Interestingly, preliminary electrophysiological studies in animals also indicate an important role for the frontal cortex (see also previous section) in the generation of scalp-recorded event-related potentials related to selective attention (Boyd, Boyd, & Brown, 1982; Knight, Hillyard, Woods, & Neville, 1981; Pirch, Corbus, & Napier, 1981; Pirch & Peterson, 1981).

Preliminary studies in man, along with aforementioned animal data, (see also previous section) have provided some support for this hypothesized role of opiate peptides in attentional processes. In normal human subjects (Arnsten, Segal, Neville, & Hillyard, 1981) and schizophrenics (Davis, 1980), naloxone has been found to alter components of the evoked potential associated with selective attention. Naloxone has also been reported in one study (Lipinski, Meyer, Kornetsky, & Cohen, 1979) to improve the performance of schizophrenic subjects on the Continuous Performance Test (CPT), a reliable measure of sustained visual attention. If replicated, this latter result would be quite important because, from Kraeplin (1919) to the present, attention dysfunction has been considered to be a fundamental defect in schizophrenia. This notion has been confirmed in various experimental paradigms: cross-modal reaction time (Sutton et al., 1965); variable interval reaction time (Zahn, Rosenthal, & Shakow, 1973); inability to maintain cognitive set (Shakow, 1977); sustained visual attention (Kornetsky & Mirsky, 1966); auditory attention; and auditory-evoked potential (Roth, Prefferbaum, Horvath, Berger, & Kopell, 1980). However, the attentional disorder of schizophrenia is clearly not confined to difficulties in the processing or filtering of external sensory input. Phenomenological descriptions by patients themselves, particularly in the acute stages, convey a profound feeling of loss of "control," engendered by an intense preoccupation with internal stimuli, intrusion into consciousness of bizarre ideation (plus affect-laden past associations) feelings of "thought insertion," auditory hallucinations or "voices within," and often a sense of difficulty in distinguishing between thoughts and memories. The intermingling of these cognitive disturbances with ongoing situations and behavior leads to disruption of the normal modulation of sensory experience, difficulty in the ability to maintain the normal focus and coherence of thought, and the profound confusion characteristic of this disorder. It is evident that in addition to disturbances in the filtering of external sensory input, the selective attentional deficit in schizophrenia also reflects an inability to process or efficiently "filter" internal stimuli. Purposeful behavior requires that external input be matched with appropriate internally filtered information, based on relevant past associations, and current motives. Stevens (1973) and Matthysse (1974) have proposed that limbic forebrain DA hyperactivity in schizophrenia is responsible for defective internal stimulus filtering.

Stevens (1973) discussed a pathological widening of the field of consciousness that engenders a sense of internal incoherence that is central to the pathology of schizophrenia. She reviews clinical and experimental data that suggest that overactivity or hypersensitivity at the site of DA terminals in the limbic striatum (nucleus accumbens, olfactory tubercle, and the nucleus of the stria terminals) is responsible for the preemption of consciousness by the characteristic sense of unreality, distorted sexual and sensual perceptions, plus other compelling internal stimuli. She draws a parallel between the limbic striatum and neostriatum on a number of points. Both are similar in terms of ultrastructure, and both receive topographically contiguous DA innervation from the mesencephalon. The two systems also manifest striking similarities in terms of their pattern of afferent input and efferent outflow. There is an orderly projection of virtually the entire neocortex on to the caudate and putamen (Kemp & Powell, 1970). The premotor and motor areas project to the anterior caudate: the parietal and occipital cortices project to ventral and posterior regions. This orderly topographic relationship is maintained by the caudate-putamen efferents to the globus pallidus (Nauta & Mehler, 1966). In a parallel manner, the limbic striatum receives orderly topographic limbic projections, including projections from the pyriform lobe, cingulate gyrus, amygdala, and the hippocampus. Again, parallel to the neostriatal afferent and efferent organization, the output of the limbic striatum, via the substantia innominata, is histologically similar to and ventrally continguous with that of the caudate, i.e., the globus pallidus (Nauta & Mehler, 1966). Electrophysiological evidence (Bunney & Agajahnian 1978; Buchwald 1969; Rolls et al., 1981) indicates that the mesencephalic DA neurons function to bias the sensitivity of single unit responsiveness to significant afferent input in the neostriatum and limbic striatum, thereby influencing their outflow. Stevens proposes that caudate-putamen interneurons (whose sensitivity level is set by mesencephalic DA projections) act as a gate or filter that normally limits and regulates the incoming sensory and motor afferents from the neocortex. In a parallel manner, the "limbic-striatal filter" (particularly the nucleus accumbens) would serve a similar function with respect to the limbic-striatal outflow. It would thus regulate the access to consciousness of information from limbic structures (e.g., amygdala, hippocampus) concerned with affect, memory, and basic drives. Hyperactivity of the DA neurons or oversensitivity to DA input in the limbic striatum would disrupt the normal outflow, thus leading to an innundation of consciousness of limbic-affective information, causing disturbances of attention. Phenomenologically, this would be experienced as an internal disturbance of attention characterized by bizarre ideation, intermingled with past affective associations.

Matthysse (1974) also noted similarities between the basal ganglia and limbic areas that receive prominent mesencephalic DA projections. He reviews evidence that indicates that the basal ganglia effectively transform subthreshold motor commands into intentional movements. DA acts by disinhibition to permit the emergence of these movements from their subthreshold state. Matthysse proposes that, in the cognitive realm, DA neurons may serve a similar function and suggests that the preconscious thoughts are similar to subthreshold motor commands. In some structures, analogous to the basal ganglia, DA neurons regulate the orderly entry of these subthreshold thoughts in consciousness. Thus, DA neurons would function to permit the emergence of ideas, in the same manner as they permit the emergence of movements. This disinhibitory function of the DA neurons is overactive in schizophrenia, resulting in internal disturbances of attention: it explains the clinical usefulness of the dopaminergic antagonists (Matthysse, 1974). Matthysse suggests (as did Stevens) that the nucleus accumbens septi be considered as a prime neural site for this disinhibitory function. (This notion will be pursued further below and in the following section.) Finally, Matthysse speculated that single units in the brain could conceivably be identified as encoding for "emotional significance" or, as he termed these, "value detectors [p. 735]." Obviously, as cited above, the reward-related units recorded in the prefrontal cingulate area (Pragay, et al., 1980; Kojima, 1980; Niki & Watanabe, 1979; Rolls et al., 1982; Rosenkilde et al., 1981; Watanabe, 1981), and amygdala (Fuster & Uyeda, 1977; Rolls et al., 1982) of monkeys, do apparently abstract information relative to "emotional" or "motivational" significance of stimuli.

To summarize, evidence has been reviewed to suggest an important role for the nucleus accumbens and its efferent DA modulated outflow via the pallidum in the regulation of internal stimuli. The nucleus accumbens has extremely high concentrations of Type II or opiate-δ receptors (Pert et al., 1980). Immunohistochemical studies, in both rat and monkey, have also demonstrated high opiate concentrations in the globus pallidus (Atweh & Kuhar, 1977; DiFiglia, Aronin, & Martin, 1982; Hiller, Pearson, & Simon, 1973; Kuhar, Pert, & Snyder, 1973; Uhl et al., 1979), and the presence of enkephalinergic terminals in limbic forebrain areas that receive dopaminergic innervation from the mesencephalon (Elde et al., 1976; Simantov, Kuhar, Uhl, & Snyder, 1977). It is worthwhile to recall the fact that the opiate-δ agonists have been demonstrated to preferentially stimulate (relative to opiate-μ agonists) DA release in vivo (Chesselet et al., 1981). Recently, there has been a plethora of studies concerned with the effects of the opiate antagonist naloxone in schizophrenia (for review see: Pickar et al., 1982). Although the results of these clinical investigations are generally negative, a number of well-controlled studies (Davis, Bunney, Defraites, Kleinman, van Kammen, Post, & Wyatt, 1977; Emrich, Cording, Pirée, Kölling, Zerssen, & Herz, 1977; Gunne, Lindstrom, & Terenius, 1977; Watson, Berger, Akil, Mills, & Barchas, 1978) have demonstrated reductions in particular attention-related symptoms, i.e., auditory hallucinations and bizarre, distracting thought content. In contrast to those studies that found naloxone ineffective, these latter studies generally employed larger doses, involved longer observation periods and, in many instances, involved patients who were concurrently receiving neuroleptic treatment. The fact that high doses of naloxone were necessary indicates involvement at site(s) other than opiate-μ receptors because naloxone, possessing great affinity for this receptor, should effectively block any action mediated via this subclass of receptors at low doses. This fact, considered in conjunction with the presence of high opiate-δ receptor densities in brain areas implicated in these specific types of schizophrenia symptoms (see above), suggests the involvement of opiate-δ neurons in these specific therapeutic effects of naloxone. It is plausible that the amelioration of certain attention-related symptoms in schizophrenia by the co-administration of neuroleptics and naloxone may be due to a synergistic antagonism of excessive dopaminergic-enkephalinergic disinhibitory action within critical limbic-forebrain circuits. This disinhibition leads to the innundation into awareness of normally subthreshold, affect-laden, internal stimuli. Experimental and clinical evidence indicate an inhibitory role for the frontal cortex (particularly orbital-frontal) in this type of limbic-mediated behavior, both overt and covert (for a review see Damasio, 1979). Pribram (1969) has suggested that at the behavioral level such inhibitory, frontally mediated, neural processes shift information processing toward internal inhibition (i.e., habituation), suppressing interference and thus rendering temporal organization to cognitive operations. In this vein it noteworthy that recent positron emission tomographic (PET) analysis of regional brain activity in unmedicated schizophrenics has revealed a pronounced "hypo-frontality," relative to other psychiatric controls (Buchsbaum, Ingvar, Kessler, Waters, Capelletti, van Kammen, King, Johnson, Manning, Flynn, Mann, Bunney, & Sokoloff, 1982). These important functional findings are consistent with the positive histopathological findings of cortical cellular loss and disruption (layers III & V) in predominantly prefrontal cingulate cortex in postmortem schizophrenic brain tissue (Weinstein, 1954), and biochemical data strongly implicating these specific cortical regions in the therapeutic action of the antidopaminergic neuroleptics (Bacoupoulos, Bustos, Redmond, Baula, & Roth, 1978; Bacoupoulos, et al., 1979). Thus, although the etiology and precise pathophysiology of schizophrenia remains obscure, these experimental and clinical studies point to an extremely important role for dopaminergic-enkephalinergic mechanisms in internal stimulus regulation.

It is worthwhile now to return to a consideration of the amygdala. As noted, this structure accomplishes a critical role in behavioral adaptation through the integration of motivationally relevant external perceptual input with internal information concerning present needs and pertinent past associations. The role of the cortical (particularly amygdaloid) opiate-μ receptors in the selective filtering of external sensory input has been discussed. However, it must be noted that the amygdala also contains a high proportion of opiate-δ (enkephalin) receptors. Enkephalin receptors have been localized on mesotelencephalic ("mesolimbic") dopaminergic axon terminals (Pollard et al., 1977a, 1977b). The DA fibers innervate forebrain areas, such as the medial prefrontal cortex, anterior cingulate, and the amygdala (Björklund & Lindvall, 1978). In addition, neurochemical (6-hydroxydopamine) lesions within the ventral mesencephalon result in decreased enkephalin receptors in both the nucleus accumbens (Pollard et al., 1977a) and the amygdala (Gardner, Zukin, & Makman, 1980). Combined horseradish peroxidase, autoradiography, and histofluorescence techniques have detailed the origin, course, and termination of DA substantia nigra (zona compacta) cells projecting to the amydala (Meibach & Katzman, 1981). Hommer, van Kammen, and Pert (1981) noted the stimulatory effect of opiates (morphine) on DA cells in the zona compacta of the substantia nigra, which sends DA projections to the central amygdaloid nucleus (Meibach & Katzman, 1981). Roberts, Woodhams, Polak, and Crow (1982) recently reported extremely dense enkephalin immunoreactivity and the identification of enkephalin cell bodies within the central nucleus of the amygdala. Further, there is firm biochemical evidence for enkephalinergic modulation of DA sensitive adenylate cyclase in monkey amygdala (Walczak, Wilkening, & Makman, 1978). Finally, as noted, Chesselet et al. (1981) demonstrated preferential mesotelencephalic dopamine release by opiate δ agonists. Thus, in brief, anatomical, electrophysiological, and neuropharmacological data establish a firm basis for a DA-enkephalinergic substrate within the amygdala for the "matching" of external input with internal information based on affective need, drive states, past associations, and cognitive expectancies.

In sum, this section has reviewed evidence suggesting that opiate-μ receptors may filter motivationally relevant sensory input at the cortical level. Conversely, it is proposed that opiate-δ receptors, through modulation of DA activity, are involved with the concurrent filtering of relevant internal stimuli based on affective state, past associations, and cognitive set. The mesotelencephalic DA neurons constitute an anatomical and functional interface for these two types of information processing. Finally, evidence has been reviewed to emphasize the importance of the amygdala and related cortico-limbic structures in these integrative processes.

THE MAINTENANCE OF BEHAVIOR

Conceptual Schema

Lesion, biochemical, and behavioral evidence indicate that the ascending ventral mesencephalic dopaminergic neurons function to bias the sensitivity of limbic-forebrain structures concerned with the integration of higher order perceptual analysis with information pertaining to stimulus significance. Thus, the DA neurons may be viewed as possessing a type of "modulatory control" over "reward-selective" attentional processes, which serve to activate the organism to orient and respond to motivationally significant stimuli. This "drive," or more accurately, "incentive induction," engages DA-opioid neurons in the mediation of exploratory, investigatory behavior. Sustained activation in dopaminergic pathways, in conjunction with modulatory influence by opiate-δ neurons, provides immediate feedback to limbic-forebrain structures, encouraging continuation of behavioral sequences that result in positive or adaptive consequences. This internal feedback, as will be indicated, is of a basic hedonic nature, which essentially modulates the affective tone of the limbic-forebrain targets, thereby influencing subsequent integrative processes involved in both overt behaviors and covert (cognitive) processes. "Re-afferent" hedonic information is relayed back to the brainstem DA neurons via a number of anatomical connections, thereby creating a completed circuit of dynamic feedback processes underlying motivated behavior. This section will briefly cover the anatomical basis for such interactions between motivational and motor systems, and review data indicating a critical role for brainstem DA and opiate-δ neurons in the maintenance of purposeful behavior.

Intention, Motivation, Action

Classical research on motor functions has concerned itself primarily with the neural mechanisms of sensory processes and their relationship to the initiation of action. The analysis of volitional movement has focused on the integrative activities of the cerebral cortex, cerebellum, and the basal ganglia in the directing of motor impulses to the spinal cord. Hierarchichal organization generally prevails, with neural signals from neocortex proceeding to the striatum (caudate-putamen), from there to the globus pallidus, and eventually to spinal outflow pathways. It is important to note that at each level, from motor cortex to spinal cord, this system has numerous complex sensory-motor integrative feedback processes (for a review, see Evarts, 1974; Kornhuber, 1974).

The appearance of associative cortex in higher animals, together with considerable elaboration of the basal ganglia and cerebellum, suggests a greater contribution of complex perceptual processes to the initiation of motor activity (i.e., sensory-motor integration). The demonstration of direct projections from virtually the entire neocortex onto the caudate nucleus (Carman, Cowan, & Powell, 1963; Kemp & Powell, 1970; Webster, 1961) further highlights the importance of cognitive processes in the elaboration of motor behavior in higher organisms. It has been proposed that the caudate nucleus (dorsal striatum) of the basal ganglia serves to "filter" motor impulse flow from the neocortex (Costa, 1977). This "filtering" function is modulated by the dopaminergic neurons of the midbrain, so that, for example, degeneration in the nigral cells and subsequent depletion of DA content in the caudate nucleus results in the profound akinesia characteristic of Parkinson's Disease (Hornykiewicz, 1966). Experimentally, single-unit studies in rats and monkeys support the notion of tonic control of the basal ganglia by DA neurons of the ventral midbrain (Bunney & Aghajanian, 1978), and phasic modulation in response to behaviorally relevant sensory stimuli (Rolls et al., 1981).

Although it seems obvious to suppose that emotional-motivational factors (in addition to "purely" perceptual-cognitive) contribute to the initiation of behavior, this area of research has been rather dormant. Recent theorists, however, (e.g., Mogenson, Jones, & Yim, 1980; Nauta & Domesick, 1978), have begun to elucidate the neural systems of this "interface" between motivation, movement, and cognition. In particular, there has been emphasis on similarity and parallels between dorsal (caudate-putamen) and ventral (nucleus accumbens) striatum. It has been proposed tat as the caudate nucleus (dorsal striatum) "filters" neocortical signals to the globus pallidus, the nucleus accumbens (ventral striatum) "filters" limbic information targeted for the globus pallidus to eventually influence behavior (Costa, 1977). This "filtering" or "gate" function of the nucleus accumbens, as that of the caudate, is regulated by dopaminergic input from the mesencephalon. On the bais of evidence reviewed in the previous section, it may be proposed that opiate-δ neurons also play a significant role in this selective filtering process by interactive activity with the DA fibers that terminate in the nucleus accumbens and other limbic structures (e.g., amygdala).

The enkephalin-rich nucleus accumbens is a critical nexus between the limbic and striatal circuitry controlling behavior. This nucleus receives direct projections from virtually all limbic-forebrain structures (Björklund & Lindvall, 1978; Moore & Bloom, 1978; Nauta & Domesick, 1978; Ungerstedt 1971) and the dopaminergic cells of the ventral mesencephalon, and in turn it projects directly, via gabergic (Jones & Mogenson, 1980; Pycock & Horton, 1976) and suspected enkephalinergic efferents, to the globus pallidus (e.g., see: Del Fiaccio, Paxinos, & Cuello, 1982; DiFiglia et al., 1982; Frey & Huffman, 1981). Recent immunocytochemical studies have also revealed the presence of enkephalinergic nerve terminals in regions of the cingulate cortex (Sar, Steumphf, Miller, Chang, & Cuatrecasas, 1978), known to receive projections from the nucleus accumbens (Powell & Leman, 1976). Thus, it has been problematical classifying the nucleus accumbens as either limbic or striatal in function. In fact, it represents the intermingling of components from both systems. The previous section has reviewed anatomical, electrophysiological, and behavioral data concerning a substrate by which mesencephalic DA neurors may "modulate" the access of forebrain activity (concerned with the per:eptual-motivational integration) to behavioral output via the opiate-δ neuronal "gates" of the enkephalin-rich nucleus accumbens and globus pallidus. Consequences of this limbic "filtered" output are fed back to the DA pathways for the purpose of maintaining or terminating a particular behavioral sequence. Thus, in terms of the present conceptualization, activity in DA-enkephalinergic "reward" pathways will be sustained or terminated on the basis of "re-afferent" internal feedback from limbic structures. Anatomical and electrophysiological experiments provide a firm basis for this type of limbic-mediated control of behavior via dopaminergic neurons.

As Nauta has noted, despite their invariable coexistence in the mammalian brain, the limbic system (i.e., hippocampus, amygdala) and corpus striatum have traditionally been regarded as functionally distinct and separate systems. However, on the basis of our present knowledge, it is in fact reasonable to suggest the limbic system as a major source of modulating influence upon the striatal motor mechanisms (Nauta & Domesick, 1978). Accordingly, anatomical work has delineated how limbic information converges on the nucleus accumbens. The prefrontal cortex, as well as much of the remaining neocortex, projects through various sequences of cortico-cortico connections, ultimately to converge on the ventromedial temporal cortex, which, in turn, projects to the amygdala and hippocampus (to the latter via the entorhinal area) (Jones & Powell, 1970; Van Hoesen & Pandya, 1975), and then to the nucleus accumbens (ventral striatum). This parallels the topographic projections of neocortex onto the caudate-putamen (dorsal striatum), and thence to the globus pallidus (Jones & Powell, 1970). Additional experiments, (e.g., Morgane, 1975; Nauta, 1958; Nauta & Haymaker, 1969) have delineated neural projections from limbic-forebrain structures to the ventral tegmental area of Tsai (the site of origin of the DA neurons of the mesotelencephalic system, or area A_{10} of Dahlström and Fuxe, 1964). A recent investigation involving microiontophoretic injections of horseradish peroxidase (HRP) into the ventral tegmental area of Tsai confirmed these previously described afferents, and in addition, noted hitherto undescribed afferents from the cerebral cortex, hypothalamus, amygdala, thalamus, superior colliculus, substantia nigra, and parabrachial nuclei (Phillipson, 1978). Thus, neuroanatomical studies continue to unravel prominent interrelationships between limbic and striatal systems. For example, Nauta and Domesick (1978) have shown that HRP injections into the striatum result in a selective labeling of cells lying within the descending pathways of components of the medial forebrain bundle. The pattern of labeling is remarkable in that it is strikingly congruent with the ascending distribution of mesotelencephalic cells, forming a virtual "crossroads" between limbic and striatal circuitry. To date, no other descending pathway matches this distribution so closely. Another major source of intercommunication between limbic and striatal motor systems consists of reciprocal mesencephalic-habenhular pathways. The habenula and its projections represent an alternative to the medial forebrain bundle, as a major source of information flow from limbic-forebrain to limbic-midbrain areas. Although the functions of the habenula system are obscure, diverse ablation and stimulation studies have implicated it in olfaction, ingestion, mating, and endocrine modulation (Sutherland, 1982). In contrast to early reports (Olds & Olds, 1963), it has also been recently demonstrated that the habenula complex supports rewarding brain stimulation

(Sutherland & Nakajima, 1981). Consistent with earlier histochemical data demonstrating the presence of DA in the lateral habenula (Lindvall et al., 1974), Domesick, Beckstead, and Nauta (1976), employing autoradiographic techniques, have demonstrated projections from area A_{10} to the lateral habenula. Further, functional mapping by the autoradiographic 2-deoxyglucose technique (Sokoloff, 1977), in conjunction with the administration of DA agonists and antagonists, has provided evidence that functional activity within the lateral habenula is regulated by dopaminergic activity (McCulloch, Savaki, & Sokoloff, 1980). Pert et al., (1980) have reported autoradiographic evidence for an opiatergic pathway projecting reciprocally from the habenula to the interpeduncular nucleus, near the site of origin of DA neurons that project to the limbic forebrain. Undoubtedly, further anatomical scrutiny will reveal even greater details concerning this important limbic-motor interface.

Electrophysiological data has also demonstrated direct or indirect connections between limbic structures and dopaminergic-linked motor mechanisms. Nigral afferents from the frontal cortex, lateral habenula, and the central nucleus of the amygdala have been identified in single-unit studies (Bunney & Aghajanian, 1978). Parallel electrophysiological findings, concerning basal forebrain projections to the ventral tegmental area, have recently been summarized by Mogenson et al. (1980). The mesencephalic DA projections to the nucleus accumbens apparently serve an important "gating" function in regulating the transmission of neuronal signals from limbic structures en route to the basal ganglia. Thus, for example, it has been noted that microiontophoretically applied dopamine, or electrical stimulation of the ventral tegmental area, attenuates the excitatory response of nucleus accumbens cells normally elicited by amygdaloid stimulation (Mogenson & Yim, 1981). In sum, ample anatomical and electrophysiological data demonstrate a substrate by which limbic mechanisms may relay information to dopaminergically linked striatal motor mechanisms.

In the behavioral realm, it has been known since the pioneering studies of Hess (1957) that electrical stimulation of limbic structures and related descending pathways (i.e., lateral hypothalamus) could elicit behaviors ranging from attack to defense, feeding, and other more complex behavioral sequences. In the past two decades, various stimulation and ablation studies, carried out in many laboratories, have confirmed the involvement of fibers passing near the lateral hypothalamus, and related limbic structures, in the initiation of goal-oriented or motivated behavior (for a critical review, see Panksepp, 1981). As noted in the introductory comments, numerous attempts have been made to relate specific fiber systems to specific behaviors, such as feeding, sexual activity, etc. In retrospect, it is clear that these attempts at neuroanatomical specificity within well-defined limbic-midbrain circuits have generally been usuccessful (for reviews, see Morgane, 1979; Valenstein, 1977). Clearly there are fiber systems related to basic drives such as hunger, thirst, etc. However, the majority of these fibers have sternly resisted repeated attempts to relate them to simple, highly localized, homeostatic mechanisms. (For example, even the "so-called" hypo-thalamic feeding and satiety "centers" have been "chased" around various diencephalic sites, even occasionally leaving entirely, only to be found "acting up" in sundry forebrain, brainstem, and even striatal sites, many of which seem to have no specific relationship to basic drives such as hunger, etc. For a review, see Morgane, 1979.) Essentially, these endeavors have yielded to more general considerations that attempt to account for the general plasticity and situational dependency of electrical stimulation to these pathways (Valenstein et al., 1968) and the theoretical difficulties of localization of stimulation effects (Kornetsky & Esposito, 1981). The high congruency between the limbic brainstem sites for elicited behaviors and the phenomenon of self-stimulation has suggested alter-native explanations. As self-stimulation behavior may be elicited from such a range of sites (many of which seem to have no specific relationship to basic drives such as hunger, etc.) and can be related to any arbitrarily chosen stimulus and operant response, it suggests a rather generalized phenomenon. Intracranial self-stimulation is readily demonstrable across diverse species, extending from fish to man, and shows a fairly good correspondence with catecholaminergic systems as delineated in rat and primate brain (German & Bowden, 1974). The artificial nature of the self-stimulation demonstration notwithstanding, it seems that by this means we are tapping into a "system(s)" that seems to subserve motivated behavior in general. It has been proposed that this "system(s)" may have evolved to amplify the effects of significant stimuli and related responses. As I suggested in my introductory comments, evolutionary parsimony alone would argue for the existence of such a unified brain system that would act as a "facilitator" for general goal-oriented or motivated behavior(s). I would further propose, on the basis of current evidence, that dopaminergic-opioid interactions within the brainstem and limbic-forebrain areas, which support rewarding brain stimulation in animals, represent a fundamental neurochemical substrate for such a generalized neuronal system concerned with aspects of reward-selective atten-tional processes and related responses.

Evidence for the critical role of the catecholamines in the mediation of self-stimulation behavior is substantial, and will not be covered here. (See Crow, 1976; German & Bowden, 1974). Recent critical evaluations of the "so-called" catecholamine theory of brain-stimulation reward have highlighted the impor-tance of dopamine (Clavier & Routtenberg, 1980; Phillips & Fibiger, 1978; Wise, 1978). As noted, the evidence implicating DA in the mediation of brain-stimulation reward, at various levels of the mesotelencephalic DA projection system, is particularly cogent (Clavier & Routtenberg, 1980). Studies employing DA antagonists have generally shown suppression of self-stimulation behavior. The difficulty with such pharmacological interventions is in trying to disentangle direct effects on reward from general effects on motor behavior (Fibiger, 1978). Recent studies, employing more elaborate behavioral measures, in combination with low doses of neuroleptics, have been able to substantiate firmly the importance of DA in self-stimulation behavior. Esposito, Faulkner, & Kornetsky (1979a) reported that extremely low doses of haloperidol, 3–20 u/kg administered systemically, will elevate the "reward thresholds" (in terms of current intensity) necessary to maintain self-stimulation behavior in rats. At these doses, haloperidol has very specific action on dopaminergic neurotransmission (Andèn, Butcher, Corrodi, Fuxe, & Ungerstedt, 1970; Andèn, Roos, & Werdenicus, 1964; Carlsson and Lindquist, 1963; van Rossum, 1966). Edmonds and Gallistel (1977) reported very similar results, in rats, after low systemic doses (0.1–0.4 mg) of the highly specific DA antagonist, pimozide. Mora, Rolls, Burton, and Shaw (1976) reported that systemic administration of the dopamine antagonist, spiroperidol (0.62–0.1 mg/kg), produced dose-related decreases in responding for self-stimulation to the orbitofrontal cortex, hypothalamus, and the locus coeruleus region of the squirrel and rhesus monkey. Intracranial microinjection of spiroperidol (6 ug), administered bilaterally into the nucleus accumbens of the hypothalamus, attenuated self-stimulation of the amygdala; microinjections into the orbitofrontal cortex reduced self-stimulation to the lateral hypothalamus and amygdala. In contrast, self-stimulation to the locus coeruleus and other sites was unaffected by these injections. The low doses and site-specific nature of these effects seem to rule out explanations based on simple neuroleptic-induced motor impairment. Further, they render strong support for a dopaminergic substrate underlying functional interrelationships between these structures. A number of recent reports have demonstrated that after withdrawal from chronically administered DA antagonists, self-stimulation is enhanced at certain brain sites, in accordance with the expected DA hypersensitivity induced by chronic administration of DA antagonists (Tarsy & Baldessarini, 1974). Self-stimulation (in rats) after chronic DA blockade has been reported to be enhanced in the hypothalamus (Ettenberg & Wise, 1976), the dopaminergic A_{10} area of the ventral midbrain (Seeger, Gardner, & Bridges, 1981b), and the prefrontal cortex (Robertson & Mogenson, 1979). Studies utilizing 6-hydroxydopamine lesions have rendered further support for a dopaminergic role in ventral tegmental, nucleus accumbens, and medial prefrontal cortex self-stimulation in the rat (Phillips & Fibiger, 1978). More direct evidence for the role of dopamine in prefrontal cortex self-stimulation has been provided by Myers and Mora (1977) and Mora and Myers (1977). These investigators had rats self-stimulate to the dopamine-rich medial prefrontal cortex, while at a region directly adjacent to the electrode site radioactive-labeled (^{14}C) dopamine was perfused repeatedly by means of a push-pull cannula. They noted enhanced release of dopamine and its metabolites associated with self-stimulation in this brain area. In sum, there is substantial support from self-stimulation studies to imply a critical role (albeit not a sufficient) role for DA in goal-directed or generalized motivational behavior.

As might be suspected on neuroanatomical and biochemical grounds, recent evidence has indicated an important role for opioids in the modulation of DA-mediated rewarding brain stimulation. Numerous studies have shown that heroin, morphine, and other euphorigenic opiates will enhance brain stimulation reward at a diversity of neuroanatomical sites (for a review, see Esposito & Kornetsky, 1978). Esposito, McLean, and Kornetsky (1979b) reported that morphine would lower the reinforcement threshold (i.e., thus, implying increased reward value of the stimulation), at a number of catecholamine-opioid receptor-rich sites in the rat brain, including placements in or near the dopaminergic A_{10} area. Kornetsky and Esposito (1979b) further reported that the opiate agonists-antagonists (drugs which to varying degrees possess both agonist and antagonist effects) also enhanced brain stimulation reward in rats, but only to the extent that the particular compound shared the euphorigenic properties of morphine. The degree to which these drugs lowered reinforcing thresholds for brain stimulation correlated strikingly with their abuse liability. This work demonstrates that the hedonic or reinforcing properties of the opiates and certain other drugs of abuse (i.e., amphetamine, cocaine—see below) lies in their ability to sensitize the fundamental neuronal substrate of reward (Kornetsky & Esposito, 1979b).

The importance of the brain's dopaminergic pathways in mediating the rewarding effects of exogenous opiates has been indicated by recent studies dealing with opiate self-administration in rats. Bozarth and Wise (1981b) demonstrated that rats will administer morphine directly into the dopaminergic ventral tegmental area but not into other brain sites also rich in opiate receptors. These same researchers demonstrated that intravenous opiate self-administration in rats could be affected by microinjection of opiate antagonists into the ventral tegmental area, but not other brain sites rich in opiate receptors (Bozarth & Wise, 1980). Finally, the intravenous self-administration of heroin in the rat is blocked by the dopamine antagonist pimozide (Bozarth & Wise, 1981a).

Considering the striking congruency between enkephalin imunofluorescence and DA cell bodies and fibers (Elde et al., 1976), it would seem likely that these peptides may play some modulatory role in DA-mediated reward-related behaviors. Byck (1976) initially speculated on this possibility and further proposed that opiate antagonists, such as naloxone, should block the pleasurable effects of drugs such as cocaine, amphetamine, and alcohol. However, the first experimental evidence that the endorphins might share the euphorigenic effects of the opiate alkaloids was the finding that rats would self-administer intraventricular injections of both met- and leu-enkephalin (Belluzzi & Stein, 1977). It is noteworthy that leucine-enkephalin (leu-enkephalin) was self-administered more avidly than met-enkephalin in spite of the greater in vitro potency of met-enkephalin. However, as the authors noted, opiate receptor binding by the leucine peptide is reduced more by sodium and enhanced more by manganese than is the case with met-enkephalin, and that similar differential sensitivity to sodium and manganese differentiates between narcotics with high and low abuse potential (Simantov & Snyder, 1976). Tortella and Moreton (1980) reported the self-administration of D-Ala²-methionine enkephalinamide (DALA-MET) in morphine-dependent rats. Mello and Mendelson (1978) reported similar findings in the rhesus monkey. A few studies have attempted to directly investigate the potential effects of endorphins themselves on self-stimulation behavior. Broekkamp et al. (1979a) reported facilitation of hypothalamic self-stimulation (rats) following intracerebral injections of a synthetic analogue of met-enkephalin (DALA-MET) into the ventral tegmental area. They suggested an endogenous opioid involvement in the dopaminergic mediated self-stimulation behavior to this area. Bain, Esposito and Kornetsky (1980) noted that low doses (under 200 ug) of alpha-endorphin (opiate active fragment amino acid sequence 61–76 of β-lippotropin) could affect self-stimulation to the ventral mesencephalon in rats. In a similar report, Dorsa, van Ree, and deWied (1979) noted that the subcutaneous administration of α-endorphin (5ug and 25ug) facilitated ventral tegmental self-stimulation in rats, but opposite effects were reported for Des-Tyr', γ-endorphin, a synthetic analogue of γ-endorphin (β-lippotropin fragment 61–77).

Opioid-induced facilitation of self-stimulation behavior derived from dopaminergic areas strongly suggests a functional relationship between the catecholamines (particularly dopamine) and the endogenous opiates. The opiate antagonist naloxone administered by itself has been shown to be devoid of effects on self-stimulation behavior in rats at a variety of catecholamine-opioid-rich sites in the brain (Esposito et al., 1981). These results seem to rule out a tonic opioid involvement in the neuronal mechanisms subserving this central reward phenomena. However, naloxone has been shown to block the reward-enhancing effect of amphetamine on brain stimulation reward (Esposito et al., 1980) while conversely potentiating the effects of chlorpromazine on this behavior (Esposito et al., 1981). The differential effects of amphetamine and chlorpromazine on self-stimulation behavior are generally believed to be related to their opposing actions on catecholaminergic neural transmission. The data concerning naloxone interactions are in accordance with the growing body of anatomical and biochemical evidence suggesting a possible neuromodulatory type of control by opioid peptides on central catecholamine neuronal functioning. Accordingly, Biggio, Casu, Corda, DiBello, and Gessa (1978) reported that met-enkephalin can, in fact, stimulate dopamine release by means of presynaptic mechanism. Because amphetamine's agonist actions are clearly mediated presynaptically (Chiueh & Moore 1975), it is reasonable to hypothesize that naloxone's blockade of the amphetamine effects may be due to its occupation of the opiate receptors located presynaptically on these mesolimbic-cortical dopamine neurons, thereby blocking the effects that enkephalins might normally have in stimulating dopamine release. This is consonant with the findings of Chesselet et al. (1981) that opiate-δ agonists preferentially stimulate presynaptic dopamine release in vivo. Thus, existing evidence would tend to suggest an opiate-δ receptor-mediated enhancement of the facilitative effects on brain stimulation reward, induced by psychostimulants such as amphetamine. The mechanism of chlorpromazine-induced potentiation of naloxone's effect on rewarding brain stimulation is presently more difficult to ascertain, given the complexity of enkephalin and striatal dopamine postsynaptic interactions. However, the data are consistent with the prediction of Diamond & Borison (1978) that naloxone should antagonize the effects of agents acting presynaptically to affect DA neurotransmission, while, conversely, potentiate the effects of postsynaptically acting agents.

Interestingly, a variety of drugs of abuse share with the opiates and with amphetamine the ability to enhance brain stimulation reward (for reviews, see Kornetsky & Esposito 1979a, 1979b). All of these agents have significant effects on dopaminergic and/or opioid systems, and these actions seem to be related to the rewarding properties of these compounds. It is not surprising, in light of its pharmacological similarities to amphetamine, that cocaine has been demonstrated to produce dose-related reductions in the threshold for rewarding brain stimulation (Esposito, Motola, & Kornetsky, 1978). Like amphetamine, the effects of cocaine on brain stimulation reward can be blocked by low to moderate doses of naloxone (Kornetsky et al., 1981). One might ask if the facilitative effects of these psychostimulants is in fact related to their rewarding properties. Current data suggest an affirmative answer to this question. The ability of cocaine to function as a discriminative stimulus for animals has been shown to be dependent on dopamine (Colpaert, Niemegeers, & Janssen, 1978), and furthermore, this stimulus or cue effect of both cocaine and amphetamine is blocked by the administration of low doses of haloperidol (Colpaert, Niemegeers, & Janssen, 1978). Risner and Jones (1976) have demonstrated the critical dependence of d-amphetamine self-administration in animals on dopaminergic mechanisms. Finally, Wald, Ebstein, and Belmaker (1978) reported that the specific dopamine antagonist pimozide blocked the euphoric effect induced by d-amphetamine in human subjects.

Acute and chronic administration of ethanol has also been found to facilitate brain stimulation reward in rats (Carlson & Lydic, 1976; Magnuson and Reid, 1977). Experimental work with rats and mice has confirmed the importance of both dopaminergic and endogenous opioid systems in the regulation of ethanol-induced neurochemical and behavioral effects (Barbaccia, Reggiani, Spano, & Trabucchi, 1980; Blum, Wallace, Eubanks, & Schwertner, 1975; Blum, Wallace, Schwertner, & Eubanks, 1976; Khanmaa, Andersson, & Fuxe, 1979). Various lines of research argue for some common biochemical mechanisms between ethanol and opioids. Examples include: The demonstration of cross-tolerance between morphine and ethanol (Venho, Eerola, Venho, & Vartiainen, 1955); the inhibition of ethanol withdrawal convulsions by morphine (Blum, et al., 1976); increased tolerance to narcotics in ethanol-tolerant animals and man (Venho et al., 1955); and the attenuation of ethanol-induced narcosis by naloxone (Blum et al., 1975). Altshuler, Phillips, & Feinhandler (1980) reported that the opiate antagonist naltrexone could attenuate intravenous ethanol self-administration in the rhesus monkey, suggesting the involvement of an opiate system in the reinforcing effects of this drug. Lorens and Sainati (1978) reported that naloxone could block the facilitative effect of ethanol on brain stimulation in rats, rendering further evidence for the hypothesis that an endogenous opiate system (in conjunction with dopaminergic mechanisms) is involved in the mediation of the rewarding effects of ethanol. Jeffcoate, Cullen, Herbert, Hastings, and Walder (1979) reported that the intravenous administration of 0.4 mg of naloxone to human subjects was capable of blocking the intoxicating effect of ethanol as assessed by tests of psychomotor performance. Lastly, a recent intriguing report (Hiller, Angel, & Simon, 1981) has indicated that ethanol binds with high specificity to opiate-δ receptors. This is the first demonstration of selectivity for one of the postulated classes of opiate receptors by an agent that is not an endogenous opioid ligand for the receptor.

Phencyclidine (PCP), another agent of abuse, produces a myriad of effects. Its profile is difficult to compare to other known drugs of abuse. It is well established that, along with its analgesic, anesthetic, and psychotomimetic properties, PCP has the ability to elicit profound euphoria in many people (Lerner & Burns, 1978). In animal tests, PCP has been found to exert effects on a number of neurotransmitter systems (e.g., Freed, Weinberger, Biny, & Wyatt, 1980), however, considerable evidence for indirect dopamine agonist activity of PCP (Meltzer, Sturgeon, Sinovic, & Fessler, 1981) may be relevant to some of the hedonic mechanisms that contribute to its abuse liability. In this context, it is noteworthy that PCP has been reported to enhance rewarding brain stimulation in rats, and interestingly, this effect has been blocked by naloxone (Kornetsky et al., 1981). In a separate study, PCP (450ug/kg) was found to elicit focal (6 cps) spike-wave complexes in the septum amygdala and cingulate cortex, paralleling the emergence of orienting, apparent sensory inattentiveness, and inappropriate searching behavior in cats (Contreras, Guzman-Flores, Porantes, Ervin, & Palmour, 1981). Naloxone had complex effects on these actions of PCP, which were dose and time dependent, suggesting an effect related to the state of "activation" of these limbic structures rather than a receptor-specific interaction. These EEG findings however, may prove particularly interesting because acute PCP administration in humans produces the most isomorphic drug-induced model of the fundamental symptoms of schizophrenia (Luby, Cohen, Rosenbaum, Gottlieb, & Kelly, 1959). Recently, Zukin and Zukin (1981) have reported that the putative ligand for the opiate-sigma receptor, the hallucinogenic opiate cyclazocine, competes with PCP for receptor binding sites. Quirion, Hammer, Herkeham, and Pert (1981b) have confirmed the specific nature of the PCP/opiate-sigma receptor and have described its distribution.

Other agents have been shown to have specific facilitative effects on brain stimulation reward that are susceptible to blockade by the opiate antagonist naloxone. Lorens and Sainati (1978) reported that naloxone could block the facilitative effects of chlordiazepoxide on lateral hypothalamic self-stimulation behavior in rats. The closely related minor tranquilizer, diazepam, (and ethanol) can produce rapid changes in enkephalin levels in both hypothalamic and striatal areas (Duka, Wuster, & Herz, 1979; Schulz, Wuster, Duka, & Herz, 1980). Seeger, Carlson, and Nazzaro (1981a) have reported that pentobarbital-induced enhancement of self-stimulation to the dopaminergic A_{10} area in rats, could be reversed by naloxone. [Many barbiturates (including pentobarbital) have recently been found to be potent in vitro inhibitors of enkephalinase, the primary degradative enzyme for endogenous opiate peptides (Alstein, Miltman, & Vogel, 1981).]

Thus, a variety of euphorigenic drugs including opiates, psychostimulants, sedative hypnotics, ethanol, and PCP share some striking commonalities. Each agent has been shown to have significant effects on either dopamine systems and opioid systems or both. Further, all of these agents share the ability to facilitate brain "reward" mechanisms in a manner that is reversible by naloxone. That is to say, each of these substances can modify the activity of mesotelencephalic DA "reward" neurons, either directly or indirectly, by modulation via endogenous opioid peptide systems, thereby effecting profound changes in internal stimulus regulation and global affective state. Thus, I would propose that the euphorigenic and abuse potential of these drugs lies principally in their ability to sensitize the fundamental biological substrate *concerned with the perception of reward*. The self-administration of prototypical opiate-δ agonists (Belluzzi & Stein, 1977; Mello & Mendelson, 1978; Tortella & Moreton, 1980), the relative insensitivity of these latter effects to naloxone blockade (Belluzzi & Stein, 1977) and the selectivity of certain agents of abuse for opiate-δ receptors (Hiller et al., 1981), suggest a critical role for the opiate-δ receptors in these changes in internal stimulus processing. In sum, current neurobehavioral and neuropharmacological data indicated that the opiate peptides may, in fact, have some type of modulatory function on the self-stimulation and undoubtedly more naturalistic behaviors mediated by this dopaminergic system, which supports brain stimulation reward. Thus, DA-opioid "reward" pathways constitute a critical link in a central neural system concerned with the correlation of exogenous and particularly endogenous stimulus of significance with appropriate overt behaviors. However, the range of evidence reviewed presently should make it evidently clear that rather than representing literal "reward fibers," these neurons are more accurately characterized as critical components or "facilitators" of a diffusely organized, but functionally unitary system including limbic, striatal, and cortical structures concerned with the perception of reward, the regulation of motivated behavior, and affective state changes.

The precise mechanism of enkephalingergic or peptidergic modulation in general of monoamine activity is far from completely understood. Studies of peptide release, electrophysiological properties, and binding properties have contributed a great deal to our characterization of these peptides, yet these achievements have barely started to provide an adequate answer concerning the basic neurophysiological roles of the enkephalins. At least a consensus has emerged which characterizes "modulation" (in a neuronal sense) as signal information that is not expressed, by itself, in terms neurotransmission or translation at the postsynaptic site. Rather, neuromodulators act to sensitize or desensitize pre- or postsynaptic elements to respond to subsequent signals. This kind of neuronal modulatory activity may be helpful, for instance, to understand the somewhat fuzzy concepts of "arousal" or "attention," classicially attributed to the mesencephalic reticular formation; or analogously, to the concept of stimulus "significance," in reference to "reward" fibers. Barker has drawn the following thoughtful analogy by comparing neurohormonal communication to that of a radio broadcast, where all properly tuned receivers may obtain information: neurotransmission is more analogous to telephone communication, where the message is private over hard-wired lines and; finally, neuromodulation may be compared to a form of gain control imposed on private conversations (Barker, Neale, Smith, & MacDonald, 1978).

SOME COMMENTS ON "REWARD" PATHWAYS, ENDOGENOUS OPIOIDS, AND MEMORY

Kety (1970) proposed that the physiological processes sensitive to the motivational or reinforcing properties of an experience may contribute to memory processes for such events. From a purely biological perspective, it would seem logical that the basic neural mechanisms concerned with the amplification of stimuli and responses that have adaptive value should also be involved with the initiation of memory consolidation for such integrative activity. Specifically, one would suspect that activity in the "reward" pathways ascending from the midbrain to innervate limbic structures, such as the amygdala or (indirectly) the hippocampus, may influence memory processes and provide some clues regarding the neuropharmacology underlying such events.

Since its discovery, it has been repeatedly demonstrated that response-contingent rewarding brain stimulation may facilitate learning in virtually any experimental paradigm. However, it has only recently been clearly demonstrated that nonresponse-contingent "rewarding" stimulation may affect the processes of learning and memory. Huston, Mueller, and Mondadori (1977) reported the facilitative effects of post-training lateral hypothalamic stimulation on both appetitive and aversively motivated learning tasks in rats. These effects were time dependent, in a manner consistent with the hypothesis that such stimulation may affect consolidation processes. Subsequently, a number of researchers have reported on the effectiveness of post-training stimulation to rewarding brain sites in altering memory. Thus, Destrade and Cardo (1975) and Major and White (1978) reported that post-training rewarding stimulation to the lateral hypothalamus in both mice and rats facilitated the retention of both appetitive and aversively motivated behaviors in a time-dependent manner. Routtenberg and colleagues (Clavier & Routtenberg 1980; Routtenberg, 1979) have demonstrated stimulation-induced memory altering effects of post-training stimulation at a number of sites including the frontal cortex, amygdala, substantia nigra, dorsal hippocampus, and the caudate nucleus. These areas all support self-stimulation and have been theoretically related to various specific and distinct memory processes (Clavier & Routtenberg, 1980). This same group has also related mesocortical stimulation-induced memory effects to specific biochemical changes (i.e., specific alterations in protein phosphorylation) in membranes of frontal cortex. Thus, mesocortical intracranial self-stimulation pathways are believed to play a specific role in the above memory processes by providing a biochemical residual following training (Routtenberg, 1979).

Interestingly, White and Major (1978b) have provided evidence for a critical difference between self-stimulation and experimenter-administered stimulation, indicating an important role for the rewarding value of the stimulation per se in the mediation of these hyperamnesic effects. This factor, considered with the time dependency of these effects, is consistent with the view that post-training rewarding effects may effect consolidation according to the "law of effect" as first documented by Thorndike (1933). Major and White (1978) have also reported some interesting site-specific stimulation effects on consolidation in rats. They noted that self-stimulation facilitated memory with electrode placements in the dorsolateral quadrant of the lateral hypothalamus and in area A_9 of the substantia nigra but not with placements in the medial part of the lateral hypothalamus or in the preoptic area. This evidence suggested that the facilitative effects of medial forebrain bundle stimulation (the site most often investigated in the previous studies) are probably mediated by the nigrostriatal fibers and are not simply due to changes in arousal level. Subsequent work by these same authors demonstrated that the specific dopamine antagonist pimozide was capable of blocking the memory/learning enhancement effect of brain stimulation (White & Major, 1978a). These data strongly implicate the midbrain dopaminergic neurons in the strengthening of learned associations and memory consolidation, presumably via a mechanism(s) related to the involvement of these pathways in the motivational aspects of behavioral regulation.

Considering the opiate modulation of dopaminergic reward-related mediated behaviors, one might suspect the endogenous opioids also may play a role in memory process. Recent experiments indicate that this is so: however, the precise role(s) of endorphins in the memory/learning process remains quite obscure. The enkephalins have been found to facilitate maze learning (Kastin, Scollan, King, Schally, & Coy, 1976) and retention for passive avoidance (Stein & Belluzzi, 1979); and to attenuate CO_2-induced amnesia in rats (Ritger, 1978). Similar effects on passive avoidance induced by post-trial morphine administration have also been reported (Staübli & Huston, 1980). deWeid, Bohus, van Ree, and Urban (1978) reported that β-endorphin (β lippotropin 61–76) facilitated passive avoidance in rats while γ-endorphin (β lippotropin 61–77) was found to have the opposite effect. Olson, Olson, Kastin, Green, Roig-Smith,

Hill, and Coy (1979) reported enhanced reversal learning after the administration of an enkephalin analogue in the rhesus monkey. These basically consistent results with opiate agonists are not complimented by converse findings with the opiate antagonist naloxone. In fact, naloxone has been found to facilitate memory consolidation processes in both mice (Izquierdo, 1979) and rats (Messing, Jensen, Martinez, Speihler, Vasquez, Soumireu-Mourat, Liang, & McGaugh, 1979) and facilitated extinction of responding in a classical conditioning paradigm in rabbits (Hernandez & Powell, 1980). In man, naloxone has produced a slowing of the averaged EEG (Volavka, 1979); blocked ethanol-induced impairment on psychomotor tasks (Jeffcoate et al., 1979); produced subtle ameliorating effects on manic symptoms; facilitated performance on simple behavioral attention tasks (Gritz, Shiffman, Jarrik, Schlesinger, & Charavastra, 1976); and evoked altered potential correlates of attention in normal subjects (Arnsten et al., 1981). Thus, although the endogenous opiates clearly have a role(s) in aspects of attention and memory processes, the precise nature of these effects, in a cognitive sense, will only be elucidated by future research. These apparent discrepancies are undoubtedly related to the ambiguities created by exogenous administration of opiate alkaloids and endogenous ligands, (which may differ markedly from physiological ligand-receptor interactions), and our present ignorance of the regulatory and feedback processes involved in normal enkephalinergic cellular activity. However, it may be hypothesized that significant reward-related effects on memory processes may actually be mediated at limbic structures that receive direct or indirect brainstem dopaminergic innervation, and have already been implicated in memory mechanisms. Structures such as the amygdala and hippocampus are prime candidates for consideration.

Recently, Gallagher, Kapp, Pascoe, and Applegate (1981) have presented evidence for opioid-μ receptor involvement in the time-dependent memory consolidation mechanisms mediated by the amygdala in rodents. Similarly, Routtenberg and colleagues (Collier, Miller, Quirk, Travis, & Routtenberg, 1981) have reported data indicative of a role for endogenous opioids in both reward and memory functions of the hippocampus. They have postulated an endogenous-opiate substrate for a reinforcement system involved in working memory. Thus, studies of the neuropharmacology of "reward" pathways may hold the promise of heralding an understanding, at the cellular level, of the memory mechanisms mediated in these limbic structures, at which decades of classical neuropsychological analysis have hinted.

REFERENCES

Alstein, M., Mittman, S., & Vogel, Z. The effect of barbiturates on the degradation of enkephalin by brain enzymes. *Life Science,* 1981, *28,* 185–191.
Altshuler, H. I., Phillips, P. E., & Feinhandler, P. A. Alteration of ethanol self-administration by naltrexone. *Life Sciences,* 1980, *26,* 679–688.

Andèn, N. E., Butcher, S. G., Corrodi, H., Fuxe, K., & Ungerstedt, U. Receptor activity and turnover of dopamine and noradrenaline after neuroleptics. *European Journal of Pharmacology,* 1970, *11,* 303–314.

Andèn, N. E., Roos, B. E., & Werdenicus, B. Effects of chlorpromazine, haloperidol, and reserpine on the levels of phenolic acids in rabbit corpus striatum. *Life Sciences,* 1964, *3,* 149–158.

Arnsten, A. T. & Segal, D. S. Naloxone alters locomotion and interaction with environmental stimuli. *Life Sciences,* 1979, *25,* 1035–1042.

Arnsten, A. T., Segal, D. S., Neville, H., & Hillyard, S. Naloxone augments electrophysiological measures of selective attention in man. *Society for Neuroscience Abstracts,* 1981, 659.

Astruc, J. Corticofugal connections of area 8 (frontal eye field) in macaca mulatta. *Brain Research,* 1971, *33,* 241–256.

Atweh, S. F. & Kuhar, M. J. Autoradiographic localization of opiate receptors in rat brain. III. The telencephalon. *Brain Research,* 1977, *134,* 393–405.

Bacopoulos, N. G., Bustos, G., Redmond, D. E., Baulu, J., & Roth, R. H. Regional activity of primate brain dopaminergic neurons to haloperiodol: Alterations following chronic treatment. *Brain Research,* 1978, *157,* 396–401.

Bacopoulas, N. G. et al. Antipsychotic drug action in schizophrenic patients: Effect on cortical dopamine metabolism after long-term treatment. *Science,* 1979, *205,* 1405.

Bain, G. T., Esposito, R. U., & Kornetsky, C. Effects of systemic administration of α-endorphin-(β-lipotropin 61-76) on intracranial self-stimulation in the rat. *Society for Neuroscience Abstracts,* 1980, 318.

Barbaccia, M. L., Reggiani, A., Spano, P. F., & Trabucchi, M. Ethanol effects on dopaminergic function: Modulation by the endogenous opioid system. *Pharmacology, Biochemistry and Behavior,* 1980, *13,* 303–306.

Barker, J. L., Neale, J. H., Smith, T. G., & MacDonald, R. L. Opiate peptide modulation of amino acid responses suggests novel form of neuronal communication. *Science,* 1978, *199,* 1451–1453.

Barrett, T. W. Studies of the function of the amygdaloid complex in macaca mulatta. *Neuropsychologia,* 1969, *7,* 1–12.

Belluzzi, J. D., & Stein, L. Enkephalin may mediate euphoria and drive-reduction reward. *Nature,* 1977, *266,* 556–558.

Ben Ari, Y., & Le Gal La Salle, G. Plasticity at unitary level: II. Modifications during sensory-sensory association procedures. *Electrocephalography and Clinical Neurophysiology,* 1972, *32,* 667–679.

Berlyne, D. E. *Conflict arousal and curiosity.* New York: McGraw-Hill, 1960.

Biggio, G., Casu, M., Corda, M. G., DiBello. C., & Gessa, G. L. Stimulation of dopamine synthesis in caudane nucleus by intrastriatal enkephalins and antagonism by naloxone. *Science,* 1978, *200,* 552–554.

Björklund, A., & Lindvall, A. The mesotelencephalic dopamine neuron system: A review of its anatomy. In K. Livington & O. Hornykiewicz (Eds.), *Limbic mechanisms.* New York: Plenum Press, 1978.

Blum, K., Wallace, J. E., Eubanks, J. D., & Schwertner, H. A. Effects of naloxone on ethanol withdrawal, preference and narcosis. *Pharmacologist,* 1975, *17,* 197. (Abstract)

Blum, K., Wallace, J. E., Schwertner, H. A., & Eubanks, J. D. Morphine suppression of ethanol withdrawal in mice. *Experientia,* 1976, *32,* 79–82.

Bonnet, K. A., Groth, J., Gigannini, T., Cortes, M., & Simon, E. J. Opiate receptor heterogeneity in human brain regions. *Brain Research,* 1981, *221,* 437–440.

Bowen, W. D., Gentleman, S., Herkenham, M., & Pert, C. B. Interconverting μ and δ forms of the opiate receptor in rat striatal patches. *Proceedings of the National Academy of Sciences, U.S.A.,* 1981, *78,* 4818–4822.

Boyd, E. H., Boyd, E. S., & Brown, L. E. Percentral cortex unit activity during the m-wave and contingent negative variation in behaving squirrel monkeys. *Experimental Neurology*, 1982, *75*, 535–554.

Bozarth, M. A., & Wise, R. A. Intracranial self-administration of morphine into various brain regions in rats. *Society for neuroscience Abstracts*, 1980, *309*.

Bozarth, M. A., & Wise, R. A. Herion reward is dependent on a dopaminergic substrate. *Life Sciences*, 1981, *29*, 1881–1886. (a)

Bozarth, M. A., & Wise, R. A. Intracranial self-administration of morphine into the ventral tegmental area in rats. *Life Sciences*, 1981, *28*, 551–555. (b)

Brodal, A. *Neurological Anatomy*. London: Oxford University Press, 1969.

Broekkamp, C. L., Phillips, A. G., & Cools, A. R. Facilitation of self-stimulation behavior following intracerebral microinjections of opioids into the ventral tegmental area. *Pharmacology, Biochemistry & Behavior*, 1979, *11*, 289–295. (a)

Broekkamp, C. L. E., Phillips, A. G., & Cools, A. R. Stimulant effects of enkephalin microinjection into the dopaminergic A10 area. *Nature*, 1979, *278*, 560–562. (b)

Brown, R. M., Crane, A. M., & Goldman, P. S. Regional distribution of monoamines in the cerebral cortex and subcortical structures of the rhesus monkey: Concentrations and in vivo synthesis rates. *Brain Research*, 1979, *168*, 133–150.

Buchsbaum, M. S., Ingvar, D. H., Kessler, R., Waters, R. N., Cappelletti, J., van Kammen, D. P., King, A. C., Johnson, J. L., Manning, R. G., Flynn, R. W., Mann, L. S., Bunney, W. E., & Sokoloff, L. Cerebral glucography with positron tomography. *Archives of General Psychiatry*, 1982, *39*, 251–259.

Buchwald, N. A. Physiological and psychological aspects of basal ganglia functions. In G. Crane & R. Gardner (Eds.), *Psychotropic drugs and dysfunctions of the basal ganglia*. Public Health Services Publication No. 1938, Government Printing Office, 1969.

Bunney, B. S., & Aghajanian, G. K. Mesolimbic and mesocortical dopaminergic systems: Physiology and pharmacology. In M. A. Lipton, A. DiMascio, & K. F. Killam (Eds.), *Psychopharmacology: A generation of progress*. New York: Raven Press, 1978.

Butter, D. M., Mishkin, M., & Mirsky, A. F. Emotional responses toward humans in monkeys with selective frontal lesions. *Physiology and Behavior*, 1968, *3*, 213–215.

Butter, C. M., Mishkin, M., & Rosvold, H. E. Conditioning and extinction of a food-rewarded response after selective ablations of frontal cortex in monkeys. *Journal of Experimental Neurology*, 1963, *7*, 65–75.

Byck, R. Peptide transmitters: A unifying hypothesis for euphoria, respiration, sleep, and the action of lithium. *N. E. Lancet*, 1976, *July*, 72.

Carlson, R. H., & Lydic, R. The effects of ethanol upon threshold and response rate for self-stimulation. *Psychopharmacology*, 1976, *50*, 61–64.

Carlsson, A. & Lindquist, M. Effect of chlorpromazine or haloperidol on formation of 3-methoxytyramine and normetanephrine in mouse brain. *Acta Pharmacologia et Toxicologica*, 1963, *20*, 140–144.

Carman, J. B., Cowan, W. M., & Powell, T. P. S. The organization of corticostriate connexions in the rabbit. *Brain*, 1963, *86*, 525–560.

Chang, K. J., Cooper, B. R., Hazum, E., & Cuatrecasas, P. Multiple opiate receptors: Different regional distribution in the brain and differential binding of opiates and opioid peptides. *Molecular Pharmacology*, 1979, *16*, 91–104.

Chesselet, M. F., Chéramy, A., Reisine, T. D., & Glowinski, J. Morphine and δ-opiate agonists locally stimulate in vivo dopamine release in cat caudate nucleus. *Nature*, 1981, *291*, 320–322.

Christopher, M., & Butter, C. M. Consummatory behaviors and locomotor exploration evoked from self-stimulation sites in rats. *Journal of Comparative Physiology and Psychology*, 1968, *66*, 335–339.

Chiueh, C. C., & Moore, K. E. Blockade by reserpine of methylphenidate-induced release of brain dopamine. *Journal of Pharmacology and Experimental Therapeutics*, 1975, 559–563.

Clavier, R. M., & Routtenberg, A. In search of reinforcement pathways: A neuroanatomical odyssey. In A. Routtenberg (Ed.), *Biology of reinforcement: Facets of brain stimulation reward.* New York: Academic Press, 1980.

Collier, T. J., Miller, J. S., Quirk, G., Travis, J., & Routtenberg, A. Remembering rewards in the environment: Endogenous hippocampal opiates modulate reinforcement-memory associations. *Society for Neuroscience Abstracts,* 1981, 369.

Colpaert, F. C., Niemegeers, J. E., & Janssen, P. A. J. Discriminative stimulus properties of cocaine and d-amphetamine, and anatagonism by haloperidol: A comparative study. *Neuropharmacology,* 1978, *17,* 937–942.

Contreras, C. M., Guzman-Flores, C., Porantes, M. E., Ervin, F. R., & Palmour, R. Naloxone and phencyclidine: Interacting effects of the limbic system and behavior. *Physiology and Behavior,* 1981, *27,* 1019–1026.

Costa, E. Introduction: morphine, amphetamine and noncataleptogenic neuroleptics. In E. Costa & G. L. Gessa (Eds.), *Advances in biochemical psychopharmacology.* New York: Raven Press, 1977.

Crow, T. J. Catecholamine-containing neurones and electrical self-stimulation: 2. A theoretical interpretation and some psychiatric inmplications. *Psychological Medicine,* 1973, *3,* 66–73.

Crow, T. J. Specific monoamine systems as reward pathways: Evidence for the hypothesis that activation of the ventral mesencephalic dopaminergic neurones and noradrenergic neurones of the locus coeruleus complex will support self-stimulation responding. In A. Waguier & E. T. Rolls (Eds.), *Brain-stimulation reward.* New York: American Elsevier Publishing Company, Inc., 1976.

Crow, T. J., & Arbuthnott, G. W. Function of catecholamine-containing neurones in mammalian central nervous system. *Nature New Biology,* 1972, *238,* 245–246.

Crow, T. J., & Gilbe, C. Brain dopamine and behavior: A critical analysis of the relationship between dopamine anatagonism and therapeutic efficacy of neuroleptic drugs. *Journal of Psychiatric Research,* 1974, *2,* 163–172.

Dahlström, A., & Fuxe, K. Evidence for the existence of monoamine-containing neurons in the central nervous system. I. Demonstration of monoamines in the cell bodies of brainstem neurons. *Acta Physiologica Scandanavica,* 1964, *62,* Supplementum 232.

Damasio, A. The frontal lobes. In K. M. Heilman & E. Valenstein (Eds.), *Clinical neuropsychology.* Oxford: Oxford University Press, 1979.

Davis, G. C. Bunney, W. E., Defraites, E. G., Kleinman, J. E., van Kammen, D. P., Post, R. M., & Wyatt, R. J. Intravenous naloxone administration in schizophrenia and affective illness. *Science,* 1977, *197,* 74–77.

Davis, G. C. Alterations of evoked potentials link research in attention dysfunction to peptide response symptoms of schizophrenia. In E. Costa & M. Tiabucchi (Eds.), *Neural peptides and neuronal communications.* New York: Raven, 1980.

Del Fiacco, M., Paxinos, G., & Cuello, A. C. Neostriatal enkephalin-immunoreactive neurones project to the globus pallidus. *Brain Research,* 1982, *231,* 1–17.

Desiraju, T. Electrophysiology of prefrontal dorsolateral cortex and limbic cortex elucidating the basis and nature of higher nervous associations in primates. In M. A. B. Brazier (Ed.), *Brain Mechanisms in Memory and Learning: From the Single Neuron to Man.* New York: Raven. 1979.

Destrade, C., & Cardo, B. Amélioration de la réméniscence par stimulation post-essai de l'hypothalamus latéral chez souris. *Academy Sci, Paris,* 1975, *280,* 1401–1404.

deWied, D., Bohus, B., van Ree, J. M., & Urban, I. Behavioral and electrophysiological effects of peptides related to lipotropin (B–LPH). *The Journal of Pharmacology and Experimental Therapeutics,* 1978, *204,* 570–580.

Diamond, B. I., & Borison, R. L. Enkephalins and nigrostriatal function. *Neurology,* 1978, *28,* 1085–1088.

DiFiglia, M., Aronin, N., & Martin, J. B. Light and electron microscopic localization of immunoreactive leu-enkephalin in the monkey basal ganglia. *Neuroscience,* 1982, *2,* 303–320.

Domesick, V. B., Beckstead, R. M., & Nauta, W. J. H. Some ascending and descending projections of the substantia nigra and ventral tegmental area in the rat. *Neuroscience Abstracts* 1976, *2,* 61.

Dorsa, D. M., van Ree, J. M., & deWied, D. Effects of [DesTyr']-γ-endorphin and α-endorphin on substantia nigra self-stimulation. *Pharmacology, Biochemistry and Behavior,* 1979, *10,* 899–905.

Duka, T. M., Wuster, M., & Herz, A. Rapid changes of enkephalin levels in rat striatum and hypothalamus induced by diazepam Naunyn-Schmiedeberg's Archives of Pharmacology, 1979, *309,* 1–5.

Edmonds, D. E., & Gallistel, C. R. Reward vs. performance in self-stimulation: Electrode-specific effects of AMPT on reward. *Journal of Comparative Physiology and Psychology,* 1977, *91,* 962–974.

Elde, R., Hökfelt, T., Johansson, O., & Terenius, L. Immuno-histochemical studies using antibodies leu-enkephalin: Initial observations on the nervous system of the rat. *Neuroscience,* 1976, *2,* 349–351.

Ellinwood, E. H., Jr. Amphetamine psychosis: A multidimensional process. *Seminars in Psychiatry,* 1969, *1,* 226.

Ellinwood, E. H., Jr., Sudilovsky, A., & Nelson, L. M. Evolving behavior in the clinical and experimental amphetamine (model) psychosis. *American Journal of Psychiatry,* 1973, *130,* 1088–1093.

Emrich, H. M., Cording, C., Pirée, S., Kölling, A., Zerssen, D. V., & Herz, A. Indication of an antipsychotic action of the opiate anatagonist naloxone. *Pharmakopsychiatry,* 1977, *10,* 265–270.

Esposito, R. U., & Kornetsky, C. Opioids and rewarding brain stimulation. *Neuroscience and Biobehavioral Reviews,* 1978, *2,* 115–122.

Esposito, R. U., Faulkner, W., & Kornetsky, C. Specific modulation of brain stimulation reward by haloperidol. *Pharmacology, Biochemistry and Behavior,* 1979, *10,* 937–940. (a)

Esposito, R. U., McLean, S., & Kornetsky, C. Effects of morphine on intracranial self-stimulation to various brainstem loci in the rat. *Brain Research,* 1979, *168* 425–429. (b)

Esposito, R. U., Motola, A. H. D., & Kornetsky, C. Cocaine: Acute effects on reinforcement thresholds for self-stimulation behavior to the medial forebrain bundle. *Pharmacology, Biochemistry and Behavior,* 1978, *8,* 437–439.

Esposito, R. U., Perry, W., & Kornetsky, C. Effects of d-amphetamine and naloxone on brain stimulation reward. *Psychopharmacology,* 1980, *69,* 187–191.

Esposito, R. U., Perry, W., & Kornetsky, C. Chlorpromazine and brain-stimulation reward: Potentiation of effects of naloxone. *Pharmacology, Biochemistry and Behavior,* 1981, *15,* 903–905.

Ettenberg, A., & Wise, R. A. Non-selective enhancement of locus coeruleus and substantia nigra self-stimulation after termination of chronic dopaminergic receptor blockade with pimozide in rats. *Psychopharmacology Communications,* 1976, *2,* 117–124.

Evarts, E. V. Sensorimotor cortex activity associated with movements triggered by visual as compared to somesthetic inputs. In F. O. Schmitt & F. G. Worden (Eds.), *The neurosciences: Third study program.* Cambridge: MIT Press, 1974.

Falck, B., Hillarp, N. A., Thieme, G., & Torp, H. Fluorescence of catecholamines and related compounds condensed with formaldehyde. *Journal of Histochemistry and Cytochemistry,* 1962, *10,* 348–354.

Fibiger, H. C. Drugs and reinforcement mechanisms: A critical review of the catecholamine theory. In R. George, R. Okun, & A. K. Cho (Eds.), *Annual Review of Pharmacology and Toxicology,* 1978.

Fink, J. S., & Smith, G. P. Mesolimbic and mesocortical dopaminergic neurons are necessary for normal exploratory behavior in rats. *Neuroscience Letters*, 1980, *17*, 61–65.

Freed, N. J., Weinberger, D. R., Biny, L. A., & Wyatt, R. J. Neuropharmacological studies of phencyclidine (PCP)-Induced behavioral stimulation in mice. *Psychopharmacology*, 1980, *71*, 291–297.

French, J. D., Hernandez-Peon, R., & Livingston, R. Projections from the cortex to cephalic brainstem (reticular formation) in monkeys. *Journal of Neurophysiology*, 1955, *18*, 74–95.

Frey, J. M., & Huffman, R. D. A comparative microiontorphoretic study on the effects of methionine-enkephalin and morphine on single unit activity in the rat globus pallidus. *Abstracts of Society for Neuroscience*, 1981, 577.

Fuster, J. M., & Uyeda, A. A. Reactivity of limbic neurons of the monkey to appetitive and aversive signals. *Electroencephalography and Clinical Neurophysiology*, 1971, *30*, 281–293.

Gallagher, M., Kapp, B. S., Pascoe, J. P., & Applegate, C. D. Administration of enkephalin analogues into the amygdala central nucleus: Effects of pavlovian conditioned heart rate in rabbits. *Society for Neuroscience Abstracts*, 1981, 525.

Gardner, E. L., Zukin, R. S., & Makman, M. Modulation of opiate receptor binding in striatum and amygdala by selective mesencephalic lesions. *Brain Research*, 1980, *194*, 232–239.

German, D. C., & Bowden, D. M. Catecholamine systems as the neural substrate for intracranial self-stimulation: A hypothesis. *Brain Research*, 1974, *73*, 381–419.

Gloor, P. Inputs and outputs of the amygdala: What the amygdala is trying to tell the rest of the brain. In K. Livingston & O. Hornykiewicz (Eds.), *Limbic mechanisms*. New York: Plenum Press, 1978.

Goodman, R. R.,Snyder, S. H., Kuhar, M. J., & Young, W. S. Differentiation of delta and mu opiate receptor localizations by light microscopic autoradiography. *Proceedings of the National Academy of Sciences of the United States of America*, 1980, *77*, 6239–6243.

Gritz, E. R., Shiffman, S. M., Jarvik, M. E., Schlesinger, M. D., & Charavastra, V. C. Naltrexone: Physiological and psychological effects of single doses. *Clinical Pharmacology and Therapeutics*, 1976, *19*, 773–776.

Gunne, L. M., Lindstrom, L., & Terenius, L. Naloxone-induced reversal of schizophrenic hallucinations. *Journal of Neural Transmission*, 1977, *40*, 13–19.

Halgren, E. Endogenous potentials generated in the human hippocampal formation and amygdala by infrequent events. *Science*, 1980, *210*, 8O3–805.

Hansch, E. C., Syndulko, K., Cohen, S. N., Goldberg, Z. I., Potvin, A. R., & Tourtellotte, W. W. Cognition in parkinson disease: an event-related potential perspective. *Annals of Neurology*, 1982, *2*, 599–607.

Heilman, K. M. Neglect and related disorders. In K. M. Heilman & E. Valenstein (Eds.), *Clinical neuropsychology*. Oxford: Oxford University Press, 1979.

Heilman, K. M., & Valenstein, E. Frontal lobe neglect in man. *Neurology*, 1972, *22*, 660–664.

Heilman, K. M., & Watson, K. M. The neglect syndrome—a unilateral defect in the orienting response. IN S. Harnard, R. W. Doty, L. Goldstein, J. Jaynes, & G. Krauthamer (Eds.), *Lateralization in the nervous system*. New York: Academic Press, 1979.

Heilman, K. M., Pandya, D. N., & Geschwind, N. Trimodal inattention following parietal lobe ablations. *Transcripts of the American Neurological Association*, 1970, *95*, 259–261.

Hernández, L. L., & Powell, D. A. Effects of naloxone on pavlovian conditioning of eyeblink and heart rate responses in rabbits. *Life Sciences*, 1980, *27*, 863–869.

Herrick, C. J. On the phylogenetic differentiation of the organs of smell and taste. *Journal of Comparative Neurology*, 1908, *18*, 157–166.

Herrick, C. J. *The brain of the tiger salamander, ambystoma tigrinum*. Chicago: University of Chicago Press, 1948.

Herzog, A. G., & Van Hoesen, G. W. Temporal neocortical afferent connections to the amygdala in the rhesus monkey. *Brain Research*, 1976, *115*, 57–69.

Hess, W. R. *The functional organization of the diencephalon.* New York: Grune & Stratton, 1957.

Hiller, J. M., Angel, L. M., & Simon, E. J. Multiple opiate receptors: Alcohol selectively inhibits binding to delta receptors. *Science,* 1981, *214,* 468–469.

Hiller, J. M., Pearson, J. & Simon, E. J. Distribution of stereo-specific binding of the potent narcotic analgesic etorphine in the human brain: Predominance in the limbic system. *Research Communications in Chemical Pathology and Pharmacology,* 1973, *6,* 1052–1062.

Hökfelt, T., Fuxe, K., Johansson, O., & Ljungdahl, A. Pharmaco-histochemical evidence of the existence of dopamine nerve terminals in the limbic cortex. *European Journal of Pharmacology,* 1974, *25,* 108–112.

Hommer, D., van Kammen, D. P., & Pert, A. Modulation of nigrostriatal dopamine activity by opiates. *Abstracts of the Society for Neuroscience,* 1981, 577.

Hornykiewicz, O. Metabolism of brain dopamine in human parkinsonism: Neurochemical and clinical aspects. In E. Costa, L. J. Côte, & M. D. Yahr (Eds.), *Biochemistry and pharmacology of the basal ganglia.* New York: Raven. 1966.

Hull, C. L. *Principles of behavior.* New York: Appleton-Century-Crofts, 1943.

Huston, J. P., Mueller, C. C., & Mondadori, C. Memory facilitation by posttrial hypothalamic stimulation and other reinforcers: A central theory of reinforcement. *Biobehavioral Reviews,* 1977, *1,* 143–150.

Iverson, S. D. Brain dopamine systems and behavior. In L. Iverson, S. D. Iverson, & S. Synder (Eds.), *Handbook of psychopharmacology, Volume 8: Drugs, neurotransmitters and behavior.* New York: Plenum Press, 1977.

Izquierdo, I. Effect of naloxone and morphine on various forms of memory in the rat: Possible role of endogenous opiate mechanisms in memory consolidation. *Psychopharmacology,* 1979, *66,* 199–203.

Jeffcoate, W. J., Cullen, M. H., Herbert, M., Hastings, A. G., & Walder, C. P. Prevention of effects of alcohol intoxication by naloxone. *The Lancet,* 1979, *December 2,* 1157–1159.

Jones, B., & Mishkin, M. Limbic lesions and the problem of stimulus-reinforcement associations. *Experimental Neurology,* 1972, *36,* 362–377.

Jones, D. L., & Mogenson, G. J. Nucleus accumbens to globus pallidus gaba projection: Electrophysiological and iontophoretic investigations. *Brain Research,* 1980, *188,* 93–105.

Jones, E. G., & Powell, T. P. S. An anatomical study of converging sensory pathways within the cerebral cortex of the monkey. *Brain,* 1970, *93,* 793–820.

Jouandet, M., & Gazzaniga, M. S. The frontal lobes. In M. S. Gazzaniga (Ed.), *Handbook of behavioral neurobiology Volume 2-Neuropsychology,* New York: Plenum Press, 1979.

Kastin, A. J., Scollan, E. L., King, M. G., Schally, A. V., & Coy, D. H. Enkephalin and a potent analog facilitate maze performance after intraperitoneal administration in rats. *Pharmacology, Biochemistry and Behavior,* 1976, *5,* 691–695.

Katz, R. J. Naltrexone antagonism of exploration in the rat. *Internal. Journal of Neuroscience,* 1979, *9,* 49–51.

Katz, R. J., & Gelbart, J. Endogenous opiates and behavioral responses to environmental novelty. *Behavioral Biology,* 1978, *24,* 338–348.

Katz, R. J., Carroll, B. J., & Baldrighi, G. Behavioral activation by enkephalins in mice. *Pharmacology, Biochemistry and Behavior,* 1978, *8,* 493–496.

Kelly, A. E., Stinus, L., & Iverson, S. D. Interactions between D-Ala-Met-enkephalin, A10 dopaminergic neurones, and spontaneous behavior in the rat. *Behavioral Brain Research,* 1980, *1,* 3–24.

Kemp, J. M., & Powell, T. P. The corticostrial projection in the monkey. *Brain,* 1970, *73,* 525–546.

Kennard, M. A. & Ectors, L. Forced circling movements in monkeys following lesions of the frontal lobes. *Journal of Neurophysiology,* 1938, *1,* 45–54.

Kety, S. S. The biogenic amines in the central nervous system: Their possible roles in arousal, emotion, and learning. In F. O. Schmitt (Eds.), *The Neurosciences: Second Study Program.* New York: Rockefeller University Press, 1970.

Khanmas, K., Andersson, K., & Fuxe, K. On the role of ascending dopamine systems in the control of voluntary ethanol intake and ethanol intoxication. *Pharmacology, Biochemistry and Behavior,* 1979, *10,* 603–608.

Kling, A., Steklis, H., & Deutsch, S. Radiotelemetered activity from the amygdala during social interactions in the monkey. *Experimental Neurology,* 1979, *66,* 88–96.

Knight, R. T., Hillyard, S. A., Woods, D. L., & Neville, H. J. The effects of frontal cortex lesions on event-related potentials during auditory selective attention. *Electroencephalography and Clinical Neurophysiology,* 1981, *52,* 571–582.

Kojima, S. Prefrontal unit activity in the monkey: Relation to visual stimuli and movements. *Experimental Neurology,* 1980, *69,* 110–123.

Kornetsky, C., & Esposito, R. U. Central reward systems of substance abuse. In E. Usdin (Ed.), *Catecholamines: Basic and Clinical Frontiers.* Elmsford, N.Y.: Pergamon Press, 1979. (a)

Kornetsky, C., & Esposito, R. U. Euphorigenic drugs: Effects on the reward pathways of the brain. *Federation Proceedings,* 1979, *38,* 2473–2476. (b)

Kornetsky, C., & Esposito, R. U. Cocaine: Reward and detection thresholds for brain stimulation: Dissociative effects of cocaine. *Brain Research,* 1981, *209,* 296–300.

Kornetsky, C., & Mirsky, A. F. On certain psychopharmacological and physiological differences between schizophrenic and normal persons. *Psychopharmacologia,* 1966, *8,* 309–318.

Kornetsky, C., Markowitz, R., & Esposito, R. U. Phencyclidine and naloxone: Effects on sensitivity to aversive and rewarding stimulation in the rat. In E. F. Domino (Ed.), *PCP: Historical and Current Perspectives.* Ann Arbor, MI: NPP Books, 1981.

Kornhuber, H. H. Cerebral cortex, cerebellum and basal ganglia: An introduction to their motor functions. In F. O. Schmitt & G. Worden (Ed.), *The neurosciences: Third Study Program.* Cambridge: MIT Press, 1974.

Kraepelin, E. *Dementia praecox and paraphrenia.* Edinburgh: E. & S. Livingstone, 1919.

Kuhar, M. J., Pert, C. B., & Snyder, S. H. Regional distribution of opiate receptor binding in monkey and human brain. *Nature,* 1973, *245,* 447–450.

Lerner, S. E., & Burns, R. S. Phencyclidine use among youth: History, epidemiology, and acute and chronic intoxication. In R. C. Peterson & R. C. Stillman (Eds.), *Phencyclidine (PCP) Abuse: An Appraisal.* Washington, D.C.: Department of Health, Education and Welfare, 1978.

Lewis, M. E., Mishkin, M., Bragin, E., Brown, R. M., Pert, C. B., & Pert, A. Opiate receptor gradients in monkey cerebral cortex: Correspondence with sensory processing hierarchies. *Science,* 1981, *211,* 1166–1169.

Lindvall, O., Björklund, A., & Divac, T. Organization of mesencephalic dopamine neurons projecting to neocortex and septum. *Advances in Biochemical Psychopharmacology,* 1979, *16,* 39–46.

Lindvall, O., Björklund, A., Moore, R. U., & Stenevi, U. Mesencephalic dopamine neurons projecting to neocortex. *Brain Research,* 1974, *81,* 325–331.

Lipinski, J., Meyer, R., Kornetsky, C., & Cohen, B. M. Naloxone in schizophrenia: Negative result. *The Lancet,* 1979, *June 16,* 1292–1293.

Llamas, C., Avendaño, C., & Reinoso-Suárez, F. Amygdala projections to prefrontal and motor cortex. *Science,* 1977, *195,* 794–796.

Lord, J., Waterfield, A., Hughes, J., & Kosterlitz, H. Endogenous opioid peptides: Multiple agonists and receptors. *Nature,* 1977, *267,* 495–499.

Lorens, S. A. & Sainati, S. M. Naloxone blocks the excitatory effect of ethanol and chordiazepoxide on lateral hypothalamic self-stimulation behavior. *Life Sciences,* 1978, *23,* 1359–1364.

Luby, E., Cohen, B. D., Rosenbaum, G., Gottlieb, J. S., & Kelly, R. Study of new schizophrenomimetic drug—Sernyl. *Archives of Neurology and Psychiatry,* 1959, *81,* 363–369.

McCulloch, J., Savaki, H. E., & Sokoloff, L. Influence of dopaminergic systems on the lateral habenular nucleus of the rat. *Brain Research,* 1980, *194,* 117–124.

McCulloch, J., Savaki, H. E., McCulloch, M. C., & Sokoloff, L. Specific distribution of metabolic alterations in cerebral cortex following apomorphine administration. *Nature*, 1979, *482*, 303–305.

Magnuson, D. J., & Reid, L. D. Addictive agents and intracranial stimulation (ICS): Pressing for ICS under the influence of ethanol before and after physical dependence. *Bulletin of the Psychonomic Society*, 1977, *10*, 364–366.

Major, R., & White, N. Memory facilitation by self-stimulation reinforcement mediated by the nigro-neostriatal bundle. *Physiology & Behavior*, 1978, *20*, 723–733.

Marshall, J. F., & Teitelbaum, P. Further analysis of sensory inattention following lateral hypothalamic damage in rats. *Journal of Comparative and Physiological Psychology*, 1974, *86*, 375–395.

Marshall, J. F., Turner, B. H., & Teitelbaum, P. Sensory neglect produced by lateral hypothalamic damage. *Science*, 1971, *174*, 523–525.

Martin, W. R., Eades, C. G., Thompson, J. A., Huppler, R. E., & Gilbert, P. E. The effects of morphine and nalorphine-like drugs in the nondependent and morphine-dependent chronic spinal dog. *Journal of Pharmacology and Experimental Therapeutics*, 1976, *197*, 517–532.

Matthysse, S. Schizophrenia: Relationships to dopamine transmission, motor control, and feature extraction. In F. O. Schmitt & F. G. Worden (Eds.), *The Neurosciences: Third study program.* Cambridge: MIT Press, 1974.

Meibach, R. C., & Katzman, R. Origin, course and termination of dopaminergic substantia nigra neurons projecting to the amygdaloid complex in the cat. *Neuroscience*, 1981, *6*, 2159–2171.

Mello, N. K., & Mendelson, J. Self-administration of an enkephalin analog by rhesus monkey. *Pharmacology, Biochemistry & Behavior*, 1978, *9*, 579–586.

Meltzer, H. Y., Sturgeon, R. D., Sinonvic, M., & Fessler, R. G. Phencyclidine as an indirect dopamine agonist. In E. F. Domino (Ed.), *PCP: Historical and current perspectives.* Ann Arbor: NPP, 1981.

Messing, R. B., Jensen, R. A., Martinez, J. L., Jr., Spiehler, V. R., Vasquez, B. J., Soumireu-Mourat, B., Liang, K. C., & McGaugh, J. L. Naloxone enhancement of memory. *Behavioral and Neural Biology*, 1979, *27*, 266–275.

Mesulam, M. M., & Van Hoesen, G. W. Limbic and sensory connections of the inferior parietal lobule (area PG) in the rhesus monkey: A study with a new method for horseradish peroxidase histochemistry. *Brain Research*, 1977, *136*, 393–414.

Miller, N. E. Some reflections on the law of effect produce a new alternative to drive induction. In M. R. Jones (Ed.), *Nebraska symposium on motivation.* Lincoln: University of Nebraska Press, 1963.

Mintz, M., Tomer, R., Radwan, H., & Myslobodsky, M. S. A comparison of levodopa treatment and task demands on visual evoked potentials in hemi-parkinsonism. *Psychiatry Research*, 1982, *6*, 245–251.

Mishkin, M., & Aggleton, J. Multiple functional contributions of the amygdala in the monkey. In Y. Ben Ari (Ed.), *The amygdaloid complex.* Elsevier/North Holland Biomedical Press, 1981.

Mogenson, G. J., Jones, D. L., & Yim, C. Y. From motivation to action: Functional interface between the limbic system and the motor system. *Progress in Neurobiology*, 1980, *14*, 69–97.

Mogenson, G. J., & Yim, C. Y. Electrophysiological and neuropharmacological behavioral studies of the nucleus accumbens: Implications for its role as a limbic-motor interface. In R. B. Chronister & J. F. DeFrance (Eds.), *The neurobiology of the nucleus accumbens.* Haer Institute, 1981.

Moore, K. E. The actions of amphetamine on neurotransmitters: A brief review. *Biological Psychiatry*, 1977, *12*, 451–461.

Moore, R. Y., & Bloom, F. E. Central catecholamine neuron systems: Anatomy and physiology of the dopmaine systems. *Annual Review of Neuroscience*, 1978, 129–169.

Mora, F., & Myers, R. D. Brain self-stimulation: Direct evidence for the involvement of dopamine in the prefrontal cortex. *Science*, 1977, *197*, 1387–1388.

Mora, F., Rolls, E. T., Burton, M. J., & Shaw, S. G. Effects of dopamine-receptor blockade on self-stimulation in the monkey. *Pharmacology, Biochemistry & Behavior*, 1976, *4*, 211–216.

Morgane, P. J. Anatomical and neurobiochemical bases of the central nervous control of physiological regulations and behavior. In G. J. Mogenson & F. R. Calaresu (Eds.), *Neural integration of physiological mechanisms and behavior*. Toronto: University of Toronto Press, 1975.

Morgane, P. J. Historical and modern concepts of hypothalamic organization and function. In P. J. Morgan & J. Panksepp (Eds.), *Anatomy of the hypothalamus (Volume 1)*. New York: Marcel Dekker, Inc., 1979.

Myers, R. D., & Mora, F. "In Vivo" neurochemical analysis, by push-pull perfusion, of the mesocortical dopaminergic system of the rat during self-stimulation. *Brain Research Bulletin*, 1977, *2*, 105–112.

Nauta, W. J. H. Hippocampal projections and related neural pathways to the midbrain in the cat. *Brain*, 1958, *81*, 319–340.

Nauta, W. J. H. Central nervous organization and the endocrine motor system. In A. V. Nalbandov (Ed.), *Advances in neuroendocrinology*. Urbana: University of Illinois Press, 1963.

Nauta, W. J. H. Some efferent connections of the prefrontal cortex in the monkey. In J. M. Watten & K. Akert (Eds.), *The frontal granular cortex and behavior*. New York: McGraw-Hill, 1964.

Nauta, W. J. H., & Domesick, V. B. Crossroads of limbic and striatal cricuitry: Hypothalamo-nigral connections. In K. Livingston & O. Hornykiewicz (Eds.), *Limbic mechanisms*. New York: Plenum Press, 1978.

Nauta, W. J. H., & Haymaker, W. Hypothalamic nuclei and fiber connexions. In W. Haymaker, E. Andersson, & W. J. H. Nauta (Eds.), *The hypothalamus*. Springfield, Ill.: C. C. Thomas, 1969.

Nauta, W. J. H., & Mehler, W. R. Projections of the lentiform nucleus in the monkey. *Brain Research*, 1966, *1*, 3–42.

Niki, H., & Watanabe, M. Prefrontal and cingulate unit activity during timing behavior in the monkey. *Brain Research*, 1979, *171*, 213–224.

Olds, J. Hypothalamic substrates of reward. *Physiological Reviews*, 1962, *42*, 554–604.

Olds, M. E., & Olds, J. Approach-avoidance analysis of rat diencephalon. *Journal of Comparative Neurology*, 1963, *120*, 259–295.

Olson, G. A., Olson, R. D., Kastin, A. J., Green, M. T., Roig-Smith, R., Hill, C. W., & Coy, D. H. Effects of an enkephalin analog on complex learning in the rhesus monkey. *Pharmacology, Biochemistry and Behavior*, 1979, *11*, 341–345.

Orona, E., Foster, K., Lambert, R., & Gabriel, M. Cingulate cortical and anterior thalamic neuronal correlates of the overtraining reversal effect in rabbits. *Behavioural Brain Research*, 1982, *4*, 133–154.

Pandya, D. M., & Kuypers, H. G. J. M. Cortico-cortical connections in the rhesus monkey. *Brain Research*, 1969, *13*, 13–36.

Panksepp, J. Hypothalamic integration of behavior: Rewards, punishments, and related psychological processes. In P. J. Morgane & J. Panksepp (Eds.), *Behavioral studies of the hypothalamus*. New York: Marcel Dekker, 1981.

Pellegrino, L. J. Amygdaloid lesions and behavioral inhibition in the rat. *Journal of Comparative Physiology and Psychology*, 1968, *65*, 483–491.

Pert, A. Personal communication, 1983.

Pert, A., & Sivet, C. Neuroanatomical focus for morphine and enkephalin-induced hypermotility. *Nature*, 1977, *265*, 645–647.

Pert, C. B. Type 1 and type 2 opiate receptor distribution in brain—what does it tell us? In J. B. Martin, S. Reichlin, & K. L. Bick (Eds.), *Neurosecretion and brain peptides*. New York: Raven Press, 1981.

Pert, C. B., Taylor, D. P., Pert, A., Herkenham, M. A., & Kent, J. L. Biochemical and auto-radiographical evidence for type 1 and type 2 opiate receptors. In E. Costa & M. Trabucchi

(Eds.), *Neural peptides and neuronal communication*. New York: Plenum Press, 1980.

Phillips, A. G., & Fibiger, H. C. The role of dopamine in maintaining intracranial self-stimulation in the ventral tegmentum, nucleus accumbens, and medial prefrontal cortex. *Canadian Journal of Psychology*, 1978, *32*, 58–66.

Phillipson, O. T. Afferent projections to A10 dopaminergic neurones in the rat as shown by the retrograde transport of horseradish peroxidase. *Neuroscience Letters*, 1978, *9*, 353–359.

Pickar, J. J., Vartanian, F., Bunney, W. E., Marier, H. P., Gastpar, M. T., Prakash, R., Sethi, B. B., Lideman, R., Belyaer, B. S., Tsutsulkovskaja, M. V. A., Jungkunz, G., Nedopil, N., Verhoeven, W., & Van Praag, H. Short-term naloxone administration in schizophrenic and manic patients. *Archives of General psychiatry*, 1982, *39*, 313–319.

Pijenberg, A. J. & van Rossum, J. M. Stimulation of locomotor activity following injection of dopamine into the nucleus accumbens. *Journal of Pharmacy and Psychopharmacology*, 1973, *25*, 1003.

Pirch, J. H., & Peterson, S. L. Event-related slow potentials and activity of single neurons in rat frontal cortex. *Internal Journal of Neuroscience*, 1981, *15*, 141–146.

Pirch, J. H., Corbus, M. J., & Napier, T. C. Auditory cue preceding intracranial stimulation induces event-related potential in rat frontal cortex: Alterations by amphetamine. *Brain Research Bulletin*, 1981, *7*, 399–404.

Pollard, H., Llorens, C., Bonnet, J. J., Costentin, J., & Schwartz, J. C. Opiate receptors on mesolimbic dopaminergic neurons. *Neuroscience Letters*, 1977, *7*, 295–299. (a)

Pollard, H., Llorens-Cortes, C., & Schwartz, J. C. Enkephalin receptors on dopaminergic neurones in rat striatum. *Nature*, 1977. *268*, 745–747. (b)

Porrino, L. J., & Goldman-Rakic, P. S. Brainstem innervation of prefrontal and anterior cingulate cortex in the rhesus monkey revealed by retrograde transport of HRP. *Journal of Comparative Neurology*, 1982, *205*, 63–76.

Porrino, L. J., Crane, A. M., & Goldman-Rakic, P. S. Direct and indirect pathways from the amygdala to the frontal lobe in rhesus monkeys. *Journal of Comparative Neurology*, 1981, *198*, 121–136.

Powell, E. W., & Leman, R. B. Connections of the nucleus accumbens. *Brain Research*, 1976, *105*, 389–403.

Pragay, E. B., Mirsky, A. F., Mirsky, C. V., & Scales, B. H. Characteristics of attention-related cells in prefrontal cortical regions. *Society for Neuroscience Abstracts*, 1980, 813.

Pragay, E. B., Mirsky, A. F., Ray, C. L., Turner, D. F., & Mirsky, C. V. Neuronal activity in the brain stem reticular formation during performance of a "go–no go" visual attention task in the monkey. *Experimental Neurology*, 1978, *60*, 83–95.

Prelević, S., Burnham, W. M., & Gloor, P. A microelectrode study of amygdaloid afferents: Temporal neocortical inputs. *Brain Research*, 1976, *105*, 437–457.

Pribram, K. H. The primate frontal cortex. *Neuropsychologia*, 1969, *7*, 259–266.

Pubols, S. M. Changes in food-motivated behavior of rats as a function of septal and amygdaloid lesions. *Experimental Neurology*, 1966, *15*, 240–254.

Pycock, C., & Horton, R. Evidence for an accumbens-pallidal pathway in the rat and its possible gabaergic control. *Brain Research*, 1976, *110*, 629–634.

Quirion, R., Bowen, W. D., & Pert, C. B. μ, δ and κ opiate receptors: Interconvertible forms of the same receptor. *Advances in Endogenous Opioids: Proceedings of the International Narcotic Research Conference*, 1981. (a)

Quirion, R., Hammer, R. P., Jr., Herkenham, M., & Pert, C. B. Phencyclidine (angel dust)/ "opiate" receptor: Visualization by tritium-sensitive film. *Procedures of the National Academy of Science, United States of America*, 1981, 78(9), 5881–5885. (b)

Ray, C. L., Mirsky, A. F., & Pragay, E. B. Functional analysis of attention-related unit activity in the reticular formation of the monkey. *Experimental Neurology*, 1982, *77*, 544–562.

Reeves, A. G., & Hagamen, W. D. Behavioral and EEG asymmetry following unilateral lesions of the forebrain and midbrain of cats. *Electroencephalography and Clinical Neurophysiology,* 1971, *30,* 83–86.

Richardson, J. S. The amygdala: Historical and functional analysis. *Acta Neurobiologiae Experimentalis,* 1973, *33,* 623–648.

Rigter, H. Attenuation of amnesia in rats by systemically administered enkephalins. *Science,* 1978, *200,* 83–85.

Risner, M. E., & Jones, B. E. Role of noradrenergic and dopaminergic processes in amphetamine self-administration. *Pharmacology, Biochemistry & Behavior,* 1976, *5,* 477–482.

Roberts, G. W., Woodhams, P. L., Polak, J. M. & Crow, T. J. Distribution of neuropeptides in the limbic system of the rat: The amygdalod complex. *Neuroscience,* 1982, 99–129.

Robertson, A., & Mogenson, G. J. Facilitation of self-stimulation of the prefrontal cortex in rats following chronic administration of spiroperidol or amphetamine. *Psychopharmacology,* 1979, *65,* 149–154.

Rodgers, R. J., & Deacon, R. M. J. Effects of naloxone on the behaviour of rats exposed to a novel environment. *Psychopharmacology,* 1979, *65,* 103–105.

Rolls, E. T., Thorpe, S. J., Perret, D. I., Boytim, M., Wilson, F. A. W., & Szabo, I. Responses of striatal neurons in the behaving monkey: Influence of dopamine. *Society for Neuroscience Abstracts,* 1981, *7,* 778.

Rolls, E. T., Caan, A. W., Griffiths, C., Murzi, E., Perret, D. I., Thorpe, S. J., & Wilson, F. A. W. Visual processing behond the inferior temporal visual cortex. *Behavioral Brain Research,* 1982, *5,* 114–115.

Rosenkilde, C. E., Bauer, R. H., & Fuster, J. M. Single cell activity in ventral prefrontal cortex of behaving monkeys. *Brain Research,* 1981, *209,* 375–394.

Roth, W. T., Prefferbaum, A., Horvath, T. B., Berger, P. A., & Kopell, B. S. P3 reduction in auditory evoked potentials of schizophrenics. *Electroencephalography and Clinical Neurophysiology,* 1980, *49,* 497–505.

Routtenberg, A. Participation of brain stimulation reward substrates in memory: Anatomical and biochemical evidence. *Federation Proceedings,* 1979, 2446–2453.

Sar, M., Steumphf, W. E., Miller, R. J., Chang, K., & Cuatrecasas, P. Immunohistochemical localization of enkephalin in rat brain and spinal cord. *Journal of Comparative Neuorolgy,* 1978, *182,* 17–38.

Schulz, R., Wuster, M., Duka, T., & Herz, A. Acute and chronic ethanol treatment changes endorphin levels in brain and pituitary. *Psychopharmacology,* 1980, *68,* 221–227.

Schwartzbaum, J. S., & Poulos, D. A. Discrimination behavior after amygdalectomy in monkeys: Learning set and discrimination reversal. *Journal of Comparative Physiology and Psychology,* 1965, *60,* 320–328.

Seeger, T. F., Carlson, K. R., & Nazzaro, J. M.   Pentobarbital induces a naloxone-reversible decrease mesolimbic self-stimulation threshold. *Pharmacology, Biochemistry and Behavior,* 1981, *15,* 583–586. (a)

Seeger, T. F., Gardner, E. L., & Bridger, W. F. Increase in mesolimbic electrical self-stimulation after chronic haloperidol: Reversal by L-Dopa or lithium. *Brain Research,* 1981. *215,* 404–409. (b)

Shakow, D. *Schizophrenia.* New York: International Universities Press Inc., 1977.

Sheffield, F. D. New evidence on the drive induction theory of reinforcement. In R. N. Haber (Ed.), *Current research in motivation.* New York: Holt, Rhinehart, & Winston, 1966.

Shizgal, P., Bielajew, C., & Yeomans, J. Behaviorally-derived estimates of conduction velocity and refractory period in a reward-related pathway differ from the characteristics of monoaminergic neurons. *Society of Neuroscience Abstract,* 1979, *5,* 352.

Shizgal, P., Bielajew, C., Corbett, D., Skelton, R., & Yeoman, J. Behavioral methods for inferring anatomical linkage between rewarding brain stimulation sites. *Journal of Comparative and Physiological Psychology,* 1980, *94,* 227–237.

Siegfried, B., & Bures, J. Asymmetry of EEG arousal in rats with unilateral 6-hydroxydopamine lesions of substantia nigra: Quantification of neglect. *Experimental Neurology*, 1978, *62*, 173–190.

Simantov, R., & Snyder, S. Isolation and structure identification of a morphine-like peptide "enkephalin" in bovine brain. *Life Science*, 1976, *18*, 781–788.

Simantov, R., Kuhar, M. J., Uhl, G. R., & Snyder, S. H. Opioid peptide enkephalin: Immunohistochemical mapping in the rat central nervous system. *Proceedings of the National Academy of Science, United States of America*, 1977, *74*, 2167–2171.

Simon, E. J., Bonnet, K. A., Crain, S. M., Groth, J., Hiller, J. M., & Smith, J. R. Recent studies on interactions between opioid peptides and their receptors. In E. Costa & M. Trabucchi (Eds.), *Neural peptides and neuronal communication. Advances in biochemical psychopharmacology (Volume 22)*. New York: Raven Press, 1980.

Sokoloff, L. Relation between physiological function and energy metabolism in the central nervous system. *Journal of Neurochemistry*, 1977, *29*, 13–26.

Spiegler, B. J., & Mishkin, M. Evidence for the sequential participation of inferior temporal cortex and amygdala in the acquisition of stimulus-reward associations. *Behavioral Brain Research*, 1981, *3*, 303–317.

Staubli, U., & Huston, J. P. Avoidance learning enhanced by post-trial morphine injection. *Behavioral and Neural Biology*, 1980, *28*, 487–490.

Stein, L., & Belluzzi, J. D. Brain endorphins: possible role in reward and memory formation. *Federation Proceedings*, 1979, *38*, 2468–2472.

Stevens, J. R. An anatomy of schizophrenia. *Archives of General Psychiatry*, 1973, *29*, 177–189.

Sutherland, R. J. The dorsal diencephalic conduction system: A review of the anatomy and functions of the habenular complex. *Neuroscience and Biobehavioral Reviews*, 1982, *6*, 1–13.

Sutherland, R. J., & Nakajima, S. Self-stimulation of the habenular complex in the rat. *Journal of Comparative Physiology and Pshchology*, 1981, *95*, 781–791.

Sutton, S., Braren, M. & Zubin, J. Evoked potential correlates for stimulus uncertainty. *Science*, 1965, *150*, 1187–1188.

Suzuki, H., & Azuma, M. Prefrontal neuronal activity during gazing at a light spot in the monkey. *Brain Research*, 1977, *126*, 497–508.

Tarsy, D., & Baldessarini, R. J. Behavioral supersensitivity to apomorphine following chronic treatment with drugs which intefere with the synaptic function of catecholamines. *Neuropharmacology*, 1974, *13*, 927–940.

Tassin, J. P., Thierry, A. M., Blanc, G., & Glowinski, J. Evidence for a specific uptake of dopamine by dopaminergic terminals of the rat cerebral cortex. *Naunyn-Schmiedeberg's Archives of Pharmacology*, 1974, *282*, 239–244.

Teuber, H. L. The riddle of frontal lobe function in man. In J. M. Warren & K. Akert (Eds.), *The frontal granular cortex and behavior*. New York: McGraw-Hill, 1964.

Teuber, H. L. Alterations of perception after brain injury. In J. C. Eccles (Ed.), *Brain and conscious experience*. New York: Springer-Verlag, 1966.

Thierry, A. M., Blanc, G., Sobel, A., Stinus, L., & Glowinski, J. Dopamine terminals in the rat cortex. *Science*, 1973, *182*, 499–501.

Thorndike, E. L. A proof of the law of effect. *Science*, 1933, *77*, 173–175.

Tortella, F. C., & Moreton, J. E. D-Ala2-methionine-enkephalinamide self-administration in the morphine-dependent rat. *Psychopharmacology*, 1980, *69*, 143–147.

Trabucchi, M., Spano, P. F., Tonson, G. C., & Eratola, L. Effects of bromocryptine on central dopaminergic receptors. *Life Sciences*, 1976, *19*, 1061–1066.

Turner, B. H., Mishkin, M., & Knapp, M. Organization of the amygdalopetal projections from modality-specific cortical association areas in the monkey. *Journal of Comparative Neurology*, 1980, *191*, 515–543.

Uhl, G., Kuhar, M. J., Goodman, R. R., & Snyder, S. H. Histochemical localization of the enkephalins. In E. Usdin, W. E. Bunney, Jr., & N. S. Kline (Eds.), *Endorphins in mental health research.* New York: Oxford University Press, 1979.

Ungerstedt, U. Sterotaxic mapping of the monoamine pathways in the rat brain. *Acta Physiologica Scandinavica, Supplement,* 1971, *367,* 1–48.

Ungerstedt, U. Brain dopamine neurons and behavior. In F. O. Schmitt & F. G. Worden (Eds.), *The neurosciences: Third study program.* Cambridge: MIT Press, 1974.

Ungerstedt, U., & Ljungberg, T. Central dopamine neurons and sensory processing. *Journal of Psychiatry Research,* 1974, *2,* 149–150.

Valenstein, E. S. Brain mechanisms in reinforcement. In W. H. Sweet, S. Obrador, J. G. Martin-Rodrigues (Eds.), *Neurosurgical treatment in psychiatry.* Baltimore: University Park Press, 1977.

Valenstein, E. S., Cox, V. C., & Kakolewski, J. W. Modification of motivated behavior elicited by electrical stimulation of the hypothalamus. *Science,* 1968, *159,* 1119–1121.

Van Hoesen, G. W., & Pandya, D. N. Some connections of the entorhinal (area 28) and perirhinal (area 35) cortices of the rhesus monkey. I. Temporal lobe afferents. *Brain Research,* 1975, *95,* 1–24.

Van Rossum, J. M. The significance of dopamine-receptor blockade for the mechanism of action of neuroleptic drugs. *Archives Internationales de Pharmacodynamie,* 1966, *160,* 492–494.

Venho, I., Eerola, R., Venho, E. V., & Vartiainen, O. Sensitization to morphine by experimentally induced alcoholism in white mice. *Annales Medicinae Experimentalis et Biologiae Fenniae,* 1955, *33,* 249–252.

Volavka, J. Electroencephalographic and other effects of naloxone in normal man. *Life Sciences,* 1979, *25,* 1267–1272.

Walczak, S. A., Wilkening, D., & Makman, M. Interaction of morphine, etorphine and enkephalins with dopamine-stimulated adenylate cyclase of monkey anygdala. *Brain Research,* 1978, *160,* 105–116.

Wald, D., Ebstein, R. P., & Belmaker, R. H. Haloperidol and lithium blocking of mood response to intravenous methylphenidate. *Psychopharmacology,* 1978, *57,* 83–87.

Walter, W. G., Cooper, R., Aldridge, V. J., McCallum, W. C., & Winter, A. L. Contingent negative variation: An electric sign of sensorimotor association and expectancy in the human brain. *Nature,* 1964, *203,* 380–384.

Watanabe, M. Prefrontal unit activity during delayed conditional discriminations in the monkey. *Brain Research,* 1981, *225,* 51–65.

Watson, R. T., Heilman, K. M., Cauthen, J. C., & King, F. A. Neglect after cingulectomy. *Neurology,* 1973, *23,* 1003–1007.

Watson, R. T., Heilman, K. M., Miller, B. D., & King, F. A. Neglect after mesencephalic reticular formation lesions. *Neurology,* 1974, *24,* 294–298.

Watson, S. J., Berger, P. A., Akil, H., Mills, M. J., & Barchas, J. D. Effects of naloxone on schizophrenia: Reduction in hallucinations in a subpopulation of schizophrenics. *Science,* 1978, *201,* 73–76.

Webster, K. E. Cortico-striate interrelations in the albino rat. *Journal of Anatomy,* 1961, *95,* 532–545.

Weinstein, M. R. Histopathological changes in the brain in schizophrenia: A critical review. *Archives of Neurology and Psychiatry,* 1954, *71,* 539–553.

Welch, K., & Stuteville, P. Experimental production of neglect in monkeys. *Brain Research,* 1958, *81,* 341–347.

Welzl, H., Flack, H. G., & Huston, J. P. Contraversive circling and facilitation of the perioral biting reflex by injection of substance P or D-Ala$_2$2-Met-enkephalinamide into the substantia nigra. *Behavioral and Neural Biology,* 1982, *34,* 104–108.

White, N., & Major, R. Effect of pimozide on the improvement in learning produced by self-stimulation and by water reinforcement. *Pharmacology, Biochemistry and Behavior*, 1978, *8*, 565–571. (a)

White, N., & Major, R. Facilitation of retention by self-stimulation and by experimenter-administered stimulation. *Canadian Journal of Psychology*, 1978, *32*, 116–123. (b)

Wise, R. A. Neuroleptic attenuation of intracranial self-stimulation: Reward or performance deficits? *Life Sciences*, 1978, *22*, 535–542.

Wright, J. J., & Craggs, M. D. Intracranial self-stimulation, cortical arousal, and the sensorimotor neglect syndrome. *Experimental Neurology*, 1979, *65*, 42–52.

Yeomans, J. S. Absolute refractory periods of self-stimulation neurons. *Physiology and Behavior*, 1979, *22*, 911–919.

Yin, T. C. T., & Mountcastle, V. B. Mechanisms of neural integration in the parietal lobe for visual attention. *Federation Proceedings*, 1978, *37*, 2251–2257.

Zahn, T. P., Rosenthal, D., & Shakow, D. Effects of irregular preparatory intervals on reaction time in schizophrenia. *Journal of Abnormal and Social Psychology*, 1973, *67*, 44–52.

Zhang, A. Z., & Pasternak, G. W. Mu and delta opiate receptors: Correlation with high and low affinity opiate binding sites. *European Journal of Pharmacology*, 1980, *67*, 323–324.

Zukin, S. R., & Zukin, R. S. In E. Domino, (Ed.), *Phencyclidine: Historical and current perspectives*, Ann Arbor: NPP, 1981.

3 Endogenous Processes in Memory Consolidation

Paul E. Gold
University of Virginia

James L. McGaugh
*Center for the Neurobiology of Learning and Memory and
Department of Psychobiology
University of California, Irvine*

INTRODUCTION

Until relatively recently, the evidence that the brain is changed by experience was based solely on indirect behavioral assessments of changes: Training can produce long-lasting changes in behavior; therefore, the brain must, it would seem, be changed by experience. There is now abundant evidence that change does occur. One of the recent major advances in neurobiology is an ever-expanding list of long-term changes in brain structure and function elicited by training procedures and neural manipulation. Early demonstrations that animals raised in enriched or impoverished conditions differ in brain weight (Rosenzweig & Bennett, 1978) were followed by anatomical evidence of precise remodeling of synaptic terminations following brain damage (Lynch & Wells, 1978; Steward, 1982), as well as evidence of changes in dendritic branching patterns produced by differential experiences (Floeter & Greenough, 1979; Juraska, Greenough, Elliot, Mack, & Berkowitz, 1980). Neurophysiological changes induced by stimulation include altered cell firing rates during conditioning (Oleson, Ashe, & Weinberger, 1975; McCormick, Clark, Lavond, & Thompson, 1982), as well as long-lasting changes produced by electrical stimulation of certain brain areas, such as long-term potentiation (Lynch, Browning, & Bennett, 1979; Goddard, 1980), and kindling (Racine, 1978; McNamara, Byrne, Dashieff, & Fitz, 1980). Finally, biochemical studies have revealed changes in neurotransmitter receptor sensitivity under a variety of experimental and endogenous conditions (Reisine, 1981) and long-term induction of transmitter-related enzyme activity and synthesis following stress or brain damage (Thoenen, 1975; Costa & Guidotti, 1978; Acheson, Zigmond, & Stricker, 1980).

As we survey the many sorts of relatively permanent brain changes induced by experience and stimulation, it seems possible that we may now know some of the changes involved in the storage of information in the brain. And yet, of course, we remain dissatisfied. Few investigators of neurobiology and memory are ready to embrace the phenomena described above as the answer to their principal question: "What brain changes underlie learning and memory?" The major reason for this dissatisfaction may be attributed to a question which, in our view, is inappropriate: "What specific memory does the specific brain change represent?" In this regard, we wish to advocate a possibly disconcerting notion. It may be possible to understand the process of memory formation and its mechanisms without ever being able to identify the neural basis of a particular memory. All memories are formed in a context that contains both species and individual elements. The evolutionary components may be conceptualized in two general forms, species-specific behavioral repertoires as well as species-specific learning and memory repertoires. In addition, the individual animal learns and remembers information within the context of that animal's individual history. These basic tenets imply simply that each organism perceives and responds to an experimental training procedure in a unique manner. Furthermore, if learning and memory occur in such contexts, it will not be possible for an animal to learn a specific association without acquiring many other associations at the same time. Thus, because the number of potential associations is very large and idiosyncratic, any attempt to identify a brain change as the basis of a specific memory seems to be a strategy without hope of success.

It may be, then, that the answer to "What specific memory does this specific brain change represent?" is unknowable. However, the biological processes by which information is stored need not be unknowable. At least two general questions remain quite reasonable: (1) What kinds of long-lasting changes are initiated by any of the variety of training procedures? The answer to this question involves continuing the cataloging of long-lasting brain changes produced by experience. (2) What biological processes regulate the brain changes? Are there neuronal systems responsible for initiating and terminating or augmenting and attenuating the changes? The latter questions provide the focus of contemporary views of memory modulation. The emphasis is on measuring and manipulating those endogenous responses to training that may be important in regulating the processes responsible for storing new information.

HISTORICAL PERSPECTIVE

It is well known that many treatments can enhance or impair later retention performance if they are administered shortly after training. These effects on memory are time-dependent. The treatments have greatest influence on memory if administered immediately after training; delayed injections are less effective (Glickman, 1961; McGaugh, 1966). These findings have generally been interpreted as supporting the view that the treatments affect retention by affecting the neural processes underlying memory consolidation (McGaugh & Herz, 1972).

The most popular traditional theory of memory consolidation is the dual-trace model, which uses short- and long-term memory traces as explanatory concepts (Hebb, 1949). According to a dual-trace hypothesis, memories are stored in a labile form, perhaps reverberating circuits, for some relatively short time after training. The short-term memory process is assumed to be necessary for the more gradual development of the relatively permanent long-term memory trace. If it is assumed that memory enhancing and impairing treatments influence the short-term trace, this theory does indeed account for a good deal of the early results. Retrograde amnesia gradients (i.e., the time after training during which memory can be disrupted) imply that a short-term memory trace precedes long-term memory. Looking back at the findings of studies of memory disruption and enhancement, it is perhaps hard to see that the results did not *have* to turn out this way. Obviously, we would have very different ideas of memory storage if memories were susceptible to impairing and enhancing agents at any time after training or if memory was not susceptible to modification at all.

Time-dependency, therefore, provides rather compelling support for the dual-trace (and multi-trace: McGaugh, 1968) models. Perhaps the major problem is the variability of retrograde amnesia gradients. A dual-trace model assumes that the longest time after training at which memory can be impaired, that is, the length of a retrograde amnesia gradient, reflects the time necessary for establishment of a long-term memory trace. According to this view, retrograde amnesia gradients should provide a time constant for the formation of long-term memory. Such a time constant could prove critical for understanding the neurobiology of memory processing. Rather early, however, it became clear that different laboratories observed very different time gradients, ranging from 0.5 sec (Lewis, 1969) to 30 sec (Chorover & Schiller, 1965) to minutes and hours (McGaugh, 1966). To some extent, the variability no doubt resulted from differences in species, or task, or age. Such results are not necessarily in conflict with dual-trace theories. However, several observations indicated that a set of retrograde amnesia gradients, ranging from minutes to hours, could be generated by merely varying the severity of the amnestic treatment (Alpern & McGaugh, 1968; Cherkin, 1969; Gold, Macri, & McGaugh, 1973; Haycock & McGaugh, 1973; Mah & Albert, 1973; Gold, McDonald, & McGaugh, 1974). More recent evidence has indicated that under some conditions amnesia can be produced by treatments administered weeks after training in rodents (Zornetzer & Gold, 1976; Zornetzer, Abraham, & Appleton, 1978; Gold & Reigel, 1980) and even years in humans (Squire, Slater, & Chace, 1975). These findings indicate that a particular retrograde amnesia gradient is a property of the treatment used to induce amnesia at least as much as it is of memory. The desired time constant of memory formation is, therefore, not provided by these experiments. These results have important implications for theories of memory storage processing. The major problem is that the time constant was thought to be a property of memory formation. Based on the above data, more empirical statements of the significance of such studies seem warranted. In particular, it seems more easily justified to speak of "susceptibility" (McGaugh & Dawson, 1971) and "resistance to interference" (Wickelgren, 1973) as the memory properties that were studied all along (See Squire, Cohen, & Nadel, this volume).

It is easy to justify modest "consolidation times" in biological terms. The brain must require time to store new information. But if the idea of a time constant is discarded, what is the biological significance of susceptibility to modification? Could susceptibility to postlearning modifying influences be beneficial for memory? These questions led us to attempt to revise the theoretical bases for studies of retrograde amnesia and memory facilitation (Gold & McGaugh, 1975). Perhaps there is a biologically important reason for time-dependent retrograde effects on memory. A consideration of the results of studies described above convinced us that dual-trace or multi-trace theories are not required in order to explain time-dependent effects in memory storage. In fact, one needs only to assume that a learning experience produces a single memory trace that reaches asymptotic strength almost immediately after training, and that the trace decays unless it is modulated by endogenous consequences of training, such as arousal level or neuroendocrine activity. According to this view, susceptibility to modification is essential for long-term maintenance of the trace.

ENDOGENOUS MODULATION OF MEMORY STORAGE: PERIPHERAL EPINEPHRINE

Constructs such as attention or arousal fit well with the theoretical notion that some endogenous neurobiological systems may regulate the storage of new information. However, it is difficult to deal with these constructs with confidence at a biological level. For this reason, much current research focuses on neuroendocrine responses that can be readily assessed. Most studies have employed a one-trial inhibitory (passive) avoidance training procedure. On the single training trial, an animal (usually rat or mouse) receives a brief footshock upon entering a dark alleyway. Retention performance is assessed at a later time by noting the latency to re-enter the shock compartment. Not surprisingly, avoidance behavior varies with the intensity and duration of the footshock. A more intense shock results in higher avoidance latencies. Of course, the cue value of the shock (the pain it produces) accounts for some of the improvement in retention performances at high shock levels. In addition, however, it is possible that some endogenous neuroendocrine responses that vary with footshock level may function to promote the storage of information about the training experience.

An early experiment provided support for this general hypothesis (Gold & van Buskirk, 1975). Animals were trained in a one-trial inhibitory avoidance task as described above. The footshock intensity was fairly low, resulting in moderate retention latencies. Immediately after training, each animal received an injection (subcutaneous) of epinephrine in one of several doses. The results are shown in Figure 3.1. Note that retention latencies in the saline control group averaged approximately 50 sec. The effects of epinephrine injections varied with the dose in an inverted-U manner. Intermediate doses facilitated retention performances; high and low doses were ineffective. In addition, a facilitatory dose of epinephrine (e.g., 0.1 mg/kg) impaired memory if more stressful training procedures (high footshock) were used. Thus, the inverted-U dose-response curve is very sensitive to endogenous consequences of training. Finally, both the memory enhancement and impairment produced by epinephrine were time-dependent. Injections delayed by 30 min or more had no effect on 24–hr retention performance. Thus, epinephrine effects on memory are similar to the composite of the major results comprising the field of memory consolidation. Epinephrine can produce both retrograde amnesia and memory enhancement in a time-dependent

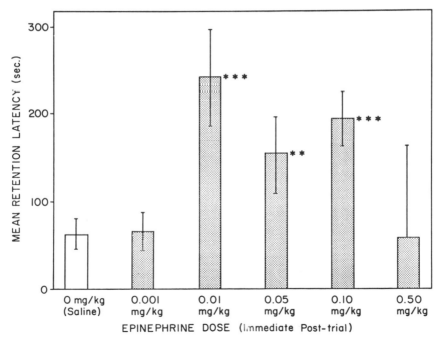

FIG. 3.1.   Retention performance for rats trained with weak footshock (0.7 mA, 0.4 sec) in a one-trial inhibitory (passive) avoidance task. Note that at several intermediate doses, post-training injections of epinephrine enhanced later retention performance. (From Gold & van Buskirk, 1975).

manner. Therefore, these findings are consistent with the view that endogenous adrenergic activity may promote or impair the storage of recent information. According to this view, weak footshock training results in poor retention performance because the endogenous modulatory systems (including peripheral epinephrine) are not sufficiently activated by the relatively innocuous training event. Thus, injections of epinephrine may facilitate memory by mimicking one component of a possible constellation of endogenous physiological responses that modulate memory. Furthermore, although the mechanism is unclear, higher epinephrine doses impair memory storage; the inverted-U relationship between circulating epinephrine levels and memory storage seems very similar to the well-known relationship between arousal level and performance in many situations (Yerkes & Dodson, 1908; Hebb, 1949; Malmo, 1959).

A recent set of experiments examined plasma catecholamine levels following training and epinephrine injections (cf. Gold, McCarty, & Sternberg, 1982a). In these experiments, rats were prepared with chronic tail-artery catheters from which blood samples could be taken without handling the animals. Using a sensitive radiometric enzyme-linked assay, the plasma was analyzed for epinephrine and norepinephrine levels. Plasma epinephrine is derived from the adrenal medulla. Norepinephrine is derived from the adrenal medulla and overflow from the sympathetic nervous system. The first issue addressed was whether peripheral catecholamines were sensitive to these training procedures. The findings indicated that both plasma epinephrine and norepinephrine were responsive to the training footshock. The results obtained with plasma epinephrine are shown in Figure 3.2. Plasma epinephrine levels increased (2x) after the animal was merely placed in the training apparatus (no footshock). Weak footshock training resulted in no further increase in plasma catecholamine. However, a strong training footshock resulted in very high catecholamine levels (10–15-fold increase in plasma epinephrine). These high levels were mimicked in magnitude, though not duration, by an injection of an epinephrine dose (0.1 mg/kg), which facilitates memory after weak footshock training (Figure 3.3). A higher amnestic epinephrine dose (0.5 mg/kg) resulted in supraphysiological plasma epinephrine levels. Another amnestic treatment of interest here, supraseizure electrical stimulation of frontal cortex, resulted in significant increases in plasma epinephrine levels beyond those elicited by intense footshock alone (Gold & McCarty, 1981). These findings indicate that: a) manipulations of peripheral catecholamine activity can modulate memory; and b) under some conditions plasma epinephrine and norepinephrine levels are correlated with later retention performance.

Other memory modulatory treatments may also act through peripheral catecholamine mechanisms. For example, there are several reports that indicate that amphetamine, which is known to influence adrenergic mechanisms, can enhance memory in a variety of tasks (McGaugh, 1973), including inhibitory avoidance (Johnson & Waite, 1971; Haycock, van Buskirk, & Gold, 1977), appetitive

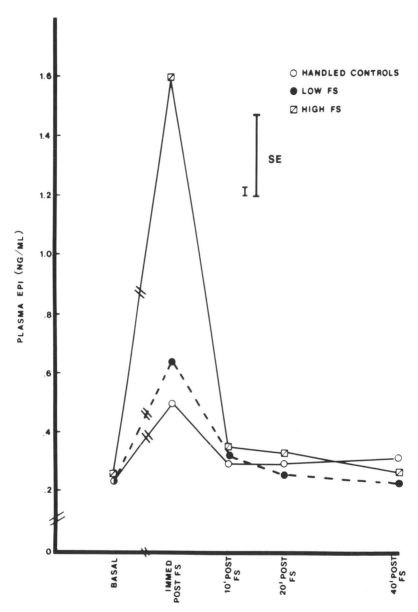

FIG. 3.2.   Plasma levels of epinephrine (ng/ml) under basal conditions (home cage) and immediately, 10, 20, and 40 min after the rats were placed in a test chamber and received a low (0.6 mA, 0.5 sec duration) or high (3.0 mA, 2.0 sec) footshock. Handled controls were placed in the apparatus but received no footshock. Values are means for 6–7 animals per group; the range of standard errors is indicated. (From McCarty & Gold, 1981).

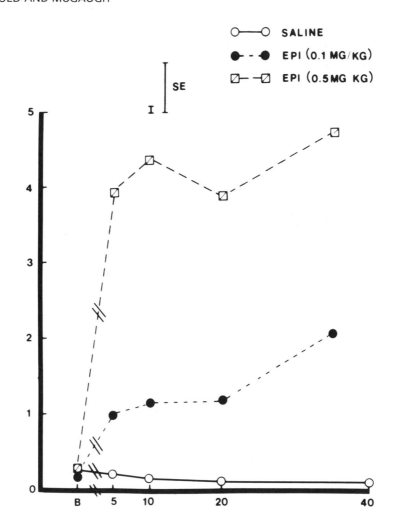

FIG. 3.3.   Plasma levels of epinephrine before (B) and at various times after a subcutaneous injection of epinephrine or saline. Values are means for 5 animals per group and the range of standard errors is indicated. Note that the epinephrine dose (0.1 mg/kg) that enhances memory for low-footshock training results in plasma epinephrine levels comparable to those shown in Fig. 3.2 immediately after high footshock training. (From McCarty & Gold, 1981).

discrimination (Krivanek & McGaugh, 1969), and discriminated active avoidance (Doty & Doty, 1966; Hall, 1969; Evangelista & Izquierdo, 1971). Amphetamine is a drug that stimulates activity of both central and peripheral catecholamine systems. Recent findings suggest that the amphetamine effects on memory may be mediated peripherally through adrenomedullary catecholamines (McGaugh, Martinez, Jensen, Hannan, Vasquez, Messing, Liang, Brewton, & Spiehler, 1982b). First, as we noted, intraperitoneal injections of amphetamine can enhance memory for inhibitory avoidance training in rats. However, central (intraventricular) injections of amphetamine are ineffective (Martinez, Jensen, Messing, Vasquez, Soumireu-Mourat, Geddes, Liang, & McGaugh, 1980a). Second, 4–OH amphetamine, a peripherally acting agonist, can also enhance performance. Third, memory facilitation with either amphetamine or 4-OH amphetamine is blocked in adrenal demedullated rats (Martinez, Vasquez, Rigter, Messing, Jensen, Liang, & McGaugh, 1980b). These results are consistent with earlier findings that amphetamine and nicotine memory enhancement for shuttle-box training are abolished in adrenal demedullated rats (Orsingher & Fulginiti, 1971).

Parallel evidence for peripheral action has been reported for amnestic drugs that interfere with catecholamine function. For example, Walsh and Palfai (1979) found that injections of syrosingopine, a peripherally acting reserpine analog, can cause retrograde amnesia. Systemic injections of catecholamines, which do not enter the brain in large amounts if at all, attenuated the memory impairment in syrosingopine-treated animals. Similarly, the amnestic effects of diethyldithiocarbamate, a norepinephrine and epinephrine synthesis inhibitor, can be blocked with peripheral injections of these amines (Meligeni, Ledergerber, & McGaugh, 1978; McGaugh, Martinez, Jensen, Messing, & Vasquez, 1980).

The findings described here suggest that peripheral catecholamine release may be a major component of an endogenous system that can regulate memory storage. In addition, adrenal medullary and sympathetic adrenergic activity may be responsible for the actions on memory of several other treatments. The generality of such mechanisms mediating all cases of memory modulation is still under investigation. One exception is adrenocorticotrophic hormone (ACTH). The effects of ACTH on memory are comparable to those described above for epinephrine. Post-training ACTH injections (subcutaneous) enhance or impair memory in an inverted-U dose-related manner (Gold & van Buskirk, 1976). However, an ACTH injection does not result in augmented plasma catecholamine levels, indicating that ACTH effects on memory are not mediated by release of adrenomedullary or sympathetic catecholamines (McCarty & Gold, 1981).

Although adrenal demedullation can block the memory enhancement produced by some treatments, an intact adrenal medullary system is not essential for learning and memory, nor does it appear to be necessary for the actions of all amnestic treatments. Adrenalectomized or adrenal demedullated animals can learn and remember avoidance tasks (Martinez et al., 1980b; Orsingher & Fulginiti, 1971; Sternberg, McGaugh & Gold, in preparation; Wendlandt & File, 1979). Also, under some conditions amnestic treatments are effective in adrenalectomized rats (Sternberg et al., in preparation).

On the other hand, several recent experiments indicate that peripheral injections of adrenergic antagonists can attenuate the amnesia produced by a variety of treatments. It is perhaps not too surprising that antagonists administered in this manner can block the memory enhancing and impairing effects of adrenergic agonists. For example, Gozzani and Izquierdo (1976) found that post-training injections of clonidine, an α-adrenergic agonist, produced retrograde amnesia. The memory impairments were blocked in animals pretreated with the α-adrenergic antagonist, phentolamine. Later, Gold and van Buskirk (1978b) reported that phenoxybenzamine or propranolol, α- and β-adrenergic antagonists, blocked epinephrine modulation of memory. More recent findings suggest the remarkable possibility that the amnestic effects of many treatments can be attenuated by adrenergic antagonists (cf. Gold et al., 1982a). In these experiments, rats received an antagonist 30 min prior to training at a dose that did not itself affect acquisition or retention performance but that was sufficiently high to block adrenergic transmission. The animals then were given an amnestic treatment shortly after training, and retention performance was tested 24 hrs or more later. With these procedures, the amnesia produced by a wide variety of treatments was attenuated by phenoxybenzamine (Gold & Sternberg, 1978; Sternberg & Gold, 1981). The amnesia was produced by diverse treatments, including supraseizure electrical stimulation of frontal cortex (similar to electroconvulsive shock), subseizure electrical stimulation of the amygdala, diethyldithiocarbamate (a norepinephrine synthesis inhibitor), and cycloheximide (a protein synthesis inhibitor). Interestingly, the attenuation of amnesia can be produced by a variety of α- and β-adrenergic antagonists if the drugs are injected peripherally (Sternberg & Gold, 1980), but not if injected into the cerebral ventricles (Sternberg & Gold, 1981).

The amnesia produced by these treatments is generally attributed to their "primary" effects, as described above. However, the fact that a single drug, phenoxybenzamine, attenuates the effects on memory of each of these treatments suggests that there may be a neurobiological mechanism common to these, and perhaps other, amnestic agents. One possibility is that the common mechanism might involve the release of high levels of peripheral catecholamines. Many amnestic treatments are physiological stressors and may well elicit supraphysiological adrenomedullary and sympathetic responses. This hypothesis suggests that many retrograde amnesias may be the result, for example, of reflexive alterations in reticular formation activity in response to blood pressure changes, altered cerebral blood flow mediated by autonomic systems, or altered brain activity in response to increased release of peripheral amines, monitored directly, via peripheral receptors, or by afferent information from sympathetic end organs.

A possible role for peripheral adrenergic amines in amnesia is supported by findings that epinephrine injections may serve a permissive function in eliciting amnesia. That is, it may be that activation of adrenergic receptors enables treatments to have modulating influences on memory. For example, the time after training at which supraseizure cortical stimulation can produce amnesia (the retrograde amnesia gradient) can be extended from a few minutes to a week or more if rats receive a subcutaneous epinephrine injection just prior to electrical stimulation (Gold & Reigel, 1980).

More recent findings suggest that epinephrine may also be important in enabling amygdala stimulation to produce amnesia (McGaugh, Liang, Bennett, Martinez, Messing, & Ishikawa, 1982a; McGaugh, 1983a). In these studies (Brewton, Liang, & McGaugh, 1981) rats with implanted amygdala electrodes, as well as unimplanted controls, were given sham adrenal surgery or adrenal demedullation or denervation. They were then trained on an inhibitory avoidance task followed by training on an active avoidance task two weeks later. Amygdala stimulation was administered immediately following the training on each task and retention was tested one day after training. Comparable findings were obtained with both adrenal demedullation and adrenal denervation and with both active and inhibitory avoidance tasks. Figure 3.4 shows the findings of denervated animals trained in the active avoidance task. In the sham-operated groups, retention of the animals given post-training amygdala stimulation was significantly poorer than that of either implanted or unimplanted controls. These results are comparable to those of many previous studies (McGaugh & Gold, 1976). In denervated rats (as well as demedullated rats) the retention of implanted controls was significantly impaired. Further, the retention performance of the animals given post-training amygdala stimulation was better than that of unstimulated animals and was comparable to that of unimplanted controls. Thus, the effects of amygdala stimulation on memory were clearly influenced by removal of the adrenal medulla. In demedullated or denervated rats amygdala stimulation appears to attenuate the retention deficit seen in implanted controls.

Other recent findings indicate that the effects produced by demedullation are also attenuated by administration of epinephrine (Bennett, Liang, & McGaugh, 1982). The retention deficit found in demedullated and implanted animals is attenuated by administration of epinephrine immediately after training. Further, demedullated rats given epinephrine immediately after training, but just prior to amygdala stimulation, show retention deficits like those seen in animals with intact adrenal medullae given post-training amygdala stimulation. However, amygdala stimulation did not produce amnesia in rats given epinephrine immediately *after* the amygdala stimulation. Thus, the findings indicate that the impairing effect of amygdala stimulation on memory seems to require the presence of peripheral epinephrine at the time of the stimulation. The enhancing effect of amygdala stimulation (or attenuation of retention deficit) seen in implanted ani-

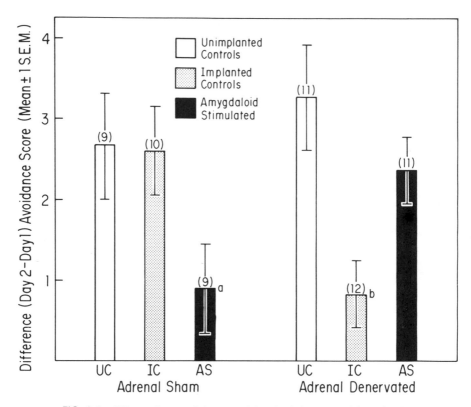

FIG. 3.4.   Effects of post-training amygdala stimulation on retention of active avoidance in adrenal-denervated and sham-operated rats. a = p < 0.05 compared with IC sham and denervated AS groups; b = p < 0.01 compared with IC sham controls and UC denervated; p < 0.02 compared with AS adrenal denervated group. (From Brewton et al., 1981; McGaugh et al., 1982a.)

mals seems not to be based on peripheral epinephrine; the effect was obtained in both demedullated and denervated rats.

The findings of these recent experiments have suggested that peripheral epinephrine might influence memory storage through influences on brain processes that are also influenced by the amygdala. This interpretation is supported by evidence (Liang & McGaugh, 1983) that post-training epinephrine does not affect retention in rats with bilateral lesions of the stria terminalis, a major amygdala pathway. It seems clear from these studies that peripheral epinephrine has effects that influence brain processes involved in memory and that such effects interact with influences from specific brain regions. We do not yet understand the mechanisms by which peripheral epinephrine influences brain processes.

CENTRAL CATECHOLAMINES

As described above, there is now considerable evidence supporting the view that peripheral catecholamines modulate memory storage processing. In many cases, examinations of central norepinephrine have led to analogous results. The general strategy for examining a possible role of central catecholamines in modulating memory is similar to that employed in peripheral studies. There are extensive demonstrations that brain norepinephrine concentrations are sensitive to many stressors, including footshock (cf. Stone, 1975). One technical problem is that, although release of peripheral amines can be measured directly, central norepinephrine release is assessed by examining transient decreases in brain norepinephrine content soon after training or treatment. The transient decrease in brain norepinephrine is believed to reflect the release and subsequent metabolism of the amine prior to its resynthesis. Generally, the decrease in norepinephrine content is most evident several minutes after the initiation of a stressor. The extent of the decrease (generally 20%–40%) varies with the magnitude and duration of the stressor. Recent findings indicate that a single training footshock is sufficient to elicit a 20% decrease in norepinephrine content measured 10 min after training. The norepinephrine concentrations return to control values within 30–90 min. The 20% decrease appears to reflect a pattern of norepinephrine release that is optimal for memory storage. Under a variety of training treatment conditions, the extent of the decrease in brain norepinephrine predicts later retention performance. For example, Gold and van Buskirk (1978a) found that a weak training footshock, which fails to produce good retention performance, does not elicit the brain norepinephrine response. However, if the weak footshock is followed by a memory enhancing peripheral epinephrine injection, brain norepinephrine levels exhibit a 20% decline. If animals receive a higher amnestic dose of epinephrine, brain norepinephrine concentrations exhibit a 40% decline. Similar results have been obtained with posttrial ACTH injections (Gold & McGaugh, 1978). This correlation between brain norepinephrine levels soon after training and later retention performance has also been observed under several other conditions. If epinephrine effects on memory are blocked by pretreatment with adrenergic antagonists, the relationship between post-training brain norepinephrine levels and later retention performance is maintained (Gold & van Buskirk, 1978b). Similarly, Gold and Murphy (1980) found that supraseizure frontal cortex stimulation, an amnestic treatment like electroconvulsive shock, produces brain norepinephrine responses that deviate from the 20% decrease seen in trained but untreated animals. Recently, Gold, Murphy, and Cooley (1982b) reported that, in young rats, the endogenous brain norepinephrine response to a training footshock matures at about the same age as does 24–hr retention of inhibitory (passive) avoidance training. Collectively, the findings support the view that memory modulation—both endogenous modulation and modulation by experimental treatments—may include a major role for central noradrenergic systems.

Although we have emphasized the role of adrenergic catecholamines in memory modulation, there is much evidence indicating that memory is also influenced by other hormones normally released by arousing stimulation including, as we have noted, ACTH (Gold & Delanoy, 1981) as well as vasopressin and oxytocin, (Bohus, Conti, Kovacs, & Versteeg, 1982), and opioid peptides (Gallagher & Kapp, 1981; Martinez, Jensen, Messing, Rigter, & McGaugh, 1981; Izquierdo, Dias, Perry, Souza, Elisabetsky, & Carrasco, 1982; McGaugh, 1983b). Further, it has been known for a number of years that retention can be influenced by electrical stimulation of the midbrain reticular formation (Bloch, 1970; Denti, McGaugh, Landfield, & Shinkman, 1970), a system normally activated by arousing stimulation. Thus, it is not yet clear whether adrenergic systems play a unique role in memory or whether they are but part of a complex and possibly redundant set of physiological responses to arousing stimulation that are involved in memory modulation. It is also not yet clear whether pituitary and adrenal medullary hormones act through influences initiated peripherally or whether they act directly on the brain. Knowledge of the site of action of peripheral hormones should lead to an increased understanding of the bases of their effects on memory storage.

CONCLUDING COMMENTS: CONSOLIDATION, TIME-DEPENDENCY, AND MODULATION

Research and theory in memory consolidation has continued to change over the years. The perservation-consolidation hypothesis (Muller & Pilzecker, 1900) was first developed as an explanation for forgetting in human memory (see Keppel, this volume). The consolidation hypothesis was subsequently considered to provide an explanation for human as well as animal retrograde amnesia (see Squire, Cohen, & Nadel, this volume). Consolidation studies were used, as we noted, in an effort to estimate time constants in the development of time-dependent processes underlying long-term memory. And a great deal of research on the neurobiology of consolidation has attempted to determine the bases of amnesia induced by various experimental treatments (McGaugh & Gold, 1974). In this chapter we have suggested that the issues might be approached from a different perspective. Memory consolidation processes may provide a mechanism by which the strength of memory is modulated by endogenous physiological systems activated by an experience (Gold & McGaugh, 1975). From this perspective, the question of interest concerns the nature of endogenous processes activated by experience and the mechanisms by which the processes act to modulate memory. There is recent evidence suggesting that the brain changes produced by experience and stimulation are influenced by hormones found to modulate memory. For example, long-term potentiation, a neurophysiological analog of memory, is influenced by electrical stimulation of the midbrain reticular formation (Laroche & Bloch, 1982) as well as by peripheral amphetamine or epinephrine injections (Gold, Delanoy, & Merrin, 1984). Understanding the bases of such modulating influences, considered together with findings of the effects of these treatments on memory, should contribute significantly to our understanding of brain systems underlying memory storage.

ACKNOWLEDGMENTS

The research in this paper was supported by National Institute of Mental Health Research Grants MH31141 and AG01642 and MH12526 and AG00538. We thank our colleagues and students for their contributions to the ideas and findings summarized in this paper.

REFERENCES

Acheson, A. L., Zigmond, J. M., & Stricker, D. M. Compensatory increase in tyrosine hydroxylase activity in rat brain after intraventricular injections of 6-hydroxydopamine. *Science*, 1980, *207*, 537–540.

Alpern, H. P., & McGaugh, J. L. Retrograde amnesia as a function of duration of electroshock stimulation. *Journal of Comparative and Physiological Psychology*, 1968, *65*, 265–269.

Bennett, C., Liang, K. C., & McGaugh, J. L. Epinephrine alters the effect of amygdala stimulation on retention of avoidance tasks. *Neuroscience Abstracts*, 1982, *8*, 459.

Bloch, V. Facts and hypotheses concerning memory consolidation. *Brain Research*, 1970, *24*, 561–575.

Bohus, B., Conti, L., Kovacs, G. L., & Versteeg, D. H. G. Modulation of memory processes by neuropeptides: Interaction with neurotransmitter systems. In C. Ajmone Marsan & H. Matthies (Eds.), *Neuronal plasticity and memory formation*. New York: Raven Press, 1982.

Brewton, C. B., Liang, K. C., & McGaugh, J. L. Adrenal demedullation alters the effect of amygdala stimulation on retention of avoidance tasks. *Neuroscience Abstracts*, 1981, *7*, 870.

Cherkin, A. Kinetics of memory consolidation: Role of amnesic treatment parameters. *Proceedings of the National Academy of Sciences*, 1969, *63*, 1094–1101.

Chorover, S. L., & Schiller, P. H. Short-term retrograde amnesia in rats. *Journal of Comparative and Physiological Psychology*, 1965, *59*, 73–78.

Costa, E., & Guidotti, A. Molecular mechanisms mediating the transynaptic regulator of gene expression in adrenal medulla. In M. A. Lipton, A. DiMascio, & K. J. Killam (Eds.), *Psychopharmacology: A generation of progress*. New York: Raven Press, 1978.

Denti, A., McGaugh, J. L., Landfield, P., & Shinkman, P. Facilitation of learning with posttrial stimulation of the reticular formation. *Physiology and Behavior*, 1970, *5*, 659–662.

Doty, B. A., & Doty, L. A. Facilitative effects of amphetamine on avoidance conditioning in relation to age and problem difficulty. *Psychopharmacologia*. 1966, *9*, 234–241.

Evangelista, A. M., & Izquierdo, I. The effect of pre- and post-trial amphetamine injections on avoidance responses of rats. *Psychopharmacologia*, 1971, *20*, 42–47.

Floeter, M. K., & Greenough, W. T. Cerebellar plasticity: Modification of purkinje cell structure by differential rearing in monkeys. *Science*, 1979, *206*, 227–229.

Gallagher, M., & Kapp, B. S. Influence of amygdala opiate-sensitive mechanisms, fear-motivated responses, and memory processes for aversive experiences. In J. L. Martinez, Jr., R. A. Jensen, R. B. Messing, H. Rigter, & J. L. McGaugh (Eds.), *Endogenous peptides and learning and memory processes*. New York: Academic Press, 1981.

Glickman, S. E. Perseverative neural processes and consolidation of the memory trace. *Psychological Bulletin*, 1961, *58*, 218–233.

Goddard, G. V. Component properties of the memory machine: Hebb revisited. In P. W. Jusczyk & R. M. Klein (Eds.), *The nature of thought: Essays in honour of D. O. Hebb*. Hillsdale, N.J.: Lawrence Erlbaum Associates, 1980.

Gold, P. E., & Delanoy, R. L. ACTH modulation of memory storage processing. In J. L. Martinez, Jr., R. A. Jensen, R. B. Messing, H. Rigter & J. L. McGaugh (Eds.), *Endogenous peptides and learning and memory processes*. New York: Academic Press, 1981.

Gold, P. E., Delanoy, R. L., & Merrin, J. Adrenergic modulation of long-term potentiation. *Brain Research*, 1984, in press.

Gold, P. E., Macri, J., & McGaugh, J. L. Retrograde amnesia gradients: Effects of direct cortical stimulation. *Science*, 1973, *179*, 1343–1345.

Gold, P. E., & McCarty, R. Plasma catecholamines: Changes after footshock and seizure-producing frontal cortex stimulation. *Behavioral and Neural Biology*, 1981, *31*, 247–260.

Gold, P. E., McCarty, R., & Sternberg, D. B. Peripheral catecholamines and memory modulation. In C. Ajmone Marsan & H. Matthies (Eds.), *Neuronal plasticity and memory formation*. New York: Raven Press, 1982. (a)

Gold, P. E., McDonald, R., & McGaugh, J. L. Direct cortical stimulation: A further study of treatment intensity effects on retrograde amnesia gradients. *Behavioral Biology*, 1974, *10*, 485–490.

Gold, P. E., & McGaugh, J. L. A single-trace, two-process view of memory storage processes. In D. Deutsch & J. A. Deutsch (Eds.), *Short-term memory*. New York: Academic Press, 1975.

Gold, P. E., & McGaugh, J. L. Endogenous modulators of memory storage processes. In: *Clinical Psychoneuroendocrinology in Reproduction*, eds. L. Carenza, P. Pancheri & L. Zichella, pp. 25–46. London: Academic Press, 1978.

Gold, P. E., & Murphy, J. Brain noradrenergic responses to training and to amnestic frontal cortex stimulation. *Pharmacology Biochemistry and Behavior*, 1980, *13*, 257–263.

Gold, P. E., Murphy, J. M., & Cooley, S. Neuroendocrine modulation of memory during development. *Behavioral and Neural Biology*, 1982, *35*, 277–293. (b)

Gold, P. E., & Reigel, J. A. Extended retrograde amnesia gradients produced by epinephrine injections administered at the time of cortical stimulation. *Physiology and Behavior*, 1980, *24*, 1101–1106.

Gold, P. E., & Sternberg, D. B. Retrograde amnesia produced by several treatments. Evidence for a common neurobiological mechanism. *Science*, 1978, *201*, 367–369.

Gold, P. E., & van Buskirk, R. B. Facilitation of time-dependent memory processes with posttrial epinephrine injection. *Behavioral Biology*, 1975, *13*, 145–153.

Gold, P. E., & van Buskirk, R. B. Enhancement and impairment of memory processes with posttrial injections of adrenocorticotrophic hormone. *Behavioral Biology*, 1976, *16*, 387–400.

Gold, P. E., & van Buskirk, R. B. Posttraining brain norepinephrine concentrations: Correlation with retention performance of avoidance training and with peripheral epinephrine modulation of memory processing. *Behavioral Biology*, 1978, *23*, 509–520. (a)

Gold, P. E., & van Buskirk, R. B. Effects of α- and β-adrenergic receptor antagonists on post-trial epinephrine modulation of memory: Relationship to post-training brain norepinephrine concentrations. *Behavioral Biology*, 1978, *24*, 168–184. (b)

Gozzani, J. M. L., & Izquierdo, I. Possible peripheral adrenergic and central dopaminergic influences in memory consolidation. *Psychopharmacology*, 1976, *49*, 109–111.

Hall, M. E. Effects of post-trial amphetamine and strychnine on learning as a function of task difficulty. *Behavioral Biology*, 1969, *4*, 171–175.

Haycock, J. W., & McGaugh, J. L. Retrograde amnesia gradients as a function of ECS-intensity. *Behavioral Biology*, 1973, *9*, 123–127.

Haycock, J. W., van Buskirk, R. B., & Gold, P. E. Effects on retention with posttraining amphetamine injections in mice: Interaction with pretraining experiences. *Psychopharmacologia*, 1977, *54*, 21–24.

Hebb, D. O. *The organization of behavior*. New York: Wiley, 1949.

Izquierdo, I., Dias, R. D., Perry, M. L., Souza, D. O., Elisabetsky, E., & Carrasco, M. A. A physiological amnestic mechanism mediated by endogenous opioid peptides, and its possible role in learning. In C. Ajmone Marsan & H. Matthies (Eds.), *Neuronal plasticity and memory formation*. New York: Raven Press, 1982.

Johnson, F. W., & Waite, K. Apparent delayed enhancement of memory following post-trial methylamphetamine hydrochloride. *Experientia*, 1971, *27*, 1316–1317.

Juraska, J., Greenough, W., Elliot, C., Mack, K., & Berkowitz, R. Plasticity in adult rat visual cortex: An examination of several cell populations after differential rearing. *Behavioral and Neural Biology*, 1980, *29*, 157–167.

Krivanek, J. A., & McGaugh, J. L. Facilitating effects of pre- and posttrial amphetamine administration on discrimination learning in mice. *Agents and Actions*, 1969, *1*, 36–42.

Laroche, S., & Bloch, V. Conditioning of hippocampal cells and long-term potentiation: An approach to mechanisms of posttrial memory facilitation. In C. Ajmone Marsan & H. Matthies (Eds.), *Neuronal plasticity and memory formation*. New York: Raven Press, 1982.

Lewis, D. J. Sources of experimental amnesia. *Psychological Review*, 1969, *76*, 461–472.

Liang, K. C., & McGaugh, J. L. Lesions of the stria terminalis attenuate the enhancing effect of posttraining epinephrine on retention of an inhibitory avoidance response. *Behavioural Brain Research*, 1983, *9*, 49–58.

Lynch, G., Browning, M., & Bennett, W. F. Biochemical and physiological studies of long-term synaptic plasticity. *Federation Proceedings*, 1979, *38*, 2117–2122.

Lynch, G., & Wells, J. Neuroanatomical plasticity and behavioral adaptability. In T. Teyler (Ed.), *Brain and learning*. Stamford, Conn: Greylock Press, 1978.

Mah, C. J., & Albert, D. J. Electroconvulsive shock-induced retrograde amnesia: An analysis of the variation in the length of the amnesia gradient. *Behavioral Biology*, 1973, *9*, 517–540.

Malmo, R. B. Activation: A neuropsychological dimension. *Psychological Review*, 1959, *66*, 367–386.

Martinez, Jr., J. L., Jensen, R. A., Messing, R. B., Rigter, H., & McGaugh, J. L. (Eds.). *Endogenous peptides and learning and memory processes*. New York: Academic Press, 1981.

Martinez, Jr., J. L., Jensen, R. A., Messing, R. B., Vasquez, B. J., Soumireu-Mourat, B., Geddes, D., Liang, K. C. & McGaugh, J. L. Central and peripheral actions of amphetamine on memory storage. *Brain Research*, 1980, *182*, 157–166. (a)

Martinez, Jr., J. L., Vasquez, B. J., Rigter, H., Messing, R. B., Jensen, R. A., Liang, K. C., & McGaugh, J. L. Attenuation of amphetamine-induced enhancement of learning by adrenal demedullation. *Brain Research*, 1980, *195*, 433–443. (b)

McCarty, R., & Gold, P. E. Plasma catecholamines: Effects of footshock level and hormonal modulators of memory storage. *Hormones and Behavior*, 1981, *15*, 168–182.

McCormick, D. A., Clark, G. A., Lavond, D. G., & Thompson, R. F. Initial localization of the memory trace for a basic form of learning. *Proceedings of the National Academy of Sciences* (USA), 1982, *79*, 2731–2735.

McGaugh, J. L. Time-dependent processes in memory storage. *Science*, 1966, *153*, 1351–1358.

McGaugh, J. L. A multi-trace view of memory storage. In D. Bovet, F. Bovet-Nitti & A. Oliverio (Eds.), *Recent advances in learning and retention*. Rome: Roma Accademia Nazionale Dei Lincei, Quaderno N. 109 Anno CCLXV, 1968.

McGaugh, J. L. Drug facilitation of learning and memory. *Annual Review of Pharmacology*, 1973, *13*, 229–241.

McGaugh, J. L. Preserving the presence of the past: Hormonal influences on memory storage. *American Psychologist*, 1983. (a)

McGaugh, J. L. Hormonal influences on memory. *Annual Review of Psychology*, 1983. (b)

McGaugh, J. L., & Dawson, R. G. Modification of memory storage processes. In W. K. Honig & P. H. R. James (Eds.), *Animal memory*, New York: Academic Press. 1971. Also revised for *Behavioral Science*, 1971, *16*, 45–63.

McGaugh, J. L., & Gold, P. E. Conceptual and neurobiological issues in studies of treatments affecting memory storage. In G. H. Bower (Ed.), *The Psychology of learning and motivation* (Vol. 8). New York: Academic Press, 1974.

McGaugh, J. L., & Gold, P. E. Modulation of memory by electrical stimulation of the brain. In M. R. Rosenzweig & E. L. Bennett (Eds.), *Neural mechanisms of learning and memory*. Cambridge, Mass.: The MIT Press, 1976.

McGaugh, J. L., & Herz, M. J. *Memory consolidation*. San Francisco: Albion Publishing Company, 1972.

McGaugh, J. L., Liang, K. C., Bennett, C., Martinez, Jr., J. L., Messing, R. B., & Ishikawa, K. Modulating influences of peripheral hormones on memory storage. In S. Saito & T. Yanagita (Eds.), *Learning and memory drugs as reinforcer*. Amsterdam: Excerpta Medica, 1982. (a)

McGaugh, J. L., Martinez, Jr., J. L., Jensen, R. A., Hannan, T. J., Vasquez, B. J., Messing, R. B., Liang, K. C., Brewton, C. B., Spiehler, V. R. Modulation of memory storage by treatments affecting peripheral catecholamines. In C. Ajmone Marsan & H. Matthies (Eds.), *Neuronal plasticity and memory formation*. New York: Raven Press, 1982. (b)

McGaugh, J. L., Martinez, Jr., J. L., Jensen, R. A., Messing, R. B., & Vasquez, B. J. Central and peripheral catecholamine function in learning and memory processes. In R. F. Thompson, L. H. Hicks & V. B. Shvyrkov (Eds.), *Neural mechanisms of goal-directed behavior and learning*. New York: Academic Press, 1980.

McNamara, J. O., Byrne, M. C., Dashieff, R. M., & Fitz, J. G. The kindling model of epilepsy: A review. *Progress in Neurobiology*, 1980, *15*, 139–159.

Meligeni, J. A., Ledergerber, S. A., & McGaugh, J. L. Norepinephrine attenuation of amnesia produced by diethyldithiocarbamate. *Brain Research*, 1978, *149*, 155–164.

Muller, G. E., & Pilzecker, A. Experimentelle Beitrage zur Lehre vom Gedachtniss. *Zeitschrift fur Psychologie*, 1900, *1*, 1–288.

Oleson, T. D., Ashe, J. H., & Weinberger, N. M. Modification of auditory and somatosensory activity during pupillary conditioning in the paralyzed cat. *Journal of Neurophysiology*, 1975, *38*, 1114–1139.

Orsingher, O. A., & Fulginiti, S. Effects of alpha-methyl tyrosine and adrenergic blocking agents on the facilitating action of amphetamine and nicotine on learning in rats. *Psychopharmacologia*, 1971, *19*, 231–240.

Racine, R. J. Kindling: The first decade. *Neurosurgery*, 1978, *3*, 234–252.

Reisine, T. Adaptive changes in catecholamine receptors in the central nervous system. *Neuroscience*, 1981, *6*, 1471–1502.

Rosenzweig, M. R., & Bennett, E. L. Experiential influences on brain anatomy and brain chemistry in rodents. In G. Gottlieb (Ed.), *Studies on the development of behavior and the nervous system*, New York: Academic Press, 1978.

Squire, L. R., Slater, P. C., & Chace, P. M. Retrograde amnesia: Temporal gradient in very long-term memory following electroconvulsive therapy. *Science*, 1975, *187*, 77–79.

Sternberg, D. B., & Gold, P. E. Effects of α- and β-adrenergic receptor antagonists on retrograde amnesia produced by frontal cortex stimulation. *Behavioral and Neural Biology,* 1980, *29,* 289–302.

Sternberg, D. B., & Gold, P. E. Intraventricular adrenergic antagonists: Failure to attenuate retrograde amnesia. *Physiology and Behavior,* 1981, *27,* 551–555.

Sternberg, D. B., McGaugh, J. L., & Gold, P. E. Amnesia in adrenalectomized rats. In preparation.

Steward, O. Assessing the functional significance of lesion-induced neuronal plasticity. *International Review of Neurobiology,* 1982, *2,* 197–354.

Stone, E. A. Stress and catecholamines. In A. J. Friedhoff (Ed.), *Catecholamines and behavior (Vol. 1).* New York: Plenum Press, 1975.

Thoenen, H. Transynaptic regulation of neuronal enzyme synthesis. In L. L. Iversen, S. D. Iversen, & S. H. Snyder (Eds.), *Handbook of psychopharmacology* (Vol. 3), *Biochemistry of biogenic amines.* New York: Plenum Press, 1975.

Walsh, T. J., & Palfai, T. Peripheral catecholamines and memory characteristics of syrosingopine-induced amnesia. *Pharmacology Biochemistry and Behavior,* 1979, *11,* 449–452.

Wendlandt, S., & File, S. E. Behavioral effects of lesions of the locus coeruleus noradrenaline system combined with adrenalectomy. *Behavioral and Neural Biology,* 1979, *26,* 189–201.

Wickelgren, W. A. The long and the short of memory. *Psychological Bulletin,* 1973, *80,* 425–438.

Yerkes, R. M., & Dodson, J. D. The relation of strength of stimulus to rapidity of habit-formation. *Journal of Comparative and Neurological Psychology,* 1908, *18,* 458–82.

Zornetzer, S. F., Abraham, W. C., & Appleton, R. The locus coeruleus and labile memory. *Pharmacology Biochemistry and Behavior,* 1978, *9,* 227–234.

Zornetzer, S. F., & Gold, M. The locus coeruleus: Its possible role in memory consolidation. *Physiology and Behavior,* 1976, *16,* 331–336.

4 The Physiology and Semantics of Consolidation

Ralph R. Miller
State University of New York at Binghamton

Nancy A. Marlin
University of Missouri—Rolla

OF MICE AND MEN

Surely the first question to be asked by our friends will be: What are a couple of nice students of rodent memory doing in a volume like this which is concerned primarily with information processing in rowdy, hairless apes? Clearly we would not be here if we felt that students of animal memory had nothing in common with researchers concerned with the psychobiology of human information processing. This is not to suggest that rodents are miniature humans save for the addition of whiskers and a tail. Rather, owing to our common evolutionary roots, it is our belief that the fundamental processes and basic structures responsible for the phenomenon of memory share certain similarities across Mammalia. Analogously, a motorcycle is not a minature car, but it is propelled by the same principles of internal combustion of hydrocarbons and translation of reciprocating motion into circular motion as is an automobile. Pushing the analogy a little further, the exposed motorcycle engine facilitates its study relative to the enclosed engine of an automobile: moreover, the absence of superfluous accessories on motorcycles relative to most automobiles would assist in focusing upon the essential principles of land transportation powered by internal combustion.

We would not think to turn to rodents if we wished to understand political science. But, just as infrahuman models greatly contributed to our understanding of human respiration and blood circulation, so we feel there is substantial merit in using animals to assist in a molecular analysis of the physiological basis of human information processing and, more specifically, memory consolidation. The examples in this chapter come principally from animal laboratories, largely our own as we best know our own research, but occasionally we cite parallel observations of human behavior in an effort to convince the reader of the plausibility of generalizing across mammals at the present level of analysis.

DEFINITIONS OF CONSOLIDATION

Much, perhaps even most, of the controversy concerned with consolidation of memory arises from the frequent use of divergent definitions of consolidation. Although the term "memory consolidation" dates back at least to Harris (1751), it was introduced to modern theorizing by Müller and Pilzecker (1900). They hypothesized that the physiological representation of newly acquired information was labile and that over time subsequent to acquisition it was slowly solidified or "consolidated" into a more stable form. Ironically, the very phenomenon that Müller and Pilzecker were trying to explain, retroactive interference between verbal items, has generally not been found to depend on short intervals between presentation of the target item and presentation of the interfering item (e.g., Archer & Underwood, 1951; Newton & Wickins, 1956). However, the idea that immediately following acquisition, information is subject to a brief period of vulnerability to disruption proved attractive to other researchers and was quickly applied to various situations, some of which are today still regarded by some investigators as evidence supportive of the consolidation theory of memory. Most commonly, the retroactive amnesia often induced by head injuries was attributed to interference with the consolidation process (e.g., McDougall, 1901; Burnham, 1903).

Owing to our limited knowledge of brain physiology at the beginning of the 20th century, Müller and Pilzecker were quite vague about the specific nature of the consolidation process. For example, they did not specify whether consolidation was a change in state within a single representational system analogous to the drying of glue, or was a transfer of information from a labile representational system to a physiologically distinct representational system that was more durable.

During the first half of this century, sufficient information was gathered concerning the physiology of the nervous system so that, in 1949, both Hebb and Gerard felt justified in proposing two-stage models of memory. Today the evidence for there being *at least* two distinctly different means of representing acquired information in the nervous system is overwhelming. Some contemporary researchers (e.g., Cherkin, 1972) have adhered to Müller and Pilzecker's empirical definition of consolidation, i.e., the memorial process that is subject to disruption soon after acquisition but not at a later time (presumably because the process has gone to completion). Other researchers, ourselves included (e.g., Miller & Springer, 1973; Miller & Marlin, 1979), have rejected this definition in the belief that it has little heuristic value. To define all retrograde disruption of acquired information as consolidation failure and then cite retrograde disruption of acquired information as evidence of consolidation failure is circular and does not add to our knowledge of underlying physiological processes. Instead, we prefer the more specific meaning of consolidation first proposed by Hebb (1949) and Gerard (1949). These researchers uniquely identified consolidation with the process of encoding the target information into a secondary physiological format less vulnerable to disruption than was the initial representation. This latter view leaves open the possibility that some forms of retroactive disruption of retention may be due to consolidation failure, whereas other forms of retroactive disruption may result from other factors.

EVIDENCE FOR AT LEAST TWO STAGES OF MEMORY

Information concerning the external world enters an organism through sensory receptors that communicate with the central nervous system via neural transmission. Thus, newly acquired information is initially encoded in the pattern of action potentials along select afferent pathways. We shall call the memory system in which acquired information is encoded in ongoing electrochemical neural transmission *active storage*. Evidence for the representation of newly acquired information in this format comes from many sources, for example, Hubel and Wiesel's (1968) observation that there is a high correlation between external stimuli and the action potentials of specific neurons in the appropriate receptive fields of the cortex. Ordinarily the induced electrophysiological activity constituting active storage appears to endure only for a brief period of time (seconds or minutes) after the termination of the stimulus. Thus, active storage, owing to both its dynamic form and temporary nature, is analogous to information in transit within a telephone wire.

As there is compelling evidence that acquired information is initially encoded in active storage, parsimony demands careful consideration of the possibility that all acquired information permanently resides in active storage. One obvious problem with this hypothesis arises from the seemingly temporary nature of representations in active storage. The observable changes in electrophysiological activity of the nervous system induced by acquired information are extremely short-lived relative to the general durability of memory. However, this could merely reflect the inadequacy of our techniques of recording and analyzing electrophysiological activity. Perhaps information endures indefinitely in active storage, but the electrochemical pattern representing any given information takes on a relatively subtle code shortly after acquisition. Arguing against this last viewpoint are considerations of the inadequate information capacity and excessive energy demands of maintaining a lifetime of information in active storage (Wooldridge, 1963). Conservative estimates of the maximal number of action potentials that could simultaneously occur in an adult human, although a large number indeed, suggest that even the most efficient neural coding of information is inadequate to encode more than a small fraction of the information commonly retained by an adult human. Moreover, the energy per unit time necessary to repolarize neurons given this large number of action potentials is vastly in excess of the basal metabolic requirements of the brain. Thus, the possibility that all memory is uniquely a consequence of active storage appears remote.

In addition to theoretical arguments concerning information capacity and energy requirements, there are compelling empirical grounds for hypothesizing a stage of memory beyond active storage. Foremost among these is the observation that animals can retain acquired information over periods of neurological electrical silence or distribution resulting from hibernation (Gerard, 1963; Mrosovsky, 1967) or electroconvulsive shock (McGaugh, 1966) provided that sufficient time has elapsed between learning and treatment. Both hibernation and the comatose state that follows electroconvulsive shock are accompanied by a radical decrease in ongoing neural transmission that depresses the frequency of action potentials by at least four orders of magnitude. The fact that acquired information can be retained over such periods of relative electrophysiological silence strongly suggests that the information must be encoded in some form other than ongoing neural transmission during this period. We shall refer to this second memory system as *passive storage* in recognition of its relatively low energy requirement and its independence from ongoing neural transmission. These arguments for independent active and passive storage systems are not meant to imply that there are but two stages of memory; rather, the evidence merely refutes the sufficiency of a one-stage model.

Passive storage is assumed to encode information through some relatively permanent chemical or structural modification of the nervous system. Currently, we know substantially less about the specific nature of encoding information in passive storage than we do about the encoding of information by action potentials in active storage. Among the mechanisms that have been entertained for coding in passive storage are modifications in hormonal balances, changes in the surface areas of select synapses, alterations in the amount of neurotransmitters released by particular synapses in response to a single action potential, modified sensitivity of certain postsynaptic surfaces, changes in select thresholds for producing an action potential, and even the formation of new synapses (e.g., Dunn, 1980; Kandel, 1976; Teyler, 1978). The general emphasis on modification at the synaptic level reflects concern for the necessarily large informational load of passive storage. Coding at the synaptic level constitutes the only mechanism(s) seriously proposed to date that appears capable of storing a lifetime of information. The rationale for this focus on synapses is based on their great number (10^{13} in the human brain). Moreover, the relatively low energy per unit time required to maintain information in the form of chemical or structural modification of synapses appears consonant with the observed basal metabolic rate of the mammalian brain. Although synaptic mechanisms of passive storage have been the subject of speculation for some time, there is currently little evidence favoring one or another particular mechanism that can be reasonably generalized beyond a few select and highly specialized preparations.

Assuming that newly acquired information is initially uniquely encoded by ongoing neural transmission and that the same information is subsequently represented by a chemical/structural modification of the nervous system, it becomes resonable to ask questions about the processes whereby information in active storage comes to be represented in passive storage. It is this process to which Hebb (1949) referred when he spoke of consolidation. One way to investigate the temporal characteristics of this consolidation process would be to disrupt it at various times following acquisition and later test for retention of the target information. Interference with the consolidation process soon after acquisition should appear as a retrograde gradient decreasing monotonically with the interval between acquisition and the disrupting event. In principle, the anticipated specific shape of this monotonic gradient depends on whether an all-or-none or incremental version of consolidation is espoused. However, the apparent organization of passive storage suggests that an event representation consists of a number of attributes (Underwood, 1969), each coded within a multidimensional network. Thus, by applying an extrapolation of Estes' (1950) stimulus elements model, both the all-or-none and incremental versions of consolidation theory can be viewed as compatible with the observation of continuously decreasing retrograde gradients rather than step functions.

In support of consolidation theory in the narrow Hebbian sense, innumerable researchers have observed continuous retrograde gradients for amnesia using any of a multitude of amnestic agents (e.g., Chorover & Schiller, 1965). These gradients demonstrate that information is decreasingly vulnerable to the effects of amnestic agents as the interval between training and the administration of the agent increases. The fundamental problem with much of this research has been the assumption that there are no other possible explanations of retrograde gradients other than the disruption of consolidation. Of course, in the broad sense of Müller and Pilzecker (1900), this assumption is true by definition. However, this broad definition of consolidation is likely to obscure the intricacies of the processes that occur during and immediately following acquisition. For this reason we prefer the more narrow definition of consolidation that delimits consolidation to the initial establishment of information in passive storage as a consequence of its representation in active storage. This is not to imply that a purely serial relationship exists between active and passive storage. Information is not a conserved quantity; in principle information can be transcribed from active storage to passive storage or vice versa without the demise of the information from the former representational stage. Moreover, our preference for a narrow definition of consolidation is not to suggest that initial consolidation is the one and only time that information concerning a particular event enters passive storage. We will discuss later the plasticity of event representations that are reactivated substantially after acquisition, that is, returned to active storage.

Our active storage/passive storage dichotomy is in many respects superficially similar to the short-term memory/long-memory dichotomy of Peterson and Peterson (1959), the short-term storage/long-term storage dichotomy of Atkinson and Shiffrin (1968), the working memory/reference memory dichotomy of Baddeley and Hitch (1974) and Honig (1978), and the active memory/inactive memory dichotomy of Lewis (1979). However, our model distinguishes itself by being predicated upon differences in underlying *physiological* processes rather than any difference in encoding at the informational level or manifestation at the behavioral level. Although it is possible that most of the differences with which these latter investigators have been concerned are themselves consequences of the physiological distinction upon which we focus, it would be a mistake with our present limited knowledge to beg the question and assume that any of these psychological dichotomies was isomorphic with the physiological distinction between active and passive storage. For this reason, we reject the use of the word "consolidation" in reference to the fixation of information in the more stable storage system of any of the psychological pairs of memories mentioned above. Instead we reserve the expression "consolidation" for the initial laying down of a chemical/structural representation of an event, and would apply "consolidation" to the entering of information into the more stable of a pair of *psychological* memory systems only when the psychological dichotomy has been proven to be no more than a behavioral manifestation of the physiological distinction between active and passive storage.

RETROGRADE AMNESIA IS NOT THE RESULT OF CONSOLIDATION FAILURE

Accepting the existence of both active and passive storage along with our definition of consolidation, there can be little doubt that consolidation occurs. However, the chain of events between a learning event and appropriate test performance includes many links, e.g., perception, acquisition, elaboration, consolidation, maintenance in passive storage, perception of retrieval cues, retrieval by active storage, integration of the retrieved information with information from the test environment, decision making, and response generation. A break anywhere in this chain of events will result in a behavioral deficit. Unfortunately there has been a tendency toward tunnel vision on the part of many students of memory. Researchers interested in perception are all too quick to attribute behavioral deficits to variations in perception, and those of us concerned with consolidation are equally overeager to attribute changes in behavior to differences in consolidation. Appropriate test performance assures that all links in the chain between input and output are intact, but a performance deficit leaves wide open the issue of which link(s) has been broken.

Amnestic agents that are alleged to disrupt consolidation processes generally fall into one of two categories. On the one hand there are treatments, such as electroconvulsive (ECS) and hypothermia, that are presumed to cause amnesia by disrupting the neural transmission constituting active storage before information can be consolidated in passive storage. On the other hand there are amnestic agents, such as antimetabolites that block protein synthesis, that allegedly induce amnesia by preventing consolidation in passive storage during the finite life of the target information in active storage. Although there is little doubt that these agents each produce the direct physiological effects with which they are identified, it is equally clear that they each also are responsible for a multitude of supposedly ancillary effects, many of which have not yet been fully identified. Over the last 15 years, an impressive amount of evidence has been gathered indicating that the most widely known physiological consequences of these amnestic agents are likely *not* the means by which these agents produce amnesia (Lewis, 1979; Miller & Springer, 1973).

Although we do not as yet know how most amnestic agents impair retention, there is now good reason to believe that these two families of amnestic agents share a physiological consequence that produces amnesia. The basis for this conclusion is that the amnesia produced by these two families of amnestic agents appears to be the same, e.g., retrograde gradient, susceptibility to recovery, immunization by pretraining familiarization, and temporarily increased vulnerability following reactivation. (Each of these effects will be reviewed later.) Moreover, the protection against an amnestic agent that is afforded by prior exposure to that amnestic agent (Hinderliter, Smith, & Misanin, 1973; Rainbow, Hoffman, & Flexner, 1980) has recently been found to work across the two families of amnestic agents: i.e., prior exposure to cycloheximide (or ECS) appears to protect rats against ECS (or cycloheximide) (Kasprow, Schachtman, Balaz, & Miller, 1983). Traditionally, the two kinds of amnestic agents were differentiated behaviorally by the effects upon retention of the interval between training and testing. In the case of the antimetabolites injected in close temporal proximity of training, retention was observed soon after acquisition but then seen to fade over a period of some minutes or hours (Agranoff, 1971; Barondes & Cohen, 1968). In the case of ECS-like amnestic agents, amnesia was commonly presumed to have an instantaneous onset contemporaneous with the amnestic treatment (McGaugh, 1966). However, a number of studies found that amnesia following ECS develops slowly in a manner similar to amnesia produced by antimetabolites (Geller & Jarvik, 1968; McGaugh & Landfield, 1970). Moreover, Miller and Springer (1971) determined that the apparent retention seen soon after ECS is truly a consequence of acquired associations rather than a change in performance variables such as activity level. If ECS obliterates information encoded in active storage as has been commonly assumed, an assumption with which we are not inclined to argue in light of the profound dimunition in electrophysiological activity of the brain that accompanies the postconvulsive coma, then manifest retention at any time after ECS must reflect information that was already encoded in passive storage at the time of treatment. And as consolidation would be necessary for information to enter passive storage, we must conclude that consolidation occurred during the interval between acquisition and ECS, a period that did not exceed 5 sec in these studies. Thus, the slow onset of amnesia after ECS indicates that consolidation must take place rapidly, and that the amnesia ultimately observed cannot be due to a consolidation failure.

The traditional consolidation failure explanations of experimental amnesia all predict that the target information is irrevocably lost; therefore, the amnesia should be permanent in the absence of new learning. The earliest tests of the permanence of experimental amnesia were inspired by the spontaneous recovery from traumatic amnesia that is well chronicled in the clinical literature (Talland, 1965). However, most attempts to obtain spontaneous recovery from experimental amnesia in animals have proved unsuccessful (e.g., Chevalier, 1965). In response to this initial failure, a number of researchers tried to restore memories in amnesic subjects by providing restorative treatments that excluded the possibility of new learning. These efforts have repeatedly met with success.

Many of these restorative treatments were designed to serve as "reminder trials" in which apparatus cues, the CS, or the reinforcer (US) from training was presented during the retention interval in a manner that prohibited new acquisition (Lewis, Misanin, & Miller, 1968; Quartermain, McEwen, & Azmitia, 1970). Other restorative treatments included chemical or electrical stimulation of the nervous system (e.g., Botwinick & Quartermain, 1974). In fact, both select physiological stimulation and reminder treatments have proven effective in restoring memory after amnesia induced by either ECS or antimetabolites. The observed restoration by physiological stimulation lays to rest any possibility that recovery following experimental amnesia depends on specific learning occurring during the restorative treatment. How any of these restorative treatments work is not yet fully understood (see Miller & Kasprow, 1982 for a discussion of some possible mechanisms). But what is overwhelmingly clear is that the target information in animals suffering from experimental amnesia is merely inaccessible at the time of testing rather than irrevocably lost. Given that ECS-like treatments obliterate active storage, the target trace must reside in some part of the amnesic animal's passive storage system, and the observed retention deficit cannot reasonably be regarded as a consolidation failure in the Hebbian sense.

If experimental amnesia is not an example of consolidation failure, one might ask if anything of value remains in the experimental amnesia literature. We believe that a number of useful insights concerning memory processes, including consolidation, can be obtained from these experiments provided biases concerning consolidation failure can be laid aside. Moreover, it should be remembered that, although we reject consolidation failure explanations of experimental amnesia, there are still strong grounds for hypothesizing a consolidation process that is responsible for the entry of acquired information into passive storage. This process, however, appears to occur much faster than is usually acknowledged.

IMPLICATIONS OF EXPERIMENTAL AMNESIA FOR CONSOLIDATION PROCESSES

We have argued that a behavioral deficit may reflect a flaw in information processing at any one of a number of different points in the necessary sequence. Thus, it is imprudent to assume that a particular behavioral deficit is a consequence of consolidation failure unless appropriate research has been conducted to discriminate between consolidation failures and failures at other points in the overall processing sequence. Moreover, experimental paradigms capable of making this distinction unequivocally have not yet been established.

This inability to conclusively identify a performance deficit as arising from consolidation failure does not, however, leave us unable to learn anything about consolidation processes from the experimental amnesia literature. An alternative strategy consists of noting that when animals display good retention, the complete information processing sequence must have occurred without disruption. If we can shut down some biological process or anatomical structure for a period of time between acquisition and testing without disrupting retention, we can conclude that the disrupted process or structure was not essential to any step in the information-processing sequence occurring during the period of time it was shut down. Thus, although we may not be able to determine precisely which biological processes or structures correspond to a particular cognitive process using this procedure, we can *exclude* a number of biological processes and structures as being essential (i.e., necessary as opposed to sufficient) at selected points in the overall information-processing sequence. By a process of elimination, this approach could guide us toward the biological basis of memory even if it is not adequate in its own right to provide ultimate answers.

As an example of this strategy, consider the previously mentioned phenomenon of animals displaying retention of acquired information if tested within a few minutes following their recovery from the comatose state produced by an ECS that immediately followed training (Geller & Jarvik, 1968; Miller & Springer, 1971). If the electrical storm and subsequent electrical silence (corresponding to the coma) induced by ECS is assumed to erase all information from active storage, the retention observed with short ECS-test intervals must reflect information that was encoded in passive storage at the moment ECS was administered. From this we may conclude that initial consolidation had gone relatively far towards completion in an interval shorter than the 5–sec delay between acquisition and ECS typical of these studies. Neural transmission for more than 5 sec after initial acquisition is apparently not essential for retention. Based on these observations, we can exclude from the list of possible biochemical and/or structural modifications that are essential for passive storage any mechanism that would require more than 5 sec to proceed far enough toward completion as to be irreversible.

Other studies particularly amenable to this type of analysis include those that entirely *fail* to obtain a retention deficit despite the administration of an amnestic agent soon after acquisition. In one such study, Carew (1970) administered ECS to rats 5 sec after passive avoidance training in a step-down apparatus. Upon testing, he found that the choice behavior (side of descent) reflected intact memory of the training event despite amnesia being seen in terms of latency scores. Still (1974), using spontaneous alternation as a measure of retention, failed to obtain amnesia with a 3.6–sec interval between acquisition and ECS. Additionally Hine and Paolino (1970), Mendoza and Adams (1969), and Springer (1975) found that, with 9–, 1.5–, and .5–sec intervals respectively between learning and ECS onset, heart rate and defecation scores indicated retention even when locomotor activity did not. Although all of these studies were basically concerned with the variation in retention seen between different measures of retention, the fact that *any* information survived ECS argues that something must have been consolidated during intervals of time shorter than those between training and ECS onset. The variation between different retention measures likely reflects differences in the particular memory attributes to which various response indices are sensitive and/or different information thresholds for activating various response indices. Why some attributes of the training event are accessible even when ECS closely follows learning whereas others are not is unclear at this time because we do not know the specific mechanism whereby ECS produces amnesia or how these various memory attributes are differentially encoded. However, the fact that any information survived ECS indicates that initial consolidation of at least some attributes was essentially complete prior to the onset of ECS, and once again points toward extremely rapid processes underlying initial consolidation.

Another study that strongly supports extremely rapid consolidation following acquisition was reported by Lewis, Miller, and Misanin (1969). These authors had previously found that 15 min of pretraining exposure to the training apparatus protected animals against the amnestic effects of ECS on one-trial passive avoidance learning even when the interval between footshock onset and ECS was as short as 5 sec (Lewis, Miller, & Misanin, 1968). They initially speculated that pretraining familiarization with the apparatus reduced the total amount of information that their rats had to consolidate at the time of training. Therefore, if the interval between footshock onset and ECS onset were sufficiently short, ECS ought be able to induce amnesia despite pretraining familiarization. To test this possibility, Lewis, Miller, and Misanin (1969) trained rats in a passive avoidance situation and parametrically varied the interval between reinforcement onset and ECS onset. They found that even at the shortest interval examined, 500 msec, animals that had received prior familiarization with the training apparatus did not display amnesia. This observation indicates that whatever processes underlie consolidation, they can occur in less than 500 msec. Although initial consolidation in other situations may take substantially more than .5 sec, the fact that consolidation can occur in less than .5 sec in even one situation indicates that the consolidation process has the potential to be extremely rapid. Of course this statement assumes that there is a single common consolidation process or sequence of processes for all information; however, there is no reason to reject this parsimonious assumption at the present time. Moreover, if an organism has the capacity to consolidate some information in less than .5 sec, it is quite possible that all initial consolidation occurs in less than .5 sec. Thus, despite the experimental amnesia literature not definitively pointing toward one or another mechanism for consolidation, it argues against any process that takes appreciably longer than .5 sec.

Ancillary support for this conclusion comes from several other sources. For example the long delay between presentation of a novel flavor (conditioned stimulus) and induction of an internal malaise (unconditioned stimulus) with which it is possible to obtain conditioned taste aversion (Garcia, Ervin, & Koelling, 1966) provides an opportunity to study the manner in which the conditioned stimulus is neurologically represented prior to the occurrence of the unconditioned stimulus. Traditionally, for learning to occur it has been assumed that a neurological trace of the CS must be retained in active storage from the time of CS presentation to the time of US presentation (e.g., Hebb, 1949). This demand for relatively long-term representation in active storage suggests that great rapidity of encoding of the CS representation into passive storage is unnecessary. On the basis of existing data, we are not inclined to challenge the need of simultaneous representation of the CS and US in active storage in order for learning to take place. However, even if this condition is accepted as a necessity for the formation of an association, it does not require that a CS representation be maintained in active storage during the entire interval between CS offset to US onset. Speaking to this issue, Roll and Smith (1972), Rozin and Ree (1972) and Buresova and Bures (1977) have all found that deep anesthesia between presentation of the CS and US in a conditioned taste aversion paradigm does not disrupt acquisition. In fact Rozin and Ree (1972) report that it prolongs the maximum interval between the CS and US that will permit the formation of a conditioned taste aversion. Similarly Ionescu and Buresova (1977) found that hypothermia induced between the CS and US presentations did not disrupt the formation of a conditioned taste aversion. As both anesthesia and hypothermia are treatments that radically attenuate ongoing neural transmission, these studies indicate that the maintenance of a CS representation in active storage from the time of CS offset to US onset is not necessary for the formation of associations between a novel taste and internal malaise.

To the extent that one can generalize between conditioned taste aversions and other types of associations (see Logue, 1979, for a compelling argument in support of qualitative equivalence between conditioned taste aversions and other types of associations), we can reject the hypothesis that, for learning to occur, a representation of the CS must be retained in active storage until the US is presented. Instead, it appears plausible that exposure to a US, at least one that induces an internal malaise and perhaps more generally, stimulates reactivation of certain CS traces selected both for their recency as determined by some sort of time tag (D'Amato, 1973) and for their appropriateness according to some sort of cue-to-consequence principle (Garcia & Koelling, 1966). These principles, although hardly proving the occurrence of rapid consolidation, are more compatible with rapid consolidation than with traditional Hebbian theory.

Further evidence indicative of extremely rapid consolidation can be found in the human literature. Shallice and Warrington (1970) report that one patient, K.F., displayed behavior suggesting that he could not retain information in short-term memory for intervals of more than a second or two (e.g., no recency effect in serial position curves and an abnormally low digit span); yet, this subject's long-term memory capabilities appeared perfectly normal. If short-term memory, at least in terms of the tests used by Shallice and Warrington, (1970) is equated with active storage, K.F.'s behavior would imply either parallel input into active and passive storage or extremely rapid passage through active storage en route to passive storage. For reasons previously discussed, we regard active storage as the sole gateway for information into the nervous system. Thus, we are strongly inclined to favor the latter possibility.

These remarks concerning K.F. suggest that the prolonged representation of information in active storage is not necessary for entry into passive storage. Moreover, there are additional data indicating that prolonged representation of acquired information in active storage is not sufficient for entry into passive storage. Craik and Tulving (1975; but see Morris, Bransford, & Franks, 1977) have reported that duration of active rehearsal is of little consequence for long-term retention, provided the rehearsal is of a rote or repetitive nature that does not appreciably change the representational level of the ongoing processing.

Although the above studies are only supportive of rapid consolidation by virtue of their disproving the necessity of processes that demand slow consolidation, the earlier mentioned familiarization experiments from the experimental amnesia literature, demonstrating retention in select circumstances even when information in active storage was obliterated fractions of a second after acquisition, speak decisively for the occurrence of rapid consolidation. We believe that this extreme rapidity of consolidation is one of the few established facts concerning the nature of consolidation.

IMPLICATIONS OF EXPERIMENTAL AMNESIA FOR MEMORIAL PROCESSES OTHER THAN CONSOLIDATION

Retrieval

Experimental amnesia was initially studied in order to better understand the consolidation process. We have pointed out that the implications of such research for consolidation, although important, are limited. We now would like to digress from our focus on consolidation and examine how modifications of retrieval processes contribute to experimental amnesia. This is valuable both in adding to our understanding of retrieval and in providing a viable alternative to consolidation-failure explanations of experimental amnesia so that we may feel less apprehension in turning away from the latter position.

The observation that experimental amnesia is generally reversible without new learning taking place during the retention interval indicates that the target information, although inaccessible, was encoded within the organism even when test performance indicated the presence of amnesia. Based on this finding we have previously interpreted experimental amnesia as an instance of retrieval failure (Miller & Springer, 1973; Miller & Marlin, 1979). However, our viewpoint conflicts with definitions of retrieval that refer solely to processes that occur when information is read out of passive storage. In the case of experimental amnesia, the interval between acquisition and the administration of the amnestic agent (i.e., the retrograde gradient) is more important in determining the behavioral impact of the amnestic agent than is the interval between the amnestic agent and testing. Using the foregoing restricted definition of retrieval processes, the retrograde gradient testifies to the independence of experimental amnesia from variations in retrieval. However, just as we doubt the usefulness of equating consolidation with everything that occurs immediately following receipt of information, we similarly question the usefulness of restricting retrieval processes by definition to the reactivation of information encoded in passive storage immediately preceding testing. Rather, we feel that it is heuristically valuable to enlarge our concept of retrieval processes to include the preparation necessary for the subsequent reactivation of information represented in passive storage. This is not to imply that preparation for retrieval should be confused with retrieval itself. However, a performance deficit resulting from a failure in either of these steps in information processing can reasonably be regarded as a retrieval failure. Such retrieval failures are distinct from storage failures that imply that the target information is not encoded in any form within the subject.

Seen in terms of the frequently used analogy between memory and a library, consolidation can be likened to the library placing a newly purchased volume on its shelves. The particular retrieval process that we hypothesize occurs around the time of acquisition would correspond to making appropriate entries in the card catalog. This latter step is essential if the volume is to be successfully located at a later time. Without being recorded in the card catalog, the book could sit on the shelf and never be found. In terms of this analogy, experimental amnesia corresponds to a degradation or obliteration of the relevant entries that would normally exist in the card catalog. A reminder treatment, such as appropriate duration exposure to the target CS, presumably facilitates later retrieval by serving as a supersalient retrieval cue that compensates for the impaired functioning of the process analogous to referencing the card catalog. Alternatively, the supersalient retrieval cue serving as a reminder stimulus could be promoting a scan of passive storage analogous to a search of the library shelves seeking the appropriate volume. Once the target memory in passive storage has been located, preparation for its later retrieval can be made anew. In the library analogy this would correspond to making a belated entry in the card catalog.

It is important to avoid confusion between the card catalog of the library analogy and the cognitive or biological corresponding mechanisms in human or animal information processing systems; however, for lack of better terminology we shall speak of a functional catalog structure and cataloging process within our information-processing model. Elsewhere we have provided a detailed discussion of some of the likely properties and implications of a reference catalog for information encoded in passive storage (Miller & Kasprow, 1982). For present purposes it will suffice for us to summarize a few of the more important implications of this viewpoint. First, the catalog system is clearly immune to amnestic agents such as ECS when the interval between acquisition and ECS is sufficiently long. This indicates that the catalog representation is of a chemical/structural format. Thus, the catalog system can be thought of as a subset of passive storage. Passive storage might be considered to consist of two subdivisions: (1) a catalog representation that encodes events only by a few of their most salient trace attributes and contains the functional storage locations of the more detailed event trace representations in the other part of passive storage; and (2) the more comprehensive representation of the event that we shall refer to hereafter as global storage. In other words, the catalog representation of an event contains the address for the global storage representation of that event. In toto, our model can be seen to be a three-stage affair consisting of active storage, catalog storage (within passive storage), and global storage (also within passive storage). Three-stage models are obviously less parsimonious than two-stage models; however, we believe that two-stage models are no longer adequate to explain the observed characteristics of memory, particularly those seen in conjunction with experimental amnesia. Moreover, our three-stage model merges an efficient retrieval system, arising from catalog storage presumably being content-addressable, with an economical mass storage system, arising from global storage being location-addressable (Miller & Kasprow, 1982).

We have already described how this three-stage model can explain experimental amnesia and its reversal by assuming that the temporary postacquisition vulnerability of the catalog trace is ordinarily of substantially greater duration than that for the global trace. One may legitimately ask why the catalog trace stays vulnerable to amnestic agents for a longer period of time than does the global trace. We believe that the reason for this stems from catalog storage being the level within the system at which the temporal boundaries of an event are defined. Global storage is believed to consist of representations of event attributes that occur simultaneously. Presumably catalog storage introduces a temporal dimension by cross-referencing sequentially occurring clusters of simultaneous attributes. From this perspective, it is plausible that the catalog representation, unlike the global representation, would stay "open," i.e., in a state of ongoing exchange of information between catalog storage and active storage. This would permit further sequential information constituting continuation of the event to be cross-referenced in catalog storage until such time as the flow of novel stimulation ceased, indicative of the end of a unitary, isolateable learning event. Our basic assumption is that as long as the catalog representation of the target event remains open to further information, it is particularly vulnerable to disruption.

Three experimental phenomena provide substantial support for the view that subsequent retrievability of newly acquired information maintains its vulnerability until the termination of the train of novel information. Studying rats in a classical conditioning preparation, Miller, Misanin, and Lewis (1969) observed that presentation of a novel stimulus of low affective value, specifically a flashing light, between the CS-US (tone-footshock) pairing and ECS, was able to prolong the postacquisition vulnerable period despite appropriate controls indicating that the flashing light alone had no disruptive effect upon retention. Presumably the flashing light was perceived as an integral part of the CS-US learning event, and the catalog representation of the event was kept open, and thus vulnerable, in anticipation of yet further sequential stimuli of consequence.

A second seemingly parallel observation is to be found in an aspect of the detention effect. Specifically, when animals are detained in the learning environment immediately following acquisition, the period of vulnerability to ECS and other amnestic agents is greatly lengthened (Davis, 1968; Robustelli, Geller, & Jarvik, 1972). Presumably the relative novelty of the training apparatus maintains the stream of novel input, thereby causing the listing of appropriate global addresses in the catalog representation to be maintained in a modifiable and thus vulnerable state.

Marlin, Berk, and Miller (1979) further explored the possibility that catalog representations were maintained in a particularly modifiable format until termination of novel events. Using a one-trial passive avoidance task, they compared retention among rats that received ECS 5 sec after the onset of the US (footshock). For some animals the US had a 1–sec duration, whereas for the other animals it lasted the full 5 sec between US onset and ECS onset. As a longer duration US ordinarily produces more robust performance, one might have expected the 5–sec duration US animals to show less amnesia than the 1–sec duration US animals. However, the opposite was observed; the 1–sec US group displayed superior retention. Apparently the 4 sec of processing time available to these animals between footshock offset and ECS onset was of greater value in terms of resistance to experimental amnesia than was the additional associative strength (or motivation) provided by four additional seconds of US presentation experienced by the 5–sec US animals. A second experiment in the same series used an appetitive US and obtained the same results, thereby demonstrating the generality of the finding. In toto, these experiments suggest that newly acquired memories are highly subject to disruption until the cessation of novel stimulation defines the end of the learning event. In conjunction with the reminder studies, which indicate that the target information is not lost by the amnesic animal but is merely inaccessible, the idea of a catalog representation (that assists in locating the global event trace) as being the memorial element subject to disruption appears particularly appealing.

The model can also explain the fact that pretraining exposure to the apparatus protects the target information against postacquisition amnestic agents, i.e., the familiarization effect. Pretraining exposure would permit the animal to make redundant representations of the appropriate entries in the catalog system. The catalog entries relevant to the target event that are specifically reactivated on the training trial may well be degraded in their potential to facilitate retrieval, but presumably these are only a small fraction of the redundant catalog entries resulting from the familiarization treatment. The residual entries, i.e., those not reactivated during the actual learning event, may well suffice to make contact with the global representation by virtue of having attributes in common with the global representation of the target event.

Before considering additional research stimulated by this model, one of its weaknesses should be noticed. We described above the relatively slow onset of amnesia seen after administration of either ECS-like treatments or antimetabolites. At its present stage of development, the model can accommodate this phenomenon only with the unsatisfying post hoc suggestion that the amnestic agents do not immediately disrupt the relevant catalog trace but initiate a slow degradation of that trace, an explanation that barely rises above paraphrasing the empirical phenomenon. However, in light of the predictive qualities of the model in respect to other phenomena, we would hope that an understanding of why degradation of the catalog trace is slow will be obtained in the future.

Reactivation

We have presented evidence supporting retrieval failure as a viable alternative hypothesis to the consolidation-failure view of experimental amnesia. Moreover, we have seen how various phenomena from within the experimental amnesia literature illuminate the nature of retrieval processes. In addition to these contributions, experimental amnesia research has been invaluable in adding to our appreciation of the long-term consequences of reactivating a trace; these consequences indirectly add to our understanding of consolidation. Thus far we have considered the actual process of retrieval (as distinct from preparation for retrieval) only as an early step in the processing sequence that immediately precedes performance on a test trial. Operationally this consists of presenting select retrieval cues, i.e., reinstating some of the cues from the training situation. Consequently a constellation of associations centered around these reinstated cues are reactivated, i.e., read from passive storage into active storage.

Reactivation is not only an essential element of a successful test trial; it has a second important consequence. The very same reactivation processes that constitute retrieval on a test trial also recreate many of the conditions in active storage that existed at the time of acquisition. This occurs independent of whether the circumstances of reinstatement permit the production of a response, thereby constituting a test trial, or exclude the possibility of responding, thereby recreating a neurological state with potential latent consequences that could only be observed on subsequent test trials.

Although any reinstatement event is operationally indistinguishable from a reminder treatment, to avoid confusion we reserve the term "reminder" for instances of reactivation in which the retrieval cues of the given retention test alone are inadequate to reactivate the target memory. In this framework, a reminder trial may be regarded as the presentation of a *supersalient* retrieval cue to a subject for whom "conventional" retrieval cues would fail to induce successful reactivation. In contrast "reinstatement" refers to the presentation of conventional retrieval cues, appropriate to the given retention tests, that are able to reactivate the target trace. Thus, reinstatement of training cues as well as reminder treatments are both potential sources of reactivation. However, it is useful to see them as different points on a continuum in terms of ease of retrievability, with "reminder" being applicable in cases of extremely difficult retrieval requiring retrieval cues that go beyond those normally defined by the retention test, and "reactivation" being applicable to relatively effortless reading of information from passive storage into active storage. It should be recognized that the basic distinction between reminder treatment and reinstatement-induced reactivation is in the state of the subject rather than in the nature of the manipulation. If an animal would do poorly on an ordinary retention test, then we would be inclined to speak of training cues serving as potential reminders; whereas, if the same animal were capable of responding appropriately on a retention test consisting of presentation of cues from the training situation, we would speak of a presentation of these same stimuli as an instance of reinstatement. Or to put it in yet another terminology, reminder treatments are a meaningful concept only when applied to animals that have forgotten the target task.

We have discussed how reminding an amnesic animal with supersalient retrieval cues might improve subsequent retrievability of the target information, thereby eliminating the memorial deficit initially observed. Intriguingly, a parallel phenomena is seen even in animals that, unlike amnesic animals, are not the obvious victims of forgetting. (See Miller & Kasprow, 1982, for a detailed discussion of some of the possible underlying mechanisms.) For example, Gordon and Spear (1973) have shown that strychnine sulfate can improve retention if it is injected either about the time of acquisition or long after acquisition, provided the injection is in temporal proximity to reinstatement of retrieval cues. Moreover, even without the aid of pharmacological agents such as strychnine, there appear to be benefits derived from repeated reactivations of a target trace. The demonstrated effectiveness of such treatments in improving infant memory both in humans (Rovee-Collier & Sullivan, 1980) and in animals (Spear, 1979) is particularly impressive. More generally Cooper and Monk (1976) describe a number of human memory studies in which reactivation of information in or out of a test situation facilitated later retention. Jacoby and Craik (1979) have elaborated on this general finding by noting that the greater the depth of level of processing at the time of reactivation during the retention interval, the greater the facilitation of later performance.

Each of the above examples describes improved retention as a function of rehearsal or pharmacological manipulation in conjunction with retention interval reactivation of the target memory. However, some of the earliest studies of reactivation took advantage of the extreme malleability of information in active storage to impair subsequent performance rather than enhance it. Misanin, Miller, and Lewis (1968) exposed animals to a CS-US contingency in a classical conditioning situation. A full day later, with the intention of reactivating the target trace, some of their animals were exposed to the CS followed immediately by an ECS. On a subsequent test trial this sequence was found to yield impaired performance relative both to animals that were not exposed to the CS immediately before the ECS and to animals that did not receive the ECS immediately after the reinstating CS. Through this early study Misanin et al. demonstrated that newly acquired memories were not unique in their vulnerability to experimental amnesia. Schneider and Sherman (1968) reported a very similar effect using an instrumental paradigm in which the reinforcer was presented during the retention interval as the reinstating cue prior to ECS. Subsequent to these early studies, this important phenomenon has been observed in a number of different laboratories with ECS as the amnestic agent (e.g., DeVietti & Holliday, 1972; Howard, Glendenning, & Meyer, 1974) as well as with anisomycin (Judge & Quartermain, 1982). Collectively these studies indicate that reactivation of a target trace can not only strengthen a representation that has been subject to forgetting, but can temporarily heighten the malleability of memory traces.

The presentation of reinstatement/reminder stimuli from the training situation during the retention interval is operationally the same whether the reminder manipulation is being used with the intent of strengthening the effective retention of a subject displaying a retention deficit or reinstatement is being performed to reactivate a target memory in a subject displaying no obvious retention deficit. Moreover, the reinstatement/reminder manipulation is also indistinguishable from operational extinction. Although there is still considerable controversy as to the processes underlying extinction (Mackintosh, 1974), there is no basic contradiction between the phenomenon of extinction and reinstatement/reminder-induced reactivation effects. Gordon, Smith, and Katz (1979) and Rohrbaugh, Riccio, and Arthur (1972) have both demonstrated that brief reinstatement of conditioned stimuli can serve as an effective reminder, strengthening subsequent performance, or an effective reactivator, temporarily heightening the malleability of a trace. However, these same researchers have also shown that prolonged exposure to conditioned stimuli in the absence of a US can produce a subsequent performance decrement corresponding to extinction. This suggests that it may prove fruitful to conceive of extinction as a retention impairment dependent upon reactivation of the target trace in close temporal proximity to potentially interfering events. In any case, whether or not extinction is viewed as one consequence of reactivation or is seen as a totally independent process that summates with the consequences of reactivation, there is no conceptual problem with reminder, reinstatement, and extinction sharing the same operational definition; they are distinguished by the state of the subject and the duration of stimulus presentation.

In reference to the three-stage model that we briefly outlined, it becomes apparent that just as information in global storage must undergo some kind of consolidation process, so too must information in catalog storage, for both catalog and global storage are passive storage systems that presumably are fed information from active storage. If the reminder phenomenon is interpreted as evidence against experimental amnesia being caused by a failure to consolidate information in global storage, is it still possible that experimental amnesia reflects a failure to consolidate information in catalog storage? This possibility is compatible with reminder treatments restoring memory, if reminder stimuli are viewed as inducing global target trace reactivation through some sort of mechanism that overcomes the lack of a robust catalog target trace. Once reactivated, a proper target trace could be laid down in catalog storage, thereby facilitating later retrieval. Unfortunately this simplifying view runs into difficulty in attempting to explain how amnestic agents are able to produce retention deficits when they are administered in conjunction with reactivation rather than acquisition (e.g., Misanin et al., 1968). Possibly experimental amnesia produced in conjunction with newly acquired information and experimental amnesia produced in conjunction with reactivated information have two fundamentally different bases; however, this is a most unparsimonious view. Alternatively one could attribute a destructive read-out feature to catalog storage such that, every time information in catalog storage is used, it must be read back into catalog storage to be subsequently available. If this were the case, amnesia produced in conjunction with reactivation or in conjunction with original learning could both reflect a failure to consolidate information in catalog storage. Thus it is conceivable that experimental amnesia reflects a failure to retrieve information from global storage owing to a consolidation failure in catalog storage. This set of hypotheses could in fact explain all the presently available data; however, the assumption of destructive read-out from catalog storage is purely speculative. Currently there are neither data nor even experimental paradigms appropriate to probe this issue, but it surely provides a target for future research.

One major implication of the preceding arguments is that much of the forgetting induced by amnestic agents, or, for that matter, caused by commonly occurring events in the natural habitat of an animal, cannot be attributed to a failure of consolidation in global storage. In support of this conclusion we have alluded to reactivation phenomena in which information acquired long ago appears subject to modification in a manner highly similar to that of newly acquired information. Furthermore, the finding that reminder treatments can effectively restore impaired memories mitigates against global storage being subject to a destructive read-out process such as we have entertained for catalog storage.

Viewed collectively, the restorability of original traces following forgetting and the modifiability of reactivated traces in some respects appear to be in conflict. If a reactivated memory is subject to modification, and if this modification is as all-encompassing as initial acquisition, then one might anticipate that these modifications would be irreversible. However, the reminder effect suggests that event representations can in large part be restored to something approximating their initial state. Loftus and Loftus (1980) have argued from human data that modification of reactivated memories irrevocably alters initial memories. This suggests that reactivation is more likely to degrade a trace through modification than are reminder consequences of stimulus reinstatement likely to strengthen the target trace. Typical of the many experiments that they cite is the case in which a subject is first presented with a narrative story and then asked a leading question about the story in which the question presupposes a condition in contradiction to the initial narrative. The subjects then are tested for recall, and the recalled narrative is seen to incorporate the variants introduced in the question stage in preference to the facts of the initial narrative.

Although the data cited by Loftus and Loftus (1980) are intriguing, their interpretation is predicated upon the notion of a unitary representation of the target information in global storage. If instead we presume that most acquired information is redundantly represented in global storage, it becomes plausible that modification of information in conjunction with reactivation may affect some representations but not others of the same target event. Thus, it becomes entirely possible that the modified trace and the original trace can coexist in the same global storage system. There are a number of studies that support this latter view, perhaps the best being a recent report by Hasher, Attig, and Alba (1981). These investigators found that if they provided human subjects first with target information, then provided input calling for the modification of that initial target information, and finally tested their subjects, they found the same effects that Loftus and Loftus (1980) described. However, if before the final test trial they told their subjects that the modifying input was erroneous, the subjects were found quite capable of returning to the original information state based on initial acquisition. Notably the modification provided in the Hasher et al. study was not merely an addition of information that could at a later time be subtracted from the total representational system but was a distinct modification including contradictions of the initial information. The fact that the subjects could recollect the initial information when the modifying input was negated indicates that the initial target information was present all along despite its not being evident in the absence of the negation. Thus we see that although reactivated memories are in some respects vulnerable to modification in a fashion similar to newly acquired memories, there is not a full correspondence. The Hasher et al. study raises the possibility that no amount of modification of information in conjunction with reactivation will suffice to obliterate the initially acquired information, although it may substantially reduce the retrievability of the initial information.

Within the animal literature, Riccio and his students (Mactutus & Riccio, 1978) have recently pointed out additional differences between newly acquired and reactivated traces. For example, they found that amnesia produced with a fixed degree of hypothermia was more readily reversible when the hypothermia immediately followed reactivation than when it immediately followed initial acquisition, thereby implying that reactivated traces are not as vulnerable to modification as newly acquired traces. This result is highly congruent with the assumed redundancy of traces and with reinstatement reactivating only some of these traces. However, they also reported that mild hypothermia was able to influence retention after reactivation but not after initial acquisition, thereby suggesting that reactivated memories are more vulnerable to modification than are newly acquired traces. There is obviously a paradox here that will not be resolved until further data are gathered. Despite the likelihood of some subtle differences between reactivated traces and traces that are active because they are newly acquired, it is clear that, at least in terms of malleability, reactivated information has much in common with newly acquired information.

SUMMARY

Experimental amnesia, whether produced by ECS-like agents or antimetabolites, is seen to be in part if not entirely the result of a retrieval failure. Thus, experimental amnesia joins the growing list of memory impairments that can be attributed primarily to retrieval failure. Miller and Kasprow (1982) have reviewed numerous additional instances of forgetting that have traditionally been attributed to consolidaton failure but have more recently been found to be a product of faulty retrieval. In retrospect these findings should not be surprising. Successful performance on a retention test represents a long sequence of events that starts with sensory input and includes encoding, consolidation in global storage, elaboration, consolidation in catalog storage, perhaps reactivation and further elaboration, sensation and encoding of retrieval cues, location of the appropriate entries in catalog storage that contain the necessary addresses in global storage, retrieval from global storage, reponse decision making, and response generation. A disruption of any link in this chain of events would suffice to produce a performance deficit during a test trial.

Early investigators concerned with consolidation processes presumed that the retention deficits they observed were a product of faulty consolidation. Not only were these early researchers in error in overlooking alternative explanations of the observed performance deficits, but the consolidation-failure hypothesis itself is inherently unsupportable using the presently available paradigms. If an organism displays retention, then we know that all essential steps in the information-processing sequence have occurred successfully. For the sake of exposition, let us assume a simple information-processing sequence consisting of only two potentially vulnerable steps, consolidation and retrieval. If a performance deficit is observed, in principle it could be attributed to either consolidation failure or retrieval failure. However, if at a later time without further training the target memory is manifest by the organism, we may presume that the initial deficit was a retrieval failure. On the other hand, if we are unsuccessful in restoring the target memory, we do not know whether the failure reflects a retrieval failure that we have been unable to reverse with our reminder treatment or a true consolidation failure. Thus retrieval failure can be definitively established with the present paradigms, whereas consolidation failure cannot be. This does not mean that consolidation failure does not occur, but that at this stage of the development of our science we are not able to identify consolidation failures. Hopefully, improved paradigms in the future will permit us to do so. However until such paradigms are developed, there appear to be no grounds for speaking of consolidation failure as more than one possible explanation for a given performance deficit, and even this possibility is restricted to retention failures in which memory restoration without additional learning has not been observed. Moreover, although there are no grounds for rejecting the possibility of consolidation failure in cases in which restorative treatments have not proven effectual, the extreme rapidity of consolidation as seen, for example, in the previously described familiarization effect, suggests that consolidation is such a fast process that interference with it is relatively unlikely.

The concept of memory consolidation is a potentially valuable one. However, we believe the usefulness of the concept would be enhanced substantially if the term were more precisely defined than is ordinarily the case. We find it advantageous to limit consolidation to the input of information into passive storage. Although we do not expect other researchers to employ our definition, we would hope that other investigators, however they use the term, would clearly define what they mean by consolidation before plunging forth. Memory consolidation as we have defined it appears to be an essential step in the overall sequence of information processing that constitutes the fundamental phenomenon of memory. As such, it behooves us to increase our knowledge concerning the nature of the phenomenon.

The present paper argues that our knowledge of consolidation processes is meager indeed. Not only do we know little about consolidation at this time, but we do not even have in our possession a respectable paradigm for investigating it. Within the framework of available paradigms, the best we can do is disrupt select physiological processes and observe whether or not our subjects still display retention. If performance is unimpaired, we can safely conclude that the disrupted process is not essential for retention during the period of disruption.

However, if a performance deficit is seen, we would have little basis for concluding that the disrupted process was essential for consolidation as opposed to one of the many other links in the overall chain of events constituting memory. We fully expect that continuing research will unveil some of the mysteries of memory consolidation. This will likely come about most rapidly if the students of human memory and the students of animal memory pay more attention to each other.

ACKNOWLEDGMENTS

The preparation of this chapter was assisted by NSF Grant BMS75–03383 and NIMH Grant MH33881. The first author was supported by NIMH Research Scientist Development Award MH–00061. Thanks are due Mary Ann Balaz and Wesley Kasprow for critically reading a preliminary version of the manuscript and Joan Wessely for her assistance in preparing the manuscript.

REFERENCES

Agranoff, B. W. Effects of antibiotics on long-term memory formation in the goldfish. In W. K. Honig & P. H. R. James (Eds.), *Animal memory*. New York: Academic Press, 1971.

Archer, E. J., & Underwood, B. J. Retroactive inhibition of verbal associations as a multiple function of temporal point of interpolation and degree of interpolated learning. *Journal of Experimental Psychology*, 1951, *42*, 283–290.

Atkinson, R. C., & Shiffrin, R. M. Human memory: A proposed system and its control processes. In K. W. Spence & J. T. Spence (Eds.), *The psychology of learning and motivation (Vol. 2)*. New York: Academic Press, 1968.

Baddeley, A. D., & Hitch, G. Working memory. In G. Bower (Ed.), *The psychology of learning and motivation (Vol. 8)*. New York: Academic Press, 1974.

Barondes, S. H., & Cohen, H. D. Arousal and the conversion of "short-term" to "long-term" memory. *Proceedings of the National Academy of Sciences (USA)*, 1968, *61*, 923–929.

Botwinick, C. Y., & Quartermain, D. Recovery from amnesia induced by pre-test injections of monoamine oxidase inhibitors. *Pharmacology, Biochemistry and Behavior*, 1974, *2*, 375–379.

Buresova, O., & Bures, J. The effect of anesthesia on acquisition and extinction of conditioned taste aversion. *Behavioral Biology*, 1977, *20*, 41–50.

Burnham, W. H. Retroactive amnesia: Illustrative cases and a tentative explanation. *American Journal of Psychology*, 1903, *14*, 382–396.

Carew, T. J. Do passive avoidance tasks permit assessment of retrograde amnesia in rats? *Journal of Comparative and Physiological Psychology*, 1970, *72*, 267–271.

Cherkin, A. Retrograde amnesia in the chick: Resistance to the reminder effect. *Physiology and Behavior*, 1972, *8*, 949–955.

Chevalier, J. A. Permanence of amnesia after a single post-trial electroconvulsive procedure. *Journal of Comparative and Physiological Psychology*, 1965, *59*, 125–127.

Chorover, S. L., & Schiller, P. H. Short-term retrograde amnesia in rats. *Journal of Comparative and Physiological Psychology*, 1965, *59*, 73–78.

Cooper, A. J. R., & Monk, A. Learning for recall and learning for recognition. In J. Brown (Ed.), *Recall and recognition*. New York: Wiley & Sons, 1976.

Craik, F. I. M., & Tulving, E. Depth of processing and retention of words in episodic memory. *Journal of Experimental Psychology: General*, 1975, *104*, 268–294.

D'Amato, M. R. Delayed matching and short-term memory in monkeys. In G. H. Bower (Ed.), *The psychology of learning and motivation (Vol. 7)*. New York: Academic Press, 1973.

Davis, R. E. Environmental control of memory fixation in goldfish. *Journal of Comparative and Physiological Psychology*, 1968, *65*, 72–78.

DeVietti, T. L., & Holliday, J. H. Retrograde amnesia produced by electroconvulsive shock after reactivation of a consolidated memory trace: A replication. *Psychonomic Science*, 1972, *29*, 137–138.

Dunn, A. J. Neurochemistry of learning and memory: An evaluation of recent data. *Annual Review of Psychology*, 1980, *31*, 343–390.

Estes, W. K. Toward a statistical theory of learning. *Psychological Review*, 1950, *57*, 94–107.

Garcia, J., Ervin, F., & Koelling, R. Learning with prolonged delay of reinforcement. *Psychonomic Science*, 1966, *5*, 121–122.

Garcia, J., & Koelling, R. A. Relation of cue to consequence in avoidance learning. *Psychonomic Science*, 1966, *4*, 123–124.

Geller, A., & Jarvik, M. E. The time relations of ECS–induced amnesia. *Psychonomic Science*, 1968, *12*, 169–170.

Gerard, R. W. Physiology and psychiatry. *American Journal of Psychiatry*, 1949, *106*, 161–173.

Gerard, R. W. The material basis of memory. *Journal of Verbal Learning and Verbal Behavior*, 1963, *2*, 22–33.

Gordon, W. C., Smith, G. J., & Katz, D. S. Dual effects of response blocking following avoidance learning. *Behavior Research and Therapy*, 1978, *17*, 479–487.

Gordon, W. C., & Spear, N. E. The effects of strychnine on recently acquired and reactivated passive avoidance memories. *Physiology and Behavior*, 1973, *10*, 1071–1075.

Harris, J. *Hermes*. London: Woodfall, 1751.

Hasher, L., Attig, M. S., & Alba, J. W. I knew it all along: Or, did I? *Journal of Verbal Learning and Verbal Behavior*, 1981, *20*, 86–96.

Hebb, D. O. *The organization of behavior*. New York: Wiley, 1949.

Hinderliter, C. F., Smith, S. L., & Misanin, J. R. Effect of pretraining experience on retention of a passive avoidance task following ECS. *Physiology and Behavior*, 1973, *10*, 671–675.

Hine, B., & Paolino, R. M. Retrograde amnesia: Production of skeletal but not cardiac response gradients by electroconvulsive shock. *Science*, 1970, *169*, 1224–1226.

Honig, W. K. On the conceptual nature of cognitive terms: An initial essay. In S. H. Hulse, H. Fowler, & W. K. Honig (Eds.), *Cognitive processes in animal behavior*. Hillsdale, N.J.: Lawrence Erlbaum Associates, 1978.

Howard, R. L., Glendenning, R. L., & Meyer, D. R. Motivational control of retrograde amnesia: Further explorations and effects. *Journal of Comparative and Physiological Psychology*, 1974, *86*, 187–192.

Hubel, D. H., & Wiesel, T. N. Receptive fields and functional architecture of monkey striate cortex. *Journal of Physiology*, 1968, *195*, 215–243.

Ionescu, E., & Buresova, O. Effects of hypothermia on the acquisition of conditioned taste aversion in rats. *Journal of Comparative and Physiological Psychology*, 1977, *91*, 1297–1307.

Jacoby, L. I., & Craik, F. I. M. Effects of elaboration of processing at encoding and retrieval: Trace distinctiveness in recovery of initial context. In L. S. Cermak & F. I. M. Craik (Eds.), *Levels of processing in human memory*. Hillsdale, N.J.: Lawrence Erlbaum Associates, 1979.

Judge, M. E., & Quartermain, D. Characteristics of retrograde amnesia following reactivation of memory in mice. *Physiology and Behavior*, 1982, *28*, 585–590.

Kandel, E. R. *Cellular basis of behavior: An introduction to behavioral neurobiology*. San Francisco: W. H. Freeman & Co., 1976.

Kasprow, W. J., Schachtman, T. R., Balaz, M. A., & Miller, R. R. Attenuation of experimental amnesia through prior administration of a dissimilar amnestic agent. *Physiology and Behavior*, 1983, *30*, 193–196.

Lewis, D. J. Psychobiology of active and inactive memory. *Psychological Bulletin*, 1979, *86*, 1054–1083.

Lewis, D. J., Miller, R. R., & Misanin, J. R. Control of retrograde amnesia. *Journal of Comparative and Physiological Psychology*, 1968, *66*, 48–52.

Lewis, D. J., Miller, R. R., & Misanin, J. R. Selective amnesia in rats produced by electroconvulsive shock. *Journal of Comparative and Physiological Psychology*, 1969, *69*, 136–140.

Lewis, D. J., Misanin, J. R., & Miller, R. R. Recovery of memory following amnesia. *Nature*, 1968, *220*, 704–705.

Loftus, E. F., & Loftus, G. R. On the permanence of stored information in the human brain. *American Psychologist*, 1980, *35*, 409–420.

Logue, A. W. Taste aversion learning and the generality of the laws of learning. *Psychological Bulletin*, 1979, *86*, 276–296.

Mackintosh, N. J. *The psychology of animal learning*. London: Academic Press, 1974.

Mactutus, C. F., & Riccio, D. C. Hypothermia-induced retrograde amnesia: Role of body temperature upon memory retrieval. *Physiological Psychology*, 1978, *6*, 18–22.

Marlin, N. A., Berk, A. M., & Miller, R. R. Vulnerability of memory to electroconvulsive shock in relation to onset and offset of reinforcement. *Physiology and Behavior*, 1979, *22*, 217–221.

McDougall, W. Experimentelle beiträge zur lehre vom gedächtniss, by G. E. Müller & A. Pilzecker. *Mind*, 1901, *10*, 388–394.

McGaugh, J. L. Time-dependent processes in memory storage. *Science*, 1966, *153*, 1351–1358.

McGaugh, J. L., & Landfield, P. W. Delayed development of amnesia following ECS. *Physiology and Behavior*, 1970, *5*, 1109–1113.

Mendoza, M. E., & Adams, H. E. Does electroconvulsive shock produce retrograde amnesia? *Physiology and Behavior*, 1969, *4*, 307–309.

Miller, R. R., & Kasprow, W. Retrieval variability: Psychobiological sources and consequences. Manuscript submitted for publication, 1982.

Miller, R. R., & Marlin, N. A. Amnesia following electroconvulsive shock. In J. F. Kihlstrom & F. J. Evans (Eds.), *Disorders of memory function*. Hillsdale, N.J.: Lawrence Erlbaum Associates, 1979.

Miller, R. R., Misanin, J. R., & Lewis, D. J. Amnesia as a function of events during the learning–ECS interval. *Journal of Comparative and Physiological Psychology*, 1969, *67*, 145–148.

Miller, R. R., & Springer, A. D. Temporal course of amnesia in rats after electroconvulsive shock. *Physiology and Behavior*, 1971, *6*, 229–233.

Miller, R. R., & Springer, A. D. Amnesia, consolidation, and retrieval. *Psychological Review*, 1973, *80*, 69–79.

Misanin, J. R., Miller, R. R., & Lewis, D. J. Retrograde amnesia produced by electroconvulsive shock after reactivation of a consolidated memory trace. *Science*, 1968, *160*, 554–555.

Morris, C. D., Bransford, J. D., & Franks, J. J. Levels of processing versus transfer appropriate processing. *Journal of Verbal Learning and Verbal Behavior*, 1977, *16*, 519–533.

Mrosovsky, N. Lowered body temperature, learning and behaviour. In K. C. Fisher, A. R. Dawes, C. P. Lyman, E. Schonbaum, & F. E. Scott, Jr., (Eds.), *Mammalian hibernation III*. London: Oliver & Boyd, 1967.

Müller, G. E., & Pilzecker, A. Experimentelle beiträge zur lehre von gedächtnis. *Zeitschfirt für psychologie und physiologie der sinnesorgane*, 1900, *1*, Suppl. 1, 1–288.

Newton, J. M., & Wickens, D. D. Retroactive inhibition as a function of the temporal position of the interpolated learning. *Journal of Experimental Psychology*, 1956, *51*, 149–154.

Peterson, L., & Peterson, M. J. Short-term retention of individual verbal items. *Journal of Experimental Psychology*, 1959, *58*, 193–198.

Quartermain, D., McEwen, B. S., & Azmitia, E. C., Jr. Amnesia produced by electroconvulsive shock or cycloheximide: Conditions for recovery. *Science*, 1970, *169*, 683–686.

Rainbow, T. C., Hoffman, P. L., & Flexner, L. B. Studies of memory: A reevaluation in mice of the effects of inhibitors on the rate of synthesis of cerebral proteins as related to amnesia. *Pharmacology, Biochemistry and Behavior*, 1980, *12*, 79–8.

Robustelli, F., Geller, A., & Jarvik, M. E. Systematic analysis of the detention phenomenon in mice. *Journal of Comparative and Physiological Psychology*, 1972, *81*, 472–482.

Rohrbaugh, M., Riccio, D. C., & Arthur, A. Paradoxical enhancement of conditioned suppression. *Behavior Research and Therapy*, 1972, *10*, 125–130.

Roll, D. L., & Smith, J. U. Conditioned taste aversion in anesthetized rats. In M. E. P. Seligman & J. L. Hager (Eds.), *Biological boundaries of learning*. New York: Appleton-Century-Croft, 1972.

Rovee-Collier, C. K., & Sullivan, M. W. Organization of infant memory. *Journal of Experimental Psychology: Human Learning and Memory*, 1980, *6*, 798–807.

Rozin, P., & Ree, P. Long extension of effective CS-US interval by anesthesia between CS and US. *Journal of Comparative and Physiological Psychology*, 1972, *80*, 43–48.

Schneider, A. M., & Sherman, W. Amnesia: A function of the temporal relation of footshock to electroconvulsive shock. *Science*, 1968, *159*, 219–221.

Shallice, T., & Warrington, E. K. Independent functioning of verbal memory stores: A neurophysiological study. *Quarterly Journal of Experimental Psychology*, 1970, *22*, 261–273.

Spear, N. E. Memory storage factors leading to infantile amnesia. In G. Bower (Ed.), *The psychology of learning and memory (Vol. 13)*. New York: Academic Press, 1979.

Springer, A. D. Vulnerability of skeletal and autonomic manifestations of memory in the rat to electroconvulsive shock. *Journal of Comparative and Physiological Psychology*, 1975, *88*, 890–903.

Still, A. W. The effect of ECS upon spontaneous alternation in rats. *Physiology and Behavior*, 1974, *12*, 301–304.

Talland, G. A. *Deranged memory*. New York: Academic Press, 1965.

Teyler, T. (Ed.). *Brain and learning*. Dordrecht, Netherlands: Reidel, 1978.

Underwood, B. J. Attributes of memory. *Psychological Review*, 1969, *76*, 559–573.

Wooldridge, D. E. *The machinery of the brain*. New York: McGraw-Hill, 1963.

5 Consolidation as a Function of Retrieval

Norman E. Spear and Christian W. Mueller
State University of New York, Binghamton

This chapter arises from consideration of "consolidation"—what it is, what its characteristics are, when it occurs, and what its consequences are at the behavioral level. We shall not discuss *how* consolidation occurs—that is, we shall not discuss the neurophysiological events presumed to lead to the neurochemical and perhaps neuroanatomical changes that have long been supposed and more recently have begun to be physically identified in vitro at the synaptic level. We could offer nothing of interest on this topic in any case, and we seek in this chapter a level of generality at the behavioral level that is as yet inconsistent with what is known about the physiological basis of learning and memory. In short, we wish to discuss human as well as animal memory, and just as the cognitive analysis of memory processing in animals may be said to lag that with human subjects, so it is that the relationship between neurophysiological functioning and memory is understood less clearly for human than animal subjects.

It does not take a great deal of courage or imagination to assert that "consolidation" exists as a time-dependent associative process. Certainly, some orderly change in a neurophysiological substrate somewhere must accompany the orderly change in behavior seen when learning occurs and a memory is acquired; and, such a process must be time-dependent in the sense that its completion requires some measurable duration, because everything biological is. We suspect that such a consolidation process typically does not outlast the duration of processing required for sensation and perception (Johnson, 1983), but even in this sense it can be "time-dependent".

"Consolidation" surely is an appropriate term for an act of bringing together into a single whole the separable attributes (Underwood, 1969), gnostic units (Konorski, 1967), nodes, or whatever are the elements that combine to form a

111

memory that represents a particular episode. For such a representation the memory must be multidimensional because at least one attribute is needed to represent the context of the episode.

One might wish to add to consolidation the secondary meaning implied by most dictionaries, that of "strengthening," although precisely what is strengthened about the particular combination of attributes and how this is accomplished is itself debatable. The term begins to lose some of its effectiveness when used only in the sense of a unidimensional strengthening consistent with metaphors such as a weld between two metal objects or a solidifying bowl of Jello. Equally difficult for the integrity of the term are notions of consolidation durations that are unreasonably lengthy. We refer here to the notion that flat gradients of retrograde amnesia indicate consolidation periods lasting hours or even a day or two. If the neural substrates of, say, learning to press a lever for food were assumed to remain active during such a period, one wonders at one level why we do not observe behavioral reflection of this during the "consolidation period," rats in their cages pressing imaginary levers or jumping nonexistent hurdles. This sort of question has been raised in a somewhat different context by W. Richie Russell (1971), whose classical work on traumatic retrograde amnesia in humans is to a large extent responsible for the development of consolidation and its related concepts. Russell asked, "If the memory of how to swim involves circuits which never rest, why are we not constantly waving our arms and legs around in response to this constant activity? [p. 67]".

It is not our intention to describe the developmental history of the concept of consolidation. There are many sources for this; still among the best are two of the earlier papers that laid out the issues and evidence in historical fashion (Glickman, 1961, and McGaugh, 1966). A few historically oriented comments about rate of consolidation seem worthwhile nevertheless to clarify the perspective of this chapter.

Retrograde Amnesia Gradient.   The slope of the retrograde amnesia gradient describes the relationship between the probability of behavioral manifestation of an acquired memory and length of the interval between the subject's exposure to an episode to be remembered and that to an amnesic agent. We assume that such gradients so far have provided no information as to the rate of consolidation of a memory. On a number of occasions and for many years, James McGaugh, the most prolific of the leaders in the experimental and theoretical analysis of consolidation, has stated this quite clearly (e.g., McGaugh & Dawson, 1971). One basic difficulty in concluding about consolidation rate from a gradient of amnesia is accounting for the gradient when the amnestic agent is shown to act on retrieval, not storage, of the memory. The doubtful value of relating consolidation rates to the slope of the gradients of retrograde amnesia can be illustrated for the case of human memory processing through recent data gathered by Squire, Slater and Chace (1975). Squire et al. assessed the influence of multiple electroshock treatments on relatively remote memories for past events of public knowledge related to TV programs and race horses. Squire's data indicate that although the deficiencies caused by these treatments are more porfound for the more recently acquired memories, significant deficits can be recorded for remembering events that occurred several years prior to the shock treatments. Surely no one today would seriously consider the interpretation that memories for events several years past are not yet consolidated by humans.

Utility of the Concept.   Another opinion we hold to be a general truth is that as a specialized, time-dependent process, consolidation has not been a particularly useful concept in studies of human memory. It would in any case seem difficult to defend the view that such a concept has formed the basis of many theories or the topic of many experiments dealing with human memory, at least in recent years (cf. Kleinsmith & Kaplan, 1963).

Nature of Consolidation.   We hold consolidation to be an explicitly automatic process that is quite impervious to competing effects of environmental events, except for those that are exceptionally traumatic physiologically. We therefore exclude from this concept all varieties of special encoding or rehearsal that are clearly sensitive to discrete stimuli, general instructions, and the like. This view is like that stated by Russell (1971), that "many memories are strengthened with the passage of time regardless of their importance to the individual [p. 64–65]" and that "the so-called on-going process of consolidation occurs unconsciously [p. 73]." While it is probably the case that no one will disagree with this characterization of consolidation as automatic and inevitable-barring trauma, we feel it needs be established here because our discussion will consider both animals and humans. Although the "controlled" or "voluntary" processing by humans obviously can have profound effects on their learning and remembering, it is in terms of relatively automatic processing that general principles of memory processing seem more likely to accommodate both human and animal data (cf. Wagner, 1981).

Consolidation Rates.   It might seem, therefore, that the time-dependent feature of consolidation would be useful only for the study of explicitly automatic processing by humans or lower animals and that the temporal parameters of consolidation will be specific to this class of processing (without, for the moment, debating whether animals might not also engage in controlled processing, as suggested by Grant, 1981 and Maki, 1981, for instance). We question such reasoning. What seems still less reasonable in comparative studies of the rate-dependent nature of consolidation is the implicit assumption that consolidation rates will be slower for phylogenetically lower animals. There has seemed little hesitancy to suggest consolidation durations on the order of an hour or longer for the rat, for example, whereas such long durations would seem unlikely for humans, for whom the estimates are more on the order of "ten seconds [p. 66]" or "within a few minutes [Russell, 1971, p. 73]." Such a simple assumption of consistent individual differences in rate of consolidation seems to us very likely wrong. The information processed by the rat is of a singular, adaptive type, as is that selected by the fish, cat or infant human, and there is no a priori reason to expect that in any of these cases, the rate of processing-what-they-select-to-process will differ from one species or age to another. In a later section, we return to this issue of individual differences in consolidation rates.

"Consolidation" and its Function.   These days one sees the term "consolidation" used perhaps most frequently in the conglomerate literature termed "neuroscience." Here the term is used almost as a sort of buzz-word substitute for "learning." Yet, a term something like "consolidation" seems needed in one aspect ot this literature. When dealing with the real prospect of a neurophysiological substrate of an animal's representation of its experience—when dealing, at least hypothetically, with a physical-entity-that-is-a-memory—it is hard to use the alternate term, "learning." One does not "learn" a memory; one acquires it or loses it, stores it or retrieves it. It seems important to recognize, however, that such language implies little more than something about the "metaphor of memory" underlying the viewpoint or conceptual framework of those using it (cf. Roediger, 1980).

Finally at the functional level, there has been little debate about what a "consolidation" process accomplishes. There has been virtual unanimity that what it accomplishes is to somehow establish the memory in storage—to "form" the memory, which is usually taken as synonymous with "storing" it initially. The point of our paper is to emphasize that, in addition, the important features of consolidation almost certainly act at the time of retrieval of a memory as well, and with very important consequences.

CONSOLIDATION ASSOCIATED WITH MEMORY RETRIEVAL: A THESIS

If our emphasis on how a consolidation process acts at the time of memory retrieval is surprising, it is because the term "consolidation" has been used conventionally in reference to the acquisition, input, initial storage, and learning of new associations, memories, episodes, and so forth. We shall argue that a similar or identical process can be anticipated to operate whenever a memory is retrieved or, more generally, made active.

The recent history of experimental psychology has taught us to be wary in supposing that a particular variable or process affects retention solely through its operation on initial storage of the memory. In terms of human memory, a warning to this effect has been stated most effectively in a large number of papers by Tulving and his associates (e.g., Tulving, 1976, 1979; Tulving & Osler, 1968; Tulving & Thomson, 1973; also, see Spear, 1976). The gist of this warning may be derived from the principle of encoding specificity. This principle states that what is remembered depends on the compatability between how an individual encodes a particular episode for storage and the stimulus circumstances at the time of retrieval. Stated more specifically (Tulving, 1979), "The compatibility relation between the trace and the cue, as a necessary condition of recollection of an event, is determined by specific encoding operations at the time of study and not by the properties of cues and target items, and their relations, in semantic memory [p. 408]." The point is that factors such as prior association strength between elements of an episode (i.e., meaningfulness) or the nature of the subject's orientation with regard to how materials are to be encoded (i.e., levels of processing) play only a secondary role in remembering. Their effectiveness depends on the requirements at the time of memory retrieval and the circumstances of the retention test. Such a principle now seems equally applicable to basic conditioning in animals (Spear, 1981). This is in one sense consistent with what has been found to determine retention and forgetting historically. For instance, task variables that affect the learning of lists of discrete verbal units—variables such as meaningfulness or intralist similarity—may have profound effects on learning efficiency and memory storage initially but little or none on later retention (e.g., Underwood, 1972). Similarly, levels or distinctiveness of processing for initial memory storage has seemed to have relatively little influence on later retention once initial memory storage is equated.

These points are presented as a precedent for the view that one cannot hope to understand remembering solely in terms of processes that occur at the time of original learning. Furthermore, the processes and events of memory retrieval must be considered in terms of their relation to those of original memory storage if we are to comprehend how a memory becomes manifested in behavior.

The point of departure from consideration of the consolidation process solely as an event of memory storage is achieved through consideration of "semantic" compared to "episodic" memory (Tulving, 1972). It is only through appeal to semantic memory, to what has been perceived and learned previously or to what we are relatively hard wired to perceive or learn, that we can interpret new episodes for storage in memory. It makes little difference whether this interpretation is said to be done through a "schema" because of "perceptual learning," or simply that to learn a set of verbal units we must at some level make contact with what we have known about the letters that make up the units. There will be general agreement that neither animals nor humans acquire totally "new" memories in the sense that all memory attributes for all aspects of an episode are experienced for the first time (perhaps even among newborns, for practical purposes). Each of the animal's attributes or representations of individual events in the episode is therefore a product of either some transfer from prior experience or a perceptual modification in accord with prior experience. Although "semantic'' memory may not be the best term for animals, it can be used to refer generally to memories that have no contextual referent as to their acquisition. On this basis, any ''consolidation'' process must always include some retrieval from some sort of semantic memory store that includes general, undatable knowledge in such a way as to provide expression of the residue of prior experience. What must occur in this process is the rearrangement of the elements in terms of their relationships, and we see no a priori reason to expect that the principles of such rearrangements should depend on the nature of the elements (e.g., Postman, 1972).

To summarize this point of departure, we assume that consolidation (initial storage into memory) must include some reprocessing of previously acquired experience, some expression of the residue of prior learning. Probably animals and persons, even young ones, never encounter a thoroughly new episode in the sense that nothing about it is consistent with their knowledge and dispositions. We do not acquire totally ''new'' memories in the sense that all attributes are experienced for the first time, with no relatable association to previously acquired attributes.

It is clearly difficult to test this sort of basic assumption. There are in any case no data that can address it directly. Probably, though, there will be little disagreement that what is learned is largely a new combination of old representations that lead to a new representation. The question then becomes: What is the ''consolidation'' process through which previously acquired memory attributes become reorganized and integrated under the heading of a particular context?

A central assumption of this paper is that whatever the consolidation process is, it operates during memory retrieval as well as memory storage; that is, consolidation takes place when output is required in the same way as when input was established. Just as previously acquired memories are accessed for interpretation of an ''episode-to-be-remembered,'' so is the previously acquired memory accessed at memory retrieval, and vice versa; for us (as per Jacoby & Craik, 1979), ''retrieval is regarded as being analogous to a second encoding [p. 18].'' From this assumption it is reasonable to expect that modification of a previously acquired memory can be accomplished in accord with contemporary events at the time of its retrieval, just as previously stored information is changed to accommodate storage of a new memory when it is acquired. There is growing evidence for this (e.g., Gordon, 1981, Loftus, 1979). It is our thesis, then, that consolidation occurs when a memory is retrieved, as well as when it was stored originally (cf. Spear, 1981).

The remainder of this paper is intended to evaluate this thesis in terms of function similarities between the consequences of retrieval and those of initial memory storage and to discuss implications of this for learning and retention. Emphasis will be given to data gathered from normal human subjects, with only the briefest allusions to experiments with animals. First, however, we should specify our orientation. We have found it difficult to discuss these issues and data without burdensome qualification to accommodate basic assumptions about how remembering proceeds. We therefore take a few sentences to describe briefly our conceptual framework for this chapter, because this will avoid the need for the repeated qualifications.

ORIENTATION AND CONCEPTUAL FRAMEWORK

We approach the issues of this chapter from the observation that storage of a memory can be revealed only through its retrieval. We recognize that the temporal relationship between when a treatment is delivered and the time of memory storage or memory retrieval is not sufficient to indicate which of the two processes, storage or retrieval, the treatment will affect. A number of treatments administered to animals at the time of memory storage have now been determined to have their effect on later manifestation of the memory, not through alteration in memory storage but, perhaps, in its retrieval (Lewis, 1969, 1979: Miller & Springer, 1973; Spear, 1971, 1981). An analogous set of results has emerged within the study of human memory. It has been determined, for instance, that a variety of manipulations at the time of testing that alter the probability of recalling or recognizing words learned earlier, do not affect retrieval absolutely, but do so only relative to the circumstances of initial memory storage (e.g., Tulving & Thomson, 1971, 1973). Similarly, variation in conditions at the time of memory storage can have effects on later recall that are not at all absolute but only relative to the circumstances of the retention test. A number of experiments illustrating this principle have been reviewed by Tulving (1979) with particular reference to the powerful effects that a subject's mnemonic operations at the time of memory storage can have on later recall. It is becoming increasingly clear that this effect on recall must depend at least in part on the sorts of mnemonic operations in which the subject engages at the time of memory retrieval (Fisher & Craik, 1977; Morris, Bransford, & Franks, 1977).

Stated simply, our position is that "retention" (degree of manifestation of an acquired memory at the time of a retention test) is governed by this simple, ancient principle: The more similar the circumstances are that comprise the episode originally learned and those present when memory retrieval is required, the greater the retention. The term "circumstances" encompasses a great deal. We do not pretend to know what these are; that is, what is necessary and what is sufficient in terms of commonality at storage and retrieval. We do know that it must take into account, for instance, contextual circumstances that are apparently redundant to acquisition of the target memory, as well as the cognitive operations of the subject (Spear, 1978; Tulving, 1979). Our fundamental assumption, then, is that retention is determined by an interaction between the conditions of memory storage and those of its retrieval. One way to state this is that retention depends on the particular number, proportion, or kinds of events noticed by the subject during the retention test in relation to those events of memory storage represented as attributes of the acquired memory. Retrieval of the particular target attribute might depend on a redintegration process, then, that promotes arousal of the target contingent upon arousal of certain other of these memory attributes (whatever number, proportion, or kind might be required). This is not certain, but such a redintegration process will be considered a possibility.

Finally, with particular reference to "consolidation" as a mechanism that converts a temporary trace into a permanent one, an active memory into a passive memory, short-term to long-term storage, or whatever, one way to characterize this chapter is in its concern for how the opposite kind of conversion might occur. Is the same kind of mechanism necessary for a memory's conversion from a passive to an active state? We therefore examine evidence that might indicate whether the same sort of "consolidation" process occurs in memory retrieval, when a passive memory is made active, as in initial perception and storage of the episode to be remembered, when an active memory becomes passive.

EXPERIMENTAL PARADIGMS AND SPECIFIC QUESTIONS

The core question in this chapter is whether processes of initial memory storage and later memory retrieval have common features. We shall therefore focus on data and ideas that indicate similarities (or differences) in the processes of storage and retrieval. Our hypothesis is that a consolidation process is common to memory storage and memory retrieval. There appear to be at least three experimental paradigms through which one might test this empirically.

Acquisition and Retrieval Similarities.   One approach is to test a corollary of this hypothesis—that characteristics of an active memory will not differ just after it is retrieved in comparison to just after it was acquired originally (cf. Spear, 1976). Tests have been conducted largely with animal subjects (one used human infants; Rovee-Collier, Sullivan, Enright, Lucas, & Fogen, 1980). The results of several of these studies have been unable to firmly reject this hypothesis. In other words, many (but not all) of these experiments indicated that recently acquired and retained memories have similar characteristics (for some reviews, see Gordon, 1981; Riccio & Ebner, 1981; Spear, 1981). It is not difficult to suggest that more studies must be completed before one can be conclusive about this, and certainly, one would like to see more experiments with human subjects on this problem. There is an advantage in using animal subjects or nonverbal infants for these studies, however, because unlike humans presented verbal materials, subjects in these experiments are presumably unable to reproduce critical stimuli for self-presentation at the time of retrieval. This circumstance permits better experimental control over the events to which the subject is exposed at the time of memory retrieval. This point is mentioned here because it becomes a problem for analysis in two of the other paradigms that have addressed our central question.

Qualitative Changes.   A second paradigm has tested qualitative changes that can occur in a memory at the time of its retrieval. Studies applying this paradigm typically have not included an explicit comparison between the consequences of retrieval and study. This paradigm includes three stages: first, establish acquisition of a memory for a particular episode; second, require retrieval of that memory in the context of new information presented to alter the supject's memorial representation of the original episode; and third, test for retention in order to determine the influence of this latter treatment (e.g., Loftus, 1979). There is no reason in principle why one could not explicitly compare the consequences of adultering a retrieved memory with those of storing the adultered memory originally, but apparently this has not been of interest.

Storage and Retrieval Outcomes   A third paradigm, the one most frequently applied, has assessed in depth a dominant common outcome of presenting a particular episode for memory storage or assessment of memory retrieval through a retention test. These studies have compared the increment in retention that follows a study (storage) compared to a test (retrieval) trial. This paradigm has been tested almost exclusively with human subjects, and there has developed a sizable literature on this problem. We shall give primary emphasis to this paradigm—comparisons of the effects of study and test trials—because this includes the largest base of data gathered with humans and so, for our purposes, provides the best opportunity for analysis. Our specific questions have emerged from this primary observation: One consequence of a test for retention of a set of verbal materials learned previously is an improvement in the retention of these materials, as assessed by a later, similar test.

A number of our questions arise because humans given a retention test have most often been required to *reproduce* the verbal units they remember; this provides the objective evidence that they have in fact remembered. This reproduction, however, could also serve as a re-presentation of the materials to the subject. The manner of presentation might differ orthographically from the occasion for original memory storage, such as, spoken by the subject at testing compared to visual presentation for study. It is no easy task analytically to answer even the simple question of whether the orthographic difference makes a difference in recall. The fundamental impediment to analysis is that the subject, not the experimenter, selects what to retrieve, and so comparisons to determine the effect of retrieval are confounded by item selection and by subject selection.

We will focus on the effects of retrieval on later recall. In doing so we will also encounter the following questions: Is re-presentation of the original materials, even if only as produced by the subject in correspondingly different form than that of original presentation, a necessary component of a test trial for an increment in subsequent retention? Does the mode of subject-produced re-presentations (e.g., visual, auditory), in relation to that of the original presentation of the material, influence the effect of a test trial on later retention? Within a given set of materials previously presented for learning, some will be remembered at the initial test and some will not; will the result of this test change in any way the subsequent retention of items *not* remembered on the first test? Does the nature of the original test (e.g., recognition vs. recall) influence the increment in retention that results from this test? How do the operations that the subjects exert for memory retrieval influence the retention increment that accompanies the test trial? Do environmental or subject variables introduced at the time of a test trial have the same effect on later retention as they have when presented during initial study? And, does retrieval of some items from a word list episode facilitate later recall of the others, as one might expect from a redintegration process, or does retrieval of some *impair* recall of others due to a process of output interference? Within the context of the following review of the literature, these and related questions are considered.

CONSOLIDATION AS A FUNCTION OF RETRIEVAL: A SELECTED REVIEW OF THE HUMAN MEMORY LITERATURE

A test for learning is both a crucial and interesting event. Even without feedback as to what is the correct answer, a learning test obliges the learner to revive past memories and to act on those that are remembered. Moreover, consequences of a test—in particular, successful remembering and the attendant expression of a reactivated memory in behavior—tend to promote later retention of the original event. In the most detailed account of this effect currently available, Cooper and Monk (1976) liken the benefits of a memory test primarily to consolidation. The same analogy has been drawn by others (e.g., Donaldson, 1971; Landauer, 1969; Rosner, 1970; Whitten & Bjork, 1977). Unfortunately, the implications of such a notion have never been fully worked out. One goal of our chapter, we hope, will be stimulate renewed efforts toward achieving these ends.

Our main purpose is to examine the claim that retrieving a memory improves its subsequent retrieval. We are particularly interested in isolating the boundary conditions that delimit this phenomenon. It is surely not universal. Though barely a handful of the relevant factors are known, nonetheless, some generalizations appear warranted. A few, indeed, may turn out to have important consequences for theories of what it takes to establish or consolidate a memory.

Background

Our major concern is with the retrieval of a to-be-remembered event, such as the occurrence of a word in a list, and what effect that has on the probability of its recovery or re-retrieval later on. We therefore do not consider extensively reaction-time measures of performance nor the effects of retrieval from semantic memory (e.g., Erdelyi, Buschke, & Finkelstein, 1977; Gardiner, Craik, &

Bleasdale, 1973; Loftus & Loftus, 1974; Slamecka & Graf, 1978). We wish, also, to focus our discussion by limiting it mainly to tests of recall.

Recognition tests are downplayed for two reasons. First, they do not entail response reproduction and so may be said to bypass or circumvent the need for subjects to use certain retrieval mechanisms (e.g., Anderson & Bower, 1972; Bahrick, 1970; Hogan & Kintsch, 1971; Underwood, 1969). Second, a test of recognition memory exposes training stimuli once again to the subject and so can lead to new learning merely because the procedure for testing is effectively the procedure for study of the list (e.g., Bowyer & Humphreys, 1979; Broadbent & Broadbent, 1977: Humphreys & Bowyer, 1980). We concede that neither of these possibilities is necessarily true. By acknowledging them, we seek merely to strengthen our analysis. Ours is but the consensus view that retrieval processes are involved, if involved at all, to a maximum in the course of recall, rather than recognition, testing. If there is no qualitative discontinuity between the two procedures (see, for example, Tulving & Watkins, 1974; Watkins & Todres, 1978), then whatever our paper has to say about recall should apply equally well in principle to recognition. That is one direction in which research may already be headed (e.g., Mandler & Rabinowitz, 1981).

To what extent retrieval of a particular memory facilitates its later retrieval is only one of a number of possible questions that could have been raised about the effects of recall testing. It is essential to the point of our review that we distinguish this issue from other, partly related issues. Three topics can be identified: test-retest reliability, potentiation, and output interference.

Reliability of Measurement

Does recall on one occasion help to predict the accuracy of a second attempt at retrieval? In part, our inquiry resembles a psychometric examination into the stability of an individual measurement over time (and situations, if the testing procedures vary). The two matters are noticeably distinct, however. The critical comparison in our case is not between successive tests. Rather it is an experimental problem we pose, for its solution requires close attention to the difference between items previously tested and those not previously tested.

Three caveats are in order regarding the kind of evidence that will be valuable to us. First, the criterion test and the initial test need not be identical and transfer between these tests may or may not coincide with the magnitude of their differences. Second, there may be surreptitious initial recall for those items not actually tested initially, depending on the effectiveness of the control task and subjects' intentions. Third, when initial recall for initially tested items is covert—for example, when subjects are asked to rehearse silently to themselves—the number of items initially retrieved is unknown and has to be inferred. Unless it is safe to assume an appreciably higher frequency of initial retrieval among those items actually tested and those not, the data will not effectively reflect the effects of such retrieval.

In the memory literature, the reliability issue has been around a long time. Witness Brown's query in 1923: "To what extent is memory measured by a single recall?" The answer continues to prove elusive. When recall is tested more than once in succession, it sometimes fails—quite dramatically in the case of items presented at the end of a single-trial free recall list (Lewis, 1971)—and it sometimes does not. When recall grows over a series of tests in the absence of repeated study, the phenomenon—as pointed out some time ago (Postman & Phillips, 1961)—is easily mistaken for reminiscence. In contemporary jargon, it has become known as "hypermnesia" (e.g., Erdelyi & Becker, 1974; Erdelyi et al., 1977). Buschke and his associates (e.g., Buschke, 1974, 1975; Fuld & Buschke, 1976) have probably traced this effect further than anyone else. They have shown that as long as the subject's motivation is maintained, free recall increases practically indefinitely with additional opportunities for recall. Roediger (1978) has reported that total recall time—the cumulative duration of attempted retrieval—contributes substantially to this pattern of results. (For similar data, see Coke, 1971; Donaldson, 1971; Nelson & MacLeod, 1974.) In comparison, recall of paired associates is relatively stable (e.g., Bregman & Wiener, 1970; Izawa, 1966, 1967, 1970) and less affected by recall time (e.g., Underwood, 1948)—although even these apparent differences must be interpreted cautiously, with proper consideration for the degree of original learning (Underwood, 1964).

Potentiation

When a subject's level of recall is observed to rise over successive tests, some of which are separated by study trials, the result is typically attributed to learning. There are various aspects to this process, of course, and one of them is that recall tests "potentiate" the learning that occurs on subsequent presentations of the study list. Potentiation, then, refers to an increment in the effectiveness of activities that enable one to learn on any given study trial. It is not so much retrieval that testing augments in this way as it is a host of encoding operations active at the time items are subsequently re-presented. The term "mathemagenesis" has been advanced to describe an analogous phenomenon in acquiring information from text (Rothkopf, 1966: Rothkopf & Bisbicos, 1967).

The ratio of study to test trials and the nature of their distribution in a training sequence are variables that contribute to the potentiation effect, i.e., the growth of recall over a series of post-input output phases. Among the classic studies in this area are those of Skaggs (1920) and Trow (1928). Tulving (1967) has done a great deal to bring back and encourage research along these lines in free recall (e.g., Birnbaum & Eichner, 1971: Bregman & Wiener, 1970: Coke, 1971; Hudson & Hudson, 1977; Hudson, Solomon, & Davis, 1972: Lachman & Laughery, 1968; Rosner, 1970; Sanford, 1979; Simmons, 1973). Other researchers (e.g., Izawa, 1968, 1969, 1970; Richardson & Gropper, 1964; Zavortink & Keppel, 1969) have undertaken comparable projects using paired associate materials—or, in one notable exception, serial lists (Martin, Fleming, & Nally, 1978).

Nearly all of the experiments just mentioned share a somewhat peculiar methodology. In a typical piece of research, subjects are assigned to groups having different arrangements of study (S) and test (T) trials. The total number of trials is held constant across groups. Thus, one group might experience a sequence of trials in the form SSTSST and another in the form STTSTT. One weakness of this design is that members of each group are liable to adopt a particular strategy in order to cope with their anticipated sequence of learning and remembering tasks. This drawback has been strongly criticized by Cooper and Monk (1976): "Some subjects will experience predominantly study trials while others will experience predominantly test trials. This may lead to the formation of learning sets that will affect performance in ways quite separate from the effects of study or test phases *per se* [p. 144]." Whitten and Bjork (1977) have recognized the same shortcoming. Furthermore, there is independent evidence from the so-called priority effect (Tulving & Watkins, 1974) that the presence or absence of a test carries over to affect subsequent acquisition of related material in a manner that goes beyond testing itself. Recent work (Allen & Arbak, 1976; Arkes & Lyons, 1979) indicates that the size of this effect is mediated by differential subject expectancies as to whether a tested list, in opposition to a list not tested initially, will or will not be subsequently tested.

By keeping the number of study and test trials constant, the research covered above has explored a form of the total-time hypothesis (Bugelski, 1962). This supposition holds, in the words of Tulving (1967), "that the amount of immediate post-input recall . . . depends primarily on the total amount of time spent on the task, and that it is relatively little affected, if at all by the distribution of this time between studying and recalling the material [p. 181]." According to Bregman and Wiener (1970), such a pronouncement suits free recall better than paired associate recall. Striking confirmation of that statement has been provided by Hudson et al. (1972, Experiment 1), who tested one group of subjects after 11 presentations of the study list and another group after an initial study phase, nine free recall tests, and a second input presentation. They report no significant difference between groups on the Trial 12 test of recall. This outcome contrasts sharply with the finding (Izawa, 1970, Experiment 5) that more than seven tests in a row are less than optimal for paired associates. One reason for the discrepancy between these outcomes is perhaps that, as we noticed earlier, cumulative recall time has more impact on free than paired associate retention.

Output Interference

Although recall of an item is a good sign of continued retention for that item, it does not always bode well for retrieval of other words in the same list. The act of recall can lower the accessibility of remaining list members. Free recall is highly susceptible to such an inhibitory effect because subjects control the order in which particular items are, or are not, remembered (Dalezman, 1976). In the earliest work on this phenomenon, Tulving and Arbuckle (1963, 1966) used paired associates to manipulate the order in which target words were probed. They found that the proportion recalled was inversely related to probe position and named their discovery "output interference."

Subsequent research has corroborated the basic phenomenon and extended it to include lists of categorized words (e.g., articles of clothing, birds, furniture, musical instruments, sports, and so on). Recall of these materials has generally been tested using the name of each category as a probe, or "retrieval cue" (Tulving & Pearlstone, 1966). At least three features of output inferences have been established. First, cued recall deteriorates across successive output positions, defined by the order of category labels at test (e.g., Dong, 1972; Roediger, 1973; Smith, 1973, Smith, D'Agostino, & Reid, 1970). This decrement cannot be ascribed merely to the passage of time (Roediger & Schmidt, 1980), nor is it the product of just any interpolated verbal activity (Smith, 1971; see especially Table 2). Second, the provision of cues for some but not all categories in a list renders less accessible the noncued categories. This effect increases with the relative number of cued categories that are recalled and is evidenced by recall of fewer and fewer noncued categories rather than fewer words within each re-called, noncued category (Parker & Warren, 1974; Roediger, 1978). Third, providing members of a target category at the time of recall—"part-set cuing" (Mueller & Watkins, 1977)—hinders retrieval for the rest of the items in the cued set (e.g., Roediger, 1973; Slamecka, 1972). Watkins (1975) has shown that roughly as much damage results whether "cues" emanate from within the study list or from outside it, although they must belong to the set whose category name is given at recall (Mueller & Watkins, 1977, Experiment 1). This effect, too, increases with the relative number of "cue" items that are supplied—that is, given free to the subject as part-set cues (Roediger, 1973: Rundus, 1973: Watkins, 1975).

The last two findings give us pause, for they bear no obvious resemblance to the first (that is, to output interference). In one case, category cues hamper recall of noncued categories; in the other, part-set cues hamper recall of items remaining within the target set. Strictly speaking, the cuing manipulations are responsible for these damages (given that subjects try to use them, of course; Roediger, 1978, Experiment 1). It is our opinion, however, that the same phenomenon underlies all three observations above and that all are capable of being understood within a single conceptual framework. The scheme we have in mind is that of cue-overload theory (Watkins, 1979; Watkins & Watkins, 1975, 1976), which has sufficient breadth to encompass retrieval deficits not only in recall of categorized lists but also in recall of pre-experimentally unrelated words (e.g., Mueller & Watkins, 1977). In the following, "cue" has two usages that are not to be confused. On the one hand, it refers to a theoretical construct—that which effectively mediates retrieval of an item; on the other, it refers to an operational definition—whatever information the subject receives on a memory test, useful or not. To differentiate these meanings, the first type of cue is sometimes called "functional" and the second "nominal."

The cue-overload principle (Watkins, 1979) maintains that "as a memory cue comes to subsume more and more events, its probability of effecting recall of any particular event declines [p. 364]." It does not rule out the possibility that recall of an item is mediated by more than one functional cue. Three supplemental and fairly routine assumptions are needed, as well, to interpret the data on output interference. First, we assume there is a cue corresponding to the study list as a whole; just as each category contains its own constituent exemplars, the list subsumes categories. Second, the contents of this cue are assumed to represent the list and not other features of the experimental situation (i.e., the context; cf. Anderson & Bower, 1972); adjunct contextual information thereby offers a source of effective retrieval cues that make contact with items in several different categories at once. Third, the receipt of a cue word is assumed to be functionally equivalent to the recall of that word; both constitute events to be subsumed by an effective retrieval cue. The immediate result of a word's occurrence—whether probe or target, experimenter-generated or subject-produced—is to overload the functional cue, whose subsequent effectiveness is proportionally reduced. As Watkins (1975) has shown, part-set cues taken from the study list and given to subjects at recall behave the same as events (i.e., probe words) occurring no where else in the experiment except at test.

The concept of cue overload helps to make sense of the results encountered above. First, within-category recall is less efficient for categories tested late in the output sequence because words recalled at early positions progressively burden the context cue (or cues); a similar idea, focusing on the breakdown of overworked spatial/temporal cues, has been tentatively put forth by Roediger (1973; also Roediger & Schmidt, 1980). Second, recall of categories is adversely affected by cuing some but not all of them because cued recall of some will load the list cue; the effectiveness of the list cue at eliciting further recall of noncued categories is then curtailed. Third, part-set cues obstruct recall because they overload the category cue governing within-set retrieval of probe and target items. In short, cue overload occurs with respect to each of three functional cues: the context, the list, and the category. Additionally, the last two detrimental effects become aggravated—in line with predictions from cue-overload theory—by increasing the number of "events" (cued categories and within-category probes, respectively) that each functional cue subsumes.

Output interference—or cue overload, assuming that is a valid conceptualization of the data—has important implications for the study of positive as well as negative effects of retrieval. Among other things, the phenomenon warns against the indiscriminate comparison of retention for items previously tested (PT) and those not previously tested (NPT). The danger resides in that the crucial aspect of this comparison is between PT items actually retrieved previously and NPT items that would have been retrieved had they been tested. In both cases, otherwise recallable items are not always recalled (for lack of time if no other reason) and the number of nonrecalled items may be rather high. Despite these obstacles, initial output ought to be more substantial among PT than NPT items. Output interference threatens, however, to offset any gains expected on the basis of prior retrieval. Specifically, it acts to depress recall of items that have not yet been retrieved. If the control task in the NPT condition is too easy relative to the memory task in the PT condition, nonrecalled items will be more easily recovered as a result of the nontesting treatment.

The following example illustrates the differential effects of test-like activities in comparison to an explicit test of learned items that later are target items for recall. Roediger (1978, Experiment 3) tested free recall of a categorized list after a period of 5 min in which subjects either read a prose passage, remembered states of the union, recalled a list of unrelated words, or were cued to recall half the target categories. The first three tasks did not involve tests of later target material, but the fourth did, with regard to only noncued categories. Though only the NPT categories had to be retrieved on the criterion test, the last group of subjects did worse than the other three groups (which did equally well). This result indicates that initial testing of some material can have a debilitating influence on subsequent recall of nonrecalled material. The impact that previous testing has in any given situation is, therefore, difficult to assess because one must take into account not only the positive effect of recall on recalled items but also the relative magnitude of the negative effects of nonrecall on nonrecalled items engendered by the PT and NPT manipulations.

We cannot safely ignore what control subjects do in place of an initial test for some items. It is perilous to assume that a demanding interpolated task has the same effect on subsequent performance as the act of recall has for nonrecalled items. As pointed out forcefully by Watkins and Todres (1978), "for any given intervening activity this assumption is almost certainly wrong (p. 623)" (see also Roediger & Schmidt, 1980). Such advice cautions us to scrutinize closely the experimental and control treatments being run. Thus alerted, we dare say that an unmet methodological challenge is to equate, in a reliable fashion, procedures used for items or subjects in an initially tested condition and those in the not tested control condition for their effects on the retention of nonrecalled but potentially recallable items.

Consolidation at Retrieval: The Experimental Evidence

Only in recent years have experimenters begun to make reasonably unbiased comparisons between PT and NPT conditions. A great deal of this research was, unfortunately, never intended to focus on the study of test effects.[1] As a conse-

---

[1](e.g., Ellis, 1977; Engle & Mobley, 1976; Masson & McDaniel, 1981; Matthews & Tulving, 1973; Poltrock & MacLeod, 1977; Watkins & Watkins, 1975).

quence, the field is badly fragmented with divergent aims and perplexing terminology. Despite the outward signs of such disorder, there may be discerned three
recurring themes: degree or completeness of retrieval, difficulty or effortfulness
of the retrieval attempt, and depth or level of retrieval processing. We would add
a fourth: distinctiveness, which highlights the interaction between successive
retrievals. Each concept specifies a different set of necessary and sufficient
conditions for consolidation to occur during retrieval. The remainder of our
chapter is devoted to an appraisal of these ideas and their empirical support.

Degree of Retrieval

There is no easy way to determine which characteristics of the retention test
take part in consolidating a memory, but one thing seems certain: Testing consolidates nothing unless something is retrieved. Exactly what and how much has to
be retrieved are questions reminiscent of the controversy surrounding incremental versus one-trial learning (e.g., Postman, 1963). Though it would be novel to
carry on such a debate in the present setting, little stands to be gained by
recounting old history. The issue is basically whether or not learned materials are
retrieved, or consolidated, in an all-or-none fashion. For lack of a better alternative, we assume they are. The alternative would have been that items vary in the
degree to which each of them is retrieved and thereby in the degree to which
retrieval benefits their subsequent retention. But no one has yet reported any
evidence to convince us that partial retrieval leads to the recollection of previously incomplete memories, however appealing this possibility might be for
retrieval theories that include a redintegration component. Indeed, "fragments"
of a memory are likely to be output consistently or not at all across successive
recall occasions (Jones, 1978).

Our position is identical to that espoused by proponents of the "reduction
method" (e.g., Ogilvie, Tulving, Paskowitz, & Jones, 1980; Tulving &
Watkins, 1975: Watkins & Tulving, 1978). This technique allows for the analysis of memory using two or more different types of probe or test format. The
object is to describe the memory trace underlying patterns of success and failure
observed on sequential tests. According to Tulving and Watkins (1975), "the
effects of retrieving a trace on one occasion on retrieving it on a subsequent
occasion represents an interesting research problem, but whatever these effects
are they are not relevant to the reduction method [p. 267]." Put somewhat more
bluntly, Watkins (1979) asserts that the method rests on "the recall-or-nothing
assumption, which says that any effects of the first set of cues on the second set
will be mediated by only those events actually recalled in the first test [p. 356]."
We are aware of no findings that compel an opposite viewpoint.

Several observations, however, are seemingly at odds with our "recall-or-
nothing" conception of test-trial effects on human memory. The first observation
is that our hypothesis may run contrary to multidimensional theories of the
memory trace (e.g., Underwood, 1969). But that is hardly the case. To conceptualize a memory as an aggregate of semi-autonomous features does not make

those features totally independent of one another; nor does it demand any special characteristics for their dependence. Their status as attributes of a single memory implies, rather, that they subserve the larger representation. It is quite likely that individual components of an item may be activated in memory, and trace retrieval may depend on the nature and the number of elements so engaged. Yet in the final analysis it is only measurement of the whole unit as remembered, or not, that provides evidence pertaining to our topic. Thus, a multi-attribute theory is compatible with the proposition that items must be recovered fairly intact in order to expedite their later retrieval.

The second observation is that tip-of-the-tongue (TOT) states at encoding have been found to predict subsequent memory performance. To be specific, Gardiner et al. (1973) demonstrated that study-word occurrences preceded by the report of a TOT experience had a significantly higher level of final recall than non-TOT target items. Notwithstanding the correlational character of such research, it is tempting to identify a TOT state with the activation of some but not all of an item's attributes (cf. Gardiner et al., 1973) and to identify the advantage of TOT items in recall with the beneficial effects of imperfect prior retrieval. That would be a mistake, however, because strictly speaking, there are item and subject selection artifacts as well as uncontrolled sources of potentiation contaminating these data. In this sense, therefore, a causal link has never been established between the TOT condition and its reputed consequences. We do not know what permits the TOT items to be rather well recalled, but whatever it is may operate in spite of—not because of—partially successful initial retrieval of target words.

The third and last observation to make here is that the evident superiority of previously tested items need not rely on their having ever been formally recalled (Whitten, 1974, Experiment 3). In this research, the criterion test was administered after a long series of two-word study lists (such as NATION, BIRD). Each list had been immediately followed by either a 4–sec test of cued recall for one of the two words or four seconds of arithmetic. On some test trials, a probe (e.g., furniture) was presented that matched neither of the target items and so neither had to be recalled. Nonetheless, more items from lists previously tested were recalled than items from nontested lists. Both Whitten (1974) and Bjork (1975) have taken this finding to mean that item "recovery" is not needed to increase criterion performance but that "search" is a sufficient condition. Such remarks are misleading, for the data do not undercut our interpretation of memory test effects. Instead, we submit, they bring to the fore certain difficulties with the type of methodology employed.

One difficulty pertains to the extent of retrieval on a "no-match" recall trial. It seems unlikely that such testing corresponds to a breakdown in recall, for presented items must be remembered even if no match is to be reported. To presume that retrieval will be unfinished under these circumstances is risky unless one has converging evidence to infer a lack of retention for list events. One generalization may be justified, however: Test effects due to remembering an item are not critically dependent on the overt production of a full, physical response. Data from other paradigms point to the same conclusion (e.g., Bjork & Geiselman, 1978: Lachman & Mistler, 1970; Johnson, Raye, Foley, & Foley, 1981).

Another difficulty and one more central to the task at hand is that immediate cued recall, with or without a match, has extremely limited utility for the study of retrieval effects. It doubtless cannot be applied beyond a narrow range of memory tasks involving very short lists and very short study-test intervals. For longer lists and intervals, a cued-recall test simply cannot be "immediate" for all items. Furthermore, this restriction brings out a fundamental ambiguity. At some point following registration of an event, initial processing directed toward the stimulus is terminated and replaced by subsequent processing that depends to a greater extent on previously stored memories. It is reasonable to presume that immediate and delayed processing will shade one into the other gradually and that retrieval on an immediate test is a special case of postpresentation processing. The unfortunate thing about any nominally immediate test is that it inevitably tends to blur any distinction between retrieval, the *re*-activation of an old memory, and continued processing or "reverberation" (Hebb, 1949). As time passes between study and recall, we grow more confident that retrieval processes are involved when the test occurs. This is not to deny that only similar processes may be involved at original encoding (e.g., Craik, 1977; Jacoby & Craik, 1979; Spear, 1981). To help decide whether they are or are not similar, however, more has to be learned about the functional characteristics, including the consequences of long-delay retrieval.

Delay—or, length of the initial retention interval—is important for yet another reason. This variable has figured prominently in numerous attempts to look at the effects of initial retrieval difficulty, a topic to which our discussion now turns.

Difficulty of Retrieval

It is clear in the phenomenology of human memory that mnemonic processes like retrieval are sometimes easy and sometimes hard to carry out. Not surprisingly, therefore, it has been hypothesized that as remembering gets harder, the pay-off in terms of subsequent retention increases for what was successfully recalled initially (e.g., Bjork, 1975: Jacoby & Craik, 1979; Landauer & Eldridge, 1967; Whitten & Leonard, 1980). This notion certainly has intuitive appeal. The catch is that few people have bothered to develop objective ways of assessing it. To do so would necessitate an index of retrieval difficulty—a measure of either cognitive effort (a motivational construct) or processing capacity (an informational construct) expended during recall—and only rudimentary steps in that direction have been taken.

The one technique used at all frequently, with an assortment of verbal materials, has been to relate length of the initial study-test retention interval ("initial delay") to subsequent memory test performance. As delay is increased, initial retrieval would be expected to become more difficult and—in keeping with the hypothesis stated above—remembered events subsequently more memorable. The pattern of results from a number of studies is in general agreement with this expectation (e.g., Bartlett, 1977; Götz & Jacoby, 1974, Landauer & Eldridge, 1967; Mazuryk, 1977; Modigliani, 1976, 1978, 1980; Whitten, 1978; Whitten & Bjork, 1977).

Unfortunately, however, data bearing on the relationship between length of initial delay and subsequent retention are not unequivocal. For one thing, length of delay has rarely exceeded 15 sec and longer delays could be expected to produce either asymptotic levels of difficulty and facilitation or, at very long lengths, no facilitation, because items would be too difficult to retrieve initially. For another, control items (i.e., those given no previous test) have routinely been omitted and they would be expected to provide an estimate of the increment in retention due to prior recall, whether delayed or immediate. The exclusion of NPT procedures means that all items are initially tested, but at various delays and with varying degrees of success. To illustrate, consider a series of Brown-Peterson trials (as in Modigliani, 1976). On each trial three words are presented, followed immediately by a variable interval of counting backwards and then by an initial attempt at recall. Performance on this test drops as a function of the interpolated period—on the one hand, attesting to an increasingly more difficult retrieval but, on the other, introducing a potential confound: item selection.

Item selection refers to individual differences among target stimuli at the time of learning, prior to any test or retention interval. Some materials are easier to learn (hence, "stronger") than others. The easiest or strongest items would be retrievable on the criterion test whether previously tested or not. As expressed by Modigliani (1976), "it can be assumed that, at time of input, items are stored with different strengths, for a variety of reasons. Therefore, the longer the interval, the stronger the initial strength of an item that is successfully recalled at the end of that interval (and) . . . the higher the probability that a successfully recalled item (will) be recalled again at a later time [p. 610.]." Only relatively weak items would thus be expected to benefit from previous retrieval.

This state of affairs entails a complicated measurement problem. The possibility that recall exercises a strengthening effect cannot be reliably assessed when initial strength is uncontrolled. As length of delay is extended, weak items drop out and the greater difficulty of retrieval of those successfully recalled is offset by their growing scarcity. Given those opponent processes, criterion recall can show an absolute increase with initial delay only if the facilitating influence of retrieval rises faster than the rate at which PT items are "lost" (that is, not initially recovered). The inclusion of NPT items serves as a control for baseline differences in initial storage (i.e., item selection). Further steps may be taken to quantify the impact of a previous test (e.g., Bartlett, 1977; Modigliani, 1976), but the validity of such indices is highly dependent on the use of NPT controls.

Given the importance of proper controls, it is distressing to note how inadequate they tend to be in most studies of delayed versus immediate recall. More often than not, as pointed out above, all items are tested. But to make matters worse, the delay itself frequently is confounded with extraneous differences. In Bartlett (1977), for example, delay covaries with the output position of an initial probe and hence the number and nature of items previously recalled. A more telling instance is the well-known phenomenon of negative recency, wherein final retention decreases with serial position (e.g., Cohen, 1970, Craik, 1970; Madigan & McCabe, 1971). The last items in a list are the most recent. Theirs is the shortest delay between initial presentation and test, but the length of their delay is not the only thing that distinguishes them from earlier members of the list. End-of-list items are liable to be encoded differently in anticipation of the test (Watkins & Watkins, 1974). The value of a test for early versus late items, then, is tangled with encoding differences. This complication has been acknowledged (Bjork, 1975), and it raises an important point. We really do not know whether the effect of testing depends on the subset of materials retrieved, whether it is amplified or curtailed for recent items, or whether it varies as a function of initial strength. It was suggested earlier that weak items stand to gain the most from recall, but we have no evidence that they do. In fact, one could argue on the basis of negative recency that a weak item gains nothing from having been remembered.

Even when NPT controls are included, they sometimes have been inappropriate for the clear interpretation we seek. Modigliani (1976, Experiment 2) had subjects listen to a series of 3–word lists and count backwards after each. Whereas PT subjects were asked to recall each list after its presentation, NPT subjects did not attempt to recall anything until the criterion test. Regrettably, to compare them at that point is fruitless. Going into the final test, these two groups had already had different amounts of exposure to a free recall situation (hence, different amounts of generalized practice at free recall). Moreover, they faced different immediate tasks and so may not even have encoded target materials in the same way originally. In order to avoid such problems, it is preferable to compare PT and NPT items within subjects and within a single list. This has been done at least twice, over a fairly wide range of initial delays: 2–34 sec in Mazuryk (1977, Experiment 3) and 0–90 sec in Landauer and Bjork (1978, Experiment 1, Uniform conditions). The intriguing result in both cases was that all nonzero delays were about equally helpful, unlike the zero-delay interval, which did very little to promote subsequent retention (see also Modigliani, 1978).

The abrupt transition from marginal to maximum facilitation with an immediate versus a delayed test suggests two things. One is the commonsense view that there is, in effect, no retrieval at no delay. Second, retrieval may not be a sufficient condition for facilitation to occur. If it were, then, because fewer items can be retrieved at longer intervals, the evident constancy of test effects at all nonzero spacings would have to mean that each item recalled initially was strengthened more at a long than a short delay. Indeed, one would have to say that the two forces—item "loss" due to delay and item "consolidation" due to recall—were almost perfectly balanced. Is that a coincidence? We do not know. But there seems to be an alternative: Only strong items might be facilitated. These items are a subset of those retrieved initially at each interval. If their retrieval were all that mattered, a fixed amount of improvement could ensue during the final test (PT minus NPT). There are no data to rule out this possibility. Though it need not be taken too seriously, we think it illustrates the current state of uncertainty surrounding such matters.

Depth of Retrieval

At first glance, this concept merely adds to our confusion. It refers to aspects of retrieval—namely, the retrieval cues—that covary with level of difficulty. In most test situations, "depth" and "difficulty" have indistinguishable operational definitions. For instance, when performance on a memory test declines with retention interval, it can be said that retrieval involves either a deeper analysis of the available information or a more difficult decision or both. Thus, the two constructs may be used interchangeably (e.g., Bjork, 1975). There is, however, a conceptual distinction worth making, for it could be argued that the effects of retrieval difficulty are actually superceded or precipitated by concomitant variation in depth (e.g., Bartlett, 1977; Gotz & Jacoby, 1974; Whitten, 1978).

The "depth" notion stems directly from the levels-of-analysis viewpoint (Craik & Lockhart, 1972). Originally formulated to describe processes at encoding, the idea has been applied more recently to events at retrieval (e.g., Jacoby & Craik, 1979; Lockhart, Craik, & Jacoby, 1976). Within this framework, level of processing and depth of retrieval both refer to the way in which information is analyzed, particularly the extent to which it is semantically analyzed. Retrieval cues are classifiable into two types on this basis. "Semantic" cues include category names (*furniture*-CHAIR), high associates (*table*-CHAIR) and meaningfully related words or synonyms (*seat*-CHAIR). "Nonsemantic" cues include rhymes (*rare*-CHAIR), initial letters (*ch*-CHAIR), and temporal coordinates (*the second item in the last list*-CHAIR). It is not always possible to specify the cues that are functional in any given situation. But, conceivably, all remembering is mediated by the use of effective retrieval cues (e.g., Tulving, 1974; Watkins, 1979). Given that assumption, the effects of having remembered are later on very likely to depend upon the nature of cues (i.e., memory attributes) employed initially. As stated by Götz and Jacoby (1974), "attributes used as retrieval cues experience an increase in cue effectiveness as a consequence. The use of short-lived attributes requires less effort so that they are employed as retrieval cues when there is a choice; immediate recall primarily uses short-lived attributes such as the acoustic trace of an item. If a filled delay precedes recall, short-lived cues will not be available and initial recall will be based on more durable attributes [p. 296]." Hence, subsequent criterion recall should be higher following delayed (semantic) rather than immediate (nonsemantic) initial retrieval.

There have been at least five direct tests of the hypothesis that the facilitating effects of retrieval will depend on the type of cue initially employed (Bartlett, 1977; Bartlett & Tulving, 1974; Mazuryk, 1977, Experiment 5: Whitten, 1974, Experiment 3; 1978). In each study, initial recall was tested for some items but not others and recalled items were emitted in response to either semantic or nonsemantic cues. Criterial performance, often including recognition as well as recall, evinced an impressively uniform pattern of results. In all cases, there was a numerical advantage for tested (PT) versus nontested (NPT) items that increased with semantic cuing. An experiment by Whitten (1978) illustrates this trend. He presented 32 four-word lists visually at a rapid pace, each followed by one probe word that was either semantically related (a synonym) or acoustically related (a rhyme) to an item in the list. His subjects had 4 sec to call out the item before another trial began. After all 32 trials plus a minute's interpolated activity, they were unexpectedly given the criterion test involving 5 min of written free recall. Every serial position had been cued prior to this test an equal number of times with synonyms and rhymes (four apiece). The effect of cuing was consistent across serial positions in showing both an advantage for PT over NPT items as well as higher retention for materials probed semantically rather than acoustically.

Not only was there an overall difference in retention for the two types of material but also the serial position curves were markedly different. In both initial and final recall, the serial position function was essentially flat for semantic retrieval but not for acoustic retrieval. In the latter condition, initial recall was bowed (U-shaped) and final recall showed evidence of negative recency. Moreover, the two recall curves crossed in initial retention so that semantic probes were more effective than acoustic probes at the first two serial positions but less effective at the last two. One interpretation for the crossover may be that semantic cues are easier to use than nonsemantic cues when recall is delayed but that nonsemantic cues are easier when recall is immediate. If ease of initial recovery were the mediating variable, then subsequent recall might have been expected to look like the inverse of that seen initially. It did not. Rather, final recall favored the semantic condition at all list positions, which implies that qualitative aspects of retrieval (i.e., depth) are more potent than amount of difficulty in determining later retention. That suggestion is reinforced by the response latencies collected during initial recall. As would be expected on the basis of increasing difficulty, the average time it took subjects to initiate their responses was longer for the items further back in the list. These data bore no relation, however, to the pattern of effects observed for previous testing, especially the effects of semantic testing, which were constant throughout the list. Thus, apparently, retrieval difficulty is less related to subsequent remembering than is the depth to which items are processed at the time they are initially recovered.

We have discussed Whitten's experiment in some detail not only because it is representative of current work demonstrating a new and important role for depth but also because it typifies a larger body of research testifying to the general, functional significance of retrieval. These investigations show that during or soon after recall, the contents of a reactivated memory are potentially quite malleable. Numerous phenomena of this sort have been uncovered using a research paradigm developed by Loftus (e.g., 1975; for a review, see Loftus & Loftus, 1980). Though less dramatic, Whitten's data permit the same conclusion. Immediately after presentation of an item, a memory for that event has to exist in some form if it is ever to be remembered. In terms of criterion recall for that item, however, full expression of the memory is not guaranteed but depends critically on the nature of postpresentation test events—particularly the presence or absence of initial retrieval and the type of retrieval cues employed. Although such interventions are mild by comparison with those ordinarily imposed to study consolidation (e.g., electroconvulsive shock, psychoactive drugs, brain lesions), they are seemingly no less effective. Whitten, for one, found target memories were upgraded in final retention by initial cued recall and that they were enhanced more by semantic than acoustic cuing. These effects evidence the power of one retrieval to rewrite, as it were, an old memory and to boost its chances for success on a subsequent test of remembering.

Whether such an updating process eradicates the old memory or partially augments it we do not know. That is one of the most basic and controversial topics in this area of inquiry. Alternative views abound. Perhaps the simplest point of view would be an accretion model, wherein something is added to a memory trace by virtue of its retrieval. The exact nature of the supplementary information is open to conjecture. It may be said, for instance (Whitten & Bjork, 1977), that "exercise of the retrieval route stabilizes availability" (of an item; [p. 474]) or that interitem organization is improved (Donaldson, 1971: Rosner, 1970). Any theory that posits a unidimensional increase in the quality of an item's representation (i.e., its "strength") is characterizable in these terms. Consolidation is generally such a notion (e.g., Crowder, 1976; Landauer, 1969). And it has been remarked (Schacter, Eich, & Tulving, 1978), that "facilitating effects of recall are almost invariably attributed to some sort of 'strengthening' process [p. 733.]."

Recall also has a less constructive side, which in large part is only now being recognized (Bjork, 1978; Bjork & Landauer, 1978). An erasure model might handle this aspect of retrieval. According to Loftus and Loftus (1980), for example, old memories can be overwritten by new information at the time they are recovered. Under these circumstances, the memory trace of a remembered episode is like a palimpsest on which the original message has been rubbed out and another inscribed. This analogy is supported by the observation that "leading" questions can mislead and alter the course of subsequent remembering even for experiences that otherwise would remain intact (e.g., Loftus, 1975). Destruction—and concurrent replacement—of the established memory is not the inevitable consequence of retrieval, however, as recent experiments have demonstrated (Dodd & Bradshaw, 1980; Hasher, Attig, & Alba, 1981). These studies are beginning to indicate when substitution of new content will occur and when it will not. We expect that trend to continue.

There is yet another way to picture the recall process which, unlike accretion and deletion models, posits more than a single representation in memory for each nominally designated target item. From this vantage point, retrieval neither strengthens nor modifies the trace of a remembered event but lays down a fresh memory in addition to the original (see, for example, Miller & Marlin, this volume). A similar concept involving the establishment of multiple memories was formulated as early as 1904 by Semon who suggested (as modern readers were not long ago reminded; Schacter et al., 1978, "that what emerges after recall is not a strengthened version of an already existing trace but rather a new, unique constellation of information in the present context plus information in the retrieved trace [p. 73]."

Maintenance of the Integrity of a Retrieved Memory

Several lines of contemporary research warrant a multitrace perspective on the function of retrieval. The most direct support has come from two research programs investigating how people keep track of their memories. One team of investigators has been concerned with "memory for remembered events" (e.g., Gardiner, Passmore, Herriot, & Klee, 1977) and one with "reality monitoring" (e.g., Johnson & Raye, 1981). Both groups have demonstrated that criterion tests of memory performance are sensitive to characteristics of initial recall as well as initial presentation. In one study (Johnson, Taylor, & Raye, 1977), for instance, the frequency with which categorized words were presented was orthogonally combined with the frequency with which they were tested for (cued) recall. The frequencies were two, five, and eight in each case. The criterion task was to judge either how often an item had been presented or how often tested. It was found that the two types of occurrence—study and test—could be judged rather accurately and independently of one another. In a different piece of research (Klee & Gardiner, 1980), categorized lists were tested either with or without category cues. Subsequently subjects tried to decide which items had been recalled earlier and which had not. Knowledge of recall varied differentially for the cued and noncued materials, suggesting "test-specific events have memorial consequences that cannot be fully understood merely in terms of the nature of the originally encoded event. That is, each act of remembering is a new event in episodic memory and results in the formation of a unique memory trace [p. 225]."

Studies involving item repetition offer an additional source of support for a multitrace hypothesis. The evidence is indirect, however, because it relies on an analogy between repetition and test effects. In this regard, we mentioned earlier in this chapter the possibility that operations performed on an item when it is physically present—encoding or storage—are functionally equivalent to activities at recall. According to other observers (e.g., Hintzman, Summers, & Block, 1975; Mandler, Worden, & Graesser, 1974; Thios & D'Agostino, 1976), any number of repetitions will be ineffective without study-phase retrieval. Consistent with such accounts, Whitten and Bjork (1977, Group B) found that repeated and retrieved items had comparable effects on subsequent retention. More generally, repetition data are quite often favorable to a multitrace approach (for a review, see Crowder, 1976, pp. 314–320). Some of the best data in that sense involve judgments of frequency (Hintzman & Block, 1971; Johnson et al., 1977) or recency (Flexner & Bower, 1974).

One finding in particular has special significance for the idea that a repeated or retrieved item will leave a unique trace "in the present context" (to reiterate Schacter et al., 1978). Thios and D'Agostino (1976, Experiment 2) presented object phrases such as EXPRESS TRAIN in the company of sentence frames: *The conductor boarded the . . . .* At intervals ranging from zero to 96 sec, they repeated the object phrase either alone or in its original context (e.g., *The conductor boarded the* EXPRESS TRAIN.). In either case, subjects had to transpose the sentence into its passive form ("The express train was boarded by the conductor.") Perfect transformations were generated at all times when context was provided (the No Retrieval condition) and at zero delay when it was not (the Retrieval condition). Study-phase retrieval dropped sharply in the second instance from 100% to asymptote (60%) after a 32–second filler delay. In the criterion test, subjects were given 5 min for written recall of all object phrases. Final performance was congruent with the assumption that repetitions are ineffective unless accompanied by retrieval processing at the time of their occurrence. Items repeated in the Retrieval condition were significantly better remembered than those in the No Retrieval condition. Moreover, the latter items showed no Melton effect (i.e., no significant increase in final recall with initial delay). "Retrieval" items did, and these data are rather exciting. They were analyzed conditional on the success or failure of initial sentence-frame retrieval and showed similar outcomes in both cases. That is, free recall increased roughly as much for phrases whose contexts could be retrieved as for those whose contexts could not. This finding indicates that original context does not have to be reactivated in order to produce an effective repetition. When contextual information was not recovered, subjects had to provide their own sentence completions. Nonetheless, items manifesting the complete recovery of that information were functionally equivalent in final retention to items repeated (retrieved?) within new and different surroundings. The implication would seem to be that retrieval will forge new links between an item and its context (i.e., a new trace) even when the old memory is still intact and perfectly available.

Further Evidence That a Memory Need Not Be Altered When Retrieved

The foregoing evidence implies that a memory will not inevitably be permanently altered, in its later accessibility or its quality, simply as a consequence of its being retrieved under circumstances different from those of learning. The question is significant because it touches upon this old, unanswered question: Is a memory forever intact as originally stored, or is it instead progressively changed whenever it is "used"? From a slightly different perspective than that discussed in the preceding section, an answer to this issue has begun to emerge from a set of rather incisive experiments by Lynn Hasher and her colleagues and also, to a lesser extent, within the study of animal memory.

How stable is memory representation for specific aspects of an episode? There are two paradigms. The first asks whether a biasing context, such as a theme provided to integrate otherwise disjunctive elements, can lead to a failure to store and remember the specific elements. The second asks whether biasing of the meaning or content of an episode after it has been learned leads inevitably to a dissolution of memory for the specific elements as originally learned.

Hasher and her colleagues have approached these issues through consideration of two general perspectives on memory processing. One is the notion that remembering occurs through a reconstruction process that is guided by abstracted features of the episode, such as its theme. This has been supported experimentally. There seems no doubt that what is recalled can depend on the theme assigned during original learning. It has been determined also that what is recalled about an episode can be altered by incorporating into a memory, upon its retrieval, new elements or new interpretations. Yet one can, with equal experimental certitude, find data that argue instead for the view that remembering is geared to a system of relatively accurate reproduction of what is learned. Among the varieties of evidence supporting this view are the following: (1) humans are extraordinarily precise in excluding what is not to be remembered, that is, intrusions, an effect encompassed in the construct, "selector mechanism"; (2) retention deficits can be reversed toward accurate reproduction by cuing that elicits the precise information acquired earlier—though the nominal cues may bear little relation to initial circumstances (e.g., Anderson & Pichert, 1978); and (3) in a quite general sense, it is impossible to deny the precision of many common instances of verbatim recall. These positions, stated by Hasher and Griffin (1978), are based on their experiments, which assessed the role of thematic information on what is recalled about a specific learned episode.

The results of Hasher and Griffin (1978) are quite clear in showing that although subjects are indeed capable of theme-induced reconstruction at the time of recall, they are equally capable of accurately reproducing specific details of what was learned, independent of the theme. The balance of these two phenomena—whether reconstruction or reproduction will prevail—depends, in Hasher and Griffin's words, "upon the demands imposed upon the system, some of which are determined by the retention situation itself. Thus, there are situations such as the present one in which one may see, given similar initial storage of information, either reconstruction or reproductive retention [p. 329]." The integrity of lexical information in memory was illustrated also by subsequent experiments (Alba, Alexander, Hasher, & Caniglia, 1981). This study determined that thematic biasing of neutral verbal material can have quite a profound effect on its comprehension and recall and yet have no influence on recognition of the specific elements of the material as learned originally.

These studies are persuasive in arguing for the relative permanence of memories. Even though a stored memory can, upon its activation, be combined with other experiences to aid in the formation of a new representation, the integrity of the memory-as-stored is maintained as a special entity. The issue is therefore not a simple one, in that both reconstruction and the capacity for reproduction can exist simultaneously. When a memory is made active, there seems little doubt that changes may result in either the probability of accessing that memory later on or the specific behavior that emerges from its access. Yet, it cannot be stated flatly that the memory originally acquired has changed in specific details. (For generally agreeable evidence with animal subjects, see Spear, 1981.)

Summarizing Comments

Does Testing Facilitate Later Retrieval For All Aspects of the Episode to be Remembered?

When the episode contains multiple elements such as a set of words, the effects of a test on later retrieval must be considered separately for two subsets of these items: those retrieved at the test and those not retrieved. For those items retrieved and produced by the subject, we may ask about the relationship between their physical reproduction and later retention scores. It would be relatively uninteresting, for instance, if the effect of retrieval of a particular item on its later recall were wholly dependent on the same physical conditions that attend its re-exposure. As one of us (Spear, 1981) has argued, the processes at storage and retrieval may be similar but they need not be identical. And as others have argued (e.g., Johnson & Raye, 1981), these processes are likely to incorporate different sources of information.

Our review indicates that physical reproduction of an item at a test is not necessary for improved retention later, although it might possibly be sufficient. But aside from physical reproduction, the special contribution of *retrieval* of an item during testing for its later accessibility is inevitably at question due to probable item selection. The weight of the evidence would seem to indicate, nevertheless, that the benefits of retrieval for accessibility later probably are too great and too general to be accounted for solely in terms of item selection.

The problem of confounding by item selection may be more difficult when evaluating the effects of *non* retrieved items that had been part of the episode tested for recall. Is accessibility of all items in an episode raised as a consequence of retrieving some of the items? Although a plausibly appealing notion, there simply is not very good evidence for this and the sort of redintegration that could be claimed if it were so. The process of output interference, however, works against manifestation of such redintegration in overt recall. Also, for most experiments so far, the items not recalled in the original test probably are simply the weaker items, perhaps so weak that small changes in their accessibility might not be detected on later tests of the type that have been used so far.

It is safe to assert that the retrieval process, or its consequences for a particular item, can promote later recall. One can then state the obvious analogy, that later recall is aided by the memory storage process or its ancillary production (implicit or explicit) of items.

Implications of a Common Consolidation Process at Storage and Retrieval

One rather obvious implication of our hypothesis is concerned with individual differences. If a common consolidation process occurs during initial storage and later retrieval of information, then we should expect that persons with high "rates of consolidation" will be especially proficient at both storing and retrieving information whereas persons with low rates of consolidation should have equal difficulty with initial storage and subsequent retrieval. We should have no individuals or groups of individuals, such as those at different ages or in different species, who learn more rapidly but retrieve more poorly than others, or vice versa.

It is unlikely that this implication holds in fact. For instance, although there are very clear and consistent individual differences in the learning of paired verbal items—slow learners and fast learners—these differences are not maintained in terms of retention 24 hours later (Underwood, 1954). Similarly, a dissociation between efficacy in initial memory storage and that of memory retrieval has been implied in the analysis of certain dysfunctions of memory, sometimes in terms of the rubric "short-term vs. long-term memory" and sometimes in terms of the storage-retrieval framework (Spear, 1978; Warrington & Weiskrantz, 1973).

There is also a problem with the reasoning. The underlying assumption that consistent individual differences in rate of consolidation will be reflected in rate of learning or resistance to retrograde amnesia is likely incorrect. This assumption exemplifies how a construct of "consolidation" in terms of, say, a change in the structure or action of a neurotransmitter at the level of a single synapse, makes little contact with the behavioral constructs of learning and retention, storage, and retrieval. For instance, infants and young children would in this view be suspected of having slower rates of consolidation than normal adults, because they learn more slowly. But, *what* they learn more slowly need not imply slower consolidation at the synaptic level. In the case of infants, whether animals or humans, it has become clear that they are a great deal more astute when learning under circumstances that might be said generally to be "consistent with their ecological niche," much more "mature" in their learning and memory capacity than was previously estimated from tests originally designed for adults (Rovee-Collier & Lipsitt, 1981; Spear, 1984; Spear & Campbell, 1979). Similarly, it seems likely that many of the ontogenetic differences observed in learning and memory among animals may be traced to differential stimulus selection rather than different rates of storing individual elements into memory (Spear, 1979). It is especially well established that when children are provided particular organizational techniques and led to use them, their recall becomes more adultlike (Ornstein, 1978). A final example is in terms of results with retention measures that tap what has been termed "automatic processing"— recognition learning, for example. These results indicate that individual differences such as those associated with ontogenetic progression, some mental disorders, or aging, simply do not occur (Hasher, 1981).

If taken to represent the physiological change responsible for establishing in memory a record of a unitary event, "consolidation" is indeed a necessary condition for learning; but it cannot be sufficient so long as "learning" involves behavioral change to more than one unitary event. In short, by equating learning rate with consolidation rate, we would have completely missed many of the factors that are in fact responsible for many individual differences in the processing of memories.

REFERENCES

Alba, J. W., Alexander, S. G., Hasher, L., & Caniglia, K. The role of context in the encoding of information. *Journal of Experimental Psychology: Human Learning and Memory*, 1981, *7*, 283–292.

Allen, G. A. & Arbak, C. J. The priority effect in the A-B, A-C paradigm and subjects' expectations. *Journal of Verbal Learning and Verbal Behavior*, 1976, *15*, 381–385.

Anderson, J. R., & Bower, G. H. Recognition and retrieval processes in free recall. *Psychological Review*, 1972, *79*, 97–123.

Anderson, R. C., & Pichert, J. W. Recall of previously unrecallable information following a shift in perspective. *Journal of Verbal Learning and Verbal Behavior*, 1978, *17*, 1–12.

Arkes, H. R., & Lyons, B. J. A mediational explanation of the priority effect. *Journal of Verbal Learning and Verbal Behavior*, 1979, *18*, 721–731.

Bahrick, H. P. Two-phase model for prompted recall. *Psychological Review*, 1970, *77*, 215–222.

Bartlett, J. C. Effects of immediate testing on delayed retrieval: Search and recovery operations with four types of cue. *Journal of Experimental Psychology: Human Learning and Memory*, 1977, *3*, 719–732.

Bartlett, J. C., & Tulving, E. Effects of temporal and semantic encoding in immediate recall upon subsequent retrieval. *Journal of Verbal Learning and Verbal Behavior*, 1974, *13*, 297–3O9.

Birnbaum, I. M., & Eichner, J. T. Study versus test trials and long-term retention in free-recall learning. *Journal of Verbal Learning and Verbal Behavior*, 1971, *10*, 516–521.

Bjork, R. A. Retrieval as a memory modifier: An interpretation of negative recency and related phenomena. In R. L. Solso (Ed.), *Information Processing and Cognition. The Loyola Synposium*. Hillsdale, N.J.: Lawrence Erlbaum Associates, 1975.

Bjork, R. A. The updating of human memory. In G. H. Bower (Ed.), *The Psychology of Learning and Motivation (Vol. 12)*. New York: Academic Press, 1978.

Bjork, R. A., & Geiselman, R. E. Constituent processes in the differentiation of items in memory. *Journal of Experimental Psychology: Human Learning & Memory*, 1978, *4*, 347–361.

Bjork, R. A., & Landauer, T. K. On keeping track of the present status of people and things. In M. M. Gruneberg, P. E. Morris & R. N. Sykes (Eds.), *Practical aspects of memory*. New York: Academic Press, 1978.

Bowyer, P. A., & Humphreys, M. S. Effect of a recognition test on a subsequent cued-recall test. *Journal of Experimental Psychology: Human Learning and Memory*, 1979, *5*, 348–359.

Bregman, A. S., & Wiener, J. R. Effects of test trials in paired-associate and free-recall learning. *Journal of Verbal Learning and Verbal Behavior*, 1970, *9*, 689–698.

Broadbent, D. E., & Broadbent, M. H. P. Effects of recognition on subsequent recall: Comments on "Determinants of recognition and recall: Accessibility and generation" by Rabinowitz, Mandler & Patterson. *Journal of Experimental Psychology: General*, 1977, *106*, 330–335.

Brown, W. To what extent is memory measured by a single recall? *Journal of Experimental Psychology*, 1923, *6*, 377–382.

Bugelski, R. R. Presentation time, total time, and mediation in paired associate learning. *Journal of Experimental Psychology*, 1962, *63*, 409–412.

Buschke, H. Spontaneous remembering after recall failure. *Science*, 1974, *184*, 579–581.

Buschke, H. Retrieval of categorized items increases without guessing. *Bulletin of the Psychonomic Society*, 1975, *5*, 71–73.

Cohen, R. Recency effects in long-term recall and recognition. *Journal of Verbal Learning and Verbal Behavior*, 1970, *9*, 672–678.

Coke, E. U. The effects of test events and spaced practice on free recall learning. *Psychonomic Science*, 1971, *22*, 335–336.

Cooper, A. J. R., & Monk, A. Learning for recall and learning for recognition. In J. Brown (Ed.), *Recall and recognition*. New York: Wiley, 1976.

Craik, F. I. M. The fate of primary memory items in free recall. *Journal of Verbal Learning and Verbal Behavior*, 1970, *9*, 143–148.

Craik, F. I. M. Similarities between the effects of aging and alcoholic intoxication on memory performance, construed within a "levels of processing" framework. In I. M. Birnbaum & E. S. Parker (Eds.), *Alcohol and human memory*. Hillsdale, N.J.: Lawrence Erlbaum Associates, 1977.

Craik, F. I. M., & Lockhart, R. S. Levels of processing: A framework for memory research. *Journal of Verbal Learning and Verbal Behavior*, 1972, *11*, 671–684.

Crowder, R. G. *Principles of learning and memory*. Hillsdale, N.J.: Lawrence Erlbaum Associates, 1976.

Dalezman, J. J. Effects of output order on immediate, delayed, and final recall performance. *Journal of Experimental Psychology: Human Learning & Memory*, 1976, *2*, 597–608.

Dodd, D. H., & Bradshaw, J. M. Leading questions and memory: Pragmatic constraints. *Journal of Verbal Learning and Verbal Behavior*, 1980, *19*, 695–704.

Donaldson, W. Output effects in multitrial free recall. *Journal of Verbal Learning and Verbal Behavior*, 1971, *10*, 577–585.

Dong, T. Cued partial recall of categorized words. *Journal of Experimental Psychology*, 1972, *93*, 123–129.

142   SPEAR AND MUELLER

Ellis, J. A. Transfer failure and proactive interference in short-term memory. *Journal of Experimental Psychology: Human Learning and Memory*, 1977, *3*, 211–221.

Engle, R. W., & Mobley, L. A. The modality effect: What happens in long-term memory? *Journal of Verbal Learning and Verbal Behavior*, 1976, *15*, 519–527.

Erdelyi, M. H., & Becker, J. Hypermnesia for pictures: Incremental memory for pictures but not words in multiple recall trials. *Cognitive Psychology*, 1974, *6*, 159–171.

Erdelyi, M. H., Buschke, H., & Finkelstein, S. Hypermnesia for Socratic stimuli: The growth of recall for an internally generated memory list abstracted from a series of riddles. *Memory and Cognition*, 1977, *5*, 283–286.

Fisher, R. P., & Craik, F. I. M. Interaction between encoding and the retrieval operations in cued recall. *Journal of Experimental Psychology: Human Learning and Memory*, 1977, *3*, 701–711.

Flexner, A. J., & Bower, G. H. How frequency affects recency judgments: A model for recency discrimination. *Journal of Experimental Psychology*, 1974, *103*, 706–716.

Fuld, P. A., & Buschke, H. Stages of retrieval in verbal learning. *Journal of Verbal Learning and Verbal Behavior*, 1976, *15*, 401–410.

Gardiner, J. M., Craik, F. I. M., & Bleasdale, F. A. Retrieval difficulty and subsequent recall. *Memory and Cognition*, 1973, *1*, 213–216.

Gardiner, J. M., Passmore, C., Herriot, P., & Klee, H. Memory for remembered events: Effects of response mode and response-produced feedback. *Journal of Verbal Learning and Verbal Behavior*, 1977, *16*, 45–54.

Glickman, S. E. Perseverative neural processes in consolidation of the memory trace. *Psychological Bulletin*, 1961, *58*, 218–233.

Gordon, W. C. Mechanisms for cue-induced retention enhancement. In N. E. Spear & R. R. Miller (Eds.), *Information processing in animals: Memory mechanisms*. Hillsdale, N.J.: Lawrence Erlbaum Associates, 1981.

Götz, A., & Jacoby, L. L. Coding and retrieval processes in long-term retention. *Journal of Experimental Psychology*, 1974, *102*, 291–297.

Grant, D. S. Short-term memory in the pigeon. In N. E. Spear & R. R. Miller (Eds.), *Information processing in animals: Memory mechanisms*. Hillsdale, N.J.: Lawrence Erlbaum Associates, 1981.

Hasher, L. A. *The automatic encoding of information into memory*. Invited address at meetings of the Eastern Psychological Association, New York, 1981.

Hasher, L., Attig, M. S., & Alba, J. W. I knew it all along: Or, did I? *Journal of Verbal Learning and Verbal Behavior*, 1981, *20*, 86–96.

Hasher, L., & Griffin, M. Reconstructive and reproductive processes in memory. *Journal of Experimental Psychology: Human Learning and Memory*, 1978, *4*, 318–330.

Hebb, D. O. *The organization of behavior: A neuropsychological theory*. New York: Wiley, 1949.

Hintzman, D. L., & Block, R. A. Repetition and memory: Evidence for a multiple-trace hypothesis. *Journal of Experimental Psychology*, 1971, *88*, 297–306.

Hintzman, D. L., Summers, J. J., & Block, R. A. Spacing judgements as a index of study-phase retrieval. *Journal of Experimental Psychology: Human Learning and Memory*, 1975, *104*, 31–40.

Hogan, R. M., & Kintsch, W. Differential effects of study and test trials on long-term recognition and recall. *Journal of Verbal Learning and Verbal Behavior*, 1971, *10*, 562–567.

Hudson, R. L., & Hudson, K. S. Effects of presentation, recall and study trials on word recall of a highly structured list. *Bulletin of the Psychonomic Society*, 1977, *10*, 60–62.

Hudson, R. L., Solomon, M. L., & Davis, J. L. Effects of presentation and recall trials on clustering and recall. *Journal of Verbal Learning and Verbal Behavior*, 1972, *11*, 356–361.

Humphreys, M. S., & Bowyer, P. A. Sequential testing effects and the relationship between recognition and recognition failure. *Memory and Cognition*, 1980, *8*, 271–277.

Izawa, C. Reinforcement-test sequences in paired-associate learning. *Psychological Reports*, 1966, *18*, 879–919.

Izawa, C. Function of test trials in paired-associate learning. *Journal of Experimental Psychology*, 1967, *75*, 194–209.

Izawa, C. Effects of reinforcement, neutral and test trials upon paired-associate acquisition and retention. *Psychological Reports*, 1968, *23*, 947–959.

Izawa, C. Comparison of reinforcement and test trials in paired-associate learning. *Journal of Experimental Psychology*, 1969, *81*, 600–603.

Izawa, C. Optimal potentiating effects and forgetting-prevention effects of tests in paired-associate learning. *Journal of Experimental Psychology*, 1970, *83*, 340–344.

Jacoby, L. L., & Craik, F. I. M. Effects of elaboration of processing at encoding and retrieval: Trace distinctiveness and recovery of initial context. In L. S. Cermak & F. I. M. Craik (Eds.), *Levels of processing in human memory*. Hillsdale, N.J.: Lawrence Erlbaum Associates, 1979.

Johnson, M. K. A multiple-entry, modular memory system. IN G. R. Bower (Ed.), *The psychology of learning and motivation*. New York: Academic Press, 1983.

Johnson, M. K., & Raye, C. L. Reality monitoring. *Psychological Review*, 1981, *88*, 677–685.

Johnson, M. K., Raye, C. L., Foley, H. J., & Foley, M. A. Cognitive operations and decision bias in reality monitoring. *American Journal of Psychology*, 1981, *94*, 37–64.

Johnson, M. K., Taylor, T. H., & Raye, C. L. Fact and fantasy: The effects of internally generated events and the apparent frequency of externally generated events. *Memory & Cognition*, 1977, *5*, 116–122.

Jones, G. V. Repeated cuing in the structure of recall. *British Journal of Mathematical and Statistical Psychology*, 1978, *31*, 1–10.

Klee, H., & Gardiner, J. M. Remembering the recall of cued and uncued words: Effects of initial accessibility. *Canadian Journal of Psychology*, 1980, *34*, 220–226.

Kleinsmith, L. J., & Kaplan, S. Paired-associate learning as a function of arousal and interpolated interval. *Journal of Experimental Psychology*, 1963, *65*, 190–193.

Konorski, J. *Integrative activity of the brain: An interdisciplinary approach*. Chicago: University of Chicago Press, 1967.

Lachman, R., & Laughery, K. R. Is a test trial a training trial in free recall learning? *Journal of Experimental Psychology*, 1968, *76*, 40–50.

Lachman, R., & Mistler, J. L. Rehearsal, test trials, and component processes in free recall. *Journal of Experimental Psychology*, 1970, *85*, 374–382.

Landauer, T. K. Reinforcement as consolidation. *Psychological Review*, 1969, *76*, 82–96.

Landauer, T. K., & Bjork, R. A. Optimum rehearsal patterns and name learning. In M. M. Gruneberg, P. E. Morris, & R. N. Sykes (Eds.), *Practical aspects of memory*. New York: Academic Press, 1978.

Landauer, T. K., & Eldridge, L. Effects of tests without feedback and presentation-test interval in paired-associate learning. *Journal of Experimental Psychology*, 1967, *75*, 290–298.

Lewis, D. J. Sources of experimental amnesia. *Psychological Review*, 1969, *76*, 461–472.

Lewis, D. J. Psychobiology of active and inactive memory. *Psychological Bulletin*, 1979, *86*, 1054–1083.

Lewis, M. Q. Short-term memory items in repeated free recall. *Journal of Verbal Learning and Verbal Behavior*, 1971, *10*, 190–193.

Lockhart, R. S., Craik, F. I. M., & Jacoby, L. L. Depth of processing, recognition and recall. In J. Brown (Ed.), *Recall and recognition*. New York: Wiley, 1976.

Loftus, E. F. Leading questions and the eyewitness report. *Cognitive Psychology*, 1975, *7*, 560–572.

Loftus, E. F. The malleability of human memory. *American Scientist*, 1979, *67*, 312–320.

Loftus, E. F., & Loftus, G. R. On the permanence of stored information in the human brain. *American Psychologist*, 1980, *35*, 409–420.

Loftus, G. R., & Loftus, E. R. The influence of one memory retrieval on a subsequent memory retrieval. *Memory & Cognition*, 1974, *2*, 467–471.

Madigan, S. A. & McCabe, L. Perfect recall and total forgetting: A problem for models of short-term memory. *Journal of Verbal Learning and Verbal Behavior*, 1971, *10*, 101–106.

Maki, W. S. Directed forgetting in animals. In N. E. Spear & R. R. Miller (Eds.), *Information processing in animals: Memory mechanisms.* Hillsdale, N.J.: Lawrence Elrbaum Associates, 1981.

Mandler, G., & Rabinowitz, J. C. Appearance and reality: Does a recognition test really improve subsequent recall and recognition? *Journal of Experimental Psychology: Human Learning and Memory*, 1981, *7*, 79–90.

Mandler, G., Worden, P. E., & Graesser, A. C. Subjective disorganization: Search for the locus of list organization. *Journal of Verbal Learning and Verbal Behavior*, 1974, *13*, 220–235.

Martin, E., Fleming, F. G., & Nally, P. D. Effect of temporal locus of a recitation attempt on learning and retention. *Memory & Cognition*, 1978, *6*, 274–282.

Masson, M. E. J., & McDaniel, M. A. The role of organizational processes in long-term retention. *Journal of Experimental Psychology: Human Learning and Memory*, 1981, *7*, 100–110.

Mathews, R. C., & Tulving, E. Effects of three types of repetition on cued and noncued recall of words. *Journal of Verbal Learning and Verbal Behavior*, 1973, *12*,.707–721.

Mazuryk, G. F. The effects of initial recall processes upon subsequent retrieval performance. Unpublished doctoral dissertation, University of Toronto, 1977.

McGaugh, J. L. Time-dependent processes in memory storage. *Science*, 1966, *153*, 1351–1358.

McGaugh, J. L. & Dawson, R. G. Modification of memory storage processes. In W. K. Honig & P. H. R. James (Eds.), *Animal Memory.* New York: Academic Press, 1971.

Miller, R. R., & Springer, A. D. Amnesia, consolidation and retrieval. *Psychological Review*, 1973, *80*, 60–79.

Modigliani, V. Effects on a later recall by delaying initial recall. *Journal of Experimental Psychology: luman Learning and Memory*, 1976, *2*, 609–622.

Modigliani, V. Effects of initial testing on later retention as a function of the initial retention interval. In M. M. Gruenberg, P. E. Morris, & R. N. Sykes (Eds.), *Practical aspects of memory.* New York: Academic Press, 1978.

Modigliani, V. Immediate rehearsal and initial retention interval in free recall. *Journal of Experimental Psychology: Human Learning and Memory*, 1980, *6*.

Morris, D. C., Bransford, J. D., & Franks, J. J. Levels of processing versus transfer appropriate processing. *Journal of Verbal Learning and Verbal Behavior*, 1977, *16*, 519–533.

Mueller, C. W., & Watkins, H. J. Inhibition from part-set cuing, A cue-overload interpretation. *Journal of Verbal Learning and Verbal Behavior*, 1977, *16*, 699–709.

Nelson, T. O., & MacLeod, C. M. Fluctuations in recall across successive test trials. *Memory & Cognition*, 1974, *2*, 687–690.

Ogilvie, J. C., Tulving, E., Paskowitz, S., & Jones, G. V. Three-dimensional memory traces: A model and its application to forgetting. *Journal of Verbal Learning and Verbal Behavior*, 1980, *19*, 405–415.

Ornstein, P. A. (Ed.). *Memory development in children.* Hillsdale, N.J.: Lawrence Erlbaum Associates, 1978.

Parker, R. E., & Warren, L. Partial category cuing: The accessibility of categories. *Journal of Experimental Psychology*, 1974, *102*, 1123–1125.

Poltrock, S. E., & MacLeod, C. M. Primacy and recency in the continuous distractor paradigm. *Journal of Experimental Psychology: Human Learning and Memory*, 1977, *3*, 560–571.

Postman, L. One-trial learning. In C. N. Cofer & B. S. Musgrave (Eds.), *Verbal behavior and learning: Problems and processes.* New York: McGraw-Hill, 1963.

Postman, L. A pragmatic view of organization theory. In E. Tulving & W. Donaldson (Eds.), *Organization of memory.* New York: Academic Press, 1972.

Postman, L., & Phillips, L. W. Studies in incidental learning: IX. A comparison of the methods of successive and single recalls. *Journal of Experimental Psychology*, 1961, *64*, 236–241.

Ratcliff, R. Theory of memory retrieval. *Psychological Review*, 1978, *85*, 59–108.

Riccio, D. C., & Ebner, D. L. Post-acquisition modification of memory. In N. E. Spear & R. R. Miller (Eds.), *Information processing in animals: Memory mechanisms*. Hillsdale, N.J.: Lawrence Erlbaum Associates, 1981.

Richardson, J., & Gropper, M. S. Learning during recall trials. *Psychological Reports*, 1964, *15*, 551–560.

Roediger, H. L. Inhibition in recall from cueing with recall targets. *Journal of Verbal Learning and Verbal Behavior*, 1973, *12*, 644–657.

Roediger, H. L. Recall as a self-limiting process. *Memory & Cognition*, 1978, *6*, 54–63.

Roediger, H. L. Memory metaphors in cognitive psychology. *Memory & Cognition*, 1980, *8*, 231–246.

Roediger, H. L., & Schmidt, S. R. Output interference in the recall of categorized and paired-associate lists. *Journal of Experimental Psychology: Human Learning and Memory*, 1980, *6*, 91–105.

Rosner, S. R. The effects of presentation and recall trials on organization in multitrial free recall. *Journal of Verbal Learning and Verbal Behavior*, 1970, *9*, 69–74.

Rothkopf, E. Z. Learning from written instructive materials: An exploration of the control of inspection behavior by test-like events. *American Educational Research Journal*, 1966, *3*, 241–249.

Rothkopf, E. Z., & Bisbicos, E. E. Selective facilitative effects of interspersed questions on learning from written prose. *Journal of Educational Psychology*, 1967, *58*, 56–61.

Rovee-Collier, C. K. & Lipsitt, L. P. Learning adaptation and memory. In P. M. Stratton (Ed.), *Psychobiology of the human newborn*. New York: Wiley, 1981.

Rovee-Collier, C. K., Sullivan, M. W., Enright, M. K., Lucas, D., & Fagen, J. W. Reactivation of infant memory. *Science*, 1980, *208*, 1159–1161.

Rundus, D. Negative effects of using list items as recall cues. *Journal of Verbal Learning and Verbal Behavior*, 1973, *12*, 43–50.

Russell, W. R. *The traumatic amnesias*. Oxford: Oxford University Press, 1971.

Sanford, J. F. Freedom of pair construction: Implications for information processing at input and retrieval. *American Journal of Psychology*, 1979, *92*, 477–488.

Schacter, D. L., Eich, J. E., & Tulving, E. Richard Semon's theory of memory. *Journal of Verbal Learning and Verbal Behavior*, 1978, *17*, 721–243.

Simmons, J. G. Patterned versus unpatterned sequences of study and recall trials in free recall of a categorizable word list. *Journal of Experimental Psychology*, 1973, *101*, 191–193.

Skaggs, E. B. The relative value of grouped and interspersed recitations. *Journal of Experimental Psychology*, 1920, *3*, 424–446.

Slamecka, N. J. The question of associative growth in the learning of categorized material. *Journal of Verbal Learning and Verbal Behavior*, 1972, *11*, 324–332.

Slamecka, N. J., & Graf, P. The generation effect, Delineation of a phenomenon. *Journal of Experimental Psychology: Human Learning and Memory*, 1978, *4*, 592–604.

Smith, A. D. Output interference in organized recall from long-term memory. *Journal of Verbal Learning and Verbal Behavior*, 1971, *10*, 400–408.

Smith, A. D. Input order and output interference in organized recall. *Journal of Experimental Psychology*, 1973, *100*, 147–150.

Smith, A. D., D'Agostino, P. R., & Reid, L. S. Output interference in long-term memory. *Canadian Journal of Psychology*, 1970, *24*, 85–89.

Spear, N. E. Forgetting as retrieval failure. In W. K. Honig & P. H. R. James (Eds.), *Animal memory*. New York: Academic Press, 1971.

Spear, N. E. Retrieval of memories: A psychobiological approach. In W. K. Estes (Ed.), *Handbook of learning and cognitive processes (Vol. 4), Attention and memory.* Hillsdale, N.J.: Lawrence Erlbaum Associates, 1976.

Spear, N. E. *The processing of memories: Foreetting and retention.* Hillsdale, N.J.: Lawrence Erlbaum Associates, 1978.

Spear, N. E., & Campbell, B. A. (Eds.). *Ontogeny of learning and memory.* Hillsdale, N.J.: Lawrence Erlbaum Associates, 1979.

Spear, N. E. Memory storage factors in infantile amnesia. In G. Bower (Ed.), *The psychology of learning and motivation (Vol. 13).* New York: Academic Press, 1979.

Spear, N. E. Extending the domain of memory retrieval. In N. E. Spear & R. R. Miller (Eds.), *Information processing in animals: Memory mechanisms.* Hillsdale, N.J.: Lawrence Erlbaum Associates, 1981.

Spear, N. E. Ecologically determined dispositions control the ontogeny of learning and memory. In R. V. Kail & N. E. Spear (Eds.), *Memory development: Comparative perspectives.* Hillsdale, New Jersey: Lawrence Erlbaum Associates, 1984.

Squire, L. R., Slater, P. C., & Chace, P. M. Retrograde amnesia: Temporal gradient in very long-term memory following electroconvulsive therapy. *Science,* 1975, *187,* 77–79.

Thios, S. J., & D'Agostino, P. R. Effects of repetition as a function of study-phase retrieval. *Journal of Verbal Learning and Verbal Behavior,* 1976, *15,* 529–536.

Trow, W. C. Recall vs. repetition in the learning of rote and meaningful material. *American Journal of Psychology,* 1928, *40,* 112–116.

Tulving, E. The effects of presentation and recall of material in free-recall learning. *Journal of Verbal Learning and Verbal Behavior,* 1967, *6,* 175–184.

Tulving, E. Cue-dependent forgetting. *American Scientist,* 1974, *62,* 74–82.

Tulving, E. Ecphoric processes in recall and recognition. In J. Brown (Ed.), *Recall and recognition.* New York: Wiley, 1976.

Tulving, E. Relation between encoding specificity and levels of processing. In L. S. Cermak & F. I. M. Craik (Eds.), *Levels of processing in human memory.* Hillsdale, N.J.: Lawrence Erlbaum Associates, 1979.

Tulving, E., & Arbuckle, T. Y. Sources of intratrial interference in paired-associate learning. *Journal of Verbal Learning and Verbal Behavior,* 1963, *1,* 321–334.

Tulving, E., & Arbuckle, T. Y. Input and output interference in short-term associative memory. *Journal of Experimental Psychology,* 1966, *72,* 145–150.

Tulving, E., & Osler, S. Effectiveness of retrieval cues in memory for words. *Journal of Experimental Psychology,* 1968, *77,* 593–601.

Tulving, E., & Pearlstone, Z. Availability versus accessibility of information in memory for words. *Journal of Verbal Learning and Verbal Behavior,* 1966, *5,* 381–391.

Tulving, E., & Thompson, D. M. Encoding specificity and retrieval processes in episodic memory. *Psychological Review,* 1973, *80,* 352–373.

Tulving, E., & Watkins, M. J. On negative transfer: Effects of testing one list on the recall of another. *Journal of Verbal Learning and Verbal Behavior,* 1974, *13,* 181–193.

Tulving, E., & Watkins, M. J. Structure of memory traces. *Psychological Review,* 1975, *82,* 261–275.

Underwood, B. J. "Spontaneous recovery" of verbal associations. *Journal of Experimental Psychology,* 1948, *38,* 429–439.

Underwood, B. J. Speed of learning and amount retained: A consideration of methodology. *Psychological Bulletin,* 1954, *51,* 276–282.

Underwood, B. J. Degree of learning and the measurement of forgetting. *Journal of Verbal Learning and Verbal Behavior,* 1964, *3,* 112–119.

Underwood, B. J. Attributes of memory. *Psychological Review,* 1969, *76,* 559–573.

Underwood, B. J. Are we overloading memory? In A. W. Melton & E. Martin (Eds.), *Coding processes in human memory*. Washington, D.C.: V. H. Winston, 1972.

Wagner, A. R. SOP: A model of automatic memory processing in animal behavior. In N. E. Spear & R. R. Miller (Eds.), *Information processing in animals: Memory mechanisms*. Hillsdale, N.J.: Lawrence Erlbaum Associates, 1981.

Warrington, E. K., & Weiskrantz, L. An analysis of short-term and long-term memory defects in man. In J. A. Deutsch (Ed.), *The physiological basis of memory*. New York: Academic Press, 1973.

Watkins, M. J. Inhibition in recall with extralist ''cues.'' *Journal of Verbal Learning and Verbal Behavior*, 1975, *14*, 294–303.

Watkins, M. J. Engrams as cuegrams and forgetting as cue overload: A cueing approach to the structure of memory. In C. R. Puff (Ed.), *Memory organization and structure*. New York: Academic Press, 1979.

Watkins, M. J., & Todres, A. K. On the relation between recall and recognition. *Journal of Verbal Learning and Verbal Behavior*, 1978, *17*, 621–633.

Watkins, M. J., & Tulving, E. When retrieval cueing fails. *British Journal of Psychology*, 1978, *69*, 443–450.

Watkins, M. J.: & Watkins, O. C. Processing of recency items for free recall. *Journal of Experimental Psychology*, 1974, *102*, 488–493.

Watkins, M. J., & Watkins, O. C. Cue-overload theory and the method of interpolated attributes. *Bulletin of the Psychonomic Society*, 1976, *7*, 289–291. Watkins, O. C., & Watkins, M. J. Buildup of proactive inhibition as a cue-overload effect. *Journal of Experimental Psychology: Human Learning and Memory*, 1975, *104*, 442–452.

Whitten, W. B. II Retrieval ''depth'' and retrieval component processes: A levels-of-processing interpretation of learning during retrieval. (Tech. Rep. No. 3). Ann Arbor: University of Michigan, Human Performance Center, 1974.

Whitten, W. B. Initial-retrieval ''depth'' and the negative recency effect. *Memory & Cognition*, 1978, *6*, 590–598.

Whitten, W. B., & Bjork, R. A. Learning from tests: Effects of spacing. *Journal of Verbal Learning and Verbal Behavior*, 1977, *16*, 465–478.

Whitten, W. B., & Leonard, J. M. Learning from tests: Facilitation of delayed recall by initial recognition alternatives. *Journal of Experimental Psychology: Human Learning and Memory*, 1980, *6*, 127–234.

Zavortink, B., & Keppel, G. Retroactive inhibition as a function of List 2 study and test intervals. *Journal of Experimental Psychology*, 1969, *81*, 185–190.

6 Consolidation and Forgetting Theory

Geoffrey Keppel
University of California, Berkeley

The concepts of neural perseveration and consolidation were used to explain learning and memory phenomena by theorists writing in the shadow of Ebbinghaus. Just a few years after Ebbinghaus published his classical monograph, Müller and Pilzecker (1900) introduced the notion of perseveration to account for a number of their experimental findings. More specifically, they found that the memory for a set of learning materials was reduced by interpolating a second set of learning materials—the phenomenon of retroactive inhibition. They saw that this loss was unaffected by the similarity of the two sets and that it was greater when the second set was presented immediately after the first set (17 sec) than after a delay of 6 min. To account for these findings, they speculated that neural activity representing the effects of learning continues, or perseverates, following the cessation of practice and continues until the neural trace is fully formed, or is consolidated. They further proposed that any activity that disrupts this consolidation process will adversely affect subsequent recall of the material and that the negative effect of this interpolated activity decreases as the interval between the two tasks lengthens.

In his review of the literature on perseverative neural processes and consolidation of the memory trace, Glickman (1961) reported that these ideas were widely held and debated by numerous psychologists during the early 1900s. To impart some of the flavor of these theoretical speculations, I will quote from one of the champions of this point of view: (DeCamp, 1915):

> From the neurological standpoint, in the learning of a series of syllables, we may assume that a certain group of synapses, nerve cells, nerve paths, centres, etc., are involved. Immediately after the learning process the after-discharge continues for a

149

short time, tending to set associations between just learned syllables. Any mental activity engaged in during this after-discharge, involving or partially involving the same neurological group, tends, more or less, to block the after-discharge, and give rise to retroactive inhibition [p. 68].''

Beginning in the 1920s, consolidation theory was replaced by various forms of interference theory as the favored explanation of retroactive inhibition. In fact, the interruption of the neural trace has never returned as a serious explanation of this phenomenon. Part of the reason was the development of theories that specified the characteristics and nature of the interference, and paradigms and methodology that permitted their direct study and measurement. (See Postman, 1971, pp. 1087–1102, for a review of this literature.) Another part of the reason was the difficulty with which a simple consolidation theory could account for *proactive* inhibition—interference attributed to material learned *prior* to the material being recalled. The theory would also have trouble explaining certain other phenomena in the memory literature, for example, spontaneous recovery—improvement in recall of the first set of material following the completion of the interpolated activity—and the detailed effects of memory following periods of sleeping and waking (see Ekstrand, Barrett, West, & Maier, 1977).

Consolidation theory did eventually return to human memory in the 1960s, but through a different methodology and a different set of paradigms. One of these developments, for example, was the interest in short-term memory and the possibility of studying retention functions very precisely for individual items presented once (see Melton, 1963). I will discuss a number of these developments and offer an assessment of the impact they have had or may have in theoretical explanations of memory phenomena. I will consider only experimental studies in this brief review and omit the relevant evidence from clinical studies on retrograde amnesia. (Larry Squire, Neal Cohen, and Lynn Nadel address this particular line of evidence in Chapter 8, this volume.)

EVIDENCE FOR CONSOLIDATION

Reminiscence

The phenomenon of reminiscence refers to an *improvement* in memory performance with time. Consolidation theory accounts for reminiscence in terms of a perseverating trace that requires time to mature and to develop into a stable and effective memory. Assessing memory before the consolidation is complete will tap a less well-formed trace and lead to less than optimal recall performance. The original demonstrations of reminiscence (see Buxton, 1943) found increases in memory for prose material and for poetry over retention intervals measured in days, but these gains were shown later to be due to the fact that the same subjects were tested repeatedly at the different retention intervals. That is, the immediate retention test is simply not a transparent assessment of the status of memory taken at the start of the retention interval but affords practice and rehearsal on the critical material: this additional study may provide sufficiently strong benefits to reverse the "normal" forgetting process and produce a net improvement on subsequent retention tests (see Ammons & Irion, 1954). As a consequence, this form of reminiscence cannot be interpreted unequivocally as evidence for the perseveration and consolidation of the memory trace because it is not possible with this sort of design to disentangle the practice effects from autonomous changes in memory storage. When the multiple testing was eliminated in subsequent studies through the use of independent groups of subjects for the immediate test and for the different delayed tests, reminiscence virtually disappeared from the literature.

In more recent times, reminiscence has been reported with short lists of paired associates that were presented once over retention intervals ranging from 0 to 24 sec (Keppel & Underwood, 1967: Peterson, 1966a). (Scheirer & Voss, 1969, found increases in recall up to 2 min. but these increases were attributed to the nature of the experimental design rather than to "bona fide"reminiscence.) Peterson (1966b) interpreted these findings in terms of a consolidation process that he believed was responsible for recall after relatively long retention intervals. Interference theory can also explain the same findings in terms of the retroactive inhibition, or input interference (see Tulving & Arbuckle, 1963), produced during list presentation, and the spontaneous recovery of these pairs during the period following presentation. In a five-pair list, for example, the first pair would be subjected to input interference generated by the presentation of the remaining four pairs for study, the second pair would be subjected to input interference from the remaining three, and so on. A retention interval introduced after the presentation of the last pair could then permit the recovery of some or all the pairs subjected to this retroactive inhibition occurring during the presentation of the list. The net result of this process, of course, would be the occurrence of reminiscence.

The analysis of recall as a function of presentation order could provide convincing support for this particular interpretation of reminiscence. For example, one might expect reminiscence to be associated with pairs presented earlier in the list, which are subjected to more potential retroaction, than those presented later in the list. The first pair might show the most recovery, that is, reminiscence, subsequent pairs less recovery, and the last pair no recovery since logically this pair is not subjected to any input interference.[1] Unfortunately, experiments have not been designed to provide unambiguous information relevant to the interpretation of reminiscence in terms of retroactive inhibition and spontaneous recovery. What is needed, of course, are data where any interference produced by the

---

[1]In this regard, it is interesting to note that Walker (1967) reported an analysis that suggests that reminiscence is due largely to the pair presented first.

testing of the pairs is carefully controlled. This may be accomplished by comparing recall probabilities as a function of presentation order and retention interval separately for each testing position. The first pair tested would provide recall data that are free from testing, or output, interference (see Tulving & Arbuckle, 1963), the remaining pairs would provide recall data obtained under increasing amounts of output interference. The ideal experiment, which would require thorough counterbalancing of pairs as well as of presentation and testing orders, to my knowledge has not yet been reported.

Another type of experimental paradigm has been used to study a reminiscence-like phenomenon that is called "hypermnesia" by Erdelyi and his associates. The basic finding originally reported by Erdelyi and Becker (1974) and replicated many times by Erdelyi and other researchers consisted of an increase in recall over a series of three recall tests given to the same group of subjects with no new presentation of the learning material. These data are not directly relevant to the consolidation question addressed in this chapter, however, because they seem adequately explained by other interpretations, such as the increased recall time afforded by the series of recall tests (Roediger & Thorpe, 1978) and by the multiple testing of subjects in the successive-recall conditions. Even the experiment reported by Shapiro and Erdelyi (1974), in which subjects received only one test after either 30 sec. or 5 min. and "reminiscence" was reported, can be explained by the active rehearsal engaged in by the subjects receiving the delayed retention test. What would be most convincing, of course, is an experiment in which rehearsal is minimized during the retention interval. It appears, then, that the phenomenon of hypermnesia reported by Erdelyi and his coworkers more closely resembles that reported by the early investigators studying reminiscence, e.g., Ballard (1913), and criticized years later by Ammons and Irion (1954) for the same use of repeated recall tests. Erdelyi and Kleinbard (1978, p. 287) seem to be of the same opinion. In any case, these interesting experiments do not provide data that are directly relevant to the perseveration and consolidation process.

Arousal and Forgetting

The major evidence responsible for the renewed interest in consolidation, however, comes from experiments in which material is acquired under different degrees of arousal and then tested for recall after varying intervals of time.[2] The primary paradigm was originally introduced by Kleinsmith and Kaplan (1963). Subjects were presented eight word-number pairs one by one. The galvanic skin response (GSR)—a measure of electrical conductivity of the skin presumed to reflect arousal—was recorded 4 sec after presentation. Pairs that showed a large

---

[2]For a detailed and comprehensive review of the earlier literature on this topic, see Uehling (1972).

decrease in skin resistance were classified as having been learned under "high arousal"; pairs that showed a small decrease were classified as having been learned under "low arousal." Different groups of subjects were tested for recall after five retention intervals ranging from 2 min to 1 week. A segregation of high and low pairs was then undertaken for each subject and recall charted over the retention intervals. The amazing finding that excited and puzzled many researchers was the *qualitatively different retention functions* observed for the two types of pairs. More specifically, low arousal pairs showed "normal" forgetting, a downward-sloped curve dropping from a high of roughly 45% recall after 2 min to essentially zero recall after 1 week. High arousal pairs, on the other hand, showed a nearly opposite trend, an upward-sloping curve rising from a low of approximately 10% recall on the 2-min test and over 40% recall on the 1-week test. Another way of expressing this dramatic gain is as a percentage based on recall obtained 2 minutes after presentation. As reported by Kleinsmith and Kaplan (1963), "After 20 min., the increase is more than 100%, and after 45 min. it has increased 400%. This high capacity for recall of high arousal pairs persists for at least a week [p. 191]." In an experiment reported a year later, covering the same retention intervals but using nonsense syllable stimuli instead of words, Kleinsmith and Kaplan (1964) found nearly identical results—rapid forgetting for low arousal pairs and extremely low recall initially, followed by striking reminiscence for high arousal pairs.

These results were interpreted in terms of the consolidation of the memory trace. The size of the GSR deflection was assumed to index the degree to which a memory trace was in the process of perseverating. High perseveration has two consequences for recall, namely, relative inaccessibility of the trace during the period of consolidation and eventually more successful transfer to long-term or permanent memory. Thus, high arousal pairs are more difficult to recall during the interval following presentation because of the perseverating trace but relatively more easy to recall later when the consolidation process has fully run its course.

Many investigators have studied this phenomenon and have experienced varying degrees of success in duplicating the provocative results. Only one researcher (Butter, 1970) found the same reverse temporal trend, however, and she found the interaction *twice*, both with the original Kleinsmith and Kaplan materials and with an entirely new set of materials varying widely in concreteness and imagery. Others have obtained the same sort of interaction between arousal and retention interval, but not as dramatically as in the original report (see, for example, Kaplan & Kaplan, 1969; McLean, 1969; Osborne, 1972; and Walker & Tarte, 1963). Still others have been unable to obtain results even remotely supporting this particular interpretation of the forgetting process (e.g., Corteen, 1969; Saufley & LaCava, 1977; Schmitt & Forrester, 1973).

The studies I have just mentioned used the GSR to identify high and low arousal pairs and generally have employed a within-subjects design in which each subject supplies an equal number of high and low pairs for the analysis. Some investigators have taken a different approach and compared the retention functions for *subjects* who differ in arousal. Howarth and Eysenck (1968), for example, selected individuals who produced scores at the two extremes of the Eysenck Extraversion Scale. According to Eysenck (1967), this division will segregate subjects in terms of their basal levels of general arousal, i.e., extroverts generally exhibiting low arousal and introverts generally exhibiting high arousal. Howarth and Eysenck found that low arousal subjects showed substantial forgetting over a 24-hr period. High arousal subjects showed a nearly identical reverse retention function, with substantial reminiscence observed over the same retention period. You will note that these results directly parallel those reported by Kleinsmith and Kaplan (1963) for high and low arousal *pairs*. Unfortunately, however, this clear-cut and impressively corroborative finding has not been reported by others attempting to replicate the phenomenon. McLaughlin (1968); for example, found no differences in forgetting for the two types of subjects in what appears to be a reasonably close replication of the Howarth-Eysenck study.

The forgetting functions for high and low arousal subjects have been studied in experiments in which subjects are classified according to differences on physiological measures rather than on the basis of scores on psychological tests. Kleinsmith, Kaplan, and Tarte (1963) used the GSR to measure arousal during the first minute of learning. Although they were interested in determining the nature of the association between GSR and recall after 6 min and 1 week, it is possible to compare the retention functions for high and low arousal subjects from the data presented in their paper. A comparison of the eight subjects producing the lowest GSRs with the eight subjects producing the highest GSRs over the two retention intervals shows better recall by the high arousal subjects, for *both* retention intervals, and no interaction. Osborne (1972) used the salivary reflex to identify low and high arousal subjects. (Low arousal subjects salivate less in response to lemon juice applied to the mouth than do high arousal subjects.) On the basis of the preliminary testing of 99 subjects, Osborne selected for study the 20 highest and the 20 lowest for the main part of the experiment. Subjects in this part were presented nonsense syllable-number pairs under incidental learning instructions and tested after either 2 min or 24 hrs. He found the expected interaction—forgetting for low arousal subjects and reminiscence for high arousal subjects—but his evidence is not strong statistically and has severe "floor" effects because of the single presentation and incidental instructions.

Finally, a number of investigators have attempted to induce differences in arousal by experimental means. One approach, taken by Berlyne and his associates (Berlyne, Borsa, Craw, Gelman, & Mandell, 1965; Berlyne, Borsa, Hamacher, & Koenig, 1966), consisted of the application of blasts of white noise during learning. Research has shown that white noise raises the GSR of a subject for at least 10–15 minutes; therefore, the procedure provides a convenient way of achieving experimental control over arousal. McLean (1969) reported similar results of slightly larger magnitude. Taken as a whole, these experiments produced results in support of the Kleinsmith and Kaplan position, but just barely. The differences on the immediate test and delayed tests were in the expected opposite directions; however, they were generally quite small in magnitude when compared with the original findings of Kleinsmith and Kaplan. These results are typically interpreted in terms of consolidation, but Hamilton, Hockey, and Quinn (1972) suggested an alternative explanation based on a consideration of serial position cues. More specifically, they speculated that aroused subjects pay more attention to the order in which the pairs are presented than do unaroused subjects. Because pairs usually are tested in a different order from that used to present them, the immediate deficit observed when white noise is presented during learning may be due to the differential use of these irrelevant cues by the aroused subjects rather than to interference with the consolidation process.

Other approaches have been used to arouse subjects differentially during the learning session. For example, Batten (1967) used drugs; Geen (e.g., 1973) employed different social settings to manipulate arousal. Although these studies have strongly supported the Kleinsmith and Kaplan analysis, they can be explained in other ways when the designs are given careful scrutiny.

In summary, I am not impressed with the robustness of the interaction between arousal and retention interval so dramatically represented in the work of Kleinsmith and Kaplan. Results *that* strong and clear-cut should have no difficulty being replicated by others, but this is exactly what has happened. Data that appeared to lend strong support to a consolidation view of forgetting and to offer real problems for other theories of forgetting now are of questioned reliability, to say it most negatively, or are of limited generality, to say it most positively.

The Effects of Repetition

Most of the research I have mentioned usually involved a single exposure of the material and a recall test administered at some point following the presentation of the stimulus material. What does the consolidation view say should happen when subjects are given multiple learning trials? What would happen to the retention functions for material learned under conditions of high and low arousal?

Walker (1967) has indicated that multiple learning trials should produce what he calls a negative effect of repetition for material learned under high arousal. That is, he expects high arousal pairs that are associated with a considerable amount of perseveration not to show as much of a gain from continued practice as do low arousal pairs. The reason for this expectation is that following presentation high arousal pairs are in a sort of "refractory period" that will not permit the full benefits of additional presentations to accrue to them. Tarte (1964) tested this notion in his dissertation, but the results were complicated and relatively unsupportive of predictions based on the consolidation position.

Osborne (1972) investigated Walker's theory in a simple, straightforward, design. He varied the number of times high and low arousal pairs were presented

(1, 2, or 3 repetitions) and assessed performance for independent groups tested immediately after the last exposure trial. He found no evidence for a negative repetition bias for the high arousal pairs. In fact, high arousal pairs produced *superior* performance after one or two repetitions. He replicated this finding in a second experiment. Several studies have provided a test of Walker's prediction by inducing arousal in an experimental setting rather than by comparing high and low arousal pairs. Berlyne (Berlyne, Borsa, Craw, Gelman, & Mandell, 1965; Berlyne, Borsa, Hamacher, & Koenig, 1966), for example, used white noise to induce arousal during learning and found a small advantage for the no-noise control condition relative to the noise conditions. Taken as a whole, these experiments are only weakly supportive of the consolidation position espoused by Walker.

I will now consider an entirely different but relevant paradigm than has been used to study the effects of repetition. These studies have been concerned with the exact timing of the second presentation. The general finding is that spaced repetitions are superior to massed repetitions and the phenomenon is called the "spacing effect." Landauer (1969) has interpreted the spacing effect in terms of a consolidation-like process. More specifically, he assumes that transfer to permanent store is accomplished some time after the presentation of the stimulus material and that an optimal interval exists after which a second presentation adds maximally to the reverberating trace and eventually to permanent store. This interval appears to be approximately 15 sec or so. A similar proposal has been offered by Peterson (1966b). These two theories view consolidation as a general property of the learning organism. Reminiscence—the gradual increase in permanent memory—is present for any type of material or subject, not just with material learned under high arousal.

Numerous other theories have been offered to account for the general appearance of a spacing effect and for the sorts of data cited by Landauer and by Peterson in favor of their own interpretations. These have been reviewed by Hintzman (1974). None of these various theories seems capable of offering a complete explanation of the phenomena associated with the spacing effect. The consolidation explanation has not attracted many followers, perhaps for the reason Hintzman suggested, namely, that researchers in the field of human memory favor explanations that specify the active involvement of the learner rather than the more-or-less automatic, involuntary, processing of the memory trace proposed by consolidation theorists.

COMMENTS

In this brief review, I have summarized and evaluated the most well-known phenomena generally offered in support of a consolidation process in human learning and memory. On the basis of this literature, I have the following observations and comments to offer.

Connection Between Behavioral Evidence and Neurological Theory

For a cognitively oriented psychologist, I find little connection between the behavioral evidence obtained from human learning experiments on the one hand and neurophysiological theory on the other. I can expesss this puzzle best with a series of questions: What exactly is being consolidated in a human learning experiment? Is it the entire stimulus complex or the products of the subject's voluntary or involuntary abstraction? Can we really extrapolate from the neurophysiological evidence based on much simpler experimental preparations to the experimental settings of the typical human learning study? As one example, are the time parameters associated with certain neurophysiological processes measured at the neuronal level of any relevance to the time factors generally studied and manipulated in the human learning laboratory? Stated from the other "direction," how do researchers at the *neurophysiological* level view the seemingly relevant data from human learning experiments? Are they convinced that the observation of reminiscence for high arousal pairs and forgetting for low arousal pairs, for instance, demands a consolidation explanation at the neurophysiological level? In short, we can ask: Is there any realistic rapprochment at this time between the two fields that differ so widely on so many important and relevant dimensions? I simply am not convinced that the concepts of perseveration and consolidation "buy" the cognitive psychologist any explanatory power, except perhaps as a metaphor and as a reasonable explanation of retrograde amnesia.

Generality and Reliability of the Arousal Effects

I believe there is sufficient cause to question the strength of the memory evidence offered in support of a consolidation theory of forgetting. Reminiscence, as defined unambiguously with independently tested groups of subjects, has yet to become an established, or reliable, phenomenon in human memory. Even the stunning effects originally reported by Kleinsmith and Kaplan have not received the widespread replication that one would expect for a phenomenon that appeared so strong, stable, and dramatic when first it was reported. But this is what I find in the literature.

If we examine the arousal experiments chronologically, we seem to see a steady washing away of the original results with the later studies. We are all aware of the urge to publish significant results and not to publish nonsignificant results, a bias generally perpetuated by journal editors who tend to reject the nonreplication or the nonsignificant finding and contributed to by researchers who tend to move on to other problems when they fail to replicate someone else's finding. Greenwald (1975) has argued that our journals may contain large numbers of undetected Type I errors stemming from exactly these sorts of decisions made by reviewers, editors, and researchers. Perhaps we need more exact replications in independent laboratories and journal policies that will permit the publishing of well-executed replication studies that reaffirm as well as question the reliability of new and potentially important findings. I do not know if the Kleinsmith and Kaplan findings represent a Type I error or if they are the result of a special combination of factors, but the relevant reports available in the literature certainly follow the temporal pattern described by Gardner (1966) in support of his proposition that the overlearning-reversal effect in the animal literature was originally the result of imprecise experimentation and Type I errors.

A more generous interpretation of the original Kleinsmith and Kaplan findings is that they lack *generality*. One reason for suggesting this possibility is an intriguing property associated with studies providing strong evidence for reverse temporal trends for high and low arousal pairs, namely, *no overall forgetting* when the data are averaged over the types of pairs or types of subjects. This clearly atypical finding—no forgetting over relatively long retention intervals— was first noted by Saufley and LaCava (1977), who also were unable to replicate the earlier findings. Countless experiments have shown significant amounts of forgetting over a 1-week period. Why are those showing an absolute increase in recall for the high arousal pairs an exception? Is there something peculiar about the testing situation, the materials, the subjects, or the instructions, to account for this unexpected failure to find overall forgetting when the results are averaged across both types of pairs? This situation reminds me of that reported by Postman, Stark, and Fraser (1968), who found that they could specify which experiments in the literature showed spontaneous recovery and which did not simply by noting the amount of forgetting exhibited by the *control group* over the recovery interval. More specifically, they discovered that experiments exhibiting large amounts of forgetting showed no spontaneous recovery, whereas those exhibiting small amounts did. Perhaps the amount of overall forgetting in the arousal studies provides a similar key.

Another reason for bringing up the question of generality is the fact that these experiments are relatively unique when compared with other retention studies. Most of the positive replications have employed the original Kleinsmith and Kaplan procedures of incidental learning instructions, a single presentation with long intervals between successive pairs, and the same set of stimulus materials. In addition, they have exhibited low recall probabilities in general. Early on, Walker (1967) admitted that these studies employed "rather unique procedures [p. 214]," but no one has attempted to pinpoint the critical characteristics responsible for producing the phenomenon. Kaplan and Kaplan (1969) introduced a number of changes in procedure, the most important of which in their opinion were the instructions for subjects to relax during presentation and the concurrent measurement of the GSR. Although they found some evidence for reminiscence of high arousal pairs, the overall results were qualitatively different from the original findings.

Consolidation and Forgetting Theory

I have shown that the evidence in support of consolidation theory obtained from the traditional human memory literature is not very strong. Straightforward studies of forgetting over relatively short retention intervals provide only a rare demonstration of reminiscence. Reminisence for high arousal pairs and for high arousal subjects have been reported, but not by later researchers who attempted to replicate the impressive findings. Other studies using experimental means to induce arousal in subjects have been moderately successful—but not as dramatic—in producing the reverse temporal trends that are critical for the argument. The effects of spaced repetitions have been interpreted in terms of consolidation, but other types of explanations have also been offered. Perhaps the strongest evidence now of a consolidation process comes from studies of retrograde amnesia. It is entirely possible, of course, that human studies will be devised that will permit the direct manipulation of consolidation processes with normal subjects in standard laboratory paradigms. At that time, I would assume that the role of consolidation in learning and forgetting will be taken more seriously than it is presently. In the meantime, I think we will find that cognitive theorists will continue to prefer cognitive explanations of learning and forgetting and to avoid explanations that view the human as a passive organism completely at the mercy of involuntary physiological processes.

REFERENCES

Ammons, H. & Irion, A. L. A note on the Ballard reminiscence phenomenon. *Journal of Experimental Psychology,* 1954, *48,* 184–186.

Ballard, P. B. Oblivescence and reminiscence. *British Journal of Psychology Monograph Supplements,* 1913, No. 2.

Batten, D. E. Recall of paired-associates as a function of arousal and recall interval. *Perceptual and Motor Skills,* 1967, *24,* 1055–1058.

Berlyne, D. E., Borsa, D. M., Craw, M. A., Gelman, R. S., & Mandell, E. E. Effects of stimulus complexity and induced arousal on paired-associate learning. *Journal of Verbal Learning and Verbal Behavior,* 1965, *4,* 291–299.

Berlyne, D. E., Borsa, D. M., Hamacher, J. H., & Koenig, I. D. V. Paired-associate learning and the timing of arousal. *Journal of Experimental Psychology,* 1966, *72,* 1–6.

Butter, M. J. Differential recall of paired associates as a function of arousal and concreteness-imaginary levels. *Journal of Experimental Psychology,* 1970, *84,* 252–256.

Buxton, C. E. The status of research on reminiscence. *Psychological Bulletin,* 1943, *40,* 313–340.

Corteen, R. S. Skin conductance changes and word recall. *British Journal of Psychology,* 1969, *60,* 81–84.

DeCamp, J. E. A study of retroactive inhibition. *Psychological Monographs,* 1915, *19*(4, Whole No. 84).

Ekstrand, B. R., Barrett, T. R., West, J. N., & Maier, W. G. The effect of sleep on human long-term memory. In R. R. Drucker-Colín, & J. E. McGaugh (Eds.), *Neurobiology of sleep and memory.* New York: Academic Press, 1977.

160   KEPPEL

Erdelyi, M. H., & Becker, J. Hypermnesia for pictures: Incremental memory for pictures but not words in multiple recall trials. *Cognitive Psychology*, 1974, *6*, 159–171.

Erdelyi, M. H., & Kleinbard, J. Has Ebbinghaus decayed with time?: The growth of recall (hypermnesia) over days. *Journal of Experimental Psychology: Human Learning and Memory*, 1978, *4*, 275–289.

Eysenck, H. J. *The biological basis of personality*. Springfield, Ill.: Charles C. Thomas, 1967.

Gardner, R. A. On box score methodology as illustrated by three reviews of overtraining reversal effects. *Psychological Bulletin*, 1966, *66*, 416–418.

Geen, R. G. Effects of being observed on short- and long-term recall. *Journal of Experimental Psychology*, 1973, *100*, 395–398.

Glickman, S. E. Perseverative neural processes and consolidation of the memory trace. *Psychological Bulletin*, 1961, *58*, 218–233.

Greenwald, A. G. Consequences of prejudice against the null hypothesis. *Psychological Bulletin*, 1975, *82*, 1–20.

Hamilton, P., Hockey, G. R. J., & Quinn, J. G. Information selection, arousal and memory. *British Journal of Psychology*, 1972, *63*, 181–189.

Hintzman, D. L. Theoretical implications of the spacing effect. In R. L. Solso (Ed.), *Theories in cognitive psychology: The Loyola symposium*. Hillsdale, N.J.: Lawrence Erlbaum Associates, 1974.

Howarth, E., & Eysenck, H. J. Extraversion, arousal, and paired-associate learning. *Journal of Experimental Research in Personality*, 1968, *3*, 114–116.

Kaplan, R., & Kaplan, S. The arousal-retention interaction revisited: The effects of some procedural changes. *Psychonomic Science*, 1969, *15*, 84–85.

Keppel, G., & Underwood, B. J. Reminiscence in the short-term retention of paired-associate lists. *Journal of Verbal Learning and Verbal Behavior*, 1967, *6*, 375–382.

Kleinsmith, L. J., & Kaplan, S. Paired-associate learning as a function of arousal and interpolated interval. *Journal of Experimental Psychology*, 1963, *65*, 190–193.

Kleinsmith, L. J., & Kaplan, S. Interaction of arousal and recall interval in nonsense syllable paired-associate learning. *Journal of Experimental Psychology*, 1964, *67*, 124–126.

Kleinsmith, L., Kaplan, S., & Tarte, R. The relationship of arousal to short-term and long-term memory. *Canadian Journal of Psychology*, 1963, *17*, 393–397.

Landauer, T. K. Reinforcement as consolidation. *Psychological Review*, 1969, *76*, 82–96.

McLaughlin, R. J. Retention in paired-associate learning related to extroversion and neuroticism. *Psychonomic Science*, 1968, *13*, 333–334.

McLean, P. D. Induced arousal and time of recall as determinants of paired-associate recall. *British Journal of Psychology*, 1969, *60*, 57–62.

Melton, A. W. Implications of short-term memory for a general theory of memory. *Journal of Verbal Learning and Verbal Behavior*, 1963, *2*, 1–21.

Müller, G. E., & Pilzecker, A. Experimentelle Beiträge zur Lehre vom Gedächtniss. *Zeitschrift für Psychologie*, 1900, Suppl. No. 1.

Osborne, J. W. Short- and long-term memory as a function of individual differences in arousal. *Perceptual and Motor Skills*, 1972, *34*, 587–593.

Peterson, L. R. Reminiscence in short-term retention. *Journal of Experimental Psychology*, 1966, *71*, 115–118. (a)

Peterson, L. R. Short-term verbal memory and learning. *Psychological Review*, 1966, *73*, 193–207. (b)

Postman, L. Transfer, interference and forgetting. In J. W. Kling & J. A. Riggs (Eds.), *Woodworth & Schlosberg's experimental psychology* (3rd ed). New York: Holt, Rinehart, & Winston, 1971.

Postman, L., Stark, K., & Fraser, J. Temporal changes in interference. *Journal of Verbal Learning and Verbal Behavior*, 1968, *7*, 672–694.

Roediger, H. L., III, & Thorpe, L. A. The role of recall time in producing hypermnesia. *Memory and Cognition,* 1978, *6,* 296–305.

Saufley, W. H., Jr., & LaCava, S. C. Reminiscence and arousal: Replications and the matter of establishing a phenomenon. *Bulletin of the Psychonomic Society,* 1977, *9,* 155–158.

Scheirer, J. C., & Voss, J. F. Reminiscence in short-term memory. *Journal of Experimental Psychology,* 1969, *80,* 262–270.

Schmitt, J. C., & Forrester, W. E. Effects of stimulus concreteness-imagery and arousal on immediate and delayed recall. *Bulletin of the Psychonomic Society,* 1973, *2,* 25–26.

Shapiro, S. R., & Erdelyi, M. H. Hypermnesia for pictures but not words. *Journal of Experimental Psychology,* 1974, *103,* 1218–1219.

Tarte, R. D. *The effects of time on reactivation or interference on trace consolidation in verbal learning* (Doctoral dissertation, University of Michigan). Ann Arbor, Mich.: University Microfilms, 1964, No. 65–5948.

Tulving, E., & Arbuckle, T. Y. Sources of intratrial interference in immediate recall of paired associates. *Journal of Verbal Learning and Verbal Behavior,* 1963, *1,* 321–334.

Uehling, B. S. Arousal in verbal learning. In C. P. Duncan, L. Sechrest, & A. W. Melton (Eds.), *Human memory: Festschrift in honor of Benton J. Underwood.* New York: Appleton-Century-Crofts, 1972.

Walker, E. L. Arousal and the memory trace. In D. P. Kimble (Ed.), *The organization of recall.* New York: New York Academy of Sciences, 1967.

Walker, E. L., & Tarte, R. D. Memory storage as a function of arousal and time with homogeneous and heterogeneous lists. *Journal of Verbal Learning and Verbal Behavior,* 1963, *2,* 113–119.

7 Departures from Reality in Human Perception and Memory

Elizabeth F. Loftus
University of Washington

John C. Yuille
University of British Columbia

INTRODUCTION: TRACE THEORY AND TRADITIONAL MEMORY RESEARCH

A quiet afternoon in a pharmacy is disrupted by the sudden appearance of a young man wielding a knife. In the presence of six customers and two staff, he threatens a female employee with the knife, demanding: "I want drugs. Give me all of your drugs and hurry up." While the pharmicist is unlocking the safe containing the controlled drugs, the intruder opens the cash register and removes all of the money. He then moves to the back of the pharmacy, and removes a quantity of drugs. He flees from the store, after which the police are called. During the three minute period between the phone call and the arrival of the police, three of the patrons of the pharmacy, who are acquaintances, have an opportunity to discuss the event with one another so that they could "cement in their minds their description of that horrible creature." Two policemen arrive and begin to separately interview the witnesses. The police are unhappy, although not surprised, to find a considerable discrepancy among the witnesses concerning the appearance of the thief as well as the sequence of events. In fact, the major consistency is among the three acquaintances. Otherwise, the witnesses are unable to agree on the height, weight, clothing, and age of the thief.

Two weeks after the incident the two employees and three of the witnesses are asked to go through a set of 400 pictures supplied by a computer sort from the library of police mug shots. One employee and one eyewitness identify the same picture. The others are unable to identify anyone. The individual identified by the two witnesses is arrested and placed in a lineup, which is viewed individually by all eight witnesses. Four of the witnesses, all of whom had previously seen pictures, identified the accused. Three of the remainder could not make a positive identification; one witness identified a police officer who was serving as a foil in the lineup.

This incident represents a synthesis of a number of case histories and is typical of memory in a "natural" crime situation. The questions that are critical here are: 1) What is it that an eyewitness perceives in such a situation? 2) In what form is that information "stored"? 3) What happens to that information between its registration and its subsequent recall? and 4) How does recall occur?

One would expect to find some of the answers to these questions in the data and theories of experimental psychology. However, this expectation is not easily met. This is not a result of a lack of effort but a reflection of the methodology that psychologists have employed in their research. During the past century, experimental psychologists have devoted considerable effort to the investigation of the nature of human learning and memory. This endeavor has been characterized by a concern for *experimental rigor* and *control*. Diverse paradigms, control procedures, and a variety of stimuli have been employed to meet both experimental and theoretical needs, resulting in a substantial body of data. Researchers have used simple materials such as nonsense syllables, single words, or sentences in their studies of memory. These stimuli were deemed to be most useful because of the capacity of the experimenter to control what were considered to be relevant attributes, such as the meaningfulness, familiarity, or concreteness of verbal materials.

As a consequence of this controlled investigation, numerous memory models have been generated, and yet the consequent theoretical disagreements have frequently led to the energetic pursuit of relatively trivial questions. In a 1970 review of memory research, Tulving and Madigan concluded: "Nothing very much has changed over the past hundred years in the understanding of how people learn and remember things. Anyone disputing this assertion is either not familiar with understanding of these phenomena, or is fixated on minor details while we are talking about the general picture [p. 476–7]."

One result of this state of affairs is that those who are concerned with the operation of human memory in everyday or real life situations find little value in the traditional research efforts of the experimental psychologist. For example, a 1976 report of a British commission, under the direction of Lord Devlin, charged with investigating issues related to eyewitness memory and identification, noted that "a gap exists between academic research into the powers of the human mind and the practical requirements of courts of law, and the stage seems not yet to have been reached at which the conclusions of psychological research are sufficiently widely accepted or tailored to the needs of the judicial process to become the basis for procedural change [p. 73]." Similarly, in a recent review of the literature related to eyewitness memory, Clifford and Bull (1978) asserted:

The theoretical models of man with which experimental psychology operates are noteworthy both for their dissimilarity one from the other and for their common dissimilarity with the reality which exists when a person sees a criminal episode and tries to remember it . . . (the models) failed for a greater or lesser number of reasons, but all were inadequate uniformly because they failed to take into account man's thinking, feeling, believing totality [p. 5].

In spite of the artificial character of traditional memory research, and the disparity among theoretical models, there has been persistently a characteristic attribute to memory: the trace. From the perspective of trace theory, an experience is assumed to involve a code (response, reaction, cell assembly, etc.) that is replicated in memory. The memory trace is something that can be revitalized at a later time, causing the event to be re-experienced. This trace view has strongly affected the dialogue between investigators of memory and those concerned with finding the physiological correlates of memorial processes. For example, a concern with the characteristics of consolidation implicitly reflects the adoption of a trace model.

Throughout psychology's history, the trace idea has intruded itself. Take William James (1892), who expressed a belief that some people have memories that are virtually permanent, wheras others do not:

The persistence or permanence of the paths is a physiological property of the brain-tissue of the individual, whilst their number is altogether due to the facts of his mental experience. Let the quality of permanence in the paths be called the native tenacity, or physiological retentiveness. This tenacity differs enormously from infancy to old age, and from one person to another. Some minds are like wax under a seal—no impression, however disconnected with others, is wiped out. Others, like a jelly vibrate to every touch, but under usual conditions retain no permanent mark [p. 293].

Sigmund Freud, too, had an opinion about the permanence of memories. In treating patients who suffered from a variety of "nervous disorders," Freud thought it necessary to trace his patients' symptoms—such as tremors, tics, and paralyses—back to more remote memories; to early and seemingly common amnesia that overlays early childhood up to the age of about five. In order to truly understand a particular hysterical symptom, Freud argued, one must reach back into the earliest years of childhood. He reasoned that these early experiences, because they are typically forgotten, must have been crucial. By forgotten, however, Freud did not mean that these memories were lost forever. Rather, in his classic work, *Psychopathology of everyday life* (1901–1960), he claimed that "all impressions are preserved, not only in the same form in which they were first received, but also in all the forms which they have adopted in their further developments. . . . Theoretically, every earlier state of the memory content could thus be restored to memory again, even if its elements have long ago exchanged all their original connections for more recent ones [p. 274–275]." Thus, Freud held the view that whatever form conscious thought might take, the underlying memory traces remained unchanged over time. With techniques such as psychoanalysis, these original memories could be retrieved and illuminated.

Based only on informal observations, the views of James and Freud were speculative. But they would eventually receive some experimental support from the work of Wilder Penfield (1951; Penfield & Perot, 1963). As is well known, Penfield was operating on epileptic patients during the 1940s, removing the damaged areas of their brains. To guide himself in pinpointing the damage, Penfield stimulated the surface of the brain with an electric current in the hope of discovering the damaged areas of the brain. Penfield (1951) noted that certain placements of the electrode apparently caused some of the patients to re-experience events from their past. From these observations, he was led to his strong belief in permanence: "Thus, it would appear that the memory record continues intact even after the subject's ability to recall it disappears [p. 22]." Penfield's work is widely known and widely cited. What is less widely known is the fact that his conclusions were based upon very few patients who seemed not so much to be reliving their experiences but reconstructing them. Some have criticized the fact that the "memories" that Penfield uncovered were not verified, but in fact, such verification is probably impossible. To determine whether a memory had changed over time, one must know how it was represented when it was originally stored, not how the event really happened. This is because, as we discuss later, the initial representation might in itself depart significantly from reality.

It should be noted that trace theory has not been unopposed. On the other side of the ring, there were the Gestalt psychologists, whose views have been nicely summarized by Riley (1962), Many of the studies performed during the 1930s and 1940s by this group of psychologists were aimed at testing the hypothesis that memory traces continually undergo changes autonomously. A few studies concerned changes that were induced by the suggestion of verbal labels. Much of this research seemed at first blush to support the notion of progressive memory changes, usually in the direction of a "better" figure. However, Riley concluded his review by arguing that the hypothesis of autonomous change could not be proven or disproven. And, in terms of the impact of suggestive verbal labels, one could just as easily argue that these affected the response rather than modifying the memory.

By the 1960s, rarely did textbooks concern themselves with the question of the permanence of memories. Adams (1967), perhaps the exception, offered 10 pages under the heading of "Hypothesis that Memory is Permanent." In addition to noting some of the famous psychologists who believed in permanence, he aptly indicated why the issue is important in the first place. If memories are permanent, then "we are confronted with the fascinating possibility that ways may be devised to stimulate responses that normally would be considered forgotten [p. 28]." This would shift the focus of memory researchers to problems of retrieval from the memory store. The practical implications would be astounding. With sufficient research, the heavy burden that forgetting gives to society could potentially be lifted. Education might be more effective; students could be made to forget less. Refresher courses would become less necessary because people would need less refreshing. Airplane pilots would have fewer accidents because they could be made to be less likely to forget the responses needed to remedy an emergency. But alas, as Adams noted, the hypothesis of permanent memory never received serious research attention, and its status in the psychological literature seemed rather minor. In ending the section, Adams noted that the hypothesis "is of large potential significance, however, and should be a stimulus for behavioral research even though ways of testing it are foggy at the moment [p. 37]."

As we enter the 1980s, what have we learned about the permanence of memory? First, a substantial number of people believe in permanence. In a recent survey, people were specifically asked about their view on how human memory works (Loftus & Loftus, 1980). Most individuals indicated a belief that information in long-term memory is there, even though much of it cannot be retrieved. The reasons for holding this view varied. The most common reason for a belief in permanence involved the occasional recovery of an idea that a person had not thought about for quite some time. A second reason, commonly given by people trained in psychology, was knowledge of the work of Penfield. Occasionally respondents offered a comment about hypnosis, and more rarely about psychoanalysis and repression, sodium pentothal, or even reincarnation, to support their belief in the permanence of memory. A few were impressed by the accounts of people who have narrowly escaped sudden death; a stream of long lost memories alledgedly flashed before these people in the few seconds' time that seemed left to them. It is no wonder that people hold this view when they are exposed to comments like the following that appeared in an article entitled "The Magic of Memory," written for a popular science magazine (Cherry, 1980): "Almost all memory researchers now agree that our brains record—and on some level remember—everything that ever happens to us [p. 61]."

Thus, there is a widespread belief in the idea that memories, once stored, remain permanently, But does any empirical evidence bear on this question? The most succinct answer is "probably not." Traditional memory research, although useful for some purposes, has done little to enhance our understanding of memory for natural events. There are two other reasons for our lack of progress on this issue. First, a dilemma exists for any researcher of "permanence" in terms of the inability to know how information initially got represented in the first place. And, secondly, even if we assume that an accurate representation of reality was stored in memory, we do not have a handle on the changes in those representations that occur over the course of time. We now examine these two problems.

THE REPRESENTATION OF AN EVENT

A consistent criticism by psychologists of their discipline is the lack of integration among various subareas of the discipline. An excellent example of this is that students of human memory have generally ignored the role of perception and attention in their investigations (and vice versa). With the traditional memory research paradigms, experimental psychologists could take perception for granted because of the relatively simplistic materials they represented (e.g., pairs of words). Attention was not an issue because of the controlled presentation formats (e.g., memory drums). However, in everyday situations a variety of factors affect the perception of an event, and the selective nature of attention affects what is perceived. Obviously, a central concern in eyewitness research is the accuracy of the recall of the event. When the recall of the witness is demonstrated as departing from the facts of the event, we cannot simply conclude, as the experimental psychologist might, that some error in memory has occurred. This conclusion presumes that the event was originally registered correctly and that some subsequent distortion occurred. Although sometimes appropriate to laboratory studies of memory, this conclusion is inappropriate in most real life situations. Often, when recall is erroneous, the memory is an accurate recall of the original registration and it was the original registration that was incorrect. Misperception often reflects the constructive nature of perception. The role of top-down processes in the organization and interpretation of sensory information is well established (c.f., Glass, Holyoak, & Santa, 1979). An event is constructed, not simply received. (We should note here that unanimity concerning the constructive nature of perception does not exist. Some researchers [e.g., Gibson, 1966] assert that the retinal image contains sufficient information to perceive and identify objects.) A consequence of the constructive nature of perception is that, depending on the circumstances, human beings may not see critical elements of an event or alternatively, may perceive things that don't exist. One frequently used demonstration of this was first employed by Bruner and Postman (1949). Subjects saw a display of playing cards, for example 12 aces from all four suits, and were asked to report everything that they saw or thought they saw. After a brief glance, most subjects reported that they saw three aces of spades. Actually, there were more than three, but the others were colored red instead of black. People did not see the red aces of spades because they were not expecting them. In concluding, Bruner and Postman remarked that when expectations are violated by the environment, "the perceiver's behavior can be described as resistance to the recognition of the unexpected or incongruous [p. 222]."

In general, context has an enormous influence on perception. The contextural interpretation that a witness has given to a situation will profoundly affect the way in which he or she perceives that situation. In many instances critical aspects may be missed because they are not relevant to the context the individual has used in perceiving the event. Similarly, factors may be exaggerated to reflect an interpretation. One witness to the armed drugstore robbery, described at the beginning of this chapter, may have "seen" the thief as taller than he was because of his threatening behavior. Another, less intimidated witness, might have had a more accurate perception.

The rules that guide the construction of a percept, together with the context and expectancy effects, can lead a witness to perceive qualities or events that don't occur. Visual illusions provide an example. The visual illusion in Figure 7.1 is an excellent demonstration of this principle. The white triangle in the center does not exist; however, the minimum features for the perceptual system to believe that a triangle is there are present. Notice that once the system has "decided" that the triangular form exists, it improves upon it. You can almost see the lines forming the sides of the figure and the triangle appears to have a slightly different shade of white than the background (e.g., Coren, Porac, & Ward, 1979).

These constructive features of the visual system are best understood by an examination of the sequences involved in the perceptual process. Images from our visual environment are inverted, reversed, and focused by the lens on the light sensitive retina. The millions of neurons that constitute the retina perform a feature analysis of the light pattern. Through the mediating network of the cells that exist between the rods and cones and the optic tract, the light pattern is converted into a code that transmits to the brain a message concerning colors, points of contrast, motion, etc. The task for the central nervous system is to attempt to construct a visual image that best fits with: a) this feature code: and b)

FIG. 7.1.   The white triangle that does not really exist.

FIG. 7.2.   Rat–man figure (created by B. R. Bugelski).

any expectations, sets, etc. that exist concerning the nature of the external environment. If the viewer is exposed to a figure like Figure 7.2 and is provided with the label "rat" for this figure, he or she will report seeing a rat. Alternatively, if the label "man" is provided, although the visual stimulus doesn't change, the perception of it generally will.

Some recent research conducted by Treisman and Schmidt (1982) has apparently tapped one stage of the feature recombination involved in the construction of a percept. The experimenter presented, via a tachistoscope, a horizontal array of five items for 150 msec. The first and fifth items were single digits printed in black. The middle three items were colored letters (e.g., a green "T", a red "N", etc.). The task was to report the numbers first, followed by anything else that was seen. Frequently, a subject reported what Triesman calls 'illusory conjunctions.' The person stated that he or she *saw* a red P, when the array actually contained a red N and a blue P. Treisman interprets these results in terms of attention. The properties of those items attended are properly conjoined, whereas the features of unattended items may be conjoined as a result of expectancies or at random.

A critical point to note about the constructive process of perception is that it is indefinite in terms of its termination. There appears to exist a set of serial operations that promote greater degrees of abstraction or conceptualization in the registration of an event. Thus, for example, we might simply note that a flower is red, or we may proceed further to register the fact that it is fresh. This latter perception, of course, involves an examination of more of the details of the incoming information as well as an interpretation of the meaning of those details. We might proceed further to conceptualize this flower as being beautiful. This idea of levels of perception corresponds to the notion of levels of processing proposed by Craik and Lockhart (1972), and elaborated by Craik and Tulving (1975). Basically, they have argued that the degree of depth of processing of information has profound memorial consequences. The deeper the processing, the better the subsequent memory. Although not without theoretical problems (e.g., Baddeley, 1978; Nelson, 1977), this model has proven of heuristic value and has obvious implications for the explication of perception, and the relationship between perception and memory.

The extent to which the observer conceptualizes or interprets the experience during its occurrence is perhaps the central determinant of the quality of subsequent memory for that event. Doob and Kirshenbaum (1973) cite a case where a witness could only remember the fact that a thief was good-looking. It appears that this was the primary registration of her perception of the individual. Subsequently, she picked an individual from a lineup possibly because he was the best looking among the group. The classic work of Bartlett (1932) on memory provided an excellent description of the selective and interpretive nature of perception using face perception as an example. "(Faces) are very rarely . . . discriminated or analyzed in much detail. We rely rather upon the general impression, obtained at the first glance, and issuing in immediate attitudes of like or dislike, of confidence or suspicion, of amusement or gravity [p. 53]." It is the interpretation of the face that is retained. Thus, the "attitudes may strongly influence recall, and may tend in particular to produce stereotyped and conventional reproduction that adequately serve all normal needs, though they are very unfaithful to their originals [p. 55]."

The role that top-down processing plays in perception means that the nature of the registration of information in consciousness in human beings will always be indeterminant in terms of its accuracy. Before we even address the issue of the accuracy of memory, we must accept the constructed, interpreted, and therefore potentially biased nature of the information that originally enters the system. Consequently, in any complex real life situation, our capacity to judge the accuracy of memory or changes in memory over time will be substantially aided if we are able to determine the possible effects of context, expectancies, and interpretations to which the observer was subject.

Consider the drugstore robbery example. The disagreements among witnesses are what one should expect, given the constructive nature of perception. It is unlikely, if not impossible, that every witness would come to this situation with the same set of expectancies and the same set of constructive rules. Their interpretation of such characteristics as height, weight, and age are considerably dependent on their own individual experiences. Their disagreements don't necessarily reflect lying or deliberate distortion but may demonstrate an honest attempt by each witness to reconstruct the event as he or she saw it.

Constructive activity in the course of perception is complicated by the selective nature of attention. It is an obvious attribute of human cognition that only a limited subset of the impinging information can be represented in consciousness. This limited attentional capacity implies that selection from the total amount of information available must be made. There appears to be a complex set of rules that govern selective attention, some of which appear to be given and others that are acquired through environmental experience (e.g., Kahneman, 1973). The best example of the former is the orienting response (see Kling & Riggs, 1971). The registration of novel information or the appearance of an unexpected sound or motion will cause the mechanisms responsible for selection to orient to this information. The biological survival value of this mechanism is self-evident it allows the mobilization of the processing capacity of the organism to determine the value of the new information.

If this information poses some threat to the organism, a stress response will follow, in which the physical and psychological capabilities of the individual are recruited to meet the perceived threat. One important consequence for this discussion is the effect of the stress response upon selective attention. Since the pioneering work of Yerkes and Dodson (1908), we have known of the curvilinear relationship between the level of arousal and performance. Extremely low levels of arousal are associated with generally inefficient processing and activity levels and, consequently, less than optimum performance on most tasks. As the arousal of the organism increases to an optimum level, availability of both processing and motor functions permit the organism to achieve better and better levels of performance. However, as the arousal level moves beyond the optimum region, and as more and more stress is experienced, performance levels begin to decline. It appears that one of the mechanisms that is primarily responsible for this stress-associated change is the fact that the selective attention becomes more focused as stress increases. That is, as the individual experiences stress, there is a tendency for the attention mechanism to concentrate greater and greater amounts of the processing capacity upon the stimuli responsible for the stress (See Idzikowsi & Baddeley, in press). Again, the biological advantage of this relationship between stress and attention appears self-evident. If an organism is threatened by a predator, for example, being able to concentrate the full perceptual capacity on escaping from or otherwise dealing with that predator is of considerable survival value.

There is an interesting consequence of the stress/attention relationship for eyewitness memory. Most frequently, a witness views an unusual and upsetting scene. Whether the incident involves a severe automobile accident or a robbery or some act of violence, it is likely that it will be stressful for the witness. Generally speaking, the more major the crime, the more likely it is that stress is elicited in the witness. The greater the stress response in the witness, the more narrow the focus of attention and, consequently, the less detail that will be consciously attended.

The construction of a perceptual image involves a series of stages of progressive abstraction based upon the assimilation of incoming sensory information to the organizational rules of the perceiver. Each stage in perception takes the perceiver further from the physical characteristics of the information. The levels-of-processing metaphor is an appropriate one for elaborating the stages and for illustrating that the deeper levels of processing (which presumably only occur with attended information) may be the critical determinants of what is stored. From the subset of any situation that we select, we abstract and interpret to "make sense" of the event. It may be that what is stored is centrally affected by the conceptualization, attribution, and organization that has occurred during the perception of the event. When we attempt to determine what is stored, we must accept that it is not the event but rather its representation, and that the latter may depart, in significant ways, from the former.

To reiterate, the human observer in a real life situation will have a selected, constructed, and interpreted impression of an event. Thus, if there is storage of information, we must approach investigation of that storage with an understanding of its complex and problematic relationship with the original event. It is likely that of the limited aspects of an event that an individual perceives, the most available in memory is the conceptualization of the event. Thus, the female witness cited by Doob and Kirshenbaum (1973) remembered the fact that the thief was good-looking because she had conceptualized the experience in that fashion. This proved to be the most durable aspect of her memory of the event and guided very strongly her recognition memory when she was asked to view a lineup. The witnesses to the drugstore robbery differed in their recall, in part, because they were each remembering a differently conceptualized event.

To return to our contrast with traditional research, the paradigms typically employed by experimental psychologists have provided a rather different interpretation about the nature of what is stored. After subjects have devoted some number of trials to the memorization of a list of words or nonsense syllables, research often reveals rather good memory for the material. Thus, the kind of storage models that have been developed have attempted to describe the relatively verbatim nature of human storage. More recently, the computer has served as a model for this type of theorizing (e.g., Norman & Rumelhart, 1975). It is our contention, however, that the activities of the subject in the laboratory as well as the typical findings of experimental research provide an inappropriate and possibly incorrect view of the typical functioning of human memory. The memory performance in laboratory situations may be an artifact of the control imposed. Well-controlled lists of words provide little opportunity for the normal constructive process to reveal itself. In addition, the typical memory experiment has provided information of a kind and at a rate well within the attentional capabilities of the typical subject. Hence, the selective nature of attention was not revealed in the experimental investigation of memory. We would argue that, given the important influence of what is selected upon the interpretation and organization of an event, attention is a central component in determining what is stored.

Even in the confines of the laboratory, the relatively good immediate memory that is typically found deteriorates substantially with time. It appears that although we may have access to the attended details of an event for minutes or perhaps hours after that event, this availability rapidly disappears. But what remains? The constructionists would argue that what remains are the conceptual, interpretive qualities attributed to the event. When we try to recall something, we reconstruct the details of the event on the basis of these qualities. However, many others believe that even though the information cannot be reported, it still resides in memory.

THE PERMANENCE OF MEMORIES

In 1950 a curious experiment was performed in Cambridge, England (Belbin, 1950). Subjects were left sitting in a waiting room for two minutes, a room that contained a poster on a wall 12 feet away from where they sat. The poster depicted a boy running across a road between two cars and contained a verbal message at the bottom. Apparently the subjects were then brought into another room whereupon they ultimately were shown the poster and asked whether they recognized it. Prior to the recognition test, some subjects were asked to recall as much of the poster as they could; others were not. The results showed that, with no prior recall, 14 out of 16 subjects correctly recognized the picture. However, when the recognition test was preceded by recall, only 4 out of 16 subjects correctly recognized the picture.

Why did recall of the poster reduce subsequent recognition? One clue to this puzzle came from an analysis of recall protocols. Many subjects inserted erroneous details into their recall; it appears that these importations were the cause of the recognition failure. For example, one subject apparently imported a third car into his recollection. Later when shown the original picture, he said "No—not this picture—the original had a third car."

The poster study was conducted without the benefit of current methodological sophistication, but the result is indeed suggestive. Could it be that the mere act of recalling an event actually changes one's memory for that event? Does any empirical evidence bear on the question that remains in memory after the storage of information in memory?

There are two classes of phenomena that may be relevant. Some studies document the fact that information that has apparently been forgotten is recovered at some later time. The second group of studies show that information that was apparently stored cannot be retrieved at some later time. What is perhaps more interesting is the subclass of cases in which people not only fail to retrieve the original information, but insist with great confidence that it was never presented. We briefly consider these experimental findings.

Forgetting With Later Recovery

> Suppose we try to recall a forgotten name. The state of our consciousness is peculiar. There is a gap therein; but no mere gap. It is a gap that is intensively active. A sort of wraith of the name is in it, beckoning us in a given direction, making us at moments tingle with the sense of our closeness, and then letting us sink back without the longed-for term [James, 1890, p. 251].

Williams James was talking about the tip-of-the-tongue state, that semi-uncomfortable period in which a piece of information that we know is in memory simply eludes us. In many cases it will come. An easy way to help it along is to find the right retrieval cue. The work of Endel Tulving has provided us with information about the power of retrieval cues. In one study (Tulving & Pearlstone, 1966) subjects read a list of category names, such as animals and fruits, along with one or more instances of the category, for example, horse and peach. The subject's task was to remember only the instances, not the category names. Later, half were handed a sheet containing all the category names. All subjects had to write down as many instances from the original list as they could remember. The results showed that those subjects given the category names as cues recalled many more instances. To get a feeling for the magnitude of improvement that is possible, consider the subjects who were given a list of 48 items, or 12 categories of four words each. Those who were given category cues recalled about 30 words on the average, but the control group recalled only about 20 words. At a later time, the control group was supplied with the category names, and these subjects were able to recall about 28 words from the list. Those extra eight or so items must have been stored in the memory, but they could not be retrieved without a special retrieval cue. In other words, they were available in memory, but not accessible. The situation is analogous to that of a person who attempts to find a particular book in the library, only to discover that the card indicating its location is missing. The book is available, but it cannot be accessed. Providing the missing card, like providing the proper retrieval cues, is one of the best ways to facilitate retrieval.

Other researchers have shown that simple changes in the testing conditions can elicit information from memory that was previously unavailable. In one study, subjects read a story from the perspective of either a burglar or a person interested in buying a home. After recalling the story from one perspective, the subjects shifted to the other. After such a shift, people recalled additional, previously unrecalled information (Anderson & Pichert, 1978). In a second study, people read prose passages under one title, and later recalled under an alternative title. Changing the title led people to recall more of the actual material in the passage than those who did not receive a different title (Hasher & Griffin, 1978). These efforts indicate that information that is apparently not influencing memory can be brought to consciousness through additional techniques.

Finally, the research on "context effects" has shown that a person's ability to remember information is heavily influenced by the relation between the storage of that information and the retrieval context. With a different context, retrieval can suffer; with the same context, retrieval is enhanced. Context has been studied in a variety of forms. For example, Carr (1925) found that changes in maze illumination disrupted maze learning performance in rats. Burri (1931) found changes due to the presence or absence of an audience. Gartman and Johnson (1972) found changes due to the nearby list words. Eich, Weingartner, Stillman, and Gillin (1975) found changes due to the presence or absence of drugs, and Smith, Glenberg, and Bjork (1978) found changes due to environmental context. In short, context has been alleged to be responsible for enhancing recall in a variety of situations.

Certain disorders of memory have been studied that bear on the human ability to recover previously inaccessible information. If a person receives some kind of head injury, such as a severe blow, memory can be affected. That person may forget events that occurred during some time period leading up to the moment of the trauma (retrograde amnesia) and also forget events that occurred after the shock (anterograde amnesia). Can this lost information ever be recovered? The answer is clearly yes. In terms of anterograde amnesia, the period of loss occasionally becomes reduced spontaneously, as in the case presented by Russell and Nathan (1946/1969). The case concerned a man who sustained a head injury in July of 1942. A few weeks later he had a momentary retrograde amnesia and six days of nearly complete anterograde amnesia. However, ten weeks after his accident he remembered some new information spontaneously: While sitting quietly in bed he suddenly remembered being on the floor of a moving truck, and this was, in fact, the way he was brought to the hospital. With other patients, the loss of memory for events that occurred after the injury is not uniformly complete. Rather, in some cases, islands of memory emerge, such as memories concerned with special events, for example, the visit of an important relative (Russell & Nathan, 1946/1969).

Similar changes occur with events that took place prior to the incident. Retrograde amnesia is found not only after injury to the head, but also after electric convulsion therapy, acute cerebral anoxia as in hanging, severe loss of blood, and other traumas. It is longer in cases with more severe insults. However, even in severe cases, retrograde amnesia frequently shrinks or clears up (Glass, Holyoak, & Santa, 1979). In one reported case of a man injured in an air raid, the duration of the retrograde amnesia covered a period of six months. About a month later, the amnesia had shrunk to a few minutes and he remembered standing by the guns on the night he was injured, and that a few shells had been fired, but he did not remember any bombs (Russell & Nathan, 1946–1969). It is these sorts of examples that have led researchers to conclude that the amnesia represents a failure in retrieval, rather than a loss of stored information. Some have suggested that the shock puts the person in a dazed state during which he or she does not associate any of the events that have just occurred with the rest of the conceptual system. As a result, the person has no effective cues for recalling the event later on (Glass, Holyoak & Santa, 1979).

Beyond these examples, it is possible to find either clinical or experimental examples of confabulations with hypotheses followed by later recoveries: hysterical amnesias followed by later recoveries: "forgotten" ideas that emerged in subsequent dreams, daydreams, doodles, free associations, and other fantasy activities; and other recoveries of particularly unbearable memories that occur through the use of therapy, hypnosis, or drugs (Erdelyi, 1970: Erdelyi & Goldberg, 1979; Kihlstrom & Evans, 1979).

Forgetting Without Later Recovery

On the other hand, there are numerous instances in which information is not accessible, and never becomes so. Russell and Nathan (1946/1969) report that anterograde amnesia is "usually more or less permanent and unchanging [p. 9]" despite the occasional exceptions. Even with drug interventions, prior memories do not emerge. This happened in the case of a man who was thrown from a horse in July of 1941 but came to himself about 24 hours later. When examined, his memory of events before the injury was normal up to the morning of the day before the injury—he clearly remembered reporting sick because of a bad knee. But that is all he remembered of that day, and he remembered almost nothing of the day of his accident. He was given sodium amytal, which made him sleepy, euphoric, and talkative, but he recovered little in the way of additional memory (Russell & Nathan, 1945/1969).

It is probably exceedingly important that brain trauma typically has its effects on recent memory, rather than remote memory. The events forgotten are often of importance to the individual, yet for a time, and occasionally forever, they do not reappear, whereas distant memories of little importance are unaffected. This has led some investigators to conclude that as memories become older they become more strongly established, irrespective of their importance to the individual, whereas more recent memories are relatively liable to "traumatic extinction," however important they may be (Russell & Nathan, 1946/1969).

Turning now to ordinary people who try to remember rather ordinary information, one does not have to look very far to find experimental demonstrations of stored information which never again sees the light of consciousness. The most interesting examples are those in which memory is altered by subsequent inputs, and those in which an altered memory persists.

Consider the experiments of Loftus (see 1979 for a summary) which showed that reports of real world complex events can undergo systematic and predictible distortions. In an experiment reported by Loftus, Miller, and Burns (1978), the subjects viewed a series of 30 color slides depicting successive stages in an auto-pedestrian accident. The auto was a red Datsun seen traveling along a side street toward an intersection. For half of the subjects, the intersection had a stop sign; for the remaining subjects, it had a yield sign. The slides show the Datusn turning right and knocking down a pedestrian who was crossing at the crosswalk. Immediately after viewing the slides, the subjects answered a series of 20 questions. For half of the subjects, Question 17 was "Did another car pass the red Datsun while it was stopped at the stop sign?" The remaining subjects were asked the same question with the words "stop sign" replaced by "yield sign." The assignment of subjects to conditions produced a factorial design in which half of the subjects received consistent or correct information, and the other half received misleading or incorrect information. After a short filler activity, a two-forced-choice recognition test was administered. Two slide projectors were used to present 15 pairs of slides, each pair being presented for about 8 sec. For each pair of slides, the subjects were asked to select the slide they had seen earlier. The critical pair consisted of a slide depicting a red Datsun at a stop sign and another slide, nearly identical, depicting the Datsun at a yield sign. The results showed that when the intervening question contained misleading information, recognition performance was hindered. In one condition, for example, over 80% of the subjects who received misleading information responded incorrectly on the forced-choice recognition test. They indicated that they had seen the slide that corresponded to what they had been told rather than the slide that they had actually seen.

In fact it is relatively easy to take someone who has seen one object, say a stop sign, and cause him or her to recollect actually seeing another object, in this case a yield sign, and many other investigators have succeeded in doing this (e.g., Dodd & Bradshaw, 1980; Dritsas & Hamilton, 1977: Lesgold & Petrush, 1977; Shaugnessy & Mand, 1982). The method of probing for a recollection seems to matter very little. We can ask, "Did you see a yield sign?" and obtain the response, "yes". We can ask, "What type of traffic sign did you see?" and obtain the response, "a yield sign." We can ask, "Was it a stop sign or a yield sign?" and obtain the answer, "yield." And, what is most impressive, we can present, side by side, pictures of the two signs and find that the yield sign is the choice. This last recognition test is particularly compelling, for the subject rejects the stimulus that is identical to the one actually seen. If recognition were assumed to be a relatively passive process of matching stimuli to specific locations in a content-addressable storage system, one would expect that a second representation of the actual and true scene would result in a match and that an alteration would fail to match. This does not occur. We have produced what we might call "memory blindness"—the failure to recognize something that was once in memory. It is quite similar to the failure that Belbin (1950) observed over 30 years ago. And probably also similar to what Herman Munk was referring to years and years ago when he talked about "mindblindness," a condition in which there is a loss of memory images of past visual experience. (See Benton, 1980 for a fuller discussion of Munk's ideas.)

In other paradigms, the intrusion of new information leads to relatively permanent changes in memory. For example, Fischhoff (1975, 1977) gave subjects a general knowledge test in which each question was to be answered by assigning a probability of correctness to one of two alternative answers. Some of his subjects were first told the correct answer and then asked to indicate the probability judgments they would have given had they not first been informed of the answers. A comparison of the judgments of these subjects with the judgments of naive subjects showed that the former group substantially overestimated their prior knowledge of correct answers. In explaining his results, Fischhoff argued that when a person hears the answer to a question such as "What is absinthe?" the answer is integrated with whatever else is known about the topic, in order to create a coherent whole out of all relevant knowledge. Sometimes integration involves reinterpreting previously held information to make sense out of it in light of the reported answer. These processes are so natural that people do not appreciate the effect that hearing the answer has on their perceptions. For this reason, they overestimate how obvious the correct answer would be before its correctness was indicated.

The deleterious impact of events that take place between the storage and retrieval of information has also been demonstrated by Brown, Deffenbacher, and Sturgill (1977). In one of their experiments, subject-witnesses viewed some strangers for a brief period of time. The subjects were told to scrutinize the strangers carefully because they might have to pick them out from mugshots later that evening and from a lineup the following week. About an hour and a half later the subjects viewed 15 mugshots, including some people who had been seen previously ("criminals") and some who had not. One week later several lineups were staged and the subjects were asked to indicate whether each person had been seen at the original "crime" scene. The results were dramatic: Of the persons in the lineup who had never been seen before, 8% were mistakenly "identified" as criminals. However, if a person's mugshot had been seen earlier, his chances of being falsely identified as one of the criminals rose to 20%. None of these people had ever been seen in person before, but were now "recognized" in the lineup because their photograph had been seen in the interim. This result was replicated and extended by Gorenstein and Ellsworth (1980). They asked whether the intervening mugshot had to be chosen by the subject, or whether merely presenting it was sufficient to enhance its chances of later recognition. Their results indicate that it is the prior choice much more than the mere familiarity that contributes to the subsequent increases in false recognition. Once this prior choice is made, the subject is likely to choose that very same incorrect face once again at a later time, even though the "true" face is also available as an alternative.

Results such as these make it tempting to view memory not as a receptacle for stored information but as a device to keep everything from being remembered. Does the notion that some memories may continually undergo changes due to subsequent inputs make sense from a physiological point of view? John (1972) has advanced a statistical configuration theory of learning and memory. The storage of new information is envisaged as the establishment of representational systems of large numbers of neurons in different parts of the brain, whose activity has been affected in a coordinating way by the spatiotemporal characteristics of the stimuli present during the encoding of that information. Later remembering of that information is not, according to John, based upon the establishment of new connections: rather, it seems to be based upon "the modification of existing relationships [p. 854]." When a specific memory is retrieved, a temporal pattern of electrical activity peculiar to that memory is released in numerous regions of the brain. That released set of waveshapes corresponds to the average firing pattern of ensembles of neurons diffusely distributed throughout these widespread anatomical areas. John summarized a substantial body of data to support his contention that these released patterns of electrical activity actually correspond to the activation of specific memories. But the notion of "average firing pattern" suggests that the pattern may be slightly different each time a specific memory is retrieved. Postevent inputs may simply cause slight modifications in the average firing pattern and this may constitute the basis for the altered memories.

Recovery Versus Nonrecovery

The previous summary indicates that many details that have apparently been forgotten are later recovered. Furthermore, many details that have apparently been forgotten are not recovered later. Do these situations tell us anything about the permanence of memory? Unfortunately no. Instances of the first sort in no way prove that all information is potentially recoverable, although this evidence has been used in just this way. And instances of the second sort in no way prove that the information could not eventually be recovered. Perhaps some memories are modified by subsequent inputs but others are not. If so, then a major question that confronts the memory theorist is: Under what circumstances does one process rather than the other occur? As a start toward answering this question, Loftus and Loftus (1980) have suggested that the mechanism responsible for updating memory both seeks efficiency and takes account of real world constraints. In some situations memories may not be tampered with by subsequent input, and these may last essentially forever. In other cases, new inputs that cannot logically coexist with earlier ones may cause an alteration to occur. In such instances, economy may dictate that one memory be dismissed in favor of another, much as a computer programmer will irrevocably destroy an old program instruction when a new one is created.

A recent distinction has been made between active and inactive memory (Lewis, 1979). Active memory (AM) is a subset of inactive memory (IM) and contains either newly formed memories or established retrieved memories or both. A body of evidence suggests that while in AM, memories are particularly open to disruption either by amnesic agents or through other forms of interference. Most of this evidence derives from the animal memory literature, yet it leads to the strong speculation that human memory may have to be evoked for it to be altered or distorted. Active memory is considered a changing subset of all permanent memories possessed by an organism. Over the course of time, numerous memories may become activated and these may be especially subject to change. Yet, at any given time, many of the permanent memories, which have the potential of being active, are in a relatively inactive state and have little effect on current behavior. Some of these memories may never be brought into an active state, and thus may not ever be subject to interfering events that could potentially cause their alteration or distortion.

SUMMARY

We have raised the topic of permanence of memory and noted that over the years many researchers have implicitly held the view that information, once stored, remains forever in memory even though it may not be accessible. Such an idea is embodied in many of the traditional statements on memory. And yet, as we have argued, this traditional memory research may have very little to tell us about the workings of memory for natural events. The traditional research left little room for constructive errors and faulty attention to play a role. What a person stores after an experience is almost certainly a departure from what really happened, and yet how much of a departure is something that is enormously difficult to know. Even assuming that an accurate representation of reality is stored as the result of perceiving a complex episode, we know very little about how this representation changes over time. One possibility is that memories that are never again activated may remain relatively the same as they were initially stored; on the other hand, memories that are evoked become fragile and subject to potential transformations.

REFERENCES

Adams, J. A. *Human Memory*. New York: McGraw-Hill, 1967.
Anderson, R. C., & Pichert, J. W. Recall of previously unrecallable information following a shift in perspective. *Journal of Verbal Learning and Verbal Behavior*, 1978, *17*, 1–12.

Baddeley, A. D. The trouble with levels: A reexamination of Craik and Lockhart's framework for memory research. *Psychological Review*, 1978, *85*, 139–152.

Bartlett, F. C. *Remembering: A study in experimental and social psychology*. London: Cambridge University Press, 1932.

Belbin, E. The influence of interpolated recall upon recognition. *Quarterly Journal of Experimental Psychology*, 1950, *2*, 163–169.

Benton, A. L. The neuropsychology of facial recognition. *American Psychologist*, 1980, *35*, 176–186.

Brown, E., Deffenbacher, K., & Sturgill, W. Memory for faces and the circumstances of encounter. *Journal of Applied Psychology*, 1977, *62*, 311–318.

Bruner, J. S., & Postman, L. On the perception of incongruity: A paradigm. *Journal of Personality*, 1949, *18*, 206–223.

Burri, C. The influence of an audience upon recall. *Journal of Educational Psychology*, 1931, *22*, 683–690.

Carr, H. A. *Psychology: A study of mental activity*. New York: Longmans Green, 1925.

Cherry, L. The magic of memory. *Science Digest*, Summer 1980, 61–63.

Clifford, B. R., & Bull, R. *The psychology of person identification*. London: Routledge & Kegan Paul, 1978.

Coren, S., Porac, C., & Ward, L. *Sensation and perception*. New York: Academic Press, 1979.

Craik, F. I. M., & Lockhart, R. S. Levels of processing: A framework for memory research. *Journal of Verbal Learning and Verbal Behavior*, 1972, *11*, 671–684.

Craik, F. I. M., & Tulving, E. Depth of processing and the retention of words in episodic memory. *Journal of Experimental Psychology: General*, 1975, *1*, 268–294.

Delvin, Honorable Lord Patric (chair). *Report to the secretary of state for the home department of the departmental committee on evidence of identification in criminal cases*. London: Her Majesty's Stationery Office, 1976.

Dodd, D. H., & Bradshaw, J. M. Leading questions and memory: Pragmatic constraints. *Journal of Verbal Learning and Verbal Behavior*, 1980, *19*, 695–704.

Doob, A. N., & Kirshenbaum, H. M. Bias in police lineups—partial remembering. *Journal of Police Science and Administration*, 1973, *1*, 287–293.

Dritsas, W. J., & Hamilton, V. L. Evidence about evidence: Effects of presuppositions, item salience, stress, and perceiver set on accident recall. Unpublished manuscript, University of Michigan, 1977.

Eich, J. E., Weingartner, H., Stillman, R. C., & Gillin, J. C. State-dependent accessibility of retrieval cues in the retention of a categorized list. *Journal of Verbal Learning and Verbal Behavior*, 1975, *14*, 408–417.

Erdelyi, M. H. Recovery of unavailable perceptual input. *Cognitive Psychology*, 1970, *1*, 99–113.

Erdelyi, M. H., & Goldberg, B. Let's not sweep repression under the rug: Towards a cognitive psychology of repression. In J. F. Kihlstrom & F. J. Evans (Eds.), *Functional disorders of memory*. Hillsdale, N.J.: Lawrence Erlbaum Associates, 1979.

Fischhoff, B. Hindsight/Foresight: The effect of outcome knowledge on judgment under uncertainty. *Journal of Experimental Psychology: Human Perception and Performance*, 1975, *1*, 288–299.

Fischhoff, B. Perceived informativeness of facts. *Journal of Experimental Psychology: Human Perception and Performance*, 1977, 349–358.

Freud, S. *Psychopathology of everyday life*. 1901. Standard Edition (Vol. 6). London: Hogarth Press, 1960.

Gartman, L. M., & Johnson, N. F. Massed versus distributed repetition of homographs: A test of the differential encoding hypothesis. *Journal of Verbal Learning and Verbal Behavior*, 1972, *11*, 801–808.

Gibson, J. J. *The senses considered as perceptual systems*. Boston: Houghton Mifflin, 1966.

Glass, A. L., Holyoak, K. J., & Santa, J. L. *Cognition.* Reading, Mass: Addison-Wesley, 1979.

Gorenstein, G. W., & Ellsworth, P. Effect of choosing an incorrect photograph on a later identification by an eyewitness. *Journal of Applied Psychology,* 1980, *65,* 612–622.

Hasher, L., & Griffin, M. Reconstructive and reproductive processes in memory. *Journal of Experimental Psychology: Human Learning and Memory,* 1978, *4,* 318–330.

Idzikowski, C., & Baddeley, A. D. Fear and performance in dangerous environments. In G. R. J. Hockey (Ed.), *Stress and fatigue in human performance.* New York: Wiley, in press.

James, W. *Psychology.* New York: Holt, 1892.

John, E. R. Switchboard versus statistical theories of learning and memory. *Science,* 1972, *177,* 850–864.

Kahneman, D. *Attention and effort.* Englewood Cliffs, N.J.: Prentice-Hall, 1973.

Kling, J. W., & Riggs, L. A. *Experimental Psychology (3rd ed.).* New York: Holt, Rinehart, & Winston, 1971.

Kihlstrom, J. F., & Evans, F. J., (Eds.) *Functional disorders of memory.* Hillsdale, N.J.: Lawrence Erlbaum Associates, 1979.

Lesgold, A. M., & Petrush, A. R. *Do leading questions alter memories?* Unpublished manuscript, University of Pittsburgh, 1977.

Lewis, D. J. Psychobiology of active and inactive memory. *Psychological Bulletin,* 1979, *86,* 1054–1083.

Loftus, E. F. *Eyewitness testimony.* Cambridge, Mass: Harvard University Press, 1979.

Loftus, E. F., & Loftus, G. R. On the permanence of stored information in the human brain. *American Psychologist,* 1980, *5,* 409–420.

Loftus, E. F., Miller, D. G., & Burns, H. J. Semantic integration of verbal information in to a visual memory. *Journal of Experimental Psychology: Human Learning and Memory,* 1978, *4,* 19–31.

Nelson, T. O. Repetition and depth of processing. *Journal of Verbal Learning and Verbal Behavior,* 1977, *16,* 151–171.

Norman, D. A., & Rumelhart, D. E. *Explorations in cognition.* San Francisco: Freeman, 1975.

Penfield, W. Memory mechanisms. *Transactions of the American Neurological Association,* 1951, *76,* 15–31.

Penfield, W., & Perot, P. The brain's record of auditory and visual experience. *Brain,* 1963, *86,* 595–696.

Riley, D. A. Memory for form. In Postman, L. (Ed), *Psychology in the making: Histories of selected research problems.* New York: Knopf, 1962.

Russell, W. R., & Nathan, P. W. Traumatic amnesia. In C. G. Gross & H. P. Zeigler (Eds.), *Readings in physiological psychology: Learning and memory.* New York: Harper & Row, 1969. (Originally published in *Brain,* 1946, *69,* 280–300.)

Shaughnessy, J. J., & Mand, J. L. How permanent are memories for real life events? *American Journal of Psychology,* 1982, *95,* 51–65.

Smith, S. M., Glenberg, A. M., & Bjork, R. A. Environmental context and human memory. *Memory and Cognition,* 1978, *6,* 342–353.

Treisman, A., & Schmidt, H. Illusory conjunctions in the perception of objects. *Cognitive Psychology,* 1982, *14,* 107–141.

Tulving, E., & Madigan, S. A. Memory and verbal learning. *Annual Review of Psychology,* 1970, *21,* 437–484.

Tulving, E., & Pearlstone, Z. Availability versus accessibility of information in memory for words. *Journal of Verbal Learning and Verbal Behavior,* 1966, *5,* 381–391.

Yerkes, R. M., & Dodson, J. D. The relation of strength of stimulus to rapidity of habit-formation. *Journal of Comparative and Neurological Psychology,* 1908, *18,* 459–482.

8 The Medial Temporal Region and Memory Consolidation: A New Hypothesis

Larry R. Squire
University of California, School of Medicine, La Jolla

Neal J. Cohen
Massachusetts Institute of Technology

Lynn Nadel
University of California, Irvine

The concept of memory consolidation—the idea that memory changes with the passage of time after learning—has been discussed and debated throughout this century in the disciplines of experimental psychology, physiological psychology, and neuropsychology. What is striking about these various inquiries is that each has had its own developmental history and that there has seldom been good correspondence among the disciplines in how memory consolidation should be viewed. It will be our contention here that converging evidence from all three disciplines now permits a new and coherent view of memory consolidation. This chapter presents evidence that memory changes for a long time after learning and describes a new framework in which the concept of memory consolidation can be placed.

Consolidation theory had its beginnings in experimental psychology as a way of explaining the detrimental effects on retention of a learning experience interpolated during the retention interval (Muller & Pilzecker, 1900). The shorter the interval between original learning and interpolated learning, the greater the deficit. It was supposed that the formation of stable memory required some change to occur after learning and that interpolated learning interfered with this stabilizing process. However, such an account of these data was eventually replaced by interference theory (see Keppel, this volume), which was deemed to provide a better explanation of both these and many other data. Current work on memory within cognitive psychology has largely ignored consolidation, focusing instead on the levels-of-processing approach to learning and memory (Craik & Lockhart, 1972) and the encoding specificity principle (Tulving & Thomson, 1973). These approaches emphasize processes operating at the time of information acquisition and at the time of retrieval and have had little to say about processes that might operate during the retention interval. What evidence exists concerning changes in memory over long time intervals (Bartlett, 1932; Freud, 1930; Rumelhart & Norman, 1978) has received little attention.

In physiological psychology, now sometimes termed behavioral neuroscience, consolidation theory grew out of and thrived on an explicit interest in processes that might operate after learning. Sherrington (1906) was among the first to appreciate the observation that nervous activity often outlasts a stimulus. Later, reverberating, self-reexciting neural circuits were postulated as a possible basis for memory storage (Hilgard & Marquis, 1940). Hebb (1949) embraced this idea as a possible mechanism for short-term memory and suggested that more stable, structural changes eventually occur in the same neural circuits to support long-term memory: "To account for permanence, some structural change seems necessary, but a structural growth presumably would require an appreciable time. . . . A reverberatory trace might cooperate with the structural change, and carry the memory until the growth change is made. . . . The conception of a transient, unstable reverberating trace is therefore useful, if it is possible to suppose also that some more permanent structural change also reinforces it [p. 62]."

A similar view, that memory takes time to be "fixed" after learning, was considered at about the same time by Gerard (1949, 1955). McGaugh and Herz (1972), commenting on these views, noted that "the hypothesized dual-trace mechanism accounted for the development of permanent or long-term memory and at the same time allowed for an initial "labile" period during which the neural processes underlying memory are subject to interference [p. 4]."

A large literature supporting this idea has come from the study of retrograde amnesia in laboratory animals. Certain experimental manipulations such as electroconvulsive shock or anoxia disrupt memory only when treatment is administered soon after training. Treatments administered at progressively longer intervals after training exert progressively less disruptive effects (for reviews, see Glickman, 1961; McGaugh & Herz, 1972). This work seemed to promise that determination of the interval during which a treatment is disruptive would lead to an estimate of the time course of consolidation. Unfortunately, it has not proven possible to identify a specific length of time during which consolidation occurs. Retrograde amnesia gradients in experimental animals vary widely in length, from seconds to hours, and sometimes days, depending on experimental conditions. These gradients have therefore come to be viewed more as evidence for changing susceptibility of memory to disruption than as a direct measure of consolidation time. Indeed, in comprehensive reviews of this work that have considered both the logic of retrograde amnesia studies as well as the available data, it was concluded that these studies do not permit measurement of the maximal time course of memory consolidation (Chorover, 1976; McGaugh & Gold, 1976). McGaugh and Gold (1976) wrote: "RA [retrograde amnesia] gradients do not provide a direct measure of the time required for the consolidation of long-term memory. . . . These results need not imply that there is a maximal amnesic gradient, but may simply indicate that the disruptive effectiveness of a given treatment is limited under the particular experimental conditions used [p. 550]." Though it has proven difficult in this tradition to address the temporal features of consolidation, much research continues to seek its neurobiological substrate (Gold & McGaugh, this volume). At the same time, because the time course of disruptive effects in experimental animals is usually short (i.e., seconds to hours), it has been possible on this evidence to maintain the view that such disruption occurs when memory is in a labile form, prior to its fixation.

In neuropsychology, the facts of human amnesia have also led to ideas about memory consolidation. Retrograde amnesia in man has long been known to affect recent events more than remote events (Ribot, 1882), and these observations have been taken in support of the idea that memory consolidates or changes in some way as time passes after learning (Burnham, 1903; McDougall, 1901; Russell & Nathan, 1946). In the case of amnesia associated with electroconvulsive therapy (ECT), formal studies have shown that memory for material learned immediately before treatment is worse than memory for material learned hours before treatment (Zubin & Barrera, 1941). The first systematic studies of traumatic amnesia also reported a temporally limited retrograde memory loss (Russell & Nathan, 1946). In 83% of 840 cases exhibiting retrograde amnesia, the period of time prior to injury that was affected was less than 30 min.

Individual cases of traumatic amnesia have also been described in which retrograde amnesia appears to cover six months or more prior to injury (Barbizet, 1970; Russell & Nathan, 1946). Moreover, the well-known amnesic case H.M., who in 1953 sustained bilateral excision of the medial temporal region for relief of intractable seizures (Scoville & Milner, 1957), has been reported to have had retrograde amnesia covering one to three years prior to surgery (Milner, Corkin, & Teuber, 1968). Yet evaluation of individual patients on the basis of clinical interviews cannot provide a compelling case that retrograde amnesia actually extends in a temporally limited way over a time course of many months or more. Coons and Miller (1960) argued forcibly that such impressions may result from sampling bias inherent in clinical interviews. That is, questions about recent events tend to be more detailed and to sample shorter time periods than questions about more remote events. Accordingly, an individual having long retrograde amnesia might always appear to have a temporally limited deficit, even if all past time periods were affected equally. It is now clear, however, on the basis of formal memory testing, that retrograde amnesia can extend a year or two into the past without affecting more remote time periods (Squire & Cohen, 1982). Following five treatments of bilateral ECT, patients developed a temporally limited retrograde amnesia that covered a few years prior to treatment without affecting earlier years. These results were consistent both with the idea that memory changes with the passage of time after learning and that these changes can occur over a time course of years.

This brief historical review shows that different points of view about memory consolidation have developed in three relevant disciplines. In experimental psychology, memory consolidation has been passed over to some extent in favor of processes that operate at the time of learning and at the time of retrieval. In behavioral neuroscience, memory consolidation has tended to refer to a relatively short-lived process that operates during an initial labile period while memory is being fixed. In neuropsychology, memory consolidation has been related to the facts of retrograde amnesia in patients, and would seem to proceed for a very long time.

In this chapter, our intention is to present a new hypothesis of memory consolidation that draws heavily on data from neuropsychological studies of amnesia and is compatible as well with developments in experimental psychology and behavioral neuroscience. A crucial aspect of this hypothesis is the idea that memory consolidation proceeds for a long time, up to several years, and that it depends on the integrity of the medial temporal region of the brain.

RELEVANT OBSERVATIONS

Retrograde Amnesia

Our assertion that memory consolidation can continue for as long as a few years after learning is based on the fact that temporally limited retrograde amnesia can occur on this time scale, affecting memories formed one or two years ago without affecting memories formed prior to that time. This section explicitly develops these inferences and shows how an alternative class of interpretations is ruled out by the data.

There have been many clinical reports of temporally limited retrograde amnesia spanning several years. The argument to be developed here, however, depends on features of the impairment that can be revealed only by objective testing. The present discussion therefore will focus on a few studies in which retrograde amnesia has been measured with formal memory tests and where quantitative aspects of the memory impairment can be considered. The relevant data come from studies of retrograde amnesia in psychiatric patients receiving bilateral ECT. Fig. 8.1 shows the results of two such studies. These studies asked patients questions about television programs broadcast for no more than one season during the past many years (Squire & Cohen, 1979; Squire, Slater, & Chace, 1975). Before ECT, the patients exhibited a forgetting curve across the time period measured by the test, performing best for the recent time periods and worst for the more remote time periods. One hour after the fifth treatment, there was a selective impairment in the ability to answer questions about programs broadcast one to two years previously and no impairment of memory for programs broadcast from 2 to 17 years previously. Similar results have been obtained in a third study involving the names of television programs (Squire, Chace, & Slater, 1976) and a fourth study involving details about past public events (Cohen & Squire, 1981).

These findings show that the susceptibility of memory to disruption decreases as time passes after initial learning. The validity of this conclusion depends of course on how well these testing methods overcome Coons and Miller's (1960) concern about sampling bias. Specifically, the test must satisfy the criterion of equivalence (Squire & Cohen, 1982), whereby the material tested from different time periods is likely to have been learned about to the same extent and then forgotten at similar rates. This critical requirement has now been validated by repeated testing with the television test during seven years (Squire & Fox, 1980).

The finding that a one- or two-year-old memory can be affected by ECT, while an older memory is spared, leads us to conclude that memory changes over long periods of time and becomes resistant to disruption as a result of this change. This conclusion depends on the specific pattern of the data, not on the mere fact that ECT affected one-year-old memories but not five-year-old memories. This point follows from consideration of the hypothetical data shown in Fig. 8.2. Here ECT has impaired one- and two-year-old memories without impairing older memories, but recall of one- or two-year-old memories after ECT is a little better than recall of three- to four-year-old memories and much better than recall of five- to six-year-old memories. These data would not require the conclusion that memory changes with time over the years. Suppose first that in each time period memories of varying durability are formed. Some of these memories concern details and will soon be forgotten: others concern important events and will last for a long time. Then, one need suppose only that ECT disrupts the less durable memories that would ordinarily be soon forgotten and spares the more durable memories that would ordinarily be retained for a long time. If this were the case, ECT would take its greatest toll on recent memories, and results like those depicted in Fig. 8.2 could be obtained. Importantly, with this scenario, ECT could never affect recent memories to such an extent that the score for the recent time period is actually lower than the score for more remote time periods. Durable, long-lasting memories are equally abundant in all time periods. If ECT disrupted only weak, easily forgotten memories, then all the durable memories should remain after the weak ones were disrupted, and performance at worst should be equivalent across time periods.

However, what can actually occur after ECT (See Fig. 8.1) is that the score for the most recent time period is significantly worse than the score for a more remote time period. To the extent that performance after ECT is worse for recent

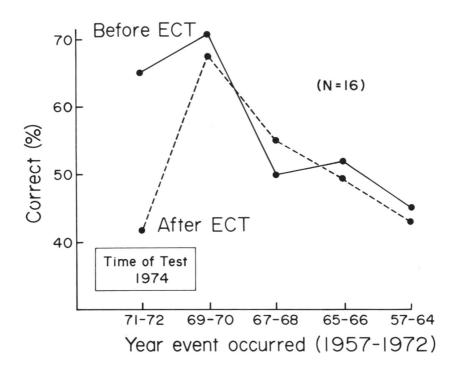

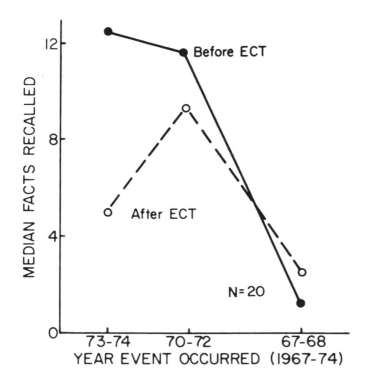

time periods than for remote time periods, the data demonstrate that changes must occur in memory on this time scale. These changes cause some memories, which can be disrupted by ECT when they are one to two years old, to become resistant to disruption during subsequent years. It is our view that these changes reflect memory consolidation. Thus, memory consolidation is a process that continues long after learning and that develops and maintains stable memory representations.

The basic idea that changes in memory continue for a long time after learning was first stated many years ago on the basis of clinical reports of extensive retrograde amnesia (Burnham, 1903): "In normal memory a process of organization is continually going on—a physical process of organization and a psychological process of repetition and association. In order that ideas may become a part of permanent memory, time must elapse for these processes of organization to be completed [p. 396]."

The well-studied neurosurgical case H.M. (Scoville & Milner, 1957) connects these ideas about memory consolidation to the medial temporal region. Case H.M. has had a profound anterograde amnesia since he sustained bilateral excision of the medial temporal region in 1953. Though it has yet not been possible to identify retrograde amnesia in this individual with formal tests, clinical interviews have given the consistent impression that he has a retrograde amnesia of one to three years, i.e., for the period 1950–1953 (Milner, Corkin, & Teuber, 1968). His memory for earlier time periods (1920–1950) is known to be good (Marslen-Wilson & Teuber, 1975). The findings from ECT show that temporally limited retrograde amnesia can occur on this time scale and raise the level of certainty that, as a result of his medial temporal surgery, H.M. indeed has this sort of retrograde amnesia. If so, it follows that the medial temporal region has a necessary role in the development and maintenance of memory that continues for as long as a few years after learning. Beyond that time, this region is less involved or not at all involved in memory. Because forgetting also occurs during this same period after learning, the changes that occur during this period apparently result in some information that has not been forgotten becoming more resistant to disruption. Of course, memory for many if not most experiences does not endure as long as a few years. We presume that the role of the medial temporal region in the consolidation of such experiences continues while information is being forgotten, during the reorganization and stabilization of what remains.

FIG. 8.1. Temporally limited retrograde amnesia for events that occurred one to two years previously in psychiatric patients receiving ECT.
A. Recognition memory for the names of former, one-season television programs.
B. Recall of details about former, one-season programs. (From Squire, Slater, & Chace, 1975; Squire & Cohen, 1979). These findings support the conclusion that memory changes during the first few years after learning and becomes resistant to disruption as a result of this change (see text).

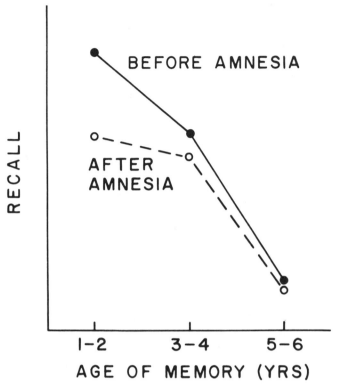

FIG. 8.2.   Hypothetical data, showing a pattern of temporally limited retrograde amnesia that would not require the conclusion that memory becomes resistant to disruption with the passage of time (see text).

Because of its time course, memory consolidation must by our view depend on changes in the neural substrates of long-term memory storage, not on transfer out of a short term, labile memory system. At the same time, this conclusion in no way denies the possible importance for long-term memory storage of events occurring during or shortly after learning. Thus it has been suggested that protein synthesis, hormonal release, and other short-term physiological consequences of training play a critical role in the formation of memory (Barondes, 1975; Gold & McGaugh, 1975; Kety, 1970; Livingston, 1967; Squire, 1975). In addition to whatever events occur near the time of training, other events continue to affect memory for a long time afterwards.

In the case of the one- to two-year retrograde amnesia associated with ECT, the memory impairment is largely temporary and is recovered substantially during the months following treatment (Squire, Slater, & Miller, 1981). Thus ECT does not erase these memories but causes them to be temporarily inaccessible in a way that depends on their age at the time of treatment. Recovery from prolonged retrograde amnesia can also occur following head trauma (Russell & Nathan, 1946). The fact that these effects of ECT are largely temporary rather than permanent is not critical to the present discussion. Apparently, the stage of resistance that memory has reached at the time of ECT will determine whether or not memory becomes inaccessible. Thus ECT reveals differences among memories of different ages that must be related to the neurological organization of these memories at different times after acquisition.

The recovery from retrograde amnesia that occurs following convulsive treatment in humans is quite compatible with the permanent retrograde amnesia reported in laboratory animals when the interval between learning and convulsive stimulation is short (McGaugh & Gold, 1976). In humans, both traumatic amnesia and ECT can also lead to long-lasting, probably permanent retrograde amnesia for information acquired just prior to the precipitating event (Russell & Nathan, 1946: Squire, Slater, & Miller, 1981). Thus these facts of amnesia are all consistent with the idea that memory grows more resistant to disruption with the passage of time. If a disruptive treatment is given sufficiently long after learning, memory will not be affected; if the treatment is given at an intermediate time after learning, memory may be reversibly affected; if the treatment is given shortly after training, memory can be permanently lost.

Rapid Forgetting

Another feature of amnesia pertinent to discussion of memory consolidation is rapid forgetting. We have described memory consolidation as a process occurring after learning that maintains and stabilizes memory representations, strengthening those that are not forgotten. In the absence of such a process, information in memory should be forgotten at an abnormally rapid rate. This possibility has now been explored rather thoroughly. Rapid forgetting was first reported experimentally by Huppert and Piercy (1979), who also developed the experimental method on which the demonstration was based. Normal subjects and case H.M. were shown 120 pictures, one at a time. The exposure duration was 1 sec for the normal subjects and 16 sec for H.M., long enough to equate his retention performance at 10 min after learning to that of the normal subjects. Having equated performance in this way, they then observed that H.M. forgot abnormally rapidly between 10 min and 7 days after learning. This method has recently been applied to patients receiving ECT who also forgot at an abnormal rate (Squire, 1981). The results with ECT confirm our expectation that temporally limited retrograde amnesia should be associated with rapid forgetting of newly learned material. H.M. exhibits rapid forgetting and presumably one- to three-year retrograde amnesia as well: therefore, dysfunction of the medial temporal region may underlie both these deficits. In the case of ECT, however, it is not possible to speak with any certainty about which brain areas are most affected by the seizure and therefore most related to the memory disorder. Nevertheless, some indirect evidence has linked ECT to medial temporal lobe dysfunction (Inglis, 1970).

In contrast to the rapid forgetting associated with dysfunction of the medial temporal region, the amnesia associated with damage to the diencephalic midline does not include this deficit. Huppert and Piercy (1978) first showed that patients with Korsakoff syndrome exhibit a normal rate of forgetting. Normal forgetting has also been observed in a second group of patients with Korsakoff syndrome, and in the case of N.A., who has a known lesion in the region of the left dorsomedial thalamic nucleus (Squire, 1981). When patients receiving ECT and Korsakoff patients all saw 120 pictures for 8 sec each, they had identical retention scores at 10 min after training. Yet during the next 32 hours, the ECT patients rapidly forgot the material; the Korsakoff patients exhibited little forgetting.

Despite this evidence for an association between rapid forgetting and medial temporal dysfunction, neuropathological information for these amnesic cases is not available. More direct evidence for this association comes from recent studies with operated monkeys (Zola-Morgan & Squire, 1982). They used the delayed nonmatching-to-sample task, which is sensitive to amnesia in man, and employed a procedure analogous to that used in the human studies. Normal monkeys were tested in the conventional way, in that they saw the sample stimulus once and then after a delay saw the sample stimulus together with a novel stimulus. Food reward was given for selecting the novel stimulus. Operated monkeys were given 10–12 successive exposures to the sample stimulus to equate their performance to that of normal monkeys at 10 min after training. Forgetting was then assessed at 1 hr and at 24 hr after acquisition. Normal monkeys remembered the sample stimulus across these delays. Monkeys with combined hippocampal-amygdala damage, who at histological examination had no abnormality in diencephalic structures, exhibited rapid forgetting. Monkeys with bilateral medial thalamic lesions that included the dorsomedial nucleus exhibited normal rates of forgetting. These results, together with the data from anmesic patients, make a strong case for the existence of two distinct entities in amnesia—diencephalic and bitemporal, and for an association between bitemporal amnesia and rapid forgetting. The normal forgetting associated with diencephalic amnesia seems to reflect a different kind of deficit (Squire, 1982; Squire & Cohen, 1982).

If both rapid forgetting and temporally limited retrograde amnesia are related deficits caused by medial temporal dysfunction, then patients with diencephalic lesions—who forget at a normal rate—might not exhibit temporally limited retrograde amnesia. Although the available data from formal tests do not yet permit a clear test of this prediction, they are consistent with it. Patients with Korsakoff syndrome exhibit an extensive remote memory deficit covering many decades, rather than temporally limited retrograde amnesia (Albert, Butters, & Levin, 1979; Cohen & Squire, 1981; Squire & Cohen, 1984). This deficit appears to depend on gradually developing anterograde amnesia and a general impairment in reconstructing past memory (Cohen & Squire, 1981; Butters & Albert, 1982: Squire & Cohen, 1984).

Case N.A., who became amnesic in 1960, exhibits generally good memory for events that occurred prior to that time (Cohen & Squire, 1981). Moreover, in two tests that revealed some deficit in his memory for the premorbid period, the deficit covered the entire period and was not temporally limited (Cohen and Squire, 1981; Zola-Morgan, Cohen, & Squire, 1983). Nevertheless, N.A. has seemed on the basis of informal conversations to have particular difficulty remembering the several months prior to his accident (Teuber, Milner, & Vaughan, 1968: Kaushall, Zetin, & Squire, 1981). Yet, these impressions, even if accurate, cannot by themselves settle the question of whether his retrograde amnesia is the type that can result from an impairment in memory consolidation. The critical issue then in reaching conclusions about memory consolidation is not whether a temporally limited retrograde amnesia occurs at all, but whether it takes the form illustrated in Fig. 8.1 rather than the form illustrated in Fig. 8.2.

If a patient had a reconstructive deficit affecting past memories, as diencephalic amnesic patients may have (Cohen & Squire, 1981), then this deficit should affect most severely the fragile memories that will be forgotten most rapidly. Because these memories are necessarily most abundant in recent time periods, patients with diencephalic amnesia should have a retrograde amnesia that affects recent memories somewhat more than remote memories. By our view, however, this amnesia would be of the type illustrated in Fig. 8.2. Only patients with bitemporal amnesia should have the kind of retrograde amnesia illustrated in Fig. 8.1, which requires the conclusion that memory changes with time after learning.

The data reviewed here suggest that rapid forgetting and temporally limited retrograde amnesia (as in Fig. 8.1) occur together in amnesia. The amnesia associated with ECT causes both these phenomena. Medial temporal dysfunction appears to be associated with rapid forgetting, and presumably with temporally limited retrograde amnesia as well. Taken together, the data suggest that the diencephalic and medial temporal regions affected in amnesia make different contributions to normal memory functions (Squire & Cohen, 1982). The medial temporal region appears to have a role in postencoding processes that operate during the retention interval and that are required for memory to develop and be maintained in a normal way. It is these processes that we here term memory consolidation, and it is for this reason that we have related the medial temporal region to memory consolidation.

Anterograde Amnesia and Retrograde Amnesia

It has long been recognized that a correlation exists between the severity of anterograde amnesia and the extent of retrograde amnesia (Russell & Nathan, 1946), and this correlation has suggested that the same deficit might underlie both phenomena (Cohen & Squire, 1981: Wickelgren, 1979). Recent computer simulation of bitemporal amnesia makes this same point more convincingly, because it links in a formal way the particular features of anterograde and retrograde amnesia that characterize medial temporal dysfunction. The simulation demonstrated that a deficit in the same mechanism can produce both rapid forgetting of newly learned material and temporally limited retrograde amnesia, as in Fig. 8.1 (McClelland & Rumelhart, 1982, personal communication). The view presented here, and explored by computer simulation, also accounts for a related feature of bitemporal amnesia—the longer the anterograde amnesia persists, the longer will be the permanent retrograde amnesia that persists after anterograde amnesia has diminished. Four related observations are consistent with this conclusion. In traumatic amnesia where the period of anterograde amnesia is often limited to a few days, the period of permanent retrograde amnesia is usually brief, involving just the seconds or minutes prior to injury (Russell & Nathan, 1946). In ECT, where anterograde amnesia can persist for several weeks, and temporary retrograde amnesia can cover the previous one or two years, there can be permanent retrograde amnesia for events that occurred during the several days prior to treatment (Squire, Slater, & Miller, 1981). In tuberculous meningitis, where anterograde amnesia can persist for a few months, permanent retrograde amnesia has been reported for events that occurred up to many months prior to illness (Williams & Smith, 1954). Finally, in case H.M., who has a permanent anterograde amnesia, retrograde amnesia appears to cover a number of years prior to surgery (Milner, Corkin, & Teuber, 1968). These observations help to clarify further the relationship between anterograde and retrograde amnesia. If the function of the medial temporal region is interrupted before its role in the development of memory is completed, memory can be irretrievably lost. The longer the disruption of function persists, the greater the loss. Unless memory is fully developed (i.e., consolidated), it will be lost at an abnormally rapid rate during the period of disruption.

Spared Learning in Amnesia.[1]

A final feature of amnesia relevant to this discussion of memory consolidation and the medial temporal region: The capacity for some kinds of learning and memory is preserved in amnesic patients. The best known examples of preserved learning and memory lie in the domain of perceptual-motor skills. For example, day-to-day learning of the hand-eye coordination skills needed for the pursuit-rotor task occurred in case H.M. (Corkin, 1968; Milner, 1962), patients with Korsakoff syndrome (Brooks & Baddeley, 1976; Cermak, Lewis, Butters, & Goodglass, 1973: Cohen, 1981), postencephalitic patients (Brooks & Baddeley, 1976), patients receiving bilateral ECT (Cohen, 1981), and case N.A. (Cohen, 1981). Of particular importance is the fact that, for some patients, learning occurred at an entirely normal rate and their performance seemed qualitatively

---

[1]This aspect of the issues under discussion was developed in a Ph.D. thesis by Cohen (1981).

indistinguishable from that of control subjects (Brooks & Baddeley, 1976: Cermak, et al., 1973; Cohen, 1981). This observation means that acquisition of perceptual-motor skills in amnesia cannot be explained merely by continued and extensive repetition of information. If repetition were responsible for the gradual acquisition of a skill over many trials, then the amnesic patients should be inferior to normal subjects during the early learning trials and catch up to normal subjects only in later trials. Yet this does not occur. Instead, the learning curves of amnesic patients and normal subjects are often superimposable. This observation of superimposable learning serves as a compelling demonstration that some form of learning is spared in amnesia and does not depend on the brain regions damaged in amnesia.

The capacity for preserved learning in amnesia appears to extend beyond perceptual-motor tasks to perceptual skills like mirror reading (Cohen & Squire, 1980) and purely cognitive skills such as the learning of a numerical rule (Wood, Ebert, & Kinsbourne, 1982) and the solution to certain puzzles (Cohen, 1981; Cohen & Corkin, 1981). A particularly clear example involves a mirror-reading task that has been studied extensively in normal subjects (Kolers, 1976, 1979). Subjects see mirror-reversed words and are asked to read them aloud as normal words. Amnesic patients (case N.A., patients with Korsakoff's syndrome, and patients receiving ECT) improved their mirror-reading skill at a normal rate on three successive days and then retained the skill at a normal level after three months. This occurred despite the fact that many patients denied having performed the task previously and all of them were amnesic for the words they had read (Cohen & Squire, 1980). It appeared that although the amnesic patients could learn the skills required for mirror reading, they could not learn the facts they would ordinarily acquire in using these skills, i.e., the words they read. Another example of preserved learning in amnesia comes from the ability of patients, including H.M., to learn the cognitive skills required for optimal solution to the Tower of Hanoi puzzle (Cohen, 1984; Cohen & Corkin, 1981), a complex problem-solving task involving at least 31 steps.

These findings have suggested to us that a significant domain of learning and memory, including motor, perceptual-motor, and cognitive skills, does not depend on the integrity of the medial temporal region. Accordingly, the ability to establish and use knowledge comprising skills can proceed normally in the brain in the absence of what we are here calling consolidation. By contrast, the development and consolidation of knowledge comprising the facts, words, faces, and shapes of conventional memory experiments depend on the integrity of the medial temporal region. We do not deny that the stabilization of memories that are independent of the medial temporal region may take some time. Nevertheless, the data do require the conclusion that the role of this region in memory consolidation applies only to some kinds of learning and memory.

The distinction between skills, which can be learned in amnesia, and the explicit knowledge gained in using those skills, which cannot be learned, is reminiscent of the distinction between knowing how and knowing that (Ryle,

1949). Similar distinctions have been proposed to address these findings from amnesia (Cohen, 1981; Cohen & Squire, 1980 [procedural/declarative]) as well as other findings in behavioral neuroscience (O'Keefe & Nadel, 1978; [taxon, locale]),[2] cognitive psychology (Bruner, 1969 [memory without record/memory with record]), and artificial intelligence (Winograd, 1975; [procedural/declarative]). Though different in some respects, the similarity among these versions has guided our understanding of what has been termed knowledge-how. It is often acquired in an incremental rather than in an all-or-none fashion, as with skill learning. It appears to be represented implicitly rather than explicitly, made accessible only by engaging in the skill in which the acquired knowledge is embedded. Thus, many skills develop despite poor access to the particular instances or events through which the skill was acquired.

We believe that, in the absence of the medial temporal region, organisms maintain the ability to acquire skills, but cannot establish a memory of the specific events that led to the perfection of the skills. That is, representations can develop that change how organisms respond to the environment, without affording access to information about the events that led to this change. Moreover, in the absence of the medial temporal region, facts that would ordinarily be acquired from such events, and knowledge that such events occurred, do not appear to be available.

In this regard, it is useful to remember that the deficit in amnesia manifests itself not merely as a breakdown of memory for specific instances of time-place information, but also includes the failure to acquire new semantic knowledge, e.g., information about public events and famous faces (Cohen & Squire, 1981; Marslen-Wilson & Teuber, 1975). In temporally limited retrograde amnesia, memory for both episodic and semantic knowledge is impaired from the period one to two years before amnesia, and both kinds of knowledge are available from earlier time periods (Zola-Morgan, Cohen, & Squire, 1983). It is now clear that both semantic and episodic memory are concerned with "knowledge that," whereas skill learning lies outside this classification (Cohen, 1981; Schacter & Tulving, 1982; Squire & Cohen, 1984; Tulving, Schacter, & Stark, 1982).

One question that needs to be asked about the kind of knowledge available to amnesic patients is how specific it can be. Are amnesic patients in a mirror-reading task acquiring and representing knowledge merely about the generic skill of reading words backwards while knowledge specific to individual words is lost or absorbed into the generic representation? Or, might amnesic patients acquire more specific information about the material that is presented? Kolers' (1976) work suggested that normal subjects not only could learn general skills of reading-transformed text but also could acquire knowledge more specific to the particular text presented. Kolers viewed both kinds of knowledge as skills because they were independent of recognition memory. Recent data suggest that

---

[2]This idea was developed in a book, coauthored by O'Keefe and Nadel (1978).

stimulus-specific information can also be available to amnesic patients under certain circumstances, and that this information might be still another example of their preserved capacity for skill learning. In one study, five patients with Korsakoff syndrome and five normal subjects were asked a question involving a homophone, e.g., "What is an example of a reed instrument?" Later, when asked to spell read/reed, the amnesic patients gave the low-frequency spelling (reed) that had been biased by the preceding question and did so with a normal, or even greater-than-normal likelihood (Jacoby & Witherspoon, 1982). Yet, the patients failed in recognition memory tests involving the same homophones. We have obtained similar results in a modified word fragment completion task (Graf, Squire, & Mandler, 1984). These results indicate that the preserved capacity for learning in amnesia can extend to specific information about the material that is presented and that the knowledge acquired by amnesic patients is not limited to generic information that is accumulated across many trials. The availability of such information need not imply the availability of episodic or semantic knowledge about these events.

In summary, the facts of spared learning and memory show that the medial temporal region is involved only in the development of a particular kind of memory. Such memory seems to afford the basis for what we have been calling "knowledge that:" knowledge about specific events, the time and place of their occurrence, and facts about the world obtained in the course of such experiences. By contrast, the medial temporal region is not required for consolidation of what has been called "knowledge how:" knowledge implicit in skills and procedures.

The Medial Temporal Region and the Hippocampal Formation

There has been great interest in the possibility of identifying specific structures within the medial temporal region that are involved in memory functions. In H.M. and in another patient who also sustained a medial temporal resection, the removal included the uncus, amygdala, and the anterior two-thirds of the hippocampus (Scoville & Milner, 1957). Several lines of evidence have suggested that damage to the hippocampal formation is responsible for the amnesia in these cases. In five of six cases, when the bilateral excision extended posteriorly only far enough to include uncus, amygdala, and anterior hippocampus, the memory loss was not so severe as in case H.M. In another case, where the excision was limited to uncus and amygdala, no memory deficit was observed (Scoville & Milner, 1957). In the case of unilateral temporal lobe resections, which are associated with verbal or nonverbal memory deficits, the severity of the deficit is correlated with the extent of involvement of the hippocampal zone (Milner, 1974). Although the medial temporal resections described above included amygdala, study of patients with circumscribed, unilateral amygdala lesions has not revealed verbal or nonverbal memory deficits (Andersen, 1978). A possible role of the temporal stem in the amnesic effects of medial temporal surgery has been ruled out in studies with monkeys (Zola-Morgan, Mishkin, & Squire, 1982). The temporal stem is a band of white matter lying in close proximity to the hippocampus. Finally, many additional examples of amnesia have been described (e.g., postencephalitic cases, vascular cases, cases of anoxic encephalopathy) that include bilateral damage to the hippocampal region.

Nevertheless, there have not been cases of bitemporal amnesia with damage clearly restricted to hippocampal formation. Based on studies of monkeys, it is possible that entorhinal cortex damage would mimic many of the effects of hippocampal damage (Moss, Mahut, & Zola-Morgan, 1981). Moreover, Mishkin (1978) has suggested that bitemporal amnesia in monkeys depends not on damage to hippocampus, but on conjoint damage to hippocampus and amygdala. His studies of a memory task given to monkeys with separate or combined lesions of these structures support this suggestion. One possibility is that these two structures contribute differently to memory functions. It also remains possible that hippocampal damage alone can cause significant memory impairment (for review, see Squire & Zola-Morgan, 1983). Because of this uncertainty about whether the hippocampal formation is the critical structure in bitemporal amnesia or whether other related brain structures also contribute to the deficit, we here use the term medial temporal region to identify the crucial brain area involved in memory consolidation. This terminology should not obscure the fact that the available data point to a necessary and important role for the hippocampal formation in this process. The next section develops some specific ideas about what memory consolidation is and how the medial temporal region might participate in consolidation.

A NEW FRAMEWORK FOR MEMORY CONSOLIDATION

Memory Storage

We presume that memory storage occurs in networks of neurons, primarily in neocortex, such that the specificity of memory is determined by which ensembles of neurons change, not by the kind of change that occurs. Plasticity depends on changes in synaptic efficacy within these ensembles. Which groups of neurons participate in memory storage is determined largely by what functions these neurons ordinarily participate in. That is, memory is stored in the same circuitry that ordinarily is involved in the perception and processing of the kind of information that is to be stored. In invertebrates like *Aplysia*, where the cellular correlates of information storage for simple forms of behavioral plasticity can be investigated rather directly, plasticity occurs as changes in circuitry that is already specialized for organizing the response that is to be modified (Kandel, 1976). Other evidence has been reviewed elsewhere (Squire & Schlapfer, 1981).

It is our contention that the neural elements participating in memory storage can undergo reorganization with the passage of time after learning. The most general way to state how this reorganization might occur is to suppose that although some elements are lost through forgetting, those that survive increase their synaptic efficacy. This notion is formally similar to the principle of competition (Purves & Lichtman, 1980), whereby when some neural elements are lost, those that remain increase their influence on target sites. By the present view, forgetting involves an actual loss of connectivity among the neural elements participating in a representation, i.e., disappearance of at least some of the changes in synaptic connectivity that originally embodied the information. In the case of long-term habituation in *Aplysia,* the relevant synaptic changes gradually disappear over a period of days and weeks in parallel with behavioral forgetting (Kandel, 1976). In this case, the neural elements remain present, but their functional connectivity changes. Loss of connectivity among elements due to forgetting is accompanied by, causes, or results from a process of reorganization of that which remains. Because there is considerable redundancy in such a representation, and because memory involves representation of many different features of an event, it is not necessary to suppose that all elements composing the memory of an event are ever lost irretrievably. Conversely, occasional success in retrieving an old memory does not require the conclusion that no connectivity has been lost among elements in the original representation. Loss of connectivity should lead, on average, to reduced efficiency, speed, or completeness of recall. As time passes after learning, one's representation of distant events loses detail through forgetting but becomes more schematized, organized, and related to other material in memory (Bartlett, 1932) during the process of consolidation.

Memory Consolidation and the Role of the Medial Temporal Region

One can imagine different formulations of how the medial temporal region is involved in consolidation. Two possibilities can be dismissed at the outset. In what might be termed a general retrieval view, the medial temporal region permits memory retrieval of all information that is stored elsewhere in the brain, e.g., in cortical cell ensembles. All memories are available in amnesia, but in the absence of the medial temporal region they cannot be retrieved. A second view is that the medial temporal region is the storage site for all memory. Neither of these views can explain why H.M. has poor memory for past events that occurred since 1953 and good memory for events that occurred prior to that time (Marslen-Wilson & Teuber, 1975). By either of these views, damage to the medial temporal region should result in a deficit in recalling all past memories, not just memories that were formed after a certain year.

By the view to be developed here, the medial temporal region plays a role that cannot be so easily labeled in terms of storage or retrieval notions. What is crucial to the present view is that the medial temporal region is required for only a limited time after learning and that its role is selective to a particular domain of information. Our proposal is that the medial temporal region establishes a relationship with distributed memory storage sites at the time of acquisition. The medial temporal region maintaines coherence of memory, permitting its retrieval during the consolidation period. Processes intrinsic to normal function at memory storage sites are responsible for consolidation, which results in changes in the system of coherent elements specified by the medial temporal region. Some elements in the representation are lost; those that remain develop better connectivity. Once this process is sufficiently complete, the medial temporal region is no longer needed either for the storage or retrieval of memory.

When the medial temporal region is damaged, the coherence of recently formed, as yet unconsolidated representations will not be maintained, and memory will be lost. Similarly, new representations cannot be established because the system that ordinarily maintains the organization of recently acquired memories and permits their retrieval and reorganization is not available. Although some neuronal changes related to memory storage may still occur when the medial temporal region is damaged, some of the information that would be embodied in the neuronal circuitry, and stabilized as a result of the participation of the medial temporal region, will be absent. That is, some of the neuronal events that subserve information storage, including changes in synaptic connectivity, will not be present.

The capacity to acquire "knowledge how" proceeds independently of the medial temporal region and, in our view, involves the modification or tuning of existing schemata or knowledge structures. The changes that underlie this kind of learning are contained entirely in the neural systems in which they develop, without need of the medial temporal region. In animals like *Aplysia,* with relatively uncomplicated nervous systems, habituation and sensitization can occur as modifications in synaptic efficacy in existing networks (Kandel, 1976) and can result in a specific change in how the organism responds to environmental stimuli. There is no evidence in such cases for the presence or availability of knowledge about the specific instances that cumulated in the behavioral change. Similarly, restricting an animal's early visual experience to horizontal lines will result in specific changes in the population of orientation-selective cells in visual cortex. Yet there is no sense in which these changes imply knowledge that the world was once composed largely of horizontal lines or knowledge of specific experiences with a horizontal world. Indeed, the capacity for this latter type of learning may have arisen relatively late in evolution with the development of the hippocampal formation. This brain region may confer upon the organism the ability to remember specific instances as separate events. That is, it affords contextual information, including information about time and place (Nadel & Willner, 1980; Nadel, Willner, & Kurz, 1984). In addition, it also affords the basis for acquiring new facts about the world which, though acquired in specific places at particular times, do not necessarily include this information, i.e., semantic knowledge.

These considerations emphasize the dissociation among different domains of knowledge and the selective role of the medial temporal region in memory consolidation. Thus, one kind of knowledge (knowledge-how) is stored in neural circuitry that does not depend on the medial temporal region and is not subject to consolidation. This knowledge consists of skills or procedures that can be embedded in already existing knowledge structures. It is accessible only by using these skills or procedures and does not by itself afford any awareness that a previous event has occurred. A second kind of knowledge (knowledge-that) depends on the medial temporal region and is contained in the interaction between the medial temporal region and neocortical storage sites. This knowledge is comprised of facts and data, including both information about specific experiences that occurred at specific places and times (episodic knowledge) and factual information about the world that is acquired as a result of these experiences (semantic knowledge). With the participation of the medial temporal region, memory for this material is consolidated during the time after learning. When memory consolidation is interrupted by damage to the medial temporal region, the semantic and episodic knowledge represented in the interaction of this region with neocortex is lost in the sense that some of the changes in synaptic efficacy that subserve its storage disappear. The knowledge that is independent of the medial temporal region, however, remains unaffected. Thus the amnesic patient, who has sustained damage to the medial temporal region, will by our view be incapable of establishing and using one kind of knowledge but will be capable of establishing and using another. To summarize, our view involves four premises:

1. The medial temporal region interacts with neocortex (and possibly other regions) in memory storage.
2. Information is embodied both in neocortical representations and in the interaction between the medial temporal region and neocortex.
3. This interaction is necessary in memory storage and retrieval for a limited time period after learning of up to a few years.
4. This interaction occurs only for certain kinds of knowledge.

Our proposal is not entirely new. Others have stressed, either separately or together, the idea that memory involves interaction between the medial temporal region and the neocortex and that the medial temporal region is concerned with particular kinds of information (Halgren, Wilson, Squires, Engel, Walter, & Crandall, 1983; Hirsh, 1974; Mishkin, 1982; Nadel & O'Keefe, 1974; O'Keefe & Nadel, 1978; Wickelgren, 1979).

There is at least one notion other than ours that could be compatible with all four premises. One might suppose that the medial temporal region does not merely permit consolidation but actually causes it to occur by exerting a neuromodulatory, or other extrinsic influence necessary for the fixation of memory (Wickelgren, 1979; McClelland & Rumelhart, 1982, personal communication). This idea supposes that the medial temporal region is the motive force for consolidation. It incorporates the selectivity of the medial temporal region's role in memory consolidation insofar as it asserts that this function is necessary only for the consolidation of some kinds of information. This selectivity might be realized in two different ways. It may be that the medial temporal region stores information about which neocortical sites it should interact with (i.e., it stores "addresses" of memories stored elsewhere [Teyler & Discenna, 1984]) and thus actively directs its interaction with the neocortical storage sites. Alternatively, the selectivity could inhere in some property of the neocortical sites, with the medial temporal region playing a more passive, nonspecific role. By the latter view, only certain neocortical sites would have the capacity or need to respond to this nonspecific, extrinsic influence. It should be noted that the "address" version of this view is closely allied with our view that the medial temporal region maintains coherence of memory. Any "coherence" model would seem to require an addressing system that contained knowledge about which particular set of elements is to be maintained by the medial temporal region. In both views, the medial temporal region directs its interaction with selected neocortical storage sites, as a result of which consolidation occurs during the time after learning for a particular domain of knowledge.

Some Neuroanatomical and Neurobiological Considerations

Our view of the role of the medial temporal region and its interaction with neocortex demands extensive and precise neural interconnections between the two. The amygdala has direct, reciprocal connections with insular cortex, all parts of the temporal lobe, including hippocampal formation, and major parts of the frontal lobe, including the orbital and medial surfaces (Price, 1982; Van Hoesen, 1981). The hippocampal formation receives much of its input from entorhinal cortex via the perforant path. The entorhinal cortex itself receives multimodal information from temporal and frontal neocortex, from the olfactory system via the prepiriform area, and has been regarded as a final link between sensory areas of neocortex and the hippocampal formation (Van Hoesen, Pandya, & Butters, 1972). Efferents from the hippocampal formation via subiculum and presubiculum, and area TH-TP (parahippocampal gyrus), reach a variety of cortical associations areas; moreover the subiculum of the hippocampal formation has direct connections with amygdala, the medial surface of frontal cortex, perirhinal cortex, and cingulate cortex (Rosene & Van Hoesen, 1977). Considering the close relationship between the medial limbic structures, i.e., amygdala and hippocampal formation, and the majority of temporal neocortex, and the relationship between temporal neocortex and other association cortices, there appears to be great opportunity for interaction between the medial temporal region and the neocortex. Thus there is evidence for the kind of connections this model would require.

Although consolidation need not continue for years for all kinds of information, the processes we are discussing last for a long time. Such processes would require neural mechanisms for maintaining and reorganizing information over long time intervals. Little is known about the neurobiological events that might underlie such processes, but examples of durable plasticity have been identified in mammalian brain. Thus, neurons in rat neocortex undergo extensive and durable changes in architecture in response to enriched environments or a series of daily training experiences (Rosenzweig, 1979; Greenough & Chang, 1984). These include changes in dendritic branching patterns, length of synaptic apposition, and number of dendritic spines—all of which could influence synaptic connectivity. In humans, growth of dendrites appears to continue throughout life (Buell & Coleman, 1979). In the medial temporal region itself and in the hippocampal formation specifically, physiological work has demonstrated a form of long-lasting synaptic plasticity, long-term potentiation (Bliss & Lomo, 1973). This effect, observed *in vitro* in hippocampal slices (Lynch & Shubert, 1980) and in the hippocampus of freely moving rats and monkeys alike (Swanson, Teyler, & Thompson, 1982) lasts for weeks or months and is associated with changes in dendritic spines (Lee, Schottler, Oliver, & Lynch, 1980). Although these forms of plasticity have not yet been clearly linked to behavioral memory, they provide potential bases for both the maintenance of an interaction between the medial temporal region and neocortex and for the changes at storage sites that we suppose subserve consolidation.

Some Cognitive Considerations

Our model of consolidation postulates that the medial temporal region maintains coherence within an ensemble of neocortical sites until such time as the coherence of these sites becomes an intrinsic property of the ensemble. It is our view that during this lengthy process certain aspects of memory for the original event are forgotten while those that remain are strengthened. But it would be simplistic to suggest that any single biological change is responsible for consolidation lasting as long as several years, as indicated by the data from retrograde amnesia. Rather, this time period, during which the medial temporal region maintains its importance, is filled with external events (such as repetition and activities related to original learning) and internal processes (such as rehearsal and reconstruction). These influence the fate of as-yet unconsolidated information through remodeling the neural circuitry underlying the original representation. The selection of which elements of a memory are forgotten and which survive and are strengthened depends on how these elements are affected by: 1) the particular events intervening between learning and retention; and 2) how the elements fit into the organism's pre-existing knowledge. During memory consolidation, some elements of memory are incorporated into pre-existing schemata; others might form the basis for new schemata; still others will be lost.

These ideas differ from the view that memories are fixed entities, traces of prior experience, uninfluenced by subsequent or prior events, and changed only by slow erosion. Memory consolidation by our view is not a relentlessly gradual or passive process. The ideas developed here fit more comfortably with a view of memory as a dynamic process, which changes over time through reorganization and assimilation to pre-existing memories, and which is affected by subsequent memory-storage episodes. This view has precedents in the work of Bartlett (1982), Rumelhart & Norman (1978), and in psychoanalytic theory (see for example, Feldman, 1977). It should be clear that we view consolidation as subserving just this sort of dynamism in memory.

ACKNOWLEDGMENTS

Supported by the Medical Research Service of the Veterans Administration, NIMH Grant MH24600, NIMH Grant MH08020, and NINCDS Grant I ROINS 17712. This paper grows out of several years of intermittent discussions among the three of us. In reaching the present perspective, a number of significant ideas evolved in ways that make them part of all of us, rather than attributable to any one individual. This paper presents our synthesis of these discussions and for us celebrates our collaboration.

REFERENCES

Albert, M. S., Butters, N., & Levin, J. Temporal gradients in the retrograde amnesia of patients with alcoholic Korsakoff's disease. *Archives of Neurology*, 1979, *36*, 211–216.

Andersen, R. Cognitive changes after amygdalotomy. *Neuropsychologia*, 1978, *16*, 439–451.

Barbizet, J. *Human memory and its pathology*. San Francisco: W. H. Freeman & Company, 1970.

Barondes, S. Protein-synthesis dependent and protein synthesis independent memory storage processes. In D. Deutsch & J. A. Deutsch (Eds.), *Short-term memory*, New York: Academic Press, 1975.

Bartlett, F. C. *Remembering*. Cambridge: Cambridge University, 1932.

Bliss, T. V. P., & Lomo, T. Long-lasting potentiation of synaptic transmission in the dentate area of the anaesthetized rabbit following stimulation of the perforant path. *Journal of Physiology*, 1973, *232*, 331–356.

Brooks, D. N., & Baddeley, A. What can amnesic patients learn? *Neuropsychologia*, 1976, *14*, 111–122.

Bruner, J. S. Modalities of memory. In G. A. Talland & N. C. Waugh (Eds.), *The pathology of memory*, New York: Academic Press, 1969.

Buell, S. J., & Coleman, P. D. Dendritic growth in the aged human brain and failure of growth in senile dementia. *Science*, 1979, *206*, 854–856.

Burnham, W. H. Retroactive amnesia: Illustrative cases and a tentative explanation. *American Journal of Psychology,* 1903, *14,* 382–396.

Butters, N., & Albert, M. S. Processes underlying failures to recall remote events. In L. Cermak (Ed.), *Human memory and amnesia,* Hillsdale, N.J.: Lawrence Erlbaum Associates, 1982.

Cermak, L. S., Lewis, R., Butters, N., & Goodglass, H. Role of verbal mediation in performance of motor tasks by Korsakoff patients. *Perceptual and Motor Skills,* 1973, *37,* 259–262.

Chorover, S. An experimental critique of "consolidation studies" and an alternative "model-systems" approach to the biophysiology of memory. In M. R. Rosenzweig & E. L. Bennett, (Eds.), *Neural mechanisms of learning and memory,* Cambridge, Mass.: MIT Press, 1976.

Cohen, N. *Neuropsychological evidence for a distinction between procedural and declarative knowledge in human memory and amnesia.* Unpublished doctoral dissertation, University of California, San Diego, 1981.

Cohen, N. Preserved learning capacity in amnesia: Evidence for multiple memory systems. In N. Butters & L. R. Squire (Eds.), *The neuropsychology of memory.* New York: Guilford Press, 1984, in press.

Cohen, N., & Corkin, S. The amnesic patient, H.M.: Learning and retention of a cognitive skill. *Society for Neuroscience Abstracts,* 1981, *7,* 235.

Cohen, N., & Squire, L. R. Preserved learning and retention of pattern analyzing skill in amnesia: Dissociation of knowing how and knowing that. *Science,* 1980, *210,* 207–209.

Cohen, N., & Squire, L. R. Retrograde amnesia and remote memory impairment. *Neuropsychologia,* 1981, *19,* 337–356.

Coons, E. E., & Miller, N. E. Conflict versus consolidation of memory traces to explain retrograde amnesia produced by ECS. *Journal of Comparative and Physiological Psychology,* 1960, *53,* 524–531.

Corkin, S. Acquisition of motor skill after bilateral medial temporal lobe excision. *Neuropsychologia,* 1968, *6,* 255–265.

Craik, F. I. M., & Lockhart, R. S. Levels of processing: A framework for memory research. *Journal of Verbal Learning and Verbal Behavior,* 1972, *11,* 671–684.

Feldman, M. M. Amnesia: A psychoanalytic viewpoint. In C. W. M. Whitty & O. L. Zangwill (Eds.), *Amnesia.* London: Butterworths, 1977.

Freud, S. S. *Civilization and its discontents* (Stand. Ed. 21). London: Hogarth Press, 1930.

Gerard, R. W. Physiology and psychiatry. *American Journal of Psychiatry,* 1949, *105,* 161–173.

Gerard, R. W. Biological roots of psychiatry. *Science,* 1955, *122,* 225–230.

Glickman, S. E. Perseverative neural processes and consolidation of the memory trace. *Psychological Bulletin,* 1961, *58,* 218–233.

Gold, P. E., & McGaugh, J. L. A single-trace, two-process view of memory storage processes. In D. Deutsch & J. A. Deutsch (Eds.), *Short-Term Memory.* New York: Academic Press, 1975.

Graf, P., Squire, L. R., & Mandler, G. The information that amnesic patients do not forget. *J. Exp. Psychol: Learning, Memory, and Cognition,* in press.

Greenough, W., & Chang, F.-L.C. Anatomically-detectable correlates of information storage in the nervous system. In C. W. Cotman (Ed.), *Neuronal plasticity,* (2nd Ed.) New York: Guilford Press, 1984.

Halgren, E., Wilson, C. L., Squires, N. K., Engel, J., Walter, R. D., & Crandall, P. H. Dynamics of the hippocampal contribution to memory: Stimulation and recording studies in humans. In W. Seifert (Ed.), *Molecular, cellular, & behavioral neurobiology of the hippocampus,* New York: Academic Press, 1983.

Hebb, D. O. *The organization of behavior.* New York: Wiley, 1949.

Hilgard, E. R., & Marquis, D. G. *Conditioning and learning.* New York: D. Appleton-Century Company, 1940.

Hirsh, R. The hippocampus and contextual retrieval of information from memory: A theory. *Behavioral Biology,* 1974, *12,* 421–444.

Huppert, F. A., & Piercy, M. Dissociation between learning and remembering in organic amnesia. *Nature*, 1978, *275*, 317–318.

Huppert, F. A., & Piercy, M. Normal and abnormal forgetting in organic amnesia: Effect of locus of lesion. *Cortex*, 1979, *15*, 385–390.

Inglis, J. Shock, surgery and cerebral asymmetry. *British Journal of Psychiatry*, 1970, *117*, 143–148.

Jacoby, L. L., & Witherspoon, D. Remembering without awareness. *Canadian Journal of Psychology*, 1982, *32*, 300–324.

Kandel, E. R. *Cellular basis of behavior.* New York: Freeman, 1976.

Kaushall, P. I., Zetin, M., & Squire, L. R. A psychosocial study of chronic, circumscribed amnesia. *Journal of Nervous and Mental Disease*, 1981, *169*, 383–389.

Kety, S. S. The biogenic amines in the central nervous system: Their possible roles in arousal, emotion, and learning. In F. O. Schmitt (Ed.), *The neurosciences: Second study program*, New York: Rockefeller University Press, 1970.

Kolers, P. A. Pattern-analyzing memory. *Science*, 1976, *191*, 1200–1281.

Kolers, P. A. A pattern-analyzing basis of recognition. In L. S. Cermak & F. I. M. Craik (Eds.), *Levels of processing in human memory*, Hillsdale, N.J.: Lawrence Erlbaum Associates, 1979.

Lee, K., Schottler, F., Oliver, M., & Lynch, G. S. Brief bursts of high-frequency stimulation produce two types of structural change in rat hippocampus. *Journal of Neurophysiology*, 1980, *44*, 247–258.

Livingston, R. B. Reinforcement. In G. C. Quarton, T. Melnechuk, & F. O. Schmitt (Eds.), *The neurosciences: A study program.* New York: The Rockefeller University Press, 1967.

Lynch, G., & Shubert, P. The use use of in vitro brain slices for multidisciplinary studies of synaptic function. *Annual Review of Neuroscience*, 1980, *3*, 1–22.

Marslen-Wilson, W. D., & Teuber, H.-L. Memory for remote events in anterograde amnesia: Recognition of public figures from newsphotographs. *Neuropsychologia*, 1975, *13*, 353–364.

McClelland, T. & Rumelhart, D. E. personal communication.

McDougall, W. Experimentelle Beitrage zur Lehre vom Gadachtniss, by G. E. Muller & A. Pilzecker. *Mind*, 1901, *10*, 388–394.

McGaugh, J. L., & Gold, P. E. Modulation of memory by electrical stimulation of the brain. In M. R. Rosenzweig & E. L. Bennett (Eds.), *Neural mechanisms of learning and memory.* Cambridge, Mass.: M.I.T. Press, 1976.

McGaugh, J. L., & Herz, M. M. *Memory consolidation.* San Francisco: Albion Publishing Company, 1972.

Milner, B. Les troubles de la memoire accompagnant des lesions hippocampiques bilaterales. In *Physiologie de l'hippocampe.* Paris: Centre National de la Recherche Scientifique, 1962.

Milner, B. Hemispheric specialization: Scope and limits. In F. O. Schmitt & F. G. Worden (Eds.), *The neurosciences: Third research program.* Cambridge, Mass.: MIT Press, 1974.

Milner, B., Corkin, S., & Teuber, H.-L. Further analysis of the hippocampal amnesic syndrome. *Neuropsychologia*, 1968, *6*, 215–234.

Mishkin, M. Memory in monkeys severely impaired by combined but not by separate removal of amygdala and hippocampus. *Nature*, 1978, *273*, 297–298.

Mishkin, M. A memory system in the monkey. *Philosophical transactions of the Royal Society*, In D. E. Broadbent L. Weiskrantz (Eds.), London, England: The Royal Society, 1982.

Moss, M., Mahut, H., & Zola-Morgan, S. Concurrent discrimination learning of monkeys after hippocampal, entorhinal, or fornix lesions. *Journal of Neuroscience*, 1981, *1*, 227–240.

Muller, G. E., & Pilzecker, A. *Experimentelle Beitrage zur Lehre vom Gedachtniss*, 1900, *1*, 1–288.

Nadel, L., & O'Keefe, J. The hippocampus in pieces and patches: An essay on modes of explanation in physiological psychology. In R. Bellairs & E. G. Gray (Eds.), *Essays on the nervous system.* A Festschrift for Prof. F. Z. Young, Oxford, England: Clarendon Press, 1974.

Nadel, L., & Willner, J. Context and conditioning: A place for space. *Physiological Psychology*, 1980, *8*, 218–228.

Nadel, L., Willner, J., & Kurz, E. M. Cognitive maps and environmental context. In P. Balsam & A. Tomie (Eds.), *Context and learning*. Hillsdale, N.J.: Lawrence Erlbaum Associates, 1984.

O'Keefe, J., & Nadel, L. *The hippocampus as a cognitive map*. London: Oxford University Press, 1978.

Price, J. L. The efferent projections of the amygdaloid complex in the rat, cat and monkey. In Y. Ben-Ari (Ed.), *The amygdaloid complex*, INSERM Synposium No. 20. Amsterdam: Elsevier/North-Holland Biomedical Press, 1981.

Purves, D., & Lichtman, J. W. Elimination of synapses in the developing nervous system. *Science*, 1980, *210*, 153–157.

Ribot, T. *Diseases of memory*. New York: Appleton, 1882.

Rosene, D. L., & Van Hoesen, G. W. Hippocampal efferents reach widespread areas of cerebral cortex and amygdala in the rhesus monkey. *Science*, 1977, *198*, 315–317.

Rosenzweig, M. R. Responsiveness of brain size to individual experience. Behavioral and evolutionary implications. In M. E. Hahn, C. & Jensen, B. Dudek (Eds.), *Development and evolution of brain size: Behavioral implications*. New York: Academic Press, 1979.

Rumelhart, D. E., & Norman, D. A. Accretion, tuning, and restructuring: Three modes of learning. In J. W. Cotton & R. Klatzky (Eds.), *Semantic factors in cognition*. Hillsdale, N.J.: Lawrence Erlbaum Associates, 1978.

Russell, W. R., & Nathan, P. W. Traumatic amnesia. *Brain*, 1946, *69*, 280–300.

Ryle, G. *The concept of mind*. London: Hutchinson, 1949.

Schacter, D. L., & Tulving, E. Memory, amnesia, and the episodic/semantic distinction. In R. L. Isaacson & N. E. Spear (Eds.), *Expression of knowledge*. New York: Plenum Press, 1982.

Scoville, W. B., & Milner, B. Loss of recent memory after bilateral hippocampal lesions. *Journal of Neurology, Neurosurgery, and Psychiatry*, 1957, *20*, 11–21.

Sherrington, C. S. *The integrative action of the nervous system*. New Haven, Conn.: Yale University Press, 1906.

Squire, L. R. Short-term memory as a biological entity. In D. Deutsch & J. A. Deutsch (Eds.), *Short-term Memory*. New York: Academic Press, 1975.

Squire, L. R. Two forms of human amnesia: An analysis of forgetting. *Journal of Neuroscience*, 1981, *1*, 635–640.

Squire, L. R. The neuropsychology of human memory. *Annual Review of Neuroscience*, 1982, *5*, 241–273.

Squire, L. R., Chace, P., & Slater, P. C. Retrograde amnesia following electroconvulsive therapy. *Nature*, 1976, *260*, 755–777.

Squire, L. R., & Cohen, N. Memory and amnesia: Resistance to disruption develops for years after learning. *Behavioral and Neural Biology*, 1979, *25*, 115–125.

Squire, L. R., & Cohen, N. Remote memory, retrograde amnesia, and the neuropsychology of memory. In L. Cermak (Ed.), *Human memory and amnesia*. Hillsdale, N.J.: Lawrence Erlbaum Associates, 1982.

Squire, L. R., & Cohen, N. Human memory and amnesia. In J. L. McGaugh, G. Lynch, N. M. Weinberger (Eds.), *Conference on the neurobiology of learning and memory*, New York: Guilford Press, 1984.

Squire, L. R., & Fox, M. M. Assessment of remote memory: Validation of the television test by repeated testing during a seven-year period. *Behavioral Research Methods and Instrumentation*, 1980, *12*, 583–536.

Squire, L. R., & Schlapfer, W. T. Memory and memory disorders: A biological and neurologic perspective. In H. M. van Praag, M. H. Lader, O. J. Rafaelsen, & E. J. Sachar (Eds.), *Handbook of biological psychiatry (Pt. IV)*. New York: Marcel Dekker, 1981.

Squire, L. R., Slater, P. C., & Chace, P. Retrograde amnesia: temporal gradient in very long-term memory following electroconvulsive therapy. *Science*, 1975, *187*, 77–79.

Squire, L. R., Slater, P. C., & Miller, P. Retrograde amnesia following ECT: Long-term follow-up studies. *Archives of General Psychiatry*, 1981, *38*, 89–95.

Squire, L. R., & Zola-Morgan, S. The neurology of memory: The case for correspondence between the findings for man and non-human primate. In J. A. Deutsch (Ed.), *The physiological basis of memory* (2nd ed.). New York, Academic Press, 1983.

Swanson, L. W., Teyler, T. J., & Thompson, R. F. (Eds.). Hippocampal long-term potentiation: Mechanisms and implications for memory, *Neurosciences Research Program Bulletin (Vol. 20)*. Cambridge, Mass.: MIT Press, 1982.

Teuber, H.-L., Milner, B., & Vaughan, H. G. Persistent anterograde amnesia after stab wound of the basal brain. *Neuropsychologia*, 1968, *6*, 267–282.

Teyler, T. J., & DiScenna, P. The hippocampal memory indexing theory. 1984, in preparation.

Tulving, E., & Thomson, D. M. Encoding specificity and retrieval process in episodic memory. *Psychological Review*, 1973, *80*, 352–373.

Tulving, E., Schacter, D. L., & Stark, H. A. Priming effects in word-fragment completion are independent of recognition memory. *Journal of Experimental Psychology: Learning, Memory, and Cognition*, 1982, *8*, 336–342.

Van Hoesen, G. W. The differential distribution, diversity and sprouting of cortical projections to the amygdala in the rhesus monkey. In Y. Ben-Ari (Ed.), *The amygdaloid complex*, INSERM Symposium No. 20. Amsterdam: Elsevier/North-Holland Biomedical Press, 1981.

Van Hoesen, G. W., Pandya, D. N., & Butters, N. Cortical afferents to the entorhinal cortex of the rhesus monkey. *Science*, 1972, *175*, 1471–1473.

Wicklegren, W. A. Chunking and consolidation: A theoretical synthesis of semantic networks, configuring in conditioning, S-R versus cognitive learning, normal forgetting, the amnesic syndrome, and the hippocampal arousal system. *Psychological Review*, 1979, *86*, 44–60.

Williams, M., & Smith, H. V. Mental disturbances in tuberculous meningitis. *Journal of Neurology, Neurosurgery, and Psychiatry*, 1954, *17*, 173–182.

Winograd, T. Understanding natural language. In D. Bobrow & A. Collins (Eds.), *Representation and understanding*. New York: Academic Press, 1975.

Wood, F., Ebert, V., & Kinsbourne, M. The episodic-semantic memory distinction in memory and amnesia: Clinical and experimental observations. In L. Cermak (Ed.), *Human memory and amnesia*, Hillsdale, N.J.: Lawrence Erlbaum Associates, 1982.

Zola-Morgan, S., Cohen, N., & Squire, L. R. Recall of remote episodic memory in amnesia. *Neuropsychologia*, 1983, *21*, 487–500.

Zola-Morgan, S., Mishkin, M., & Squire, L. R. The neuroanatomy of amnesia: Amygdala-hippocampus versus temporal stem. *Science*, 1982, *218*, 1337–1339.

Zola-Morgan, S., & Squire, L. R. Two forms of amnesia in monkeys: Rapid forgetting after medial temporal lesions but not diencephalic lesions. *Society for Neuroscience Abstracts, 8*, 1982, p. 24.

Zubin, J., & Barrera, S. E. Effect of electric convulsive therapy on memory. *Proceedings of the Society of Experimental Biology and Medicine*, 1941, 48, 596–597 (abstract).

9

Implications of Different Patterns of Remote Memory Loss for the Concept of Consolidation

Marilyn S. Albert
Harvard Medical School

At the beginning of the century, Müller and Pilzecker (1900) proposed their "perserveration-consolidation hypothesis," which stated that activity in the nervous system triggered by an event did not stop immediately but instead "perseverated." When this perseveration was complete, a stable memory trace was established. Hebb, in his seminal work *The Organization of behavior,* restated and expanded this theory. He proposed that two processes were necessary for the brain to retain information: First, the continual reverberation of a neural circuit and second, a structural change in neural patterns. The reverberating activity had to continue for a period of time in order for the structural change to take place. Consolidation was defined as the transformation of this temporary reverberating circuit into a permanent memory trace. Both theories therefore predicted that events that disturbed this continuing neural activity would prevent retention.

In order to evaluate the utility of this theory for an understanding of memory function, several questions need to be answered. Does a theory of consolidation make any predictions about retrograde amnesia? Are these predictions satisfied by the types of retrograde amnesia seen in animals and man? Are there patterns of remote memory loss that cannot be explained by the consolidation hypothesis?

Consolidation theory would predict that CNS intervention of an electrical, chemical, or traumatic nature that quickly follows an experience produces a memory deficit for that event. It would also predict that the duration of susceptibility to disruption is brief (i.e., seconds, minutes, or hours). The theory suggests that once reverberating neural activity has been transformed into a permanent memory trace, no loss would be expected. The study of retrograde amnesia in patients and experimental animals has produced considerable evidence for the first of these predictions but not the second. There seems no question that electrical, chemical, or other traumatic intervention at certain stages of the learning process will permanently disrupt or abolish retention in a wide variety of species. However, long reversible and nonreversible retrograde amnesias occur in man that would not be predicted by a narrow interpretation of consolidation theory.

Ribot's Law (Ribot, 1882), which states that recent memories are more vulnerable to disruption than remote memories, has often been used as an addendum to consolidation theory to explain these extensive retrograde amnesias. Recent evidence indicates that this addition to the theory is also insufficient to explain the range of remote memory impairments that occur. These data indicate that retrograde amnesia is not a unitary process and that at least three distinct patterns of remote memory loss exist. One of these, an extensive ungraded loss of remote memories, is a phenomenon that has only recently been described and is clearly not predicted by consolidation theory, even with the emendation of Ribot's Law. The following chapter will discuss the patterns of remote memory loss that have been described in animals and man and the underlying mechanisms that may be responsible for their occurrence with particular regard to the accuracy of the consolidation hypothesis.

RETROGRADE AMNESIA IN ANIMALS

A large number of behavioral experiments with animals have been used to study the time course of retrograde amnesia and the experimental factors that influence retention of remote events. These investigations have generally substantiated the narrow interpretation of the consolidation hypothesis in that retention is disrupted by post-training treatments and the extent of retrograde loss is brief. Most experiments have employed a paradigm in which a single trial on a learning task is followed by a treatment that is intended to interfere with learning. For example, an animal may be placed in a two-compartment chamber and then given foot shock in the compartment that had previously been determined to be the preferential choice of the animal. Then, at varying intervals and in varying intensities, a disruptive treatment is administered to the brain (e.g., electrical stimulation, cortical spreading depression, convulsant drugs, etc.). The critical response measure employed is usually the time it takes the animal to cross into the compartment where he had previously received foot shock. If the animal's latency is long, it is assumed that he remembers the shock. If instead he quickly moves to the other side, it is concluded that something has interfered with his memory of the shock. In general, this research has shown that the severity of a particular amnestic treatment varies inversely with the interval between the initial experience and the disruptive treatment. That is, treatments are most effective if they are administered shortly after the training experience. The impairment decreases as the interval between training and treatment increases. This time-dependent effect produced by post-training treatments on retention is referred to in the animal literature as the retrograde amnesia gradient.

At first it was thought that the temporal characteristics of the retrograde amnesia gradient reflected the time course of memory consolidation. There is now, however, extensive evidence to indicate that the specific parameters of the gradients depend on the methodological constraints of the experiment. A figure taken from Chorover (1976) illustrates this point (Fig. 9.1). It demonstrates that the duration of electrically induced retrograde amnesia can vary from several seconds to several hours. Chorover reports that differences in duration of electrically induced retrograde amnesia can be attributed to the strain, sex, and previous experience of the subject; the nature and the complexity of the learning task: the kind and amount of deprivation and reinforcement used; the physical parameters of the stimulus and the mode of administration.

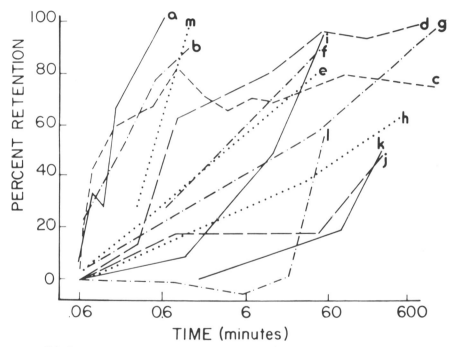

FIG. 9.1. The temporal characteristics of retrograde amnesia gradients in animals as reported in 13 different experiments. Values were recalculated by Chorover (1976) to conform to a semilogarithmic plot. References are: a) Chorover & Schiller, 1965; b) Quartermann et al., 1965; c) Lee Teng & Sherman, 1966; d) Duncan, 1949; e) McGaugh & Alpern, 1966; f) Dorfman & Jarvik, 1968; g) Alpern & McGaugh, 1968; h) Kopp et al., 1966; i) King, 1965; j) Chorover & Schiller, 1966; k) Bures & Buresova, 1963; l) Herriort & Coleman, 1966; m) Schiller & Chorover, 1966.

These retrograde amnesia gradients therefore indicate the effectiveness of a given treatment, administered at a particular time and measured following a specified delay. They do not, as pointed out by McGaugh and Gold (1976), provide a direct measure of the time required for the consolidation of long-term memory. The retrograde amnesia gradients should therefore *not* be interpreted to mean that following a certain specified time behavior is impervious to disruption. They may simply indicate that the disruptive effectiveness of a given treatment is limited under the particular experimental conditions used.

SHORT REVERSIBLE RETROGRADE AMNESIAS IN HUMANS

Amnesic syndromes in man are invariably accompanied by a disturbance in the ability to recall events that occurred prior to the onset of the illness. Such a disturbance may encompass events that transpired hours, days, or years before pathology ensued. Not only is general knowledge of current events impaired but experiences of close personal meaning are lost as well. In one of the earliest discussions of retrograde amnesia following head trauma, Russell and Nathan (1946) describe a 22–year-old man who had been thrown from a motorcycle in August, 1933. "A week after the accident he was able to converse sensibly, and the nursing staff considered that he had fully recovered consciousness. When questioned, however, he said that the date was in February 1922, and that he was a schoolboy [p. 271]." In cases of this sort, the retrograde amnesia generally shrinks so that after full recovery, the remote memory loss is usually quite short, often encompassing only a few seconds before the injury and only rarely exceeding a few minutes (Benson & Geschwind, 1967).

Clinical reports also indicate that the retrograde amnesias of head trauma patients recover in a temporally graded fashion (Benson & Geschwind, 1967; Russell & Nathan, 1946). That is, knowledge about remote events becomes accessible to the patient before knowledge about recent events is recalled. Thus, Russell and Nathan describe the recovery of their 22–year-old patient in the following manner.

> He had no recollection of five years spent in Australia, and two years in this country working on a golf course. Two weeks after the injury he remembered the five years spent in Australia and remembered returning to this country, the past two years were, however, a complete blank as far as his memory was concerned. . . . About ten weeks after the accident the events of the past two years were gradually recollected and finally he was able to remember everything up to within a few minutes of the accident [p. 291].

These results have been taken as confirmation of Ribot's Law that recent memories are more vulnerable than remote memories. Because knowledge of early life seems to be preserved intact in head trauma patients, this conclusion seems warranted. However, Ribot also argued that remote memories grow more resistant to disruption as time passes after learning. Reports that, in head trauma patients, memory recovers in temporally organized stages, still leave unanswered the issue of whether there is a gradation of memory loss within a given amnesic period. In this regard, at least two alternatives seem possible:

1. A patient's memory recovers in temporally graded stages, but within each stage remote events are as difficult to recall as recent events. For example, if a patient is amnesic for three years prior to a precipitating traumatic episode, information throughout that three year period is equally inaccessible to the individual.
2. Not only does memory recover in a series of stages but, within any given stage of recovery, memories are temporally graded. Thus, the patient with a three year retrograde amnesia has more recall of events that occurred two years premorbidly than of events that occurred one year prior to the accident.

The clinical reports of islands of memory during recovery (Russell, 1959; Whitty & Zangwill, 1966) have not clarified which of these possibilities may be true. In order to clarify these issues, objective tests of remote memory need to be administered to head trauma patients at repeated intervals during the course of recovery. If patients show a temporally organized gradation of recall within each stage of recovery, then we would have further evidence in support of Ribot's Law.

Patients who have been given electroconvulsive therapy (ECT) for severe depression present symptoms that directly parallel those following severe head trauma. First, the extent of retrograde amnesia both before and after recovery is similar in both groups. Before recovery, impairments exist for as much as 1–7 years prior to shock or trauma. After recovery, the residual retrograde amnesia extends for minutes or hours (Russell & Nathan, 1946; Squire, Slater, & Miller, 1981). Second, the nature of the loss is similar. Patients regain the ability to recall remote events as recovery proceeds. This may reflect the fact that retrieval mechanisms are disturbed or that engrams are temporarily in a state of degradation. In either case, established memories are not permanently lost. Third, the retrograde amnesias of both groups may be temporally graded. Depressed patients are always scheduled in advance for ECT treatments; therefore, it is possible to test them before and after such treatments have been administered. Squire and his associates have taken advantage of this medical procedure to investigate the recovery of retrograde amnesia. They have administered a variety of remote memory tests (Squire, Chace, & Slater, 1976; Squire, Slater & Chace, 1975; Squire & Cohen, in press) both before and after a series of 5 ECT treatments and have clearly shown that ECT patients are impaired in their ability to recall recent events (e.g., 1970s) but unimpaired in their ability to recall remote events (e.g., 1950s). Though objective tests such as those utilized by Squire have not been employed with head trauma patients, clinical reports indicate (as mentioned) that their retrograde amnesia is also temporally graded.

There is a third similarity between ECT and head trauma patients. When these individuals first demonstrate symptoms of retrograde amnesia, they also show difficulty in learning new material (i.e., anterograde amnesia). After ECT treatments, patients perform normally on intelligence tests but are clearly impaired on a variety of memory tasks (Squire & Chace, 1975; Squire & Miller, 1974). Furthermore, among head trauma patients, these deficits are said to parallel one another so that an anterograde impairment of long duration is generally seen in a patient with a severe retrograde impairment (Barbizet, 1970; Russell, 1959). This has been interpreted to mean that the same processes underlie all retrograde and anterograde amnesic difficulties (Benson & Geschwind, 1967; Rozin, 1976). It is, however, important to note that among post-traumatic amnesic patients, anterograde and retrograde impairments may be discontinuous. Most reports indicate that the anterograde deficits terminate long before the retrograde impairments are reduced (Benson & Geschwind, 1967; Russell & Nathan, 1946). Furthermore, the discontinuity between the severity of anterograde and retrograde loss is even more striking among patients with permanent memory disorders. Evidence will be presented later that demonstrates that amnesic patients may have a severe remote memory loss in the presence of a mild learning deficit.

SIMILARITIES BETWEEN HUMANS AND ANIMALS

Extent of Loss

It is striking that despite the variability in the duration of retrograde deficits in experimental animals (as shown in Fig. 9.1) the broad time limits correspond precisely to those of the residual retrograde deficits reported in head trauma and ECT patients. There seems to be a period of seconds to hours in which a memory is fragile and may be permanently lost. This appears to be the period of consolidation spoken of by Müller and Pilzecker (1900) and Hebb (1949), in which neural activity that has not formed a permanent memory trace can be abolished.

There is, however, in humans, a longer period in which, though the memory is consolidated, recall may be impaired. This corresponds to the reversible loss of days to years seen in head trauma and ECT patients. The finding that this retrograde amnesia can be temporally graded indicates that whether the remote memory loss is caused by a disturbance of retrieval (perhaps related to changes in membrane permeability or the capacity of the synapse to release transmitter substances) or a temporary degradation of engrams (possibly a disruption of the arrangement of enzymes within the cell), the potential for disruption appears to decrease as time passes after learning. How this occurs is still unclear.

It is not surprising that reversible losses are not generally seen in animals because the nature of most animal training trials differs radically from the human learning experience. Most consolidation experiments have limited themselves to one-trial training paradigms (e.g., an animal has one experience with foot shock in a particular place at a particular time). The most difficult item on a remote memory test used with humans does not compare in briefness of exposure to such a paradigm (e.g., a question may be asked about a television show with a Neilsen rating of 12 that was on the air for a year in 1957). The only experiments that have demonstrated a reversible loss in animals (Deutsch & Deutsch, 1966) utilized a learning task in which subjects were trained to criterion. Although performance was disrupted for as long as 14 days after the initial training, memory for the task eventually returned to normal. In order to see more extensive temporal gradients, one would expect that animals would have to be trained on a number of tasks consecutively arranged over time. If there is continuity between animals and humans, one would also expect that such a procedure would produce losses of remote memory that recover in a temporally graded fashion.

Neuoranatomical Considerations

There are some areas of overlap between the brain regions that have been shown to cause retrograde amnesia in animals and in man. Post-trial disruptive treatments applied to the hippocampus, caudate nucleus, substantia nigra, thalamus, midbrain reticular formation, and amygdala have all produced retrograde amnesia gradients in lower mammals. In man, damage at various points in the limbic system (i.e., the mammillary bodies, the hippocampus, the fornix) and in the medial thalamus have produced amnesic syndromes. This does not, however, enable one to define the critical neural structures in remote memory. Lynch (1976) has shown that even localized lesions cause widespread biochemical and morphological reactions in the brain so that changes in behavior may involve different regions from those damaged. Electrical stimulation of a particular site may similarly affect memory storage through alterations in other brain regions. Likewise, lesions or stimulation may cause nonspecific neural alterations by influencing arousal or hormonal states (Kety, 1976). Nevertheless, the overlap is intriguing. As will be shown in following sections, there is considerable evidence to indicate that amnesia is not a unitary disorder. Differences between patients of differing etiologies may well be a function of the particular combination of either immediate or remote neural systems affected. If appropriate animal models could be developed, their use could improve our understanding of these various factors in amnesic disorders.

SHORT NONREVERSIBLE RETROGRADE AMNESIAS IN HUMANS

Two intensively studied amnesic patients, the patient H.M. and the patient N.A., are known to have extensive and permanent anterograde amnesias accompanied by short, stable retrograde amnesias. The patient H.M. (Scoville & Milner, 1957) has been amnesic since 1953, when his mesial temporal lobes were bilaterally removed as a treatment for intractable epilepsy. The patient N.A. (Teuber, Milner, & Vaughan, 1968) has been severely amnesic for verbal material since 1960, when he sustained a stab wound to the brain with a miniature fencing foil. A recent CT scan (Squire & Moore, 1979) shows a lesion in the left dorsomedial thalamus although, of course, other lesions not seen in the scan may be present in this case. Though the IQ of both patients has remained intact, H.M. continues to be severely impaired on a variety of short-term memory tasks (Milner, 1967; 1970) and N.A. has a severe impairment in learning new verbal materials (Squire & Slater, 1978).

The interesting point with regard to the present discussion is that the retrograde amnesias of these patients is of brief duration. H.M. has difficulty recalling events 2–3 years prior to his operation (Marslen-Wilson & Teuber, 1975). N.A. appears to have a retrograde amnesia of approximately 6 months (Squire & Slater, 1978). Although the duration of these stable retrograde amnesias clearly exceeds the permanent memory loss seen in head trauma and ECT patients (i.e. several hours), it does coincide with the extent of reversible loss seen in these same individuals. This may indicate that similar phenomena are involved.

It is unfortunate that though it has been documented that H.M. and N.A.'s retrograde amnesia are short, their memory loss has not yet been demonstrated to be temporally graded. This information is necessary in order to make any assumptions about the underlying mechanisms of their remote memory loss. Their recent memories are more vulnerable than remote memories, so that H.M. and N.A. reconfirm the broad interpretation of Ribot's Law. Nevertheless, without knowing whether, within the period of amnesia, recall for remote events is better than recall for more recent ones (e.g. whether H.M. recalls more about 1951 than 1952), it cannot be determined whether Ribot's prediction that remote memories grow more resistant to disruption as time passes after learning is borne out by these patients.

The symptoms of H.M. and N.A. also highlight an aspect of amnesia that is extremely pertinent to both human and animal investigations of amnesia. There is a clear discontinuity between their anterograde and retrograde deficits. Although it may be true (as mentioned earlier) that these phenomena are linked in cases of reversible memory loss, there is now considerable evidence that this is not the case in numerous permanent amnesic states. Patients who have survived attacks of herpes simplex encephalitis have anterograde and retrograde amnesic difficulties that have been attributed primarily to damage in the hippocampus (Drachman & Adams, 1962; Drachman & Arbit, 1966), although widespread damage in the limbic system often occurs as well. Individuals with alcoholic Korsakoff's disease also exhibit anterograde and retrograde impairments, but their disorder derives from alcohol abuse and thiamine deficiency, which produces damage to the mammillary bodies and the dorsomedial nuclei of the thalamus (Victor, Adams & Collins, 1971). Two sets of investigators (Butters, & Cermak, 1976; Lhermitte & Signoret, 1972) have found that postencephalitics were superior to Korsakoff patients on tests of short-term memory. However, encephalitic patients have recently been shown to be inferior to alcoholic Korsakoff subjects on tests of remote memory (Albert, Butters, & Levin, 1980). This dissociation of anterograde and retrograde capacities is striking but not unique.

Williams and Smith (1954) and Wood, McHenry, Roman-Campos and Posner (1980) have described similar discontinuities in their patients. The former study presents four tuberculous meningitis patients who, on initial examination, had severe anterograde and retrograde deficits. After recovery, no measurable anterograde deficits were found, despite the fact that the retrograde deficits extended for 1–4 years. Similarly, Wood et al. report a case of remitted global amnesia in which retrograde deficits extended 10 years prior to the illness but no impairments of new learning persisted. These dissociations not only emphasize possible differences among amnesic populations (Mattis, Kovner, & Goldmeier, 1978), but also suggest that anterograde and retrograde amnesic symptoms need not be correlated.

Fedio and Van Buren (1975) have demonstrated that anterograde and retrograde deficits may be separated by stimulation along the anterior-posterior axis of the left temporal lobe. The subjects in their study were patients who were being considered for surgery to relieve intractable epileptic seizures. The results showed that stimulation of the anterior sectors of the left temporal lobe resulted in a failure to store verbal materials presented simultaneously with the stimulation (i.e., anterograde amnesia). In contrast, stimulation of the posterior sectors of the temporal lobe resulted in an inability to recall verbal material that had been presented shortly before the onset of stimulation (i.e., retrograde amnesia).

LONG, GRADED PERMANENT RETROGRADE AMNESIAS IN HUMANS

The longest known example of the amnesic syndrome is alcoholic Korsakoff's disease (Korsakoff, 1887). This disorder occurs among chronic alcoholics and is generally thought to result from thiamine deficiency (Talland, 1965), although recent evidence has suggested that the memory disorder in these individuals may be produced by an interaction of thiamine deficiency and the direct neurotoxic effects of alcohol (Freund & Walker, 1971). The syndrome consists of two distinct stages. The first is the Wernicke syndrome stage characterized by confusion, ataxia (i.e., gait disorders), opthalmoplegia (i.e. occular motor disturbances), polyneuropathy of the extremities (i.e., pain, sensory loss, weakness as a result of damage to peripheral nerves). It is generally thought that the acute Wernicke encephalopathy phase is precipitated by hemorrhagic damage to the diencephalon, which produces lesions primarily in the mammillary bodies and the dorsomedial nuclei of the thalamus (Victor, Adams, & Collins, 1971). If thiamine is administered during this time, the major encephalopathic symptoms are markedly reduced but a severe anterograde and retrograde amnesia persists. This stable memory impairment typifies the second and chronic stage of the illness.

There have been a number of extensive neuropsychological studies of Korsakoff patients (for a review see Butters & Cermak, 1980). These studies have focused upon the patient's short-term memory capacities and the role of interference, encoding, and storage in their retention problems. Though there have been far fewer studies of the Korsakoff patients retrograde amnesia, a recent interest in this area has begun to clarify the factors responsible for their memory deficit.

During clinical examination, the retrograde amnesia of alcoholic Korsakoff patients is usually characterized by a gradient in which memories acquired in the remote past are better preserved than those acquired during the past 10 or 15 years. It is, for example, not unusual for a Korsakoff patient to correctly recall that Roosevelt and Truman were the American presidents during World War II but be unable to recall correctly the names of the two presidents immediately preceding the incumbent.

Though an early experimental study (Sanders & Warrington, 1971) cast doubt upon whether there was a differential sparing of very remote memories, numerous investigators have now reported that alcoholic Korsakoff patients have significantly superior recall of events from the 1930s and 1940s than of events from the 1960s and 1970s (Albert, Butters, & Levin, 1979; Marslen-Wilson & Teuber, 1975; Seltzer & Benson, 1974; Squire & Cohen, in press). The disagreement concerning the existence of a temporal gradient in Korsakoff patients hinged on the contention of Sanders and Warrington that investigators had used relatively easy and overlearned items to assess remote events but more difficult and less exposed items to assess recent events. In an effort to evaluate this possibility, Albert, Butters, and Levin (1979) designed a remote memory battery in which the difficulty level of the questions was statistically controlled. The battery consisted of three tests: a facial recognition test, which included 180 photographs of famous individuals from the 1920s to the 1970s; a recall questionnaire, that consisted of 132 questions about public events and people famous from 1920 to 1975; and a multiple-choice questionnaire, which also contained 132 items about people and events from 1920 to 1975. "Hard" and "easy" items were selected on the basis of the performance of a group of controls and an equal number of both were included among questions for each decade.

When this battery was administered to alcoholic Korsakoff patients, Albert et al. found that regardless of item difficulty, the retrograde amnesia of these subjects was severe, extended over many past decades, and was characterized by a temporal gradient in which memories of very remote events were more accessible to the subjects than memories of recent events (Fig. 9.2). These data were then reanalyzed (Butters & Albert, in press) so that "easy" items from the recent

Retrograde Amnesia Battery

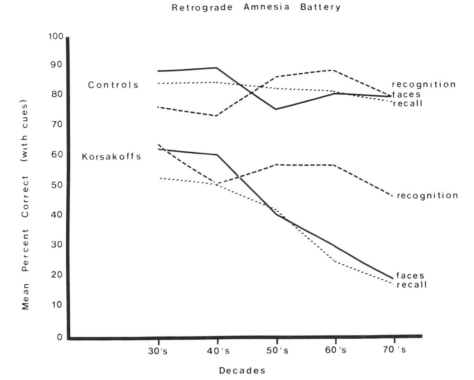

FIG. 9.2.   The overall performance of normal controls and alcoholic Korsakoff patients on Albert et al.'s (1979) remote memory battery.

past were compared to "hard" items from the remote past. The alcoholic Korsakoff patients continued to demonstrate a relative preservation of events and people from the early decades of their lives. These findings have subsequently been replicated in their entirety by Squire and Cohen (in press). It therefore appears that the temporal gradient of alcoholic Korsakoff patients cannot be reduced to an artifact of differential item difficulty.

Although these data provided a convincing description of the Korsakoff patients' loss of remote memories, they did not explain the origin of this temporally graded deficit. It seemed possible that the alcoholic Korsakoff's impaired recall of remote events could appear acutely, as with ECT and head trauma patients, or it could develop slowly as a result of many years of alcohol abuse. This latter "chronic" explanation appeared particularly viable because there is now considerable evidence that chronic alcoholics have information processing deficits that resemble those of Korsakoff patients (Parker & Nobel, 1977; Ryan & Butters, 1980). When long-term (10 or more years of alcohol abuse), but intact alcoholics are compared to alcoholic Korsakoff patients and nonalcoholic controls on verbal and nonverbal short-term memory tasks, the alcoholics' performances fall midway between the scores of the other two groups. Furthermore, the severity of the alcoholics' learning deficits is positively correlated with years of alcohol abuse. One might thus predict that if the chronic alcoholic acquired less information each year due to an increasing anterograde deficit, at the time the patient was finally diagnosed as an "alcoholic Korsakoff" he would have what appeared to be a retrograde amnesia with a temporal gradient. This would not, however, be a true retrograde amnesia but a remote memory deficit that was the result of a progressively severe anterograde impairment.

To evaluate this chronic explanation of the Korsakoff patients' remote memory losses, Albert, Butters, & Levin's (1979) memory battery was administered to chronic alcoholics, whose average period of excessive drinking was 25 years, and to nonalcoholic control subjects (Albert, Butters, & Brandt, in press, a). They found that the chronic alcoholics were impaired relative to the controls but only on the hardest recall items from the 1960s and 1970s. If the Korsakoff patients' retrograde amnesia were primarily due to a chronic and progressive deficit in new learning, the long-term alcoholics should have had far more pervasive and severe deficits on this test battery. Because they did not, Albert, Butters, & Brandt concluded that the alcoholic Korsakoff's remote memory loss probably has both an anterograde and a retrograde component. The anterograde component is the impact of alcohol abuse on the alcoholic's ability to acquire new information. The retrograde component is the loss that appears acutely during the Wernicke stage of the illness and produces a severe and equal loss for all time periods prior to the onset of the disease. It is hypothesized that when this retrograde loss of remote memories is superimposed on the patient's already deficient store, a severe retrograde amnesia with a temporal gradient should result. Patients should be impaired with respect to controls for all time periods, but memory for recent events should be most severely affected because less had been learned initially about this period. This is, in fact, what one observes in patients with alcoholic Korsakoff's disease.

LONG, UNGRADED RETROGRADE AMNESIA IN HUMANS

The major implication of this two-factor model is that patient populations should exist who demonstrate severe and equal losses for all time periods prior to the onset of disease, i.e., a "flat" retrograde amnesia. Just such a result has been found in testing patients with Huntington's disease (Albert, Butters, & Brandt, in press, b). Huntington's Disease (HD) is a genetically transmitted dementing disorder that results in atrophy of basal ganglia and cerberal cortex (Bruyn, Bots, & Dom, 1979). It is characterized by the early appearance of involuntary choreic movements and memory deficits followed by a progressive intellectual decline

(Butters, Sax, Montgomery, & Tarlow, 1978; Caine, Ebert, & Weingartner, 1977). The alcoholic Korsakoff patient retains the ability to manipulate knowledge acquired prior to the onset of his illness (e.g., proverb interpretations, arithmetic computations, vocabulary definitions), but the HD patient progressively declines in his ability to carry out such tasks. The impairments of HD patients are, however, selective. Like the alcoholic Korsakoff patient, the HD patient has a severe memory problem but normal performance on confrontation-naming tasks.

Such moderately advanced, noninstitutionalized HD patients are severely impaired on Albert et al.'s remote memory battery, but there are important and significant differences between their pattern of remote memory loss and that of patients with alcoholic Korsakoff's syndrome. The remote memory loss of alcoholic Korsakoff patients is (as previously mentioned) characterized by a temporal gradient in which facts pertaining to the distant past are more accurately retrieved

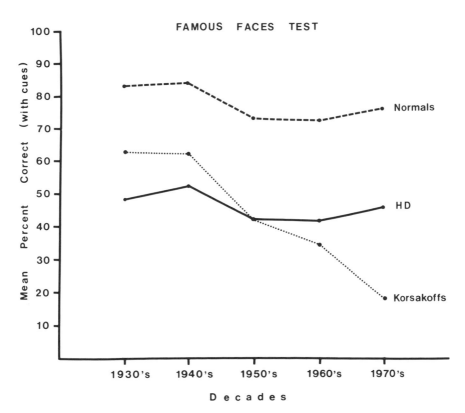

FIG. 9.3.   The performance of patients with Huntington's disease (HD), alcoholic Korsakoff's syndrome, and normal controls on the Famous Faces Test of Albert et al.'s (1979) remote memory battery.

than facts concerning events that occurred just prior to the onset of their illness. HD patients have as much difficulty identifying faces and events from the 1930s and 1940s as faces and events from the 1960s and 1970s. Thus, their pattern of remote memory loss is "flat," that is, equal for all time periods sampled. When the performances are contrasted, as in Fig. 9.3, a dramatic interaction is evident.

Furthermore, the pattern of loss of the HD patients cannot be attributed to their progressive intellectual decline, because recently diagnosed HD patients also demonstrate a "flat" remote memory curve (Albert, Butters, & Brandt, in press, c) The most prominent cognitive deficit of these recently diagnosed HD patients (i.e., tested within 12 months of diagnosis) was their impairment on short-term memory tests. In the early stages of the illness, they retain the capacity to manipulate old knowledge (Butters et al., 1978). The remote memory deficits of the recently diagnosed HD patients were, as might be expected, less

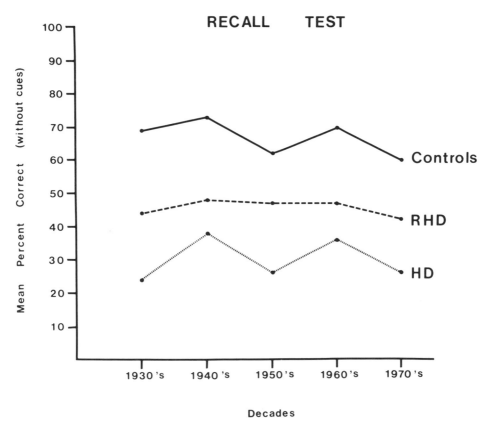

FIG. 9.4.   The performance of recently diagnosed Huntington's disease patients (RHD), advanced Huntington's disease patients (HD), and normal controls on the Recall Test of Albert et al.'s (1979) remote memory battery.

severe than those of the more advanced patients, but they extended over many decades, with approximately equivalent losses for each decade interval (Fig. 9.4). It therefore appears that HD, during all periods of its progression, involves a form of retrograde amnesia characterized by an *extensive ungraded* loss of remote memories.

These results are of considerable theoretical significance because they suggest that retrograde amnesia is not a unitary disorder. The evidence indicates that remote memory patterns may be characterized in at least three ways.

The first of these is exemplified by the remote memory losses seen in ECT (Squire et al., 1975), head trauma patients (Russell & Nathan, 1946), and animal experiments (McGaugh & Gold, 1976). There is a period, lasting seconds to hours, in which memories are completely abolished. There is also evidence of an additional period, lasting as long as 6 or 7 years, in which remote memories seem to be particularly susceptible to disruption. In ECT and head trauma patients the ability to recall remote events recovers with time, whereas amnesic patients with relatively small focal lesions (e.g., H.M. and N.A.) have short, but permanent, retrograde amnesias.

Alcoholic Korsakoff patients typify the second type of remote memory loss. Numerous studies now indicate that the remote memory loss of these patients covers many decades and is characterized by a temporal gradient (Albert et al., 1979; Marslen-Wilson & Teuber, 1975; Seltzer & Benson, 1974; Squire & Cohen, in press).

The performance of the recently diagnosed and advanced HD patients demonstrates the third pattern of impairment. Their retrograde amnesia extends over many decades but with equivalent losses in remote memory for all periods of the patients' lives. A preliminary report of remote memory deficits in patients with senile dementia (Wilson, Kaszniak, & Fox, 1980) indicates that, like HD patients, these subjects retrieve equivalent amounts of information for each decade.

Although these findings demonstrate that different patterns of remote memory loss occur in different patient populations, it is not clear what aspects of the differences between them are critical determinants of their varying retrograde amnesias. First, one must consider the fact that each of these groups has a different set of central nervous system lesions (i.e., basal ganglia, thalamus, hippocampus) and that these lesions vary in size. Moreover, perhaps for the same reason, these patients vary in the number of cognitive defects that they show. H.M. and N.A. have a severe but fairly isolated memory problem; alcoholic Korsakoff patients have subtle but significant visuoperceptive and complex problem-solving impairments. HD patients have severe deficits in several cognitive areas. These patients also differ in the suddenness with which their lesions have occurred. It is well known that gradually progressive central nervous system lesions produce a different pattern of impairments from acute lesions of the same size (Stein, 1974). Because the types of CNS damage among the patient populations discussed here differ in size as well as in speed of onset, a combination of these factors may well be important in determining their remote memory patterns.

The theoretical mechanisms underlying the differences between these groups are also unclear. A consolidation impairment seems to explain the period of seconds to hours during which memories are abolished by a disruption of neural transmission, but it does not account for the graded, reversible disturbance of recall seen in ECT patients. It may be, as Ribot's Law suggests, that for a period of about six years after learning, memory becomes more resistant to disruption. Chorover (1976) has argued that the engrams of long-term memory are not permanently fixed but may be periodically reorganized as time passes. The ECT data indicate that such reprogramming may continue for several years but that after this occurs, considerable destruction of brain tissue may be necessary to disrupt older memory traces.

The long remote memory impairments of the alcoholic Korsakoff patients and the patients with Huntington's disease seem to support this contention. They have permanent cortical and subcortical damage and their remote memory impairments cannot be attributed to a consolidation deficit. The most liberal interpretation of the consolidation hypothesis would not predict a loss of memories for events that occurred 40 years prior to the onset of disease. Some other process must be present to explain the pattern of loss of these amnesic and dementing patients. In fact, the same mechanism may underlie the remote memory loss of both patient populations, despite the difference in the appearance of their remote memory curves. If the two-factor theory of the alcoholic Korsakoff's deficit is correct (i.e., that the retrograde component of remote memory impairment produces equal losses at all time periods and the anterograde component produces a graded loss), then the retrograde component of both groups may be "flat." Both a storage and a retrieval hypothesis would predict this pattern of loss; therefore, it is not currently possible to determine which explanation seems more appropriate. Damage either to the neuroanatomical structures necessary for storing old information, or to those needed to retrieve it, would be expected to result in remote memory losses that were severe and equally distributed over time.

It should be noted that hypotheses regarding losses of remote memory need not agree with hypotheses seeking to explain anterograde memory deficits. If, as the evidence suggests, anterograde and retrograde memory problems are dissociable from one another and dependent upon different neural circuits, one would not expect the same mechanisms to underlie both impairments.

Much has been learned about remote memory and memory consolidation by contrasting the performance of carefully defined populations of neurologic patients. These data indicate that at least one form of retrograde amnesia falls within the framework of the consolidation hypothesis. Animal experiments corroborate this finding. Though both sets of data exist on different levels of magnitude from one another, the theoretical issues regarding underlying processes and possible brain structures involved appear to be similar. Thus, an analysis of memory consolidation at different levels of detail is beginning to produce a set of interlocking facts that should ultimately enable us to understand this complex phenomenon.

ACKNOWLEDGMENTS

The preparation of this paper was supported by Grant # P01–AG–02269 from the National Institute on Aging to Beth Israel Hospital and the Harvard Medical School.

The author wishes to thank Dr. Nelson Butters, Dr. Norman Geschwind, and Dr. Mark Moss for their assistance in the preparation of the manuscript.

REFERENCES

Albert, M., Butters, N., & Brandt, J. Memory for remote events in chronic alcoholics. *Journal of Studies on Alcohol,* in press. (a)

Albert, M., Butters, N., & Brandt, J. Patterns of remote memory in amnesic and dementing patients. *Archives of Neurology,* in press. (b)

Albert, M., Butters, N., & Brandt, J. The development of remote memory loss in patients with Huntington's Disease. *Journal of Clinical Neuropsychology,* in press. (c)

Albert, M., Butters, N., & Levin, J. Temporal gradients in the retrograde amnesia of patients with alcoholic Korsakoff's Disease. *Archives of Neurology,* 1979, *36,* 211–216.

Albert, M., Butters, N., & Levin, J. Memory for remote events in chronic alcoholics and alcoholic Korsakoff patients. In H. Begleiter (Ed.), *Advances in experimental medicine and biology: Biological effects of alcohol.* New York: Plenum Press, 1980.

Alpern, H. P., & McGaugh, J. L. Retrograde amnesia as a function of duration of electroshock stimulation. *Journal of Comparative and Physiological Psychology* 1968, *65,* 265–269.

Barbizet, J. *Human memory and its pathology.* Translated by D. K. Jardine. San Francisco, Calif.: W. H. Freeman, 1970.

Benson, D. F., & Geschwind, N. Shrinking retrograde amnesia. *Journal of Neurology, Neurosurgery, and Psychiatry,* 1967, *30,* 539–555.

Bruyn, G., Bots, G., & Dom, R. Huntington's Chorea: Current neuropathological status. In T. Chase, N. Wexler, & A. Barbeau (Eds.), *Advances in Neurology.* New York: Raven Press, 1979.

Bures, J., & Buresova, O. Cortical spreading depression as a memory disturbing factor. *Journal of Comparative and Physiological Psychology,* 1963, *56,* 268–272.

Butters, N., & Albert, M. Processes underlying failures to recall remote events. In L. Cermak (Ed.), *Amnesia and human memory.* Hillsdale, N.J.: Lawrence Erlbaum Associates, 1981.

Butters, N., & Cermak, L. S. Neuropsychological studies of alcoholic Korsakoff patients. In G. Goldstein & C. Neuringer (Eds.), *Empirical studies of alcoholism.* Cambridge, Mass.: Ballinger, 1976.

Butters, N., & Cermak, L. S. *Alcoholic Korsakoff's Syndrome.* New York: Academic Press, 1980.

Butters, N., Sax, D., Montgomery, K., & Tarlow, S. Comparison of the neuropsychological deficits associated with early and advanced Huntington's Disease. *Archives of Neurology,* 1978, *35,* 585–589.

Caine, E. D., Ebert, M. H., & Weingartner, H. An outline for the analysis of dementia: The memory disorder of Huntington's Disease. *Neurology,* 1977, *27,* 1087–1092.

Chorover, S. L., & Schiller, P. H. Short-term retrograde amnesia in rats. *Journal of Comparative and Physiological Psychology,* 1965, *59,* 73–78.

Chorover, S. L., & Schiller, P. H. Reexamination of prolonged retrograde amnesia in one-trial learning. *Journal of Comparative and Physiological Psychology,* 1966, *61,* 34–41.

Chorover, S. L. An experimental critique of the "consolidation studies" and an alternative "model-systems" approach to the biophysiology of memory. In M. R. Rosensweig & E. L. Bennett (Eds.), *Neural mechanisms of learning and memory.* Cambridge, Mass.: MIT Press, 1976.

Dorfman, L. J., & Jarvik, M. E. A parametric study of electroshock–induced retrograde amnesia in mice. *Neuropsychologia,* 1968, *6,* 373–380.

Deutsch, J. A., & Deutsch, D. *Physiological psychology.* Homewood, Ill.: Dorsey Press, 1966.

Drachman, D. A. & Adams, R. D. Herpes simplex and acute inclusion body encephalitis. *Archives of Neurology,* 1962, *7,* 45–63.

Drachman, D. A. & Arbit, J. Memory and the hippocampal complex. *Archives of Neurology,* 1966, *15,* 52–61.

Duncan, C. P. The retroactive effect of electroshock on learning. *Journal of Comparative and Physiological Psychology,* 1949, *42,* 32–44.

Fedio, P., & Van Buren, J. M. Memory and perceptual deficits during electrical stimulation in the left and right thalamus and parietal subcortex. *Brain and Language,* 1975, *2,* 78–100.

Freund, G. & Walker, D. W. Impairment of avoidance learning by prolonged ethanol consumption in mice. *Journal of Pharmacology and Experimental Therapeutics,* 1971, *179,* 284–292.

Hebb, D. O. *The organization of behavior.* New York: Wiley, 1949.

Heriott, J. T., & Coleman, P. D. The effect of electroconvulsive shock on retention of a modified "one-trial" conditioned avoidance. *Journal of Comparative and Physiological Psychology,* 1962, *55,* 1082–1084.

Kety, S. S. Biological concomitants of affective states and their possible role in memory processes. In M. R. Rosensweig & E. L. Bennett (Eds.), *Neural mechanisms of learning and memory.* Cambridge, Mass.: MIT Press, 1976.

King, R. A. Consolidation of the neural trace in memory: Investigation with one-trial avoidance conditioning and electroconvulsive shock. *Journal of Comparative and Physiological Psychology,* 1965, *59,* 283–254.

Kopp, R., Bohdanecky, Z., & Javvik, M. E. Long temporal gradient of retrograde amnesia for a well discriminated stimulus. *Science,* 1966, *153,* 1547–1549.

Korsakoff, S. S. Disturbance of psychic function in alcoholic paralysis and its relation to the disturbance of the psychic sphere in the multiple neuritis of non-alcoholic origin. *Vestnik Psichiatrii,* 1887, *4,* 2–32.

Lee-Teng, E., & Sherman, S. M. Memory consolidation of one-trial learning in chicks. *Proceedings of the National Academy of Sciences (USA)* 1966, *56,* 926–931.

Lhermitte, F., & Signoret, J. L. Neurological analysis and differentiation of amnesic syndromes. *Revue Neurologique,* 1972, *126,* 161–178.

Lynch, G. Some difficulties associated with the use of lesion techniques in the study of memory. In M. R. Rosensweig & E. L. Bennett (Eds.), *Neural mechanisms of learning and memory.* Cambridge, Mass.: MIT Press, 1976.

Marslen-Wilson, W. D. & Teuber, H. L. Memory for remote events in anterograde amnesia: Recognition of public figures from news photographs. *Neuropsychologia,* 1975, *13,* 347–352.

Mattis, S., Kovner, R., & Goldmeier, E. Different patterns of mnemonic deficits in two organic amnestic syndromes. *Brain and Language,* 1978, *6,* 179–191.

McGaugh, J. L., & Alpern, H. P. Effects of electroshock on memory: Amnesia without convulsion. *Science,* 1966, *152,* 665–666.

McGaugh, J., & Gold, P. E. Modulation of memory by electrical stimulation of the brain. In M. R. Rosensweig & E. L. Bennett (Eds.), *Neural mechanisms of learning and memory.* Cambridge, Mass.: MIT Press, 1976.

Milner, B. Amnesia following operation on the temporal lobes. In F. L. Darley (Ed.), *Brain mechanisms underlying speech and language*. New York: Grune & Stratton, 1967.

Milner, B. Memory and the medial temporal regions of the brain. In K. H. Pribram & D. E. Broadbent (Eds.), *Biology of memory*. New York, Academic Press, 1970.

Müller, G. E. & Pilzecker, A. Experimentale beitrage zur lehre vom gedachtnis. *Zeitschrift fur Psychologie Suppl.*: 1900, 1–288.

Parker, E., & Nobel, E. Alcohol comsumption and cognitive functioning in social drinkers. *Journal of Studies on Alcohol*, 1977, *38*, 1224–1232.

Quartermain, D., Paolino, R. M., & Miller, N. E. A brief temporal gradient of retrograde amnesia independent of situational change. *Science*, 1965, *149*, 1116–1118.

Ribot, T. *Diseases of memory*. New York: Appleton, 1882.

Rozin, P. The psychobiological approach to human memory. In M. R. Rosensweig & E. L. Bennett (Eds.) *Neural mechanisms of learning and memory*. Cambridge, Mass.: MIT Press, 1976.

Russell, W. R. *Brain, memory, learning: A neurologist's view*. Oxford: Oxford University Press, 1959.

Russell, W. R. & Nathan, P. W. Traumatic amnesia. *Brain*, 1946, *69*, 280–300.

Ryan, C., & Butters, N. Further evidence for a continuum-of-impairment encompassing male alcoholic Korsakoff patients and chronic alcoholic men. *Alcoholism: Clinical and Experimental Research*, 1980, *4*, 190–198.

Sanders, H. L., & Warrington, E. K. Memory for remote events in amnesic patients. *Brain*, 1971, *94*, 661–668.

Schiller, P. H., & Chorover, S. L. Short-term amnestic effects of electro-convulsive shock in a one-trial maze learning paradigm. *Neuropsychologia*, 1967, *5*, 155–163.

Scoville, W. B. & Milner, B. Loss of recent memory after bilateral hippocampal lesions. *Neuropsychologia*, 1957, *20*, 11–21.

Seltzer, B. & Benson, D. F. The temporal pattern of retrograde amnesia in Korsakoff's disease. *Neurology*, 1974, *24*, 527–530.

Squire, L. R., & Chace, P. M. Memory functions six to nine months after electroconvulsive therapy. *Archives of General Psychiatry*, 1975, *32*, 1557–1564.

Squire, L. R., Chace, P. M., & Slater, P. C. Retrograde amnesia following electroconvulsive therapy. *Nature* (London), 1976, *260*, 775–777.

Squire, L. R., & Cohen, N. J. Remote memory, retrograde amnesia, and the neuropsychology of memory. In L. Cermak (Ed.), *Amnesia and human memory*. Hillsdale, N.J.: Lawrence Erlbaum Associates, 1981.

Squire, L. R. & Miller, P. L. Diminution of anterograde amnesia following electroconvulsive therapy. *British Journal of Psychiatry*, 1974, *125*, 490–495.

Squire, L. R. & Moore, R. Y. Dorsal thalamic lesions in a noted case of chronic memory dysfunction. *Annals of Neurology*, 1979, *6*, 503–506.

Squire, L. R. & Slater, P. C. Anterograde and retrograde memory impairments in chronic amnesia. *Neuropsychologia*, 1978, *16*, 313–322.

Squire, L. R., Slater, P. C., & Chace, P. M. Retrograde amnesia: Temporal gradient in very long term memory following electro-convulsive therapy. *Science*, 1975, *187*, 77–79.

Squire, L. R., Slater, P. C., & Miller, P. L. Retrograde amnesia following ECT: long term follow-up studies. *Archives of General Psychiatry*, 1981, *1*(38) 89–95.

Stein, D. *Plasticity and recovery of function in the central nervous system*. New York: Academic Press, 1974.

Talland, G. *Deranged memory*. New York: Academic Press, 1965.

Teuber, H. L., Milner, B., & Vaughan, H. G. Persistent anterograde amnesia after stab wound of the basal brain. *Neuropsychologia*, 1968, *6*, 267–282.

Victor, M., Adams, R. D., & Collins, G. H. *The Wernicke-Korsakoff syndrome*. Philadelphia: F. A. Davis, 1971.

Whitty, C. W. M., & Zangwill, O. Traumatic amnesia. In C. W. M. Whitty & O. Zangwill (Eds.), *Amnesia.* London: Butterworth, 1966.

Williams, M., & Smith, H. Mental disturbances in tuberculous meningitis. *Journal of Neurology, Neurosurgery and Psychiatry,* 1954, *17,* 173–182.

Wilson, R., Kaszniak, A., & Fox, J. *Remote memory in senile dementia.* Paper presented at the International Neuropsychological Society Meeting, San Francisco, 1980.

Wood, F., McHenry, L., Roman-Campos, G., & Posner, C. M. Regional cerebral blood flow response in a patient with remitted global amnesia. *Brain and Language,* 1980, *9,* 123–128.

10 Retrograde Facilitation of Human Memory by Drugs

Elizabeth S. Parker
National Institute on Alcohol Abuse and Alcoholism

Herbert Weingartner
National Institute of Mental Health

INTRODUCTION

> The emotion then would seem to have the power to go behind mere imagery into these dispositions or traces, and to strengthen them and the connections by which they may be called into life. And not only the traces of the experience which aroused the emotion, but also of the trivial and neutral events antecedent to the emotion itself (Stratton, 1919, p. 486)

Hidden in the archives of psychopharmacological research lies information about a curious phenomenon: Human memory can be enhanced when certain drugs are administered *after* a subject studies a to-be-remembered event. This defines operationally the retrograde facilitation effect that has been observed with diverse agents that powerfully affect emotions and have a high liability for abuse (e.g. alcohol, valium, nitrous oxide). It is an interesting phenomenon both in its own right and because of the questions it raises about the mechanisms and cognitive significance of human consolidation processes.

The present chapter draws together data bearing on drug-induced memory facilitation and analyzes its possible explanations. The basic thesis will be that certain drugs enhance memory consolidation through the activation of systems related to reward and reinforcement. We shall propose that stimulation of neural systems subserving reward enhances consolidation of memory traces that have already been encoded at the conceptual level. Keeping in mind that drugs have multiple actions, a stimulating action of a drug on memory consolidation could be mediated separately and partially independently from depressant effects on encoding and retrieval.

Memory involves separate processes that include: (1) the formation of an event representation (encoding); (2) the translation of encodings into stable, lasting form; and (3) the reawakening of the representation under particular conditions (retrieval). Consolidation is considered with reference to the period after encoding but before retrieval, a period that, in humans, is also importantly influenced by rehearsal and mediational processes. Classically, consolidation is thought of as a physiological process, namely neural activity, that persists after an experience and serves as a basis for long-term storage (Hebb, 1949; McGaugh, 1966; Müller & Pilzecker, 1900). There is abundant evidence that memory processing is not complete as soon as an event has occurred, that memory traces remain open to physiological modulation shortly after acquisition, and that changes in the state of the organism can enhance or disrupt retention. The most dramatic evidence of time-dependent storage processes comes from clinical cases of retrograde amnesia following head injury, where patients suffer permanent loss of memory for events experienced just before the traumatic incident (Russell & Nathan, 1946).

Why should memory traces remain open to modulation once a representation or encoding has been formed? Such a period of vulnerability may, according to recent theorists, serve very real survival functions for the organism (Gold & McGaugh, 1975; Gold & McGaugh, this volume; Kety, 1970). Recently acquired traces might remain open to receive information from the physiological state of the animal that in turn can influence whether or not the trace will be remembered. Biologically significant state changes provide a primitive mechanism through which recent experiences are selected and driven for long-term storage. One way that memory for recent events can be influenced is through the neural systems involved in reinforcement and reward (Clavier & Routtenberg, 1980; Huston, Mueller, & Mondadori, 1977; Landauer, 1969; Major & White, 1978; Thorndike, 1933). Stimulation of reward systems by drugs during the critical postencoding period could account for the retrograde facilitation effect in humans. A noncontingent drug-induced change in emotional state, and specifically an enhancement in hedonic processes, might enhance storage of memories for events that preceded the state change.

A Curious Finding

The retrograde facilitation effect was discovered with the consolidation paradigm widely used in animal experiments. In a typical experiment the animal is trained on a one-trial passive-avoidance task, the drug is administered at different points after training, and retention is later tested when the drug effects have worn off. Because the animal is in the nondrugged state both at acquisition and at test, the effects of the drug on "performance" variables are eliminated and changes in performance are attributed to effects on consolidation (Weissman, 1967).

Human studies have been interested in drug effects on encoding and more recently on retrieval. Animal studies, in contrast, assess the consequences of administering a drug shortly after encoding. Only a handful of studies on humans have examined how memory is affected when a drug is administered shortly after initial acquisition. Current theories of human memory view the memory trace as the record of mental analyses performed during the perception of the stimulus (Craik & Lockhart, 1972). It is not surprising that there has been strong interest in how cognitive operations are influenced by drugs because these are powerful determinants of what is remembered. Manipulation of cognitive encoding operations can enhance memory performance by as much as 400% (Craik & Tulving, 1975, Exp. 9).Psychopharmacological studies in man have been concerned with how drugs alter encoding and retrieval, the very stages of memory that are excluded in animal consolidation studies. For the investigator interested in human memory, the retrograde facilitation effect provides a window for looking into a potentially important but relatively unexplored component of memory.

For the investigator of drug effects on animal memory who might want to equate consolidation with memory, it is indeed surprising that drugs such as alcohol, which are known to produce amnesia when given *before* training, can facilitate memory when given *after* training. The fact that the same drug, given in the same dose, can have opposite effects depending on whether it is given before or after training, indicates that consolidation and encoding involve different processes. Information derived about a drug effect on consolidation cannot be extrapolated to its effects on encoding or retrieval.

CHARACTERISTICS OF THE RETROGRADE FACILITATION EFFECT

The following review is selective with a focus on drug effects on postencoding processes in man. We do not, therefore, review research on consolidation enhancement by nonpharmacologic treatments such as arousal (Weingartner, Hall, Murphy, & Weinstein, 1976), sleep (Ekstrand, 1972) or olfactory stimulation (Frank, 1931). We also omit discussion of drug studies in man where interpretation is limited by methodological problems such as lack of a control group (e.g., Jarvik, 1964) or tasks that are at ceiling and insensitive to measuring improvement (e.g., Osborn, Bunker, Cooper, Frank, & Hilgard, 1967).

Admittedly, research on postencoding enhancement in man represents a new area of drug research and the data base is still limited. Nevertheless, after reviewing most studies, certain characteristics of enhancement by drugs will be discussed. It will be noted that:

1. Retrograde facilitation occurs with agents that produce deficits in the formation of new memories (anterograde amnesia) as well as with a drug that facilitates the formation of new memories (anterograde hypermnesia).
2. Retrograde facilitation is time dependent.

3. Enhancement of memory lasts over time and is evident as long as three months after original learning.
4. The conceptual structure of facilitated memories is preserved.
5. Novel stimuli may be particularly susceptible to enhancement by certain drugs.

SUMMARY OF CONSOLIDATION EFFECTS BY DRUGS (TABLE 10.1)

Alcohol.   Understandably, initial studies on the effects of alcohol hypothesized that this drug would impair consolidation, not enhance it. Alcohol is known to disrupt the formation of new memories and impaired consolidation has been one key hypothesis to explain its amnesic effects (Goodwin, Othmer, Halikas, & Freemon, 1970; Jones, 1973; Parker, Birnbaum, & Noble, 1976). The critical test for the consolidation-deficit hypothesis requires that alcohol be

TABLE 10.1
Summary of Studies on Retrograde Facilitation by Drugs in Humans

Agent	Retrograde Effect	Anterograde Effect	Reference
alcohol	+	−	Kalin, 1964
			Parker, Birnbaum, Weingartner, Hartley, Stillman, & Wyatt, 1980
			Mueller & Lisman, 1981
			Parker, Morihisa, Wyatt, Schwartz, Weingartner, & Stillman, 1981
diazepam	+	−	Clarke, Eccersely, Frisby, & Thornton, 1970
			Brown, Lewis, Brown, Horn, & Bowes, 1978
			Clark, Glanzer, & Turndorf, 1979
			Hinrichs, Mewalt, Ghoneim, & Berie, 1981
			Hinrichs, Mewalt, & Ghoneim, 1982
nitrous oxide	+	−	Summerfield & Steinberg, 1957
arecoline	+	+	Weingartner, Sitarim, & Gillin, 1979
methylphenidate	0	−	Wetzel, Squire, & Janowsky, 1981

administered immediately after original learning, with both acquisition and retrieval being in the nondrug state. When such a hypothesis is tested it turns out that a drug that impairs acquisition does not necessarily impair consolidation.

Retrograde facilitation has been reported in four published studies with alcohol, using both visual and verbal materials as well as intentional and incidental instructions (Kalin, 1964; Parker, Birnbaum, Weingartner, Hartley, Stillman, & Wyatt, 1980, Exp 1 & 2; Parker, Morihisa, Wyatt, Schwartz, Weingartner, & Stillman, 1981). One as yet unpublished study was presented at a scientific meeting (Mueller & Lisman, 1981). In addition, animal studies have also described the facilitative effect of alcohol when administered after training (Alkana & Parker, 1979; Colbern, Gorelick, & Zimmerman, 1980). An explanation of the effect cannot invoke uniquely human processes.

Recently we came across an experiment which is, as far as we know, the first documented instance of retrograde facilitation with alcohol (Kalin, 1964). The study was concerned with memory for events encoded under the influence of alcohol. To assess baseline memory, subjects were given materials to study before drinking. Fraternity brothers were randomly assigned to wet or dry parties. Before ad libidum drinking commenced, each subject wrote a story in response to a Thematic Apperception Test (TAT) picture. During the course of drinking, which in the wet group consisted of an average of 13.8 ounces of liquor (roughly 2 ml absolute alcohol/kg body weight), or soft drinks in the dry group, two more TAT stories were obtained from the subjects. The next day, as many students as possible from the night before (N=18 in the wet group and N=17 in the dry group) were asked to provide written recall for the stories they wrote the night before.

Although drug administration and other experimental parameters were not tightly controlled, the recall for the TAT story written before drinking was better in the wet group than in the dry. Story recall was about 10% better for predrinking events, prompting Kalin to note that alcohol consumption might actually improve memory for events experienced just before heavy drinking.

In another experiment (Parker et al., 1980, Exp 1), subjects viewed 10 scenic slides before drinking 1 ml absolute alcohol per kilogram body weight. Several hours later, when the intoxicating effect of alcohol had subsided, they tried to recognize which member of pairs of slides they had seen before. Recognition performance was 12% higher after alcohol than in the nondrug condition. Another, more clearly interpretable experiment, examined the effect of alcohol in 72 male, social drinkers (Parker et al., 1980, Exp. 2). All subjects sorted a set of words into semantic categories (e.g., round things, soft things, and so on). Immediately after the sorting task, half the subjects ingested alcohol (1 ml/kg) and the other half a placebo mix. Twenty-four hours later, all subjects returned to the laboratory for an unexpected recall test of the words they had sorted the day before. Subjects who had ingested alcohol recalled about 24% more words than placebo controls.

Facilitation was seen in another study with a picture recognition task (Parker et al., 1981). This was a dose-response study involving 16 subjects who participated under four different conditions: In each session subjects received either placebo, 0.25, 0.50, or 1.0 ml/kg. Each subject participated in all four conditions. Long-term recognition of pictures was significantly improved when subjects ingested either 1.0 or 0.5 ml/kg after original learning.

Diazepam (Valium).   Clear retrograde facilitation was seen when valium (.24 mg/kg) was administered intravenously to normal volunteers immediately after they had studied a list of words (Clarke, Eccersely, Frisby, & Thornton, 1970). Of 12 normal subjects, 6 received valium and another 6 were given intravenous saline as a control. One and a half hours after injection, their recall was tested. The investigators noted the number of subjects in each group that recalled 75% or more of the words presented before injection. Only 1 of 6 subjects from the control group reached this criterion, whereas 5 of 6 subjects from the drug group recalled 75% or more words from the predrug list. In this same experiment, there was dense anterograde amnesia for materials learned under the influence of valium. The anterograde amnesia with valium has been noted in a number of investigations; retrograde facilitation has been looked at less often.

Brown and coworkers (Brown, Lewis, Brown, Horn, & Bowes, 1978) found that recall of words studied before treatment was significantly enhanced by diazepam (7.5 mg, I.V.) and nonsignificantly enhanced by lorazepam (3.0 mg, I.V.) compared to saline (2 ml I.V.) controls. Subjects studied a list of words that was presented visually and auditorily. Materials were presented about 12 min before and at a number of points after drug administration. The expected amnesic effects of benzodiazepines were observed for information acquired under the drug. Nevertheless, those subjects who received diazepam recalled an average of 50% of the predrug list compared to 30% recall by saline controls. This enhancement was markedly attenuated when measured by a recognition test.

At least three other instances of retrograde facilitation with valium have been reported. In one instance improved memory for predrug materials was shown by the reported data but not mentioned by the investigators (Clark, Glanzer, & Turndorf, 1979). In another report, the facilitative effects were noted but not emphasized (Hinrichs, Mewaldt, Ghoneim, & Berie, 1981). In 1982, Hinrichs, Mewaldt, and Ghoneim presented clear evidence of retrograde facilitation of human memory with diazepam using a free-recall task and attributed it to a reduction in retrograde interference.

Despite the widespread use and abuse of benzodiazepines, there have been very few studies of their effect on consolidation in animals. In one study, valium (10 mg/kg) impaired retention only when administered before training (anterograde amnesia) but not when given immediately after (Jensen, Martinez, Vasquez, & McGaugh, 1979). Possibly retrograde facilitation would not be expressed with the strong training footshock used in that particular experiment. Now that the retrograde facilitation effect has been identified, it would not be at all surprising to see it noted more often in future studies.

Nitrous Oxide (N₂O). In 1957, Summerfield and Steinberg reported enhancement of memory with nitrous oxide. The beneficial effect of N_2O (30% administered through a face mask for 12½ min) was equivalent to about two additional learning trials. Twenty subjects learned a nonsense syllable task. Half of the subjects were then given N_2O and the other half received air through a face mask. The groups did not differ before drug administration. After the drug period, the N_2O group was superior and they maintained this superiority during subsequent trials. Because both groups of subjects performed a color-naming task during the drug administration period, the improved memory could not be attributed to some sort of differential practice effect.

Arecoline. Low doses of arecoline, a central, muscarinic, cholinergic agonist, facilitates new learning in man (Sitaram, Weingartner, & Gillin, 1978). In one experiment on its retrograde effects on memory, subjects listened to and organized a set of 27 words presented as nine clusters of three words each (Weingartner, Sitarim, & Gillin, 1979). After hearing each cluster of words, subjects were asked to think up a label to organize the three words. These labels were later used to cue their memory. Subjects participated in both a drug day and a placebo session. On the drug day, arecoline was administered (4 mg subcutaneously) immediately after the words had been studied and organized. When the effects of arecoline, a drug that is rapidly metabolized, had worn off, free and cued recall were tested. Compared to the placebo condition, arecoline produced about a 33% improvement in free recall. Significantly, more words were recalled in both the free and cued conditions.

Methylphenidate. One study on postencoding response to the stimulant, methylphenidate, in normal volunteers found no significant effect with doses of 0.1, 0.25, or 0.50 mg/kg (Wetzel, Squire, & Janowsky, 1981). Before the drug was administered intravenously, subjects studied and recalled lists of paired associate words and stories that were recalled again the next day. They also studied a set of 20 pictures after the paired-associate task but before stories. Pictures were tested only once the next day. It appears surprising that facilitation was not observed; however, anterograde enhancement by methylphenidate was not observed on tasks studied under the influence of the drug. In fact, the highest dose (0.50 mg/kg) significantly impaired new learning. We shall discuss subsequently the importance of testing retrograde facilitation with multiple tasks, a procedure which may be insensitive to postencoding enhancement. There is not, as far as we know, any research on the effects of stimulants in normal subjects where a brief, one-trial task has been presented just before drug administration. This would be expected to produce facilitation with appropriate doses.

RETROGRADE FACILITATION OVER TIME

McGaugh and Herz (1972) argued that the effects of consolidation persist over time. The enhancing effect of drug administration after an event experience should be permanent if consolidation has been affected. The issue of permanence of postprocessing treatments, such as the amnesic effects of electrocortical shock in animals, has been discussed throughly in the chapter by Miller and Marlin (this volume).

Regarding studies in humans, the lasting effect of a given treatment can be addressed by examining memory after long delays but not by administering different types of retention tests. It is tempting to infer that a treatment has affected retrieval rather than consolidation if, for example, an effect is observed on one method of testing such as recall but it is not observed on another method such as recognition. For example, electrocortical shock therapy produces amnesia for events that occur just before treatment and this amnesia is considerably more dramatic when patients are asked to recall materials than when they attempt a recognition test (Mayer-Gross, 1943; Zubin & Barrera, 1941). Nevertheless, deficits persist over time (Mayer-Gross, 1943), indicating that the consolidation was disrupted.

The fact that an enhancing or amnesic postprocessing treatment might be evidenced under one test condition but not under another could simply indicate that there is specificity to the memory processes that have been affected. Recent research in human memory demonstrates that distinctly different processes can be employed for remembering (e.g. Mandler, 1980), and quite likely different neural systems can be activated under various retention conditions. It would, therefore, be premature to reject a consolidation interpretation if a postprocessing treatment was more pronounced on one retention test than on another.

To examine the long-term persistence of memory enhancement when alcohol was administered after original learning, we attempted to follow subjects three months after they had been in one of our studies. The original study involved 16 male normal volunteers who had participated in four sessions spaced a week apart (Parker et al., 1981). Although subjects had not expected to be recontacted, we were able to locate and test 12 subjects of the original 16. Recognition was retested on the four sets of 30 pictures. Each set of pictures had been presented before one of four different doses. Three months earlier, significant enhancement occurred when either 0.5 or 1.0 ml/kg alcohol was ingested after original learning. Three months later, retention was still higher when alcohol had been consumed after original learning. The mean recognition score for pictures in the placebo condition was 18.6. Recognition for the 0.25, 0.50, and 1.0 ml/kg conditions was 20.6, 20.2, and 19.9 respectively. These data suggest that alcohol has a lasting facilitative effect on memory storage processes.

TRAINING-TREATMENT GRADIENT

The hallmark of consolidation is the temporal gradient: The effectiveness of a treatment is greatest when it is given immediately after training and diminishes with an increase in the interval between training and treatment (McGaugh, 1966). There is no single gradient that is general across tasks or treatments (Gold & McGaugh, this volume); nevertheless, clinical studies of retrograde amnesia indicate that memories are particularly vulnerable during the seconds to minutes after initial acquisition (Mayer-Gross, 1943; Russell & Nathan, 1946). The memory-enhancing effects of alcohol also are time dependent. That is, retrograde facilitation occurs when alcohol is administered immediately after training but not 30 min later.

In an unpublished pilot study, we administered alcohol 30 min after subjects had studied a set of 10 pictures. Subjects ingested either alcohol or a placebo on different days. As can be seen in Table 10.2, 30–min post-training alcohol administration did not improve recognition. In fact, subjects recognized significantly fewer pictures after alcohol. Memory of these same pictures had been enhanced when there was no delay between training and treatment with alcohol. These opposite effects of alcohol at two different times of postprocessing administration suggest that over time different neural structures can affect consolidation. A recent study on post-training stimulation of the entorhinal cortex in rats found that stimulation at 30 min after training affected retention; entorhinal

TABLE 10.2
Mean Number of Pictures
Recognized Out of a Set of 10

	Placebo	Alcohol
Study immediately before treatment[1]	8.1 (n = 12)	9.1 (n = 12)
Study 30 minutes before treatment	8.4 (n = 8)	7.3 (n = 8)

[1]Parker et al., 1980, Exp. 1.

stimulation either immediately or one hr after training had no effect. (Gauthier, Destrade, & Somiereau-Maurat, 1982).

Although our finding—that alcohol facilitates retention when administered immediately after training but not 30 min later—provides evidence for a temporal gradient of effect and hence the involvement of consolidation processes, factors other than time are important. Figure 10.1 presents alcohol's retrograde effects as a function of input position of 30 items. These pictures were studied during a 2½–min period before ingesting a .5 ml/kg dose of alcohol. Recognition was enhanced but not for those pictures presented last, just before the drug (input position 5). Although retrograde facilitation is clearly portrayed in these results, the gradient of susceptibility is more a function of encoding strength than it is of time before treatment. The input positions associated with the lowest probability of recognition after placebo were most likely to be enhanced by alcohol. Time between training and treatment is important for the retrograde facilitation effect; however, it is not the sole determinant.

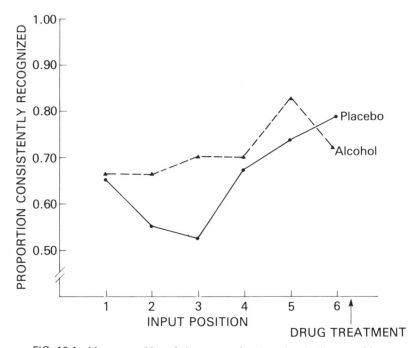

FIG. 10.1   Mean recognition of pictures as a function of study (input) position. Sixteen subjects studied 30 pictures immediately before ingestion of alcohol (0.5 ml/kg) or placebo. Each input position is the average of five consecutive pictures. Recognition performance is based on pictures which were recognized correctly on both of two sober retention tests; one test was on the input day and the other test was during the last day of four sessions (See Parker et al., 1981 for methods).

CHARACTERISTICS OF FACILITATED TRACES

One interesting feature of the retrograde facilitation effect is that it offers a window for examining the cognitive consequences of alterations in memory due to drug treatment. What aspects of predrug events are enhanced? If drugs induce some gross aberration in the structure of predrug memories, this would raise doubts about the hypothesis that drugs are acting via an endogenous system involved in remembering.

There are some limited data to indicate that the original conceptual structure of facilitated memories is well-preserved. By conceptual structure, we refer to the organization and meaning imposed on incoming stimuli. A particular to-be-remembered item, such as a word, is not just a sensory-perceptual representation; it is encoded and interpreted within its surrounding context. When, for example, the word ''coke'' is presented with words like milk, juice, coffee, and water, it is encoded and organized differently than when it is presented in the context of words like coal, iron, gold, silver. The most effective retrieval cue is one that matches the original encoding context according to the principle of encoding specificity (Tulving & Thomson, 1973). Cuing subjects with a hint that the to-be-remembered word is a beverage would not be effective if the word ''coke'' had been encoded in the context of minerals.

In two experiments, one with arecoline and the other with alcohol, the organized nature of structured word lists was maintained in both drug-treated and placebo conditions (Parker et al., 1980, Exp 2; Weingartner et al., 1979). When subjects were presented words that could be organized around conceptual labels and were cued with these labels at test, drug-treated subjects showed the same benefit in recall as controls. In both experiments, the drug-treated groups were superior in free, as well as cued recall. In both studies, improved performance after drug administration was due to an increase in the number of clusters recalled, not in the number of words per cluster. It appears that drugs retroactively enhance memory in such a way as to enhance the conceptual organization of the original representation. Interestingly, Weingartner and coworkers (1976) found that postencoding arousal and rehearsal enhanced the number of words per cluster or intrastructure salience specifically. This suggests that arousal affects consolidation differently from drugs like alcohol and arecoline.

SENSITIVITY TO RETROGRADE FACILITATION

Although very little is known about enhanced consolidation processes in humans, it will be interesting to discover what the characteristics of facilitation-sensitive stimuli are. It may well be that novel or rewarding experiences are particularly sensitive to enhancement, but habitual or repetitive stimuli are not.

This would be the case if stimuli that activate reward systems sensitize these systems for enhancement when certain drugs reach them.

The elegant research by Garcia and coworkers on conditioned taste aversion in animals demonstrates that there is a selective relation between the nature of a training stimulus and the subsequent treatment (unconditioned stimulus or reinforcer; see Garcia & Koelling, 1966: Garcia, McGowan, Ervin, & Koelling, 1968). For example, animals can be conditioned to avoid sweet water if it is followed by illness and to avoid bright, "clicking" water if it is followed by shock. Shock is not effective, however, in developing aversion to sweet water, nor is illness effective in getting animals to avoid bright, "clicking" water. Thus if certain drugs stimulate neural systems involved in affective elaboration, then stimulating conditions that activate and prepare reward systems may be particularly likely to be enhanced.

There are rewarding features to novel or unusual events. When monkeys are allowed to choose between an object they have seen before and a new object, they prefer one that is new (Mishkin & Delacour, 1975). Not only is there a natural preference for novelty, but animal studies have shown that the novelty of a training situation can affect consolidation. The chapter by Miller and Marlin (this volume) describes their extremely provocative studies on novelty and familiarization related to retrograde amnesia from electrocortical shock (ECS). When animals are familiarized with the training apparatus, they do not exhibit amnesia from immediate post-training ECS (Lewis, Miller, & Misanin, 1969). Apparently, novelty can increase vulnerability to post-training treatment. In reviewing research on drugs and retrograde amnesia, Weissman (1967) noted that the most sensitive task for animal research was one-trial passive-avoidance. Clearly, a one-trial task has a higher novelty load than does a multitrial task.

In one experiment, when subjects were given multiple lists one hr before drug administration, alcohol did not facilitate memory. The design of an unpublished experiment from our laboratory differs from most studies on the retrograde

TABLE 10.3
Mean Number of Pictures Correctly
Recognized for Three Sets of 30 Pictures
Studied on Same Day and Tested
One Week Later

	Treatment	
Time before treatment	Placebo $n = 12$	Alcohol $n = 12$
60 min	21.4	21.3
30 min	21.3	19.6
immediate	19.9	19.3

facilitation effect in humans. Typically, facilitation is observed when brief training conditions are used. The results of the discrepant study are presented in Table 10.3, which presents one-week recognition of three sets of predrug materials. In this study subjects studied three different sets of material at 1 hr, 30 min, and just before they consumed 0.5 ml/kg of alcohol. Recognition of the pictures shown immediately before the administration of the drug was not improved in the alcohol subjects.

INTERFERENCE AND CONSOLIDATION: TWO DISTINCT POSTENCODING PROCESSES

The retrograde facilitation effect might not have anything at all to do with consolidation or reward systems in the brain. In fact the seemingly most parsimonious explanation is that memories for predrug events are facilitated because subjects enter a depressed state that protects them from the detrimental effects of additional cognitive activities. Facilitation, according to this explanation, is not due to a stimulating action of drugs, but results from a reduction in cognitive activities after original learning. This was once thought to explain why memory is enhanced when subjects sleep after they have learned something (van Ormer, 1932; Ekstrand, 1972). It should be noted that a consolidation explanation for the sleep effect eventually replaced the interference explanation (see Ekstrand, 1972 for review).

In our view, consolidation and interference theories deal with different postencoding processes; we shall elaborate our rationale for this distinction. First, let us summarize the data that are not readily explained by an interference theory. One problem with an interference explanation is that retrograde facilitation has been observed when subjects had no additional task-related sources of interference in the post-training period. Interference effects do not arise simply from the generalized state of the organism; rather, they arise from additional task-related activities. We therefore conducted a study with alcohol where there were no additional tasks after the critical predrug training set. In that study, subjects were given one and only one memory task that was encoded before drug ingestion. Nevertheless, the retrograde facilitation effect occurred (Parker et al., 1981).

According to an interference explanation, retrograde facilitation with certain drugs occurs if and when subjects enter into a depressant state following encoding of the to-be-remembered materials. A drug that enhances cognitive activities after training should not be expected to induce retrograde facilitation. The fact that arecoline—a drug that enhances new learning as well as inducing retrograde facilitation—has both forward and backward facilitative actions, raises problems for an interference approach (Weingartner et al., 1979). Moreover, animal studies have repeatedly demonstrated facilitation when psychostimulants such as amphetamines are administered after training (McGaugh, 1973). Retrograde facilitation can, therefore, be produced with drugs that enhance as well as depress postencoding cognitive activities.

Interference theory predicts that the degree of retrograde facilitation depends on the degree of depression of cognitive activities following encoding. In the case of a drug like alcohol, anterograde impairment of cognitive tasks increases with the dose administered (Parker et al., 1976). The higher the dose of alcohol, the greater should be the facilitation of predrug traces because there is less and less interference with increasing dosage. This prompted us to conduct a dose-response study where facilitation was observed with two doses of alcohol (0.5 and 1.0 ml/kg) that differed greatly in direct effects on cognitive performance (Parker et al., 1981). Both doses of alcohol produced the same degree of retrograde facilitation, yet 1.0 ml/kg induces greater anterograde amnesia than 0.5 ml/kg.

And should the reader comtemplate the idea that facilitation results from differential rehearsal of some sort such that subjects who receive certain drugs after encoding try to compensate for the drug effect by working harder or expending more effort rehearsing materials, we remind you of the study with nitrous oxide by Steinberg and Summerfield (1957). In that study, subjects engaged in a distractor task while under the influence of the drug so they could not rehearse. Nevertheless, retrograde facilitation with N_2O still occurred.

Research on interference effects clearly demonstrates that memory for a set of target materials is affected by memory tasks that are given after original learning (Keppel, 1972; Postman, 1972). This does not mean that additional cognitive activities and consolidation processes are the same, that they operate according to the same laws, or that they involve identical neural systems. Cognitive activities, for example, refers to the impact of additional mental representations acquired through the course of new memory tasks and are, therefore, cognitively driven. Consolidation processes are modulated by physiological events, such as ECS or drugs, that can affect neural systems while circumventing cognitive input. It seems appropriate to consider interference effects as being driven by conceptual processes, whereas consolidation effects are driven by electrochemical events. Each describes a different aspect of postencoding influences on memory.

The distinction between cognitive interference and consolidation is substantiated by the fact that the same variable, time, affects the two differently. The importance of time for variables affecting consolidation has been discussed earlier. The change in the state of the organism must be in close temporal proximity to the acquisition of the affected trace and, in general, the effectiveness of a consolidation treatment diminishes as the training-treatment interval increases.

When the ''treatment'' is an additional memory task rather than a drug, such a temporal gradient has not been observed. Retroactive interference, or the detrimental effect that a second list can have on recalling the first list, does not follow the temporal gradient of neurobiological treatments. Consider an experiment in which subjects learned a target that was followed immediately, 24 hrs later, or 48 hrs later, by an interpolated task. The detrimental effect of the interpolated task on memory for the target task showed no relation to the point of interpolation (Archer & Underwood, 1951). Consider another experiment in which maximum retrograde interference was obtained when an interpolated task was given two days after original training, just before retention testing. No impairment was observed when the task was given immediately after original learning (Newton & Wickens, 1956). Although interference effects are not increased when a second task is given soon after the first, interference is greatly increased when there is a close conceptual relation between two memory tasks. When the first and second lists are composed of words with similar meaning, the degree of interference can be overwhelming (McGeogh, 1942).

If it is agreed that there are two different types of postencoding influences on human memory, one being consolidation and the other being interference effects, then it is theoretically possible that a drug could affect both types of processes. A drug, like alcohol, could facilitate consolidation of recently acquired materials through stimulating actions on reward systems. In addition, alcohol could reduce retroactive interference when an additional learning task is administered under an alcohol-induced depressed state. Consolidation effects should be time dependent, whereas interference effects should not. Consolidation effects should occur without the imposition of additional verbal memory tasks, whereas interference effects occur because of such tasks. At a more general level, retrograde facilitation by enhanced consolidation should occur with both depressants and stimulants if they share stimulating actions on reward systems. Retrograde effects of drugs via interference mechanisms should differ for depressants and stimulants: Depressants should reduce retroactive interference and facilitate memory for predrug events; whereas, stimulants should increase retroactive interference and depress memory for predrug events. These predictions can be examined in future studies. It is clear, however, that an interference explanation of the retrograde facilitation effect leaves unexplained a number of findings that can be accounted for by a consolidation explanation.

DRUGS, REWARD SYSTEMS, AND ENHANCED MEMORY CONSOLIDATION

Our proposal is that drugs enhance memory consolidation through their actions on brain reward systems, systems that exist to amplify the significance of recent experience and hence increase the probability that the experience will be remembered. We are emphasizing a strong interaction between emotions and memory in general, and between reward systems and consolidation in particular. The paradox of the retrograde facilitation effect is the odd relation between the drug effect and the memories that are enhanced. It appears that drugs can work backwards to facilitate memory in a noncontingent manner.

In the recent past, human memory research relegated the study of reward and reinforcement to the area of motivation, and therefore defined it as a topic with little relevance to memory in humans (see Kintsch, 1970). This has not always been the case. Thorndike's studies of human verbal learning led him to propose the law of effect in 1933. Although written in dated language, the message is remarkably timely. Thorndike stated that "the after-effects of a modifiable connection work back upon it, and that, in particular, a satisfying state of affairs accompanying or directly following a connection strengthens it (p. 173)." He anticipated a physiological explanation and would surely have been intrigued by current discoveries about the neural substrates of reward.

A similar unfortunate separation of emotions and memory occurred in consolidation research in animals. Consolidation once was viewed as an autonomous fixation process separate from motivational artifacts and explanations (see McGaugh & Herz, 1972). Discoveries in the neurosciences on the biological substrates of reward have kindled new interest in the scientific study of hedonic emotional processes and paved the way for serious inquiry about their involvement in memory.

Discoveries about the neuroanatomy and neurochemistry of structures involved in motivated behaviors have not only affected approaches to memory but have also catalyzed a major theoretical shift in understanding drug use in humans. Classically, theories of drug abuse emphasized avoidance control features of drug-taking behavior. Drugs were viewed as agents that were ingested to reduce negative states (Vogel-Sprott, 1972), and drug-seeking behavior was thought to be sustained by avoidance of the unpleasant aversive state of withdrawal (Lindesmith, 1947). Theories of drug abuse have begun to emphasize the importance of euphorogenic and rewarding properties of sustained drug-seeking behavior (Kornetsky, Esposito, McLean, & Jacobson, 1979; McAuliffe & Gordon, 1974; Wise, 1980). Psychotropic drugs such as alcohol, opiates, benzodiazepines, cocaine, and amphetamines, despite obvious differences, may share stimulating and euphoric effects.

Although the pieces to the puzzle are far from complete, there is a beginning of an understanding of neural structures involved in the processing of affectively important input. These structures, we propose, may represent the neural mechanisms underlying the hypermnesic effects of alcohol and other euphorogenic drugs of abuse. There is a wealth of data indicating that central catecholamines (dopamine and norepinephrine) are integral to the systems that enable an organism to selectively attend to and respond to significant (i.e., worth remembering) stimuli (Crow & Arbuthnott, 1972; Kety, 1970). These may be regarded as specific neurochemical components of the "reticular activating system" that is involved in arousal and motivational state changes. Recently, neuropeptides, particularly endorphins (endogenous opioids), have been implicated in these same processes (Stein & Belluzzi, 1979). Esposito (this volume) has summarized evidence showing the involvement of dopamine and enkephalins in the modulation of limbic activity and memory consolidation.

Particularly interesting for the memory enhancing effects of euphorogenic drugs is the diffuse but perhaps unitary reward system which extends from the brainstem to the frontal cortex (Crow & Arbuthnott, 1972). This reward system has been investigated through self-stimulation studies in animals. In 1954, Olds and Milner discovered that rats will work to obtain electrical stimulation when electrodes are placed in specific brain regions, presumably because of the rewarding effects these impulses provide. Separate neural systems may be involved in rewarding and aversive stimulation (Nelson, 1970).

Drugs with a high abuse potential in humans facilitate brain stimulation reward (BSR) in animals. This BSR enhancement occurs with alcohol (Lorens & Sainati, 1978), morphine (Esposito & Kornetsky, 1977), benzodiazepines (Lorens & Sainati, 1978), amphetamines (Esposito, Perry, & Kornetsky, 1980; Holzman, 1976) and cocaine (Esposito, Motola, & Kornetsky, 1978). Drugs of abuse can have stimulating effects on reward systems while having simultaneous depressant effects on other neural structures.

The neurochemical and neuroanatomic substrates of the reward system have been implicated in memory, particularly memory consolidation (Huston, et al., 1977; Major & White, 1978; Routtenberg, 1979; Stein & Belluzzi, 1979). When animals are allowed to self-stimulate after training, long-term retention memory performance can improve (White & Major, 1978). Memory facilitation by lateral hypothalamic self-stimulation is time dependent: It occurs when it follows training immediately, but not with a one-hr delay after training (Major & White, 1978). The critical demonstration for the involvement of reward systems in memory consolidation is derived from studies where memory is enhanced when animals are allowed to self-stimulate after training. Experimenter-delivered stimulation can be aversive even though the level of stimulation and the neuroanatomic sites are the same as those in self-stimulation (White & Major, 1978).

SUMMARY AND CONCLUSIONS

The present chapter has focused on a memory facilitating effect that certain drugs exert on human memory. The retrograde facilitation effect has been observed with alcohol, valium, nitrous oxide, and arecoline. Studies on post-encoding effects of psychostimulants such as cocaine and amphetamines have rarely been conducted in humans, but our prediction is that they too would facilitate consolidation under appropriate test conditions.

With depressant drugs, amnesic effects are obvious and easier to measure than are facilitative effects on memory. Impaired memory is the major effect when subjects encode and retrieve new information under drugs such as alcohol or valium. This may reflect separate and partially independent effects of the same drug on: (1) the acquisition or retrieval of conceptually driven traces; and (2) the neural systems involved in consolidation. Drugs may interfere with the acquisition and retrieval of conceptually driven memories and enhance other memory systems that are more difficult to study in humans.

Enhanced remembering of predrug experiences may reflect drug-induced stimulation of reward-driven consolidation processes. Even in humans, the neural substrates of recently formed representations remain labile shortly after encoding. Drugs with a high liability for abuse have reinforcing and rewarding effects that may enhance trace consolidation. This particular action of drugs could stimulate research on memory systems more relevant to drug-seeking behavior than research on conceptually driven memory systems. Individuals who are particularly susceptible to rewarding effects of drugs and to the retrograde facilitation effect may be at risk for alcohol or drug abuse.

In a purely speculative vein, we suggest that the retrograde facilitation effect may reflect a precognitive system that enabled primitive organisms to identify significant features of their environment. Through phylogenetic development, with growth and elaboration of the cerebral cortex in humans, conceptual encoding systems evolved to permit rapid, flexible, and structured analysis of experience. Discrete representations could occur almost simultaneously with the event. These more recent, conceptual systems reduced dependence on responsively driven consolidation processes. However, the fact that certain drugs facilitate memory indicates that these primitive systems continue to function and affect cognition. It is a challenge to think about strategies to examine experimentally this component of human memory that has hitherto eluded our scrutiny but not our behavior.

ACKNOWLEDGMENTS

We thank Ralph U. Esposito, Shahin Hashtroudi, Mortimer Mishkin, and Barbara Schwarz for their critiques, advice, and discussions surrounding earlier versions of this manuscript.

REFERENCES

Alkana, R. L., & Parker, E. S. Memory facilitation by post-training injection of ethanol. *Psychopharmacology*, 1979, *66*, 117–119.

Archer, E. J., & Underwood, B. J. Retroactive inhibition of verbal association as a multiple function of temporal point of interpolation and degree of interpolated learning. *Journal of Experimental Psychology*, 1951, *42*, 283–290.

Brown, J., Lewis, V., Brown, M. W., Horn, G., & Bowes, J. B. Amnesic effects of intravenous diazepam and lorazepam. *Experientia*, 1978, *39*, 501–502.

Clarke, P. R. F., Eccersley, P. S., Frisby, J. P., & Thornton, J. A. The amnesic effect of diazepam (valium). *British Journal of Anaesthesia*, 1970, *42*, 690–696.

Clark, E. O., Glanzer, M., & Turndorf, H. The pattern of memory loss resulting from intravenously administered diazepam. *Archives of Neurology*, 1979, *36*, 296–300.

Clavier, R. M., & Routtenberg, A. In search of reinforcement pathways: A neuroanatomical odyssey. In A. Routtenberg (Ed.), *Biology of reinforcement: Facets of brain stimulation reward*. New York: Academic Press, 1980.

Colbern, D. L., Gorelick, D. A., & Zimmerman, E. G. Post-training ethanol improves retention of passive-avoidance in mice. *Substance and Alcohol/Misuse*, 1980, *1*, 181–186.

Craik, F. I. M., & Lockhart, R. S. Levels of processing: A framework for memory research. *Journal of Verbal Learning and Verbal Behavior*, 1972, *11*, 671–684.

Craik, F. I. M., & Tulving, E. Depth of processing and the retention of words in human episodic memory. *Journal of Experimental Psychology: General*, 1975, *104*, 268–294.

Crow, T. J., & Arbuthnott, G. W. Function of catecholamine-containing neurones in the mammalian central nervous system. *Nature*, 1972, *238*, 245–246.

Ekstrand, B. R. To sleep, perchance to dream (about why we forget). In C. P. Duncan, L. Sechrest, & A. W. Melton (Eds.), *Human memory: Festschrift for Benton J. Underwood*. New York: Appleton-Century-Crofts, 1972.

Esposito, R., & Kornetsky, C. Morphine lowering of self-stimulation thresholds: Lack of tolerance with long term administration. *Science*, 1977, *195*, 189–191.

Esposito, R. U., Motola, A. H. D., & Kornetsky, C. Cocaine: Acute effects on reinforcement thresholds for self-stimulation behavior to the medial forebrain bundle. *Pharmacology, Biochemistry and Behavior*, 1978, *8*, 437–439.

Esposito, R. U., Perry, W., & Kornetsky, C. Effects of d-amphetamine and naloxone on brain stimulation reward. *Psychopharmacology*, 1980, *69*, 187–191.

Frank, J. D. Affective value vs. nature of odors in relation to reproduction. *American Journal of Psychology*, 1931, *43*, 479–483.

Garcia, J., & Koelling, R. A. Relation of cue to consequence in avoidance learning. *Psychonomic Science*, 1966, *4*, 123–124.

Garcia, J., McGowan, B., Ervin, R. F., & Koelling, R. A. Cues: Their relative effectiveness as a function of the reinforcer. *Science*, 1968, *160*, 794–795.

Gauthier, M., Destrade, C., & Soumireu-Mourat, B. Late post-learning participation of entorhinal cortex in memory processes. *Brain Research*, 1982, *233*, 255–264.

Gold, P. E., & McGaugh, J. L. A single-trace, two process view of memory storage processes. In D. Deutsch & J. A. Deutsch (Eds.), *Short term memory*. New York: Academic Press, 1975.

Goodwin, D. W., Othmer, E., Halikas, J. A., & Freemon, F. Loss of short term memory as a predictor of the alcohol "blackout". *Nature*, 1970, *227*, 201–202.

Hebb, D. O. *The organization of behavior*. New York: Wiley, 1949.

Hinrichs, J. V., Mewaldt, S. P., Ghoneim, M. M., & Berie, J. L. *Diazepam and human memory: Acquisition vs. retention*. Paper presented at the meeting of the Psychonomic Society, Philadelphia, November 1981.

Hinrichs, J. V., Mewaldt, S. P., & Ghoneim, M. M. Retrograde enhancement of recall with diazepam. Paper presented at the meeting of the Psychonomic Society, Minneapolis, November 1982.

Holzman, S. G. Comparison of the effects of morphine, pentazocine, cyclazocine, and amphetamine on intracranial self-stimulation in the rat. *Psychopharmacologia*, 1976, *46*, 223–227.

Huston, J. P., Mueller, C. C., & Mondadori, C. Memory facilitation by posttrial hypothalamic stimulation and other reinforcers: A central theory of reinforcement. *Biobehavioral Reviews*, 1977, *1*, 143–150.

Jarvik, M. E. The influence of drugs upon memory. In H. Steinberg (Ed.), *Animal behavior and drug action*. Boston: Little, Brown, 1964.

Jensen, R. A., Martinez, J. L., Jr., Vasquez, B. J., & McGaugh, J. L. Benzodiazepines alter acquisition and retention of an inhibitory avoidance response in mice. *Psychopharmacology*, 1979, *64*, 125–126.

Jones, B. M. Memory impairment of the ascending and descending limbs of the blood alcohol curve. *Journal of Abnormal Psychology*, 1973, *82*, 24–32.

Kalin, R. Effects of alcohol on memory. *Journal of Abnormal and Social Psychology*, 1964, *69*, 635–641.

Keppel, G. Forgetting. In C. P. Duncan, L. Sechrest, & A. W. Melton (Eds.), *Human memory: Festschrift for Benton J. Underwood*. New York: Appleton-Century-Crofts, 1972.

Kety, S. S. The biogenic amines in the Central Nervous System: Their possible roles in arousal, emotion and learning. In F. O. Schmitt (Ed.), *The Neurosciences second study program*. New York: Rockefeller University Press, 1970.

Kintsch, W. *Learning, memory, and conceptual processes*. New York: Wiley, 1970.

Kornetsky, C., Esposito, R. U., McLean, S., & Jacobson, J. O. Intracranial self-stimulation thresholds. *Archives of General Psychiatry*, 1979, *36*, 289–292.

Landauer, T. K. Reinforcement as consolidation. *Psychological Review*, 1969, *76*, 82–96.

Lewis, D. J., Miller, R. R., & Misanin, J. R. Selective amnesia in rats produced by electroconvulsive shock. *Journal of Comparative and Physiological Psychology*, 1969, *69*, 136–140.

Lindesmith, A. R. *Opiate addiction*. Bloomington, Ind.: Principia, 1947.

Lorens, S. A., & Sainati, S. M. Naloxone blocks the excitatory effect of ethanol and chlordiazepoxide behavior. *Life Sciences*, 1978, *23*, 1359–1364.

Major, R., & White, N. Memory facilitation by self-stimulating reinforcement mediated by the nigro-neostriatal bundle. *Physiology and Behavior*, 1978, *20*, 723–733.

Mandler, G. Recognizing: The judgement of previous occurrence. *Psychological Review*, 1980, *87*, 252–271.

Mayer-Gross, W. Retrograde amnesia. *Lancet*, 1943, *245*, 603–605.

McAuliffe, W. E., & Gordon, R. A. A test of Lindesmith's theory of addiction: The frequence of euphoria among long-term addicts. *American Journal of Sociology*, 1974, *79*, 795–840.

McGaugh, J. L. Time-dependent processes in memory storage. *Science*, 1966, *153*, 1351–1358.

McGaugh, J. L. Drug facilitation of learning and memory. *Annual Review of Pharmacology*, 1973, *13*, 229–241.

McGaugh, J. L., & Herz, M. J. *Memory consolidation*. San Francisco: Albion Publishing Company, 1972.

McGeogh, J. A. *The psychology of human learning: An introduction*. New York: Longmans, Green & Co., 1942.

Mishkin, M., & Delacour, J. An analysis of short-term visual memory in the monkey. *Journal of Experimental Psychology: Animal Behavior Processes*, 1975, *1*, 326–334.

Mueller, C. W., & Lisman, S. A. *Alcohol, rehearsal, and decrements in recognition memory*. Paper presented at the meeting of the Psychonomic Society, Philadelphia, November 1981.

Müller, G. E., & Pilzecker, A. Experimentelle beitrage zur lehre vom gedachtniss. *Zietschrift fur Psychologie mit Zietschrift fur Angewandte Psychologie*, 1900, *1*, 1–288.

Nelson, J. M. *Single dose tolerance to morphine sulphate: Electroencephalographic correlates in central motivational systems*. Unpublished doctoral dissertation, University of Boston, 1970.

Newton, J. M., & Wickens, D. D. Retroactive inhibition as a function of the temporal position of interpolated learning. *Journal of Experimental Psychology*, 1956, *2*, 149–154.

Olds, J., & Milner, P. M. Positive reinforcement produced by electrical stimulation of septal area and other regions of rat brain. *Journal of Comparative and Physiological Psychology*, 1954, *47*, 419–427.

Osborn, A. G., Bunker, J. P., Cooper, L. M., Frank, G. S., & Hilgard, E. R. Effects of thiopental sedation on learning and memory. *Science*, 1967, *157*, 574–576.

Parker, E. S., Birnbaum, I. M., & Noble, E. P. Alcohol and memory: Storage and state dependency. *Journal of Verbal Learning and Verbal Behavior*, 1976, *15*, 691–702.

Parker, E. S., Birnbaum, I. M., Weingartner, H., Hartley, J. T., Stillman, R. C., & Wyatt, R. J. Retrograde enhancement of human memory with alcohol. *Psychopharmacology*, 1980, *69*, 219–222.

Parker, E. S., Morihisa, J. M., Wyatt, R. J., Schwartz, B. L., Weingartner, H., & Stillman, R. C. The alcohol facilitation effect on memory: A dose-response study. *Psychopharmacology*, 1981, *74*, 88–92.

Postman, L. Transfer, interference and forgetting. In J. W. Kling & L. A. Riggs (Eds.), *Woodworth and Schlosberg's experimental psychology: Vol. 2, Learning and motivation*. New York: Holt, Rinehart & Winston, 1972.

Routtenberg, A. Participation of brain stimulation reward substrates in memory anatomical and biochemical evidence. *Federation Proceedings*, 1979, *38*, 2446–2453.

Russell, W. R., & Nathan, P. W. Traumatic amnesia. *Brain*, 1946, *69*, 280–300.

Sitaram, N., Weingartner, H., & Gillin, J. C. Human serial learning: Enhancement with arecoline and choline and impairment with scopolamine. *Science*, 1978, *201*, 274–276.

Stein, L., & Belluzzi, J. D. Brain endorphins: Possible role in reward and memory formation. *Federation Proceedings*, 1979, *38*, 2468–2472.

Steinberg, H., & Summerfield, A. Influence of a depressant drug on acquisition in rote learning. *Quarterly Journal of Experimental Psychology*, 1957, *9*, 138–145.

Stratton, G. M. Retroactive hypermnesia and other emotional effects on memory. *Psychological Review*, 1919, *26*, 474–486.

Summerfield, A., & Steinberg, H. Reducing interference in forgetting. *Quarterly Journal of Experimental Psychology*, 1957, *9*, 146–154.

Thorndike, T. K. A proof of the law of effect. *Science*, 1933, *77*, 173–175.

Tulving, E., & Thomson, D. M. Encoding specificity and retrieval processes in episodic memory. *Psychological Review*, 1973, *80*, 352–373.

van Ormer, E. B. Retention after intervals of sleep and of waking. *Archives of Psychology*, 1932, *137*, 5–49.

Vogel-Sprott, M. Alcoholism and learning. In B. Kissin & H. Begleiter (Eds.), *Biology of alcoholism: Physiology and behavior (Vol. 2)*. New York: Plenum Press, 1972.

Weingartner, H., Hall, B., Murphy, D. L., & Weinstein, W. Imagery, affective arousal and memory consolidation. *Nature*, 1976, *263*, 311–312.

Weingartner, H., Sitaram, N., & Gillin, J. C. The role of the cholinergic nervous system in memory consolidation. *Bulletin of the Psychonomic Society*, 1979, *13*, 9–11.

Weissman, A. Drugs and retrograde amnesia. *International Review of Neurobiology*, 1967, *10*, 167–198.

Wetzel, D. A., Squire, L. R., & Janowsky, D. S. Methylphenidate impairs learning and memory in normal adults. *Behavioral and Neural Biology*, 1981, *31*, 413–424.

White, N., & Major, R. Facilitation of retention by self-stimulation and by experimenter-administered stimulation. *Canadian Journal of Psychology*, 1978, *32*, 116–123.

Wise, R. A. Action of drugs of abuse on brain reward systems. *Pharmacology, Biochemistry and Behavior*, 1980, *13*, 213–223.

Zubin, J., & Barrera, S. E. Effect of electric convulsive therapy on memory. *Proceedings of the Society for Experimental Biology and Medicine*, 1941, *48*, 596–597.

Author Index

Numbers in *italics* denote pages with bibliographic information.

Foley, M. A., 129, *143*
Forrester, W. E., 153, *161*
Foster, K., 27, 29, *58*
Fox, J., 225, *230*
Fox, M. M., 189, *209*
Frank, G. S., 233, *251*
Frank, J. D., 233, *249*
Franks, J. J., 96, *109,* 117, *144*
Fraser, J., 158, *160*
Freed, N. J., 45, *54*
Freemon, F., 234, *249*
French, J. D., 27, *54*
Freud, S., 165–66, *182,* 186, *207*
Freund, G., 219, *228*
Frey, J. M., 37, *54*
Frisby, J. P., 234, 236, *249*
Fuld, P. A., 122, *142*
Fulginiti, S., 73, 74, *82*
Fuster, J. M., 26, 29–31, 33, *54, 60*
Fuxe, K., 17, 21, 41, 44, *50, 52, 55, 56*

G

Gabriel, M., 27, 29, *58*
Gallagher, M., 49, *54,* 78, *80*
Gallistel, C. R., 41, *53*
Garcia, J., 95, 96, *108,* 242, *249*
Gardiner, J. M., 120–21, 128, 135, *142, 143*
Gardner, E. L., 35, 41, *54, 60*
Gardner, R. A., 158, *160*
Gartman, L. M., 176, *182*
Gastpar, M. T., 33, *59*
Gauthier, M., 240, *249*
Gazzaniga, M. S., 31, *55*
Geddes, D., 73, *81*
Geen, R. G., 155, *160*
Geiselman, R. E., 129, *141*
Gelbart, J., 23, 24, *55*
Geller, A., 91, 93, 99, *108, 110*
Gelman, R. S., 154, 156, *159*
Gentleman, S., 19*n, 50*
Gerard, R. W., 86–87, 88, *108,* 186, *207*
German, D. C., 16, 17, 40, *54*
Geschwind, N., 25, *54,* 214, 216, *227*
Gessa, G. L., 43, *50*
Ghoneim, M. M., 234, 236, *249*
Gibson, J. J., 168, *182*
Gigannini, T., 19, *50*
Gilbe, C., 22, 23, *52*
Gilbert, P. E., 18, 19*n, 57*
Gillin, J. C., 176, *182,* 234, 237, 241, 243, *251*
Glanzer, M., 234, 236, *249*

Glass, A. L., 168, 176, 177, *182*
Glenberg, A. M., 176, *183*
Glendenning, R. L., 102, *108*
Glickman, S. E., 67, *80,* 112, *142,* 149, *160,* 186, *207*
Gloor, P., 28, 29, *54, 59*
Glowinski, J., 17–18, 24, 33, 35, 43, *51, 61*
Gotz, A., 130, 132, *142*
Goddard, G. V., 65, *80*
Gold, M., 67, *83*
Gold, P. E., 11, 67–75, 77, 78, *79, 80, 81, 82, 83,* 187, 192, 193, *207, 208,* 214, 225, *228,* 232, 239, *249*
Goldberg, B., 177, *182*
Goldberg, Z. I., 28, *54*
Goldman, P. S., 18, *51*
Goldman-Rakic, P. S., 18, 25, 29, *59*
Goldmeier, E., 219, *228*
Goodglass, H., 196–97, *207*
Goodman, R. R., 18, 19, 33, *54, 61*
Goodwin, D. W., 234, *249*
Gordon, R. A., 246, *250*
Gordon, W. C., 101, 102, *108,* 116, 118, *142*
Gorelick, D. A., 235, *249*
Gorenstein, G. W., 179, *183*
Gottlieb, J. S., 45, *56*
Gozzani, J. M. L., 74, *80*
Graesser, A. C., 136, *144*
Graf, P., 121, *145,* 199, *207*
Grant, D. S., 113, *142*
Green, M. T., 48–49, *58*
Greenough, W., 65, *80, 81,* 205, *207*
Greenwald, A. G., 157, *160*
Griffin, M., 137–38, *142,* 176, *183*
Griffiths, C., 26, 29–31, 33, *60*
Gritz, E. R., 49, *54*
Gropper, M. S., 122, *145*
Groth, J., 19, *50, 61*
Guidotti, A., 66, *79*
Gunne, L. M., 34, *54*
Guzman-Flores, C., 45, *52*

H

Hagamen, W. D., 26, *59*
Halgren, E., 29, *54,* 203, *207*
Halikas, J. A., 234, *249*
Hall, B., 13, *14,* 233, 241, *251*
Hall, M. E., 73, *81*
Hamacher, J. H., 154, 156, *159*
Hamilton, P., 155, *160*
Hamilton, V. L., 178, *182*

Subject Index